GW00643439

www.Explorer-Publishing.com

Passionately Publishing...

**Geneva Explorer   1st Edition**

**First Edition 2005   ISBN 976-8182-44-x**

**Copyright © Explorer Group Ltd**, 2005
All rights reserved.

Front Cover Photograph — Pamela Grist

Printed and bound by Emirates Printing Press, Dubai, United Arab Emirates.

**Explorer Publishing & Distribution LLC**
PO Box 34275, Dubai
United Arab Emirates
**Phone**        (+971 4) 335 3520
**Fax**          (+971 4) 335 3529
**Email**        Info@Explorer-Publishing.com
**Web**          www.Explorer-Publishing.com

**Promoguide SA**
Régie Publicitaire
Rue des Bains, 35
Case Postale 5615, 1211 Genève 11 Suisse
**Phone** (+41 22) 809 94 94
**Fax**  (+41 22) 809 94 00
**Email** info@promoguide.ch
**Web**  www.promoguide.ch

Plan reproduit avec l'autorisation de la Direction cantonale de la mensuration officielle
du 8 décembre 2004. Autorisation: 59/2004

# EXPLORER

www.Explorer-Publishing.com

## Publishing
Publisher — Alistair MacKenzie
Alistair@Explorer-Publishing.com

## Editorial
Editors — Claire England
Claire@Explorer-Publishing.com
Jane Roberts
Jane@Explorer-Publishing.com
Proofreader — Jo Holden-MacDonald
Authors — Katy Anderson
Stormy Berney
Susan Broomfield
Jed Payne
Beth Watts
Researchers — Helga Becker
Helga@Explorer-Publishing.com
Tim Binks
Tim@Explorer-Publishing.com
David Quinn
David@Explorer-Publishing.com
Yolanda Singh
Yolanda@Explorer-Publishing.com
Louise Mellodew

## Design
Graphic Designers — Jayde Fernandes
Jayde@Explorer-Publishing.com
Zainudheen Madathil
Zain@Explorer-Publishing.com
Sayed Muhsin
Muhsin@Explorer-Publishing.com
Photography — Pamela Grist
Pamela@Explorer-Publishing.com

## Sales & Advertising
Media Sales Manager — Alena Hykes
Alena@Explorer-Publishing.com
Media Sales Executive — Laura Zuffová
Laura@Explorer-Publishing.com
Sales/PR Administrator — Janice Menezes
Janice@Explorer-Publishing.com
Advertising Sales — Switzerland Promoguide SA
Info@promoguide.ch
Corporate Sales — Virginie Belamaric
Virginie@Explorer-Publishing.com

## Distribution
Distribution Manager — Ivan Rodrigues
Ivan@Explorer-Publishing.com
Distribution Supervisor — Abdul Gafoor
Gafoor@Explorer-Publishing.com
Distribution Executives — Mannie Lugtu
Mannie@Explorer-Publishing.com
Stephen Drilon
Stephen@Explorer-Publishing.com
Rafi Jamal
Rafi@Explorer-Publishing.com

## Administration
Accounts — Kamal Basha
Kamal@Explorer-Publishing.com
Sohail Anwar
Sohail@Explorer-Publishing.com
Administration Manager — Nadia D'Souza
Nadia@Explorer-Publishing.com

## Geneva 'Guru'
Addison Holmes

Bienvenue, Geneva Guys and Girls,

Here it is! We've swum the length and breadth of Lake Geneva and scaled the highest Alpine peaks in our efforts to present you with a refreshing, informative guide to living in Geneva. Our intrepid researchers have explored the city from top to bottom and infiltrated the legendary Swiss aloofness to bring you this book, which has more information on current events than the UN, and more oomph than the Jet d'Eau. These tireless detail addicts, all residents of Geneva themselves, have uncovered the secrets of Genevois life and reported back to us, motivated purely by their love for the city (and the promise of a large box of the finest Swiss chocolates).

Our **New Residents'** section, packed with information on things like accommodation, residence permits and transport, will help you unlock the labyrinth of Swiss bureaucracy that at times would make even the most patient of souls run screaming into the hills. The **Exploring** and **Shopping** sections will tell you exactly where to go and what to buy when you get there. And after you've read the **Activities** section crammed with info on what clubs to join, what mountains to climb and what sports to play, you'll have no excuses left for being a timid couch potato.

**Going Out** covers restaurants, bars, nightclubs and more, and includes reviews on some of Geneva's hottest spots. We'll help you pack more fun into your fondue and more ra-ra into your raclette, as well as give you the low-down on getting the hang (and hangovers) of the Geneva nightlife. Your social life, as you know it, is about to change forever!

After all the arduous work and skin-of-our-teeth deadlines we endured to bring you this guide, we are ever so proud of it. What do you think? Fill in the reader response form on our Website (www.Explorer-Publishing.com), send us an email (Info@Explorer-Publishing.com) or just pick up the phone... we're listening.

Enjoy!

**The Explorer Team**

A thousand words
in one photograph...
A world of beauty in one city.

*Passionately Publishing...*

And the fun doesn't stop there! If you're a budding food critic we want to hear from you. Check out www.EatOutSpeakOut.com and give us your take on the restaurants,

# Four Easy Ways...

In order to make the **Geneva Explorer** the best guidebook in the history of the universe we need you to tell us what you think - whether it's good, bad or ugly!

The more we know about you and your loves, hates, gripes and wishes the better job we can do - especially as everything we do, we do it for you!

**1** If you're a surfer you can fill in the Reader Response form on our website
www.Explorer-Publishing.com

**2** If you're a talker you can phone us on (+971 4) 335 3520

**3** If you're a scribbler you can fax (+971 4) 335 3529 or we can fax you the response form

**4** If you're an Outlooker you can email
Info@Explorer-Publishing.com

# & WIN!

## 'But what's in it for me?' you ask

Firstly you'll be helping us to help you by making the next edition even better than this one, and as a reward everyone who fills in a Reader Response form will be entered into a super prize draw!

Secondly, five lucky readers will win the breathtaking **Images of Geneva** photography book, as well as the fully updated 2nd edition of the **Geneva Explorer**.

rs and nightclubs featured in the book. Who knows - you could be enjoying a few free dinners yourself as an undercover food reporter for our next edition.

## Alistair MacKenzie
### Media Mogul

If only Alistair could take the paperless office one step further and achieve the officeless office he would be the happiest publisher alive. Remote access from a remote spot within the Hajar mountains would suit this intrepid explorer. The only problem could be staffing – unless he can persuade Midnight Cafeteria to deliver!

## Claire England
### Poached Ed

No longer able to freeload off the fact that she once appeared in a Robbie Williams video, Claire now puts her creative skills to better use – looking up rude words in the dictionary! A child of English nobility, Claire is quite the lady – unless she's down at Jimmy Dix.

## David Quinn
### Sharp Shooter

After a short stint as a children's TV presenter was robbed from David because he developed an allergy to sticky back plastic, he made his way to sandier pastures. Now that he's thinking outside the box, nothing gets past the man with the sharpest pencil in town.

## Alena Hykes
### Sales Supergirl

A former bond girl, Alena speaks more languages than we've had hot dinners and she's not afraid to be heard. She dresses to kill and has a sales pitch to die for with everything she touches turning to gold – must be that Goldfinger!

## Pete Maloney
### Graphic Guru

Image conscious he may be, but when Pete has his designs on something you can bet he's gonna get it! He's the king of chat up lines, ladies – if he ever opens a conversation with 'D'you come here often?' then brace yourself for the Maloney magic.

## Zainudheen Madathil
### Map Captain

Often confused with football star Zinedine Zidane because of the equally confusing name, Zain tackles design with the mouse skills of a star striker. Maps are his goal and despite getting red-penned a few times, when he shoots, he scores!

---

**But we couldn't have done it without....**
Frances & Robert MacKenzie, John Marriott, Addison Holmes, Scott Bilquist, Henrich Duriaux, Susan Broomfield, Katy Anderson, Stormy Be

## Sayed Muhsin

### Design Drummer

They say it's the quiet ones that you want to watch and Mushin is no exception. Laying low behind his layouts, what many of you don't know is that he used to be the drummer for Led Zepellin. Now he drums up designs that are music to our eyes.

## Yolanda Singh

### Fast Talker

With an iron will and a heart of gold, Yoyo manages to bounce back from every hurdle and still finds time for a good gossip. If you want to get a memo around she's far quicker than email.

## Jayde Fernandes

### Pop Idol

When he isn't secretly listening to Britney Spears or writing to Blue to become their fifth member, Jayde actually manages to get a bit of designing done (but not before he has got through his well practised list of 'the dog ate my homework' excuses). He's The Man, and all because the ladies love his in-tray!

## Janice Menezes

### Materials Girl

How does Janice manage to whiz round the office so efficiently chasing ads and artwork and generally keeping on top of the books? Rollerskates of course! When she's not practising her toe-stops, she spreads the Explorer message to over a thousand people a day.

## Jane Roberts

### Word Wizard

meticulous is her middle name and after creatively shrivelling in a dingy government office, Jane thankfully found her way to the Explorer offices with her red pen in tow. She's learning by other people's mistakes and teaching the rest of us that quantity and quality can live in harmony.

## Helga Becker

### Fantasy Foodist

From alfresco eateries to burger joints, and cocktail bars to nightclubs, Helga has been around the Dubai block a few times (in the culinary sense of course). A walking restaurant and bar guide, Helga is the goddess of going out and makes Explorer look good enough to eat.

e, Beth Watts and the Mystery Boat Man!

### Tim Binks

#### Cookie Monster

After flying the Explorer nest at the beginning of the Millennium in search of sushi, Tim eventually tired of egg rolls and flew back with the promise of a more calorific career. When the cookie crumbles Tim is the man to gather the pieces – as long as it's chocolate chip of course! Thankyou please.

### Louise Mellodew

#### The Phantom

Louise hasn't been seen at her desk for months now, and while she tells us she's on the road doing essential research, we know she's actually curled up at home, watching 'Buffy' re-runs with her cat.

### Nadia D'Souza

#### Mother Hen

Poor Nadia has the displeasure of sitting opposite the toilet, but like the Explorer adopted mother that she is she soon takes charge of any sticky toilet situations – humorous or not. When she isn't giving the boys a telling off, Nadia can be found navigating new recruits through telephonic technology.

### Mannie Lugtu

#### Distribution Demon

When the travelling circus rode into town their master juggler, Mannie, decided to leave the Big Top and explore Dubai instead. He may have swopped his balls for our books but his juggling skills still come in handy.

Dubai
TOMORROW'S CITY TODAY

-Road
EXPLORER

### Pamela Grist

#### Happy Snapper

If a picture can speak a thousand words then Pam's photos say a lot about her – through her lens she manages to find the beauty in everything – even this motley crew. And when the camera never lies, thankfully Photoshop can.

### Kamal Basha

#### Chief Calculator

Kamal has the best bottom line in Dubai and makes many an accountant jealous with his mean index finger. In fact, he's been the UAE calculator champion in the Mathematic Games for the last three years, and now has the world title in his sights. Go Kamal!

### Joe Nellary

#### Head Hacker

While we once blamed the system for all our technical hiccups we can now turn to Joe for much needed support. And if he doesn't have the answer a bit of techno jargon fools us into thinking he does.

### Ivan Rodrigues

**Head Honcho**

After making a mint in the clip board market, Ivan came to Explorer out of the goodness of his heart. Distributing joy across the office he is the man with the master plan – if only we could understand his spreadsheets.

### Abdul Gafoor

**Ace Circulator**

After a successful stint on Ferrari's Formula One team Gafoor made a pitstop at our office and decided to stay. As Explorer's most cheerful employee, he's the only driver in Dubai yet to succumb to road rage.

### Rafi Jamal

**Soap Star**

After a walk on part in The Bold and the Beautiful, Rafi swapped the Hollywood Hills for the Hajar Mountains. Although he left the glitz behind, he is frequently spotted practising his pensive to-camera pose in the office's bathroom mirror.

We like to think that our team is like no other. Many media and publishing companies may sell you an image of dedication and efficiency when in fact it is all work and no play with an unhealthy dose of office politics. We, on the other hand just work hard... then play hard! Our hearts and souls are laid bare on the plentiful pages that follow. The end result is books that we're proud of and that you will hopefully put in pride of place!

### Stephen Drilon

**Record Breaker**

Not to be outdone by the Burj tower, Stephen sits alongside Nakheel in the record books for successfully stacking the highest book tower ever constructed, even if it did only stand for 0.03 seconds. He has now moved his sights on to calendar castles.

### Sohail Butt

**Abacus Ace**

By day he may be cooking the books but by night Sohail cooks up a storm at the local Karaoke bar – while his routine includes the entire back catalogue of Abba hits, it's his heartfelt rendition of 'Money Money Money' that really brings the house down.

## Explorer Insiders' City & Country Guides

These are no ordinary guidebooks. They are your lifestyle support system, medicine for boredom, ointment for obstacles, available over the counter and prescribed by those in the know. An essential resource for residents, tourists and business people, they cover the what, the how, the why, the where and the when. All you have to do is read!

### Abu Dhabi Explorer

The ultimate guide to the UAE's capital just got bigger and better. Now covering Al Ain you'll wonder how you ever managed without it.

### Bahrain Explorer

The inside track on where and how to experience everything this fascinating gulf state has to offer.

### Dubai Explorer

The original, and still the best by far. Now in its 9th year, this is the only guide you'll ever need for exploring this fascinating city.

### Geneva Explorer

Your very own personal guide giving the low-down on everything to do and see in this European gem of a city and its surroundings.

### Oman Explorer

All the insider info you'll ever need to make the most of this beautiful, beguiling country.

## Explorer Photography Books

Where words fail, a picture speaks volumes. These award-winning photography books take you across landscapes and seascapes, through bold architecture, the past and the present, introducing a wonderland of diversity. They're an optical indulgence as well as stimulating additions to bookshelves and coffee tables everywhere.

### Dubai: Tomorrow's City Today

A photography book showcasing the sheer splendour and architectural audacity of this stunning city.

### Images of Geneva

From snow-capped mountains and azure waters to historic cobbled streets and contemporary architecture, the beauty of Geneva and its surroundings is captured in a stunning collection of photographs.

### Sharjah's Architectural Splendour

Magnificent photographs show how modern-day Sharjah has remained true to its cultural heritage.

### Images of Dubai & the UAE

Breathtaking images from this land of contrasts - from unspoilt desert, to the truly 21st century city of Dubai.

### Images of Abu Dhabi & the UAE

Awe inspiring images of exquisite natural beauty and ancient cultures juxtaposed with the modern metropolis of Abu Dhabi.

## Explorer Activity Guides

Why not visit stunning marine life and mysterious wrecks, or stand poised on the edge of a natural wadi or pool in the mountains? Get a tan and a life with our activity guidebooks.

### Off-Road Explorer (UAE)

Let's off-road! Over 20 adventurous routes covered in minute detail. Go off the beaten track and discover another side to the UAE.

### Underwater Explorer

Dive dive dive! Detailed info on all the underwater action, from reefs to wrecks, all around the UAE.

### Family Explorer (Dubai & Abu Dhabi)

The only family-friendly guide of its kind for the UAE – just add kids!

### Trekking Guide (Oman)

A booklet and individual cards detailing amazing walks through spectacular scenery. The maps correspond to waypoints that are actually painted on the ground to aid navigation.

### Street Map Explorer (Dubai)

Never get lost again. A first of its kind for Dubai, this handy map book lists every highway and byway in crystal clear detail.

SFr 10 ~ € 6          1ˢᵗ Edition  GENEVA EXPLORER

## Explorer Other Products

With such an incredible array of insiders' guides and photography and activity books you'd think we wouldn't have the time or energy to produce anything else. Well think again! Here are some of our other products – no home should be without them.

### 2005 Calendar (Abu Dhabi)

Spend a whole year in the company of stunning images of the capital of the Emirates.

### 2005 Calendar (Dubai)

A 12-month visual feast, featuring award-winning images of Dubai's finest sights.

### Starter Kit (Dubai)

Three great books - the Dubai Explorer, Zappy Explorer and Street Map - everything you need to get started and sorted.

### Images Collection (UAE)

A combination of award-winning excellence, containing both the Images of Dubai and Images of Abu Dhabi photography books (limited edition).

### Zappy Explorer (Dubai)

Page after page of fuss-free advice on getting things done in Dubai. All the info you'll ever need to get yourself sorted.

# General Information

# New Residents

# Exploring

# Shopping

# Activities

# Going Out

# Maps

# Everything you need to know in Geneva on

# www.~~cnn.com~~

tdg.ch
and click
" English Corner "

# General
# Information

**EXPLORER**

# General Information

## MUST KNOW

*A true Genevois is always on time, and will expect the same courtesy from you. The obsession with being on time stretches to the buses, trains and trams – they follow their timetables rigidly, so don't expect a kindly bus driver to wait at the stop for you if you're a few seconds late, no matter how frantically you are waving your arms!*

## MUST SEE

*When it comes to navigating your way around Geneva, don't just rely on your scanty sense of direction. At the back of this book you'll find a stack of maps so informative, so interesting, and so detailed, that you need never be lost again. If you are truly 'directionally challenged', you can always use the lake and mountains as points of reference!*

## MUST GO

*Geneva and its surrounding areas is host to several exciting annual events. Don't miss the International Motor Show (held at the Palexpo in March) where you can drool over sleek, curvaceous or classy models... we're talking about the cars, of course! If you're in the market for a new car, this is a good time of year to buy, since many dealers offer special show discounts and if you're a seasoned bargainer, you should manage to bag yourself a good deal.*

## Country Overview

### Geography

Switzerland is renowned for its breathtaking scenery. While you may find similarly attractive landscapes in other corners of the world, few places offer so much cultural variety in such a relatively small area. From high mountain peaks to low lying pastures, from lakes and rivers to glaciers, and from beautiful plants and cute furry animals to Gothic cathedrals and old towns steeped in history, Switzerland just about has it all.

Nestled in the heart of Europe, Switzerland shares borders with five countries: Italy to the south, France to the west, northwest and southwest, Germany to the north and northeast, and Austria and Liechtenstein to the east. Part of the border comprises Lac Léman and Lake Constance. Switzerland's capital, Bern, is in the north, roughly half way between the eastern and western most points of Switzerland.

The Alps occupy 60% of the country, the Swiss plateau (Mittelland) another 30%, and the Jura mountains, the remaining ten percent. Forests, rocks, lakes, settlements, rivers and glaciers cover approximately two thirds of the country's surface area and the leftover arable land is slowly being replaced with roads and buildings.

The country is divided into 26 'cantons' (semi-independent states), of which three are divided into half cantons. Each canton is then subdivided into 'communes' (municipalities). However, all 26 cantons are united under the Federal State, which has overall responsibility for national matters, such as the military, telecommunications and foreign policy.

> **Definition of a canton**
>
> *A canton is a semi-independent state with its own laws, customs, constitution and political peculiarities, and each one has a distinctive culture as well as its own traditions.*

Geneva sits in a horseshoe shaped basin, partially enclosed by the mountains of the Jura to the west and north, and the French Salève mountain to the south and southwest. The east opens out onto the rest of Switzerland. The name 'Geneva' originates from the Latin meaning 'mouth of the waters', which accurately describes Geneva's geographical location at the western tip of Lac Léman (where the waters of Lac Léman flow back into the river Rhône). The Rhône, which rises in central Switzerland, flows through Lac Léman from east to west. The canton of Geneva occupies 282 square km and has 45 communes. Its geographic co-ordinates are 46° 12' north and 6° 9' east, and its altitude is 375 metres above sea level. The canton shares 103 km of border with France (including 20 customs controlled crossings) and only 4.5 km of border with the rest of Switzerland.

### History

#### Switzerland

Over 2,000 years ago the central and eastern parts of Switzerland were known as Helvetii (hence the name Helvetic Confederation). Following the decline of the Roman Empire, various Germanic clans moved into Helvetii (the Italian speaking 'Lombards' to the south, French speaking 'Burgondes' to the west, and German speaking 'Alamans' to the north and east).

The country's political history dates back over 700 years to August 1291, when three Helvetian peasants from the valleys of Uri, Schwyz and Unterwald met on the Grütli meadow and took an oath of mutual assistance whilst maintaining their political, economic and legal independence. Their alliance marked the creation of the Helvetic Confederation.

After a series of wars and a period of occupation, Switzerland became a confederation of 22 cantons in 1815. Its first constitution, drawn up in 1848, has been revised several times; the current constitution was adopted in the year 2000.

> **Maps**
>
> *In addition to the maps at the back of this guidebook you can refer to the maps published by Editions MPA Verlag, including a substantial street guide with detailed maps charting every nook and cranny of the canton and city, as well as single page fold out options that range from the inner city centre to the whole canton. All these maps include (Unireso) the public transport network. The fold out city map by Kummerly+Frey gives visitors a good overview. Maps are very easily available from bookshops and department stores around Geneva. Alternatively, log onto www.geneva.ch/map and familiarise yourself with the region online.*

#### Geneva

Because of its convenient geographical location at the converging point of major roads and waterways connecting northern and southern Europe, Geneva became an important economic centre early on. The city was a major seat of the Roman Empire until the 6th century AD and following that, the seat of an Episcopal principality of almost 7,000 square km until the 16th Century.

St. Pierre Cathedral

In 1536 French religious reformer Guillaume Farel brought the Christian Reformation (that was spreading throughout Switzerland) to the citizens of Geneva. The old regime was abolished and the independent and autonomous Republic of Geneva was established. Farel convinced a visiting French scholar, Jean Calvin, to take on the task of implementing the Reformation. The new protestant republic attracted and welcomed many religious refugees who were persecuted in their own countries (especially France and Italy). The knowledge and various trades they brought with them contributed to the economic growth of the new Republic.

By the age of 26 Calvin had acquired a reputation as a brilliant jurist, theologian and writer, famous for his reformist views. In Geneva he promoted public education, instigated stringent laws and developed the economy in his fight against poverty and idleness. He was a relentless worker despite resistance from the Genevois who saw him as another oppressive ruler. As a result of Calvin's two decades of influential presence, Geneva became known as the 'Protestant Rome' and later, the 'City of Calvin'.

Upon Calvin's death in 1564, another Frenchman, Théodore de Bèze, took over Calvin's work. Besides becoming another important figure of Protestantism, he made a key contribution to the future of democracy by arguing that citizens should have the power to limit the authority of governors, since the latter only existed to represent the people. Bèze's work, however, was censored for fear of antagonising the House of Savoie with whom relations were already strained. Indeed, the Duke of Savoy, Charles-Emmanuel, attempted to invade the city on several occasions.

Probably the most internationally known of Geneva's great personalities is Jean-Jacques Rousseau, born in Geneva in 1712. Like Bèze he too argued for the limitation of leaders' powers but it was only after his death that his contributions to society were recognised.

In fact some of Rousseau's later works were considered so scandalous that he was accused of attempting to destroy the establishments of the Church and State and was therefore banned from Geneva and most other places in Europe. He spent the last fifteen years of his life in solitary exile.

The 18th century saw several uprisings and incidents related mainly to demands for increased political rights and freedoms. As a result of civil unrest the French occupied Geneva from April 1798 until it regained its freedom and celebrated its restoration as an independent Republic on the 31st of December 1813. It then joined Switzerland in 1815.

### The Escalade

In December 1602 Charles-Emmanuel made a surprise attack on Geneva during the night. The townsfolk however, fought off the assailants. Legend has it that Catherine Cheynel threw a cauldron of hot vegetable soup from her window on to the head of an invader. Today the annual 'Nuit de l'Escalade' celebrations kick off by breaking a chocolate cauldron filled with marzipan vegetables and shouting 'that is how to deal with the enemies of the Republic!'

Geneva earned its reputation as the 'Capital of Human Rights' following the creation (in 1864) of the International Red Cross by Henri Dunant (born in Geneva in 1828). In 'Un Souvenir de Solferino' (A Memory of Solferino), he described the sufferings he had seen in the aftermath of the battle and laid out a plan for rescuing wounded soldiers in the future. On the basis of this document European governments, monarchs and other influential persons supported the creation of the organisation.

Shortly after creating the International Red Cross, Dunant's life took a turn for the worse and in 1867 he was bankrupt. His business ventures had suffered due to his attention being concentrated on humanitarian pursuits and he was used as the company scapegoat. After this he was no longer welcome in Geneva society and spent the rest of his life in exile in a small Swiss village.

Although great changes did not occur in the 19th century itself, the ideas and philosophies that emerged from the period had important repercussions later on. Thus, Geneva entered the 20th century with a prestigious reputation as the 'cradle of great ideas'. During the two World Wars Switzerland maintained its neutrality, but just like other countries it suffered economically. Geneva continued to experience much political turmoil until the middle of the 20th century and thereafter the economy boomed. Geneva's reputation as the 'Capital of Human Rights' amidst Switzerland's neutrality made it an ideal platform for the League of Nations, and subsequently the United Nations and many other international organisations.

## Economy

### Switzerland Overview

For over 150 years, especially between 1948 and 1975, Switzerland experienced fairly strong and steady economic growth. During the 1980s the economy began to plateau and by the early 1990s, growth of the GDP (gross domestic product) had virtually ground to a halt. The economy picked up again after 1996, albeit with a modest average annual GDP growth of about 2.3 % between 1996 and 2000. Since 2000 the GDP growth has slowed further, hitting -0.5% in 2003. However, in mid 2003 an economic recovery began with a strengthening of the external environment and a gradual decline in unemployment. In 2004 the GDP growth rate rose to 1.8% and is estimated at two percent growth for 2005 by the Swiss State Secretariat for Economic Affairs.

Despite meagre GDP growth Switzerland has one of the highest per capita incomes in Europe, if not the world. According to the World Bank, Switzerland's per capita income for 2003 was SFr 47,925, though this figure varies from less than SFr 35,000 in some cantons to well over SFr 50,000 in others.

There has never been enough arable land available for Switzerland to become self-sufficient in terms of food production – the soil is not naturally fertile and peasants always had to work especially hard to produce crops – in fact currently only two percent of the country's GDP is derived from agriculture. Switzerland's mineral resources are practically non existent, with the exception of salt, so the country has to rely heavily on imports. Consequently the country has had to develop its own niche industries, such as clock and watch making, banking, insurance, pharmaceuticals, precision machines and instruments, hydroelectricity and, of course, chocolate and cheese. In the 17th century Switzerland was famous for its textile industry, having developed highly specialised precision machines. Such levels of industrial and economic development were achieved mainly because of a hardworking and well trained work force, and also by focusing on quality and precision rather than quantity.

With this background it's no surprise that Switzerland favours the principles of free trade with low customs taxes on industrial goods and few limitations on imports. The Swiss have also been cooperating closely with various international economic organisations, such as the WTO (World Trade Organisation), the United Nations and the European Union, for many years. They recently signed seven bilateral conventions with the European Union, which came into effect in June 2002 and which should help to boost Switzerland's free trade economy, considering exports are mainly to neighbouring European countries.

Geveva's Cultural Affairs Office

Swiss companies related to technology, electricity and metals account for over 40% of all export industries. It is also no secret that Swiss banks and insurance companies are predominant at an international level as well as being major contributors to the Swiss economy. Approximately half of the country's work force is employed in tertiary industries that account for two thirds of Switzerland's GDP.

Large Swiss companies such as Nestlé and Novartis actually only make a comparatively tiny portion of their revenue in Switzerland. Small businesses actually play a far more important role in the Swiss economy. A survey in 1998 revealed that 98.2% of companies had less than 50 employees but provided employment for about 1.45 million people overall (53% of the private sector workforce) and contributed approximately two thirds of Switzerland's economic performance.

Tourism also remains a considerable source of revenue, accounting for 44% of GDP in 2003, as visitors flock to this breathtaking mountainous country for hiking, skiing and all kinds of other sports, or simply to enjoy the stunning scenery.

### Geneva Overview

Geneva's 'Gateway to Europe' location has proved beneficial to the city's economic development for centuries. Place du Bourg-de-Four in the Old Town attracted travellers from all over and street stalls and small workshops sprouted along the 'rues basses' near the lakeshore and on the banks of the Rhône, attracting foreign tradesmen and bankers from all over Europe. Lac Léman and the Rhône have also been used from very early times to transport goods to and from northern and southern Europe.

| Driving Distances | |
| --- | --- |
| From Geneva to: | |
| • Brussels | 674 km |
| • Frankfurt | 585 km |
| • Luxembourg | 484 km |
| • Lyon | 162 km |
| • Marseille | 443 km |
| • Milan | 412 km |
| • Munich | 591 km |
| • Nice | 483 km |
| • Paris | 546 km |
| • Zurich | 278 km |

The cantonal income for Geneva in 2003 was SFr 20,763 million, averaging SFr 49,969 (€32,642) per capita. The economy is diverse and spread across several sectors. Banking and insurance obviously play an important role, but relatively low taxes and Geneva's central location have encouraged multinationals to set up their headquarters in the area. There are approximately 200 non governmental organisations in Geneva and some 200 diplomatic missions. Geneva's role as a meeting place and banking centre attracts many visitors each year, 70% of whom are business travellers. In addition to the thousands of meetings and sessions held by various organisations and the world famous international motor show, The huge exhibition centre Palexpo attracts 1.37 million visitors each year. The combined direct and indirect benefits to Geneva from tourism amount to SFr 1.8 billion annually.

Geneva also boasts a number of precision watchmakers from world renowned companies such as Rolex, to small artisans like Golay Spierer, who make custom watches to order. Geneva canton produces almost 13,000 hectolitres of wine a year but very little makes it across the border, as most of it is consumed locally! Other industries include pharmaceuticals, precision instruments and cosmetics.

### Travel & Tourism

Swiss tourism is a healthy industry with ecotourists and adventure seekers flocking to the country for skiing and snowboarding (in winter) and hiking, biking and water sports (in summer).

There is plenty to see and do in Geneva and its surrounding countryside. There are about 30 museums as well as plenty of historical buildings and archaeological findings. Culture buffs will enjoy the numerous theatres, concert halls and the opera house, while sports junkies can bike, walk, swim, sail, canoe, raft, paraglide and climb to their hearts' content.

With its rich past and beautiful natural assets, investments in Geneva's tourism industry aim to enhance what history and nature have already provided. Ecotourism is strongly promoted with free bicycle rental, solar powered mini train tours, and numerous city and country walks. There is also a plethora of parks, a botanical garden that boasts over 60,000 plant species, and boat trips to medieval villages around the lake.

Geneva has an excellent infrastructure in terms of accommodation and transport and is suitable for all kinds of tourists, from those with bulging pockets to those on a shoestring. It is also possible to stay in rural lodgings on farms in the villages surrounding Geneva, where you can taste and buy the products grown on site as well as learn about wine production and farming.

The beautiful sights of Geneva's Old Town

Getting around is fairly easy with an extensive and reliable bus, tram, boat and train network, and numerous taxis. Geneva is also a great starting point for many day trips to other parts of Switzerland or France. Besides sampling cheese, wine or chocolate you can visit mountain peaks, glaciers or beautiful countryside, not to mention the thermal spas where you soak in hot baths or have your body pummelled by therapeutic jets of hot water while you admire the stunning panoramic scenery.

Geneva is a renowned international meeting place, and there is no shortage of conference and gala venues. The city hosts thousands of international meetings, seminars, exhibitions and sporting events each year. The annual International Motor Show alone attracts over 700,000 visitors from over 100 different countries. A list of the main annual events can be found on [p.45.

## International Relations

Despite joining the UN and signing bilateral agreements with the European Union Switzerland remains firmly attached to its famous neutrality, which is inscribed in international law. This basically means that it cannot assist or provide military support to a country or party at war. However, it can participate in non military sanctions ordained by the UN or other international institutions such as the European Union. It can also participate in and allow the transit of peacekeeping operations. It may also collaborate with European partners with regard to equipment and training as this is not directly linked to assistance in armed conflict.

In the new Federal Constitution that came into effect on the first of January 2000 the Federal Council defined five priority areas in its foreign policy for the first decade of the new millennium. These policies include: (i) making a substantial and visible contribution to the prevention of violent conflicts and to the furtherance of democracy and rule of law, (ii) enhancing intercultural dialogue to promote cultural diversity both at national and international levels, (iii) pursuing a humanitarian policy that promotes respect for and promotion of human rights, (iv) making the fight against poverty a central element of its development cooperation activities through good governance, sustainable use of natural resources, debt relief, social balance, promotion of income and employment, and integration into world trade, and (v) safeguarding Switzerland's economic interests at international level by promoting exports of small and medium sized businesses, and establishing the country's position as a centre for research and education as well as a competitive financial centre. Switzerland is also engaged in consolidating existing international treaties to protect natural resources.

The recent move to join the UN should allow the country to safeguard its economic interests abroad in light of intensifying international collaboration between states. Switzerland is also a member of many other international bodies such as the Food and Agriculture Organization (FAO), International Labour Organization (ILO), United Nations Educational, Scientific and Cultural Organization (UNESCO), World Health Organization (WHO), Universal Postal Union (UPU), the UN Organization for Industrial Development, the World Bank, the

The perfect postcard

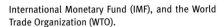

International Monetary Fund (IMF), and the World Trade Organization (WTO).

The bilateral agreements signed between Switzerland and the European Union in June 2002 regulate their cooperation in terms of research, public markets, eliminating technical obstacles to commerce, agriculture, air and land transportation, and free movement of people. For many years Switzerland has also been collaborating with other organisations such as the European Council, the Organization for Security and Cooperation in Europe (OSCE) and the Organization for Economic Cooperation and Development (OECD). Geneva also houses the European Organization for Nuclear Research (CERN), which is spread across the Swiss-French border.

There are around 200 diplomatic missions and consulates in Geneva itself and just about all major embassies and consulates are represented in Bern or Geneva.

| Consulates | |
|---|---|
| Australia | 022 799 91 00 |
| Austria | 022 319 72 88 |
| Belgium | 022 730 40 00 |
| Canada | 022 919 92 00 |
| France | 022 319 00 00 |
| Germany | 022 730 11 11 |
| Italy | 022 839 67 44 |
| Portugal | 022 791 76 36 |
| Russia | 022 734 79 55 |
| Spain | 022 749 14 60 |
| United Kingdom | 022 918 24 00 |
| USA | 022 840 51 60 |

A full list of consulates in Geneva can be found on www.geneva.ch

## Government & Politics

Switzerland has a federal structure with no central power and Swiss citizens have the right to intervene directly or indirectly in all political matters. This situation is largely thanks to a long political history, a high rate of literacy, and strong media, as well as a relatively small surface area and population. The country's political system has evolved over seven centuries and its sophistication is more a result of adaptations and modifications than a major revolution. The concept of an alliance of states that maintain their respective autonomy and sovereignty dates back to the formation of the Helvetic Confederation in 1291.

Switzerland's government, the Federal Council, has seven ministers drawn from the four strongest political parties. Each year a different minister becomes Federal President. The President holds no special powers and all members of the Federal Council take collective responsibility for decisions. In addition each Federal Councillor, including the President, runs a department. When a Federal Councillor retires or dies, a replacement is elected by Parliament. The Federal Council receives assistance and advice from the Federal Chancellery and the Federal Chancellor attends weekly cabinet meetings on a consultative basis.

The Federal Assembly is made up of two chambers that have equal weight. The National Council represents the people and consists of 200 seats divided between the cantons in proportion to their size. The Council of States represents the cantons and consists of 46 seats, two for each canton and one for each half canton. These chambers supervise government and approve federal laws. The members of these two councils are elected every four years and can propose new laws or decrees or put questions to the Federal Council. Collectively they elect the members of the Federal Council and other state officials. The speakers of these councils rotate annually and the speaker of the National Council is the highest ranking person in the country!

The 26 cantons and half cantons also have a federalist structure that allows for considerable political freedom and autonomy in terms of their administration. Cantons (and some communes) have their own constitution and laws, which are based on the Federal Constitution but include some variants. Federal duties are clearly defined and mainly consist of ensuring national and international security, guaranteeing cantonal constitutions and maintaining foreign diplomatic relations. The Federal State is also responsible for customs, post and telecommunication networks, the monetary system, the military and the development of the national economy.

Swiss men and women have equal legal and voting rights. The Federal Constitution guarantees popular rights in terms of property, trade, association, petitions, beliefs and freedom of the press. From the age of 18, Swiss citizens have the right to vote on referendums or even organise and submit petitions to change constitutional laws. Any modification to the Federal Constitution has to be voted by the citizens, while changes to federal laws and decrees need only be voted on if, 100 days following official publication of the proposed modifications, eight cantons or 50,000 citizens specifically request a vote. The cantonal referendum system varies from one canton to another.

In Geneva the executive power is made up of seven State Councillors (ministers), a State Chancellor and five Administrative Councillors (magistrates). Each year one of the State Councillors is elected President and one of the Administrative Councillors is elected Mayor. The legislative body is made up of the High Council at cantonal level with 100 members and the Municipal (town) Council consisting of 80 members who are elected every four years. Geneva has 11 seats on the National Council and two on the Council of States. Communes also have their own political structure, parties and representatives.

With so many referendums and elections of presidents, councillors, representatives, magistrates and so on, there's always voting going on for one thing or another all year round!

## Facts & Figures

### Population

A national census has been held in Switzerland every ten years since 1850. The last one was held in 2000 and revealed that the population stood at 7,288,010 as compared to 6,873,687 ten years earlier. In the canton of Geneva the population stood at 413,673 in 2000 compared to 379,190 in 1990. This represents a growth of just over six percent for Switzerland but a growth of approximately nine percent for Geneva.

Switzerland now faces a major challenge in terms of social security for several reasons. Life expectancy in Switzerland has shot up over the last century, more so among women (82.5 years in 1998) than men (76.5 years in 1998). The number of people over 64 has doubled in the last 50 years and the number of people aged over 80 has quadrupled. Meanwhile, the number of under twenties has declined over the same period, now representing only about 25% of the population compared with 30% in 1950. Consequently, the number of people contributing to social security is decreasing while the number receiving benefits is increasing.

Housing is also becoming a problem in a country with limited space because the average size of households is decreasing. In 1960 only 15% of

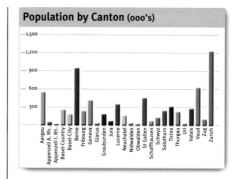

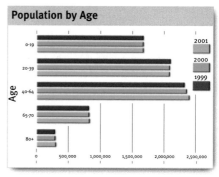

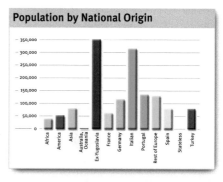

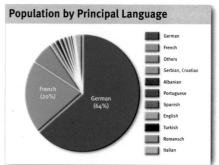

households consisted of a single person, compared to 30% by 1990. Two person households have increased from 26% to 33% over the same period, while the number of households with four or more persons is declining.

In 2001 about 20% of the population of Switzerland was foreign. The percentage varies between cantons, but Geneva has the highest proportion of foreigners (37.6%).

## National & Cantonal Flag

The Swiss national flag is a white cross on a red background. Geneva's flag is divided vertically into two parts. On one half is a representation of a half eagle on a yellow background symbolising Geneva's empirical past, and on the other is an outlined pale gold key on a red background, representing the city as an Episcopal seat.

Flags at Town Hall

## Local Time

Switzerland is in the Central European time zone (CET) which is one hour ahead of UTC (UTC +1). Like other countries in Europe Switzerland observes daylight saving time in the summer months so clocks go forward one hour on the last Sunday of

March (UTC +2), and back one hour on the last Sunday of October. Not accounting for any daylight saving time, when it is 12:00 midday in Geneva it is 06:00 in New York, 11:00 in London, 16:30 in New Delhi, 20:00 in Tokyo and 21:00 in Sydney.

## Social & Business Hours

The Swiss are a hard working nation and the working week is officially 42 hours. A referendum was held a few years ago to reduce it to 40 hours but the Swiss voted against it! People rise early and start work between 07:30 and 09:00. Lunch hours are typically between 12:00 midday and 13:30. Dinner is usually eaten quite early in the evening and there are not many restaurants where you can get a meal after 22:00.

Sunday is a day of absolute rest and all noisy activities are forbidden including drilling, hammering and cutting grass. Between 22:00 and 07:00 daily, no noisy activity is allowed, including running baths and flushing toilets in apartment buildings!

Government offices are open from 07:30 to 16:00 while in the private sector office hours are usually between 08:00 and 18:00. Small businesses may close between 12:00 and 14:00 for lunch.

Shops open around 08:30 and close around 19:00, except on Thursday when most shops remain open until 21:00. On Saturday shops close at 18:00. The only shops open on Sunday are some newsagents, bakeries and a few petrol station shops. However there is a shopping centre at the airport railway station that is open seven days a week from 08:00 until 20:00, which has a supermarket selling fresh produce. A mini market and pharmacy at Cornavin railway station are open seven days a week.

Bank timings are usually from 08:30 to 16:30, Monday to Friday. They are closed Saturdays, Sundays and public holidays.

Post offices are open from 07:30 to 12:00 and from 13:00 (or 14:00 in some cases) to 18:00, Monday to Friday; and 08:00 to 11:00 on Saturdays. The post office in Montbrillant (Rue des Gares, 16) is open seven days a week (Monday to Friday from 07:30 to 22:45, Saturday from 07:30 to 20:00 and Sunday from 12:00 to 20:00).

Opening times of embassies and consulates vary so it is best to call them directly.

## Public Holidays

Besides the longer average working week, Switzerland also has fewer public holidays than most other countries. Swiss National Day (1st August) was only made an official public holiday in 1993 even though it celebrates an event that took place over 700 years ago! Some holidays, such as Christmas and Swiss National Day, have fixed dates while others, such as Easter, Ascension and Whit Monday, vary. Occasionally, different cantons also have different public holidays. In Geneva for instance, the Jeûne Genevois (Geneva Fast) is on the Thursday following the first Sunday in September while the rest of Switzerland has the day off for the 'Federal Fast' on a Monday, ten days later. School holidays can also vary slightly from one canton to another.

Public holidays, such as Whit Monday, Ascension and Easter, are usually an excuse for a long weekend break and Christmas is a very quiet family affair. In some parts of Switzerland the New Year is a much more festive occasion and people party so extensively in some cantons that the second of January is also a public holiday! In Geneva the 31st of December is Restoration Day, which celebrates the day the Republic regained its independence after a period of French occupation and thus, is an official public holiday. Most of the larger shops (especially supermarkets) open on the second of January but some businesses and banks remain closed.

Banks, shops, offices and even some restaurants close on public holidays.

| Public Holidays – 2005 | |
| --- | --- |
| New Year's day | Jan 1 |
| Good Friday | Mar 25 |
| Easter Monday | Mar 28 |
| Ascension | May 5 |
| Whit Monday | May 16 |
| Swiss National Day | Aug 1 |
| Jeûne Genevois (Geneva Fast) | Sep 8 |
| Christmas | Dec 25 |
| Stephenstag (Boxing Day) | Dec 26 |
| Restoration Day | Dec 31 |

## Electricity & Water

Electricity and water services in Geneva are excellent. Electricity cuts and water shortages are almost unheard of so when they do occur, they make headline news! The electricity supply is 220 volts and sockets take small, two or three pin, non fused plugs.

Tap water is highly purified and perfectly safe to drink. Many different brands of bottled carbonated or still mineral water are also available. Hotels and restaurants will generally serve bottled water. You can also ask for tap water but somehow waiters tend to 'forget' to bring it and you may need to remind them (sometimes more than once)! Some restaurants may add a small surcharge (about SFr 2) if you don't order other drinks.

Electricity Works

## Photography

Normal tourist photography is perfectly acceptable although some places may not allow it. This is usually indicated, for example, in museums or places of worship. Obviously, just like anywhere else, it is courteous to ask permission before photographing people.

You will find just about any type of film and photographic equipment in Geneva and there are places all over town where you can have films and slides processed, including APS film. Several places will process films within one hour, although for APS films this is only possible in labs with Kodak processing equipment. Films and processing are not cheap and the quality of processing can vary. Most places can also transfer your photos onto a CD-ROM (which is cheaper than prints).

## Climate

Switzerland's geographically central position in Europe means that its climate has oceanic, northern, Mediterranean and continental influences. These, along with the differences in altitude, result in a number of regional and local microclimates. Although average precipitation (rain and snow) may be higher than in other European countries it is distributed very unevenly. Montreux had an average yearly precipitation of 138 cm between 1961 and 1990 while 270 cm was recorded on the Säntis (2,503 metres) for the same period. Temperatures also vary widely depending on altitude, wind exposure and hours of sunlight. The climate in Southern Switzerland is mild year round with subtropical vegetation.

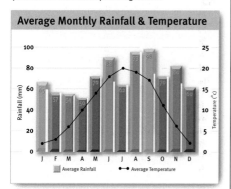

### Average Monthly Rainfall & Temperature

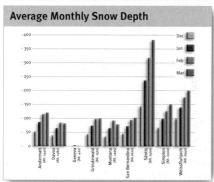

### Average Monthly Snow Depth

**Source:** Météo Suisse

On the whole however, Switzerland has a moderate climate with well defined seasons. In summer the average temperature in Geneva is 23 degrees Celsius, while the average winter temperature falls to around ten degrees. Temperatures have been known to reach the high 30s in summer, or dip below zero in winter. The temperature in spring and autumn ranges between ten and 20 degrees. It is not unusual to have flurries of snow in Geneva at any time from November to April, although it is most common in December, January and February. Aside from the odd freak snowfall, it is rare to get more than a few centimetres of snow in Geneva.

There are no extremes in humidity although the air in Geneva tends to be fairly dry which results in a lot of static electricity, particularly in winter.

## Flora & Fauna

As a result of its varied climatic influences and landscapes, Switzerland has a wide range of flora and fauna. The countryside around Geneva is a mixture of farmland, vineyards and forests. The Swiss Agency for Environment, Forests and Landscape estimates that Switzerland is home to more than 50,000 species of animals, plants and macro fungi.

While Edelweiss may be the most famous alpine flower, and an emblem of Switzerland, sadly it is now an endangered species and it is very rare to see one. Other alpine flowers to look out for are the alpine anemone, hawkweed, spring gentian, bearded bellflower, fragrant orchid, rust leaved Alpen rose, the mountain houseleek and many more (you'll find pictures of all these and more at www.switzerland-in-sight.ch).

While there are no absolutely enormous forests in Switzerland, the high number of smaller forests cover a lot of land. Deciduous trees, such as beech and oak, grow at altitudes of up to 1,300 metres, while coniferous forests (pine, Scots pine and spruce) can flourish at altitudes of up to 1,900 metres. Chestnut forests only grow on the Southern side of the Alps.

When it comes to animals, you'll find much more than just cows! Most of the animal species found here are small – out of the 40,000 or so species, around 30,000 are insects. Some 83 mammal species are found in Switzerland, but these are mainly bats and small mammals. In the Alps many species have had to adapt to harsh climatic conditions. Marmots, ibex, chamois, mountain hare and white field mouse are characteristic of the Alps where they can be found at altitudes of up to 2,200 metres. Marmots tend to hibernate in winter and other alpine animals, such as the chamois and ibex, have adapted to the steep mountainous terrain. Whilst walking through the Geneva countryside you may also come across squirrels and foxes, and on the lake and the rivers you can see swans as well as many different types of ducks and birds.

Geneva boasts a number of beautiful parks with a wonderful variety of trees and plants. You'll find two animal parks inside the Bois de la Bâtie (Bâtie Woods), and the 'La Garenne' animal park in Le Vaud (in the neighbouring canton of Vaud) has over 180 animal species, including local birds and mammals. Several species of fish and shellfish live in the rivers and the lake. Perch and trout are the most common.

## Protection

The lack of space in Geneva has resulted in conflict between those in favour of economic development and groups who are trying to preserve the country's natural heritage. Fortunately, despite ongoing urban development, protecting the environment is high on Switzerland's list of priorities and several environmental protection laws have been introduced in past years. For example, a tree may only be felled if a new one is planted to replace it, hunting is only permitted at certain times of the year, and several endangered animals and plant species are protected.

### The Kyoto Protocol

*The objective of the United Nations Framework Convention on Climate Change is to stabilise greenhouse gas concentrations in the atmosphere at a level that no longer poses a threat to the climate system. The Kyoto protocol to this Convention sets specific targets and timetables for the reduction of emissions of certain pollutants in developed countries. It affects almost all sectors of the economy and is said to be the most far reaching agreement, regarding the environment, ever adopted.*

Switzerland has ratified the Kyoto protocol to the United Nations Convention on Climate Change and is party to many other environmental agreements. At a local level many actions are being taken to improve the quality of the air and water and a massive campaign is underway to educate people about environmental issues and encourage environmentally friendly lifestyles. New taxes are being introduced in an attempt to reduce carbon dioxide emissions. Farmers too are being encouraged to use environmentally friendly methods and restrict their use of pesticides and herbicides (which eventually run into rivers and streams and harm fauna and flora). In addition, ecotourism is being promoted throughout the country, encouraging people to use non polluting (and healthier) means of transport such as walking and biking. Not only can you borrow bicycles free of charge in certain parts of town, but many maps with walking and cycling itineraries can be found and new bike lanes are being created regularly.

A lot of work has been undertaken in recent years to clean up the lakes and rivers and reduce the levels of phosphates in the water. Although further efforts are still needed the quality of the water in most swimming areas around the lake is good.

Two major environmental bodies, the World Wide Fund for Nature (WWF) and the World Conservation Union (IUCN) have their world headquarters near Geneva, in the small town of Gland. In Geneva itself offices of numerous other international and local environmental organisations are present and most of these are grouped under the Geneva Environment Network.

## Culture & Lifestyle

## Culture

With over a third of its population coming from about 200 different countries, Geneva is decidedly cosmopolitan. This is reflected in its culture, which is quite distinctive from the German-Swiss or Italian-Swiss culture.

In general Genevois are courteous but reserved, and it is often said that it is difficult to get to know them. It may take a little patience and a lot of perseverance before you manage to break the ice. While they may seem cold, distant and uncaring, this outward appearance has more to do with the fact that they are reluctant to bother others and so they tend to be very discreet. Only once they feel a certain amount of camaraderie has been established will they open up slightly and share more personal information. As a result your early conversations with Swiss people may seem overly superficial and you'll need plenty of 'small talk' to keep going!

The Swiss have built their entire economy on reliability, efficiency, quality and perfection, and this is reflected in people's daily lives. Respecting these values is important when dealing with the Swiss, whether in a business or personal context. When the Swiss say they will do something by a certain time, they mean it and they expect the same of others. They will not commit themselves to anything until they have collected all the facts and

3 LAND ROVER
YEAR
100,000km
WARRANTY

## IT'S FITTING THAT THE MOST BEAUTIFUL PLACES ON EARTH CAN ONLY BE ACCESSED BY A VEHICLE THAT ADDS TO THE VIEW.

Where would we be without technology? Technology that can take us to the most remote areas, and guarantee our return? Electronic Traction Control, Dynamic Stability Control, Electronic Air Suspension, Hill Descent Control, advanced GPS/TV navigation system. All part and parcel of one of the most beautiful vehicles ever seen. You have it all with Range Rover. **Above it all.**

**RANGE ROVER**

are sure that they can keep their word. Trams and buses arrive and depart exactly on time, even if that means reserving a substantial amount of the urban road network solely for these vehicles. In fact, drivers are, at times, so obsessed with sticking to the timetable that, even if someone is sprinting to catch the bus, they will still drive off!

With so many nationalities and religions represented Genevois can be said to be tolerant. But in return, it is expected that visitors and foreign residents respect local customs and laws (this includes sticking to peaceful activities on Sunday). If you cause a disturbance you will soon be put straight whether it is by the police force or its extension, the law abiding citizens.

## Language

Switzerland has four official languages: German, French, Italian and Romansch. German is the most widely spoken language in Switzerland (63.9%), followed by French (19.5%), Italian (6.6%) and Romansch (0.5%). Other languages are spoken by the remaining 9.5% of the population. This differentiation in languages dates back to the period when various Germanic peoples settled in the different regions after the decline of the Roman Empire. German is spoken mainly in the northern and northeastern parts of the country, French in the western part, Italian in the southern canton of Tessin and only a tiny proportion of the population in the Grisons speak Romansch.

The official language in Geneva is French but German and English are also common. Like anywhere else, efforts to speak a few words of the local language are always appreciated (and sometimes necessary).

## Religion

The main religions in Switzerland are Christian (Catholic and Protestant). Based on the last census in 2000, 41.8% of the population in Switzerland are Roman Catholic, about 33% are Reformed Church (Protestant) and another 4.3% are of other Christian religions. Islamic communities make up about 4.3% of the total population but 18.3% of the foreign population. Jewish communities represent 0.2% of the population.

Despite its past reputation as the 'Protestant Rome' there are more than twice as many Catholics as Protestants in Geneva. Many other religious groups have their own places of worship.

All over the city, and in every commune and village, you will hear church bells ringing throughout the day. You could be mistaken for thinking that religious worship is widespread, but the reality is that a considerable proportion of the population will only set foot in a church on special occasions such as marriages, deaths and baptisms. In fact, church bells traditionally also served a practical purpose by informing peasants working in the fields of the time of day (i.e., lunch, rather than prayers!).

Saint Pierre Cathedral

## National Dress

In Geneva the traditional dress is rarely worn, except at cultural events. Towards the end of the 19th Century, and as a result of industrialisation, lifestyles saw a number of changes and typical rural dress was abandoned in favour of the fashions followed by city dwellers. Gradually the original handmade individual pieces were supplanted by mass produced articles that were cheaper and more fashionable. However, when Geneva joined the National Federation of Swiss Costumes, the popular choice for a traditional dress was the one representative of the Restoration period (1813). This is the costume that you will most commonly see at special events. For women it is dresses with silk aprons and hats and for men, elegant mid length coats, silk waistcoats and scarves or ties. At Escalade, however, the costumes are representative of the city dwellers of that particular period (1602).

## Basic French

### General

| Yes | oui |
|---|---|
| No | non |
| Please | s'il vous plaît |
| Thank you | merci |

### Greetings

| Hello | bonjour |
|---|---|
| Have a good day | bonne journée |
| Have a good afternoon | bon après-midi |
| Have a good evening | bonne soirée |
| Enjoy your meal | bon apétit |
| How are you? | comment allez-vous? |
| Fine, thank you | bien, merci |
| Welcome | bienvenue |
| You are welcome (in reply to thank you) | de rien |
| Cheers! | santé! |
| Goodbye | au revoir |
| See you soon | à bientôt |

### Introduction

| My name is | je m'appelle ... |
|---|---|
| What is your name? | comment vous appelez-vous? |
| Where are you from? | d'où venez-vous? |
| I am from ... | je suis ... |
| America | américain (m), américaine (f) |
| Britain | britannique |
| Canada | canadien (m), canadienne (f) |
| Germany | allemand (m), allemande (f) |
| The Netherlands | hollandais (m), hollandaise (f) |

### Questions

| How many / much? | combien? |
|---|---|
| Where? | où? |
| When? | quand? |
| Which? | quel? |
| Which one? | lequel (m)?, laquelle (f)? |
| How? | comment? |
| What? | quoi? |
| Why? | pourquoi? |
| Who? | qui? |
| To / at | à |
| For | pour |
| In / inside | dans / dedans |
| Out / outside | hors / dehors |
| From | de, depuis |
| And | et |
| Also | aussi |
| There isn't | il n'y a pas |

### Taxi / Car Related

| Is this the road to ... | est-ce que cette route mène à ... |
|---|---|
| Stop | arrêt / stop |
| Right | droite |
| Left | gauche |
| Straight ahead | tout droit |
| North | nord |
| South | sud |
| East | est |
| West | ouest |
| Turning | tournant |
| First | premier |
| Second | deuxième |
| Road | route |
| Street | Rue |
| Roundabout | rond-point |
| Signals | signaux |
| Close to | près de |
| Petrol station | station d'essence |
| Lake | lac |
| Mountain | montagne |
| River | rivière |
| Airport | aéroport |
| Hotel | hotel |
| Restaurant | restaurant |
| Slow down | ralentir |

### Accidents

| Police | police |
|---|---|
| Driving licence | Permis de conduire |
| Accident | accident |
| Papers | papiers |
| Insurance | assurance |
| Sorry | pardon |

### Numbers

| Zero | zéro |
|---|---|
| One | un |
| Two | deux |
| Three | trois |
| Four | quatre |
| Five | cinq |
| Six | six |
| Seven | sept |
| Eight | huit |
| Nine | neuf |
| Ten | dix |
| Hundred | cent |
| Thousand | mille |

General Info

Culture & Lifestyle

Today however, dressing tends to follow European or Western trends and fashions, and in the streets, you're likely to see anything from eccentric to very formal business attire. School children do not have to wear uniforms.

## Food & Drink

There is more to Swiss cuisine than cheese and chocolate! In fact, food in Switzerland is very diverse and seasonal and most towns and regions will have their own specialities. Eating out is very common, and it can be a rarity to chance upon a free table. Not that there is any shortage of restaurants – they are spread all over the city, and can even be found on mountain tops and ski slopes!

Geneva has more than 1,100 restaurants and an extremely vast range of global cuisine, including regional or seasonal specialities. On most wine lists, you will find a choice of wines from all over the world, including Geneva.

At lunchtime, most restaurants offer a 'plat du jour' (dish of the day). These are usually well balanced meals that are good value for money by Swiss standards. A plat du jour plus a soft drink and tea or coffee will cost around SFr 20.

### Swiss Cuisine

On the whole, typical Swiss cuisine does not use many exotic herbs or spices, and tends to be a little on the rich side. One of Switzerland's most famous dishes, the cheese fondue, was originally a way to use up stale bits of cheese and bread. The cheese (usually a mix of Gruyère and Vacherin) is melted in a cast iron pot with white wine and kirsch, and then placed on a burner on the table. Armed with a small elongated fork, people then dip small pieces of bread into the cheese. Other cheese based dishes include 'raclette', which is basically melted cheese scraped from a huge lump held near a fire until a layer melts. 'Croûte au fromage' is a thick slice of bread soaked in wine, smothered in Gruyère cheese and baked until sizzling. Malakoffs are deep fried cheesy balls (a speciality from the Canton of Vaud) that are usually only found on the menu of specialised restaurants (the Auberge de Luins in the village of Luins is famous for them).

Rösti is a shredded potato pancake served either as an accompaniment, or as a main meal when made with bacon and topped with a fried egg. An 'assiette valaisanne' is a dish consisting of cold meats, including dried beef, dried sausage and smoked bacon.

The Swiss eat muesli any time of the day, not just for breakfast. Other sweet treats include epiphanies cake, brünsli, chocolate chip Tyrol cake, Engadine walnut tart ('nusstorte') and, of course, chocolate in all forms. Be sure to try some of the hand made chocolates from the 'chocolateries' – if you're not a chocoholic already, you may well become one!

Switzerland produces many of its own wines. In Geneva, red wines made from the Gamay grape and aged in oak casks are excellent, as are several of the white wines from the vineyards on the northern shores of Lac Léman, and the red Humagne from the Valais region. Fendant (white wine, also from Valais) is popular with fondue. The local beer should definitely be sampled but probably won't stop you from ordering your usual internationally brewed beer.

Coffee in Geneva is usually good but it is less easy to find a good cup of English tea. On the other hand there is hardly a herb or flower that the Swiss have not infused in some concoction or another with medicinal, relaxing or stimulating properties.

## Entering Switzerland

### Visas

Foreign nationals require a valid and accepted travel document to enter Switzerland. Furthermore, sufficient funds must be available, or procurable by legal means, to cover the cost of the stay. Nationals of the European Union and EFTA countries do not require visas, while most other nationalities do and the visa requirements vary greatly. Some nationalities may need visas in all cases, while others are released from the obligation of holding a visa if their stay in Switzerland does not exceed three months and serves one of the following purposes: tourism, visit, education, business, medical treatment and recuperation, participation in scientific, economic, cultural, religious or sporting events, transportation of persons or goods

**No Visa Required**

*Citizens from the following countries do not need a visa to enter Switzerland for a stay of less than 3 months:*

*All EU member countries, Argentina, Australia, Barbados, Brazil, Bulgaria, Canada, Chile, Costa Rica, Croatia, El Salvador, Guatemala, Guyana, Honduras, Israel, Jamaica, Korea (South), Mexico, Nicaragua, Panama, Paraguay, South Africa, Suriname, Trinidad and Tobago, United States of America, Uruguay, and Venezuela.*

SFr 10 ~ € 6

1ˢᵗ Edition | GENEVA **EXPLORER**

to or through Switzerland effected by a driver in the service of a company seated abroad, temporary reporting for foreign media and lastly, gainful occupation without taking up employment not exceeding eight days within a period of 90 days.

For more information on visa requirements call the Swiss embassy or consulate in your country of residence. Alternatively just log on to www.etrangers.ch or call +41 (0)31 325 95 11. Travellers requiring a visa should ensure that it allows them to re-enter Switzerland after visiting neighbouring countries (popping over the border to France for shopping, eating or excursions is all part of life in Geneva).

Foreign nationals coming to Switzerland as tourists (and who will not be gainfully employed) can stay in the country for up to two non consecutive periods of three months in any one year period. However they may be required to either prove that they have sufficient funds to cover their costs or request their host to act as financial guarantor during their stay.

## Visa Renewals

In principle it is not possible to renew a Swiss visa. However, in very exceptional circumstances, such as for medical reasons, a visa extension can be requested by contacting the local office of the Police des Etrangers in the canton in which you are staying. In Geneva you will have to present yourself personally, with your passport, to the Office Cantonal de la Population, Rue David-Duffour, 3 Geneva (022 327 7663), at least four days before your visa expires. You will also need to complete a form requesting an extension of your visa. The form can be printed from the Website (see below). If you are requesting an extension for medical reasons, you will need to present a medical certificate stating the nature of the illness and a document from the institution where you are being treated, indicating the cost of treatment. Again, you will either have to prove that you have sufficient funds to cover the cost of your stay (and any medical treatment), or provide a written guarantee from someone living in Geneva who will act as financial guarantor.

**Website:** *www.ge.ch/ocp gives detailed information in English on visas, residency permits and official forms.*

## Meet & Greet

There are two exits from the baggage reclaim area to the arrivals hall but both exits meet up so you shouldn't have any trouble finding the person who has come to collect you.

A special assistance service is available for the disabled. Disabled travellers should specify their requirements for assistance at the time of reservation and the airline should make the request. It is also possible to request the service 24 hours ahead by calling 022 799 3345. There is a meeting point for disabled passengers requiring assistance on departure, next to check-in desk 40.

There is a relatively new service at Geneva International Airport offering personalised treatment on arrival. When the passenger leaves the aircraft, he or she is escorted by a hostess all the way to the arrivals hall. Passport control formalities are fast-tracked and a private room is provided in the baggage claim area, while a porter takes care of your luggage. Reservations for this VIP service

### The Airport

*The airport is about 5 km from the centre. By car this can take anywhere between 15 to 30 minutes, depending on traffic. There are usually plenty of taxis waiting in front of the airport, on the same level as arrivals. Taxi drivers may refuse to take you to a hotel very close to the airport, so if you don't want to trudge all the way there with your bags, check with the hotel if they have a regular courtesy bus service (nearly all hotels close to the airport have one).*

*The number 10 bus connects the airport to the centre of town in about 20 to 25 minutes. The bus stop is one floor above arrivals on the same level as the check-ins. You will need coins (SFr 2.60) to purchase a ticket from the vending machine before boarding.*

*Adjacent to the airport is a train station. Trains leave almost every ten minutes and take just six minutes into Geneva's railway station (Cornavin). It can be a bit of a trek but you can take your airport trolley all the way up to the platforms. A one way, second class ticket costs SFr 5.60, and you can purchase them from the self service machines or the ticket office.*

*There is a bank located just next to arrivals, which is open seven days a week, along with ATMs that accept most major credit cards and an automatic change machine that accepts a variety of foreign bank notes.*

*If you are travelling to Geneva on business and need somewhere to work or hold a meeting, the SKYCOM Business Centre has eight private offices with access to PCs, faxes and modems, eleven conference rooms and secretarial and catering services. They are open 08:00 to 18:00 Monday to Friday (022 788 14 30).*

*Need to freshen up on arrival or before leaving? Showers are available in the baggage reclaim area and in the arrivals area, after customs (SFr 15).*

should be made 24 hours in advance by email (accueil@gva.ch). The cost is SFr 100 per welcome (for up to four passengers), which includes two items of luggage per person. There is a charge of SFr 20 per additional passenger and SFr 5 per extra piece of luggage. Payment is by credit card only.

## Customs

No customs duty is levied on any personal effects or sports equipment brought into the country, but it is forbidden to import drugs. Personal effects and goods bought in Switzerland can be exported without customs duty, whatever their value.

## Leaving Switzerland

Check in times vary from one airline to another, but generally you should aim to have completed your check in formalities with an hour to an hour and a half to spare before the departure of your flight. The last thing you want is to watch as your plane taxis down the runway while you are still stuck in the security queue!

Children travelling alone should be accompanied by a parent until the time they board the aircraft, so the parent will have to present their ID. At the check in desk the accompanying parent will be given a special form allowing them to go through passport and security controls.

Hôtel Beau Rivage

## E-tickets and Electronic Check-in

Electronic ticketing is becoming more and more common and several airlines operating out of Geneva International Airport now offer this convenient service. Basically you can buy your ticket online or over the phone, pay by credit card, receive confirmation of your reservation by email or post, and then when you check in for your flight you just need to present your ID and in some cases a confirmation number.

Geneva Airport also has some self service check in machines, which can be used if you have only one piece of hand luggage. To use these machines, which are located near check in desks 79 and 80, you will need an ATB type ticket (with a magnetic strip on the back), and a SWISS Travel Club card or the credit card that you used to pay for your ticket.

### Duty Free Allowances

- Tobacco – 200 cigarettes or 50 cigars or 250 grams of pipe tobacco
- Alcohol – 2 litres of wine and 1 litre of spirits
- Presents for a value of up to SFr 100.

## Travellers' Info

## Health Requirements

There are no vaccinations that you need to have before you enter Switzerland. Geneva is relatively free from diseases and the most you are likely catch while you're there is a common cold or the odd tummy bug. There are absolutely no medical precautions that you need to take, except of course to make sure that you have adequate medical insurance for accidents and general illness. Food hygiene standards are high, and even the water is perfectly safe to drink.

## Health Care

Health care in Switzerland is of a very high standard, and if you need medical assistance while you are visiting, you can just go to one of the hospitals or outpatient clinics ('permanence médicale'). However, medical care is very, very expensive, and all visitors should make sure they have adequate health and accident insurance. It is probably a good idea to carry proof of your medical cover with you when you go to the hospital or clinic. If you are a national of an EU country, you are entitled to free medical treatment under the bilateral Reciprocal Health Agreement. However, to make use of this benefit you should present a signed E-111 form, which can be obtained from the post office in your home country. If you don't have proof of medical cover or a signed E-111 form you will be expected to pay for medical services upfront. However, hospitals and clinics will not turn away any emergency case.

There are no specific health risks facing visitors and the climate is moderate, but a high factor sunscreen is strongly recommended on the ski slopes as well as for water sports.

Red Cross Statue

## Travel Insurance

Visitors to Switzerland should have travel insurance to cover the costs of any emergency that may arise during your visit. Choose a reputable insurer and a policy that meets your needs, especially if you are planning any 'high risk' activities like skiing, mountain climbing or even hiking. Some policies may not cover you for very dangerous activities. Always read the small print – in some cases you may not qualify for cover if you were under the influence of alchol at the time of your mishap, for example.

## Female Visitors

Aggression against women is rare in Geneva but it is still not advisable to walk through parks or along poorly lit streets if you are alone. As with just about any city in the world these days, pickpockets operate in Geneva, so stay alert and keep your handbag safe. In car parks, try to park close to the pedestrian exits and have your keys ready before returning to your car. These are all precautions that you should take in any city, and are not Geneva specific.

In the centre of Geneva, there is a hostel specifically for women (see Youth Hostels [p.28, 62]).

## Travelling with Children

Geneva is fairly child friendly with lots of parks and playgrounds all around town. When the weather is warm enough for swimming, the open air pools have separate sections for toddlers. The tourist information office on Pont de la Machine sells a small booklet (SFr 3) listing the playgrounds in Geneva and what they have to offer. In summer there are usually plenty of temporary amusement parks and fairgrounds which should keep the kids happy. For more information on what you can do in Geneva with children, refer to the Activities section [p.169].

Some shopping malls have babysitting facilities for toddlers and young children (they don't usually take babies). Many of the hotels are more welcoming to business travellers than tourists so you should check what services they offer for children before you confirm your booking. Similarly, not all restaurants have highchairs, but there are quite a few that do, and most family restaurants have children's menus.

## Physically Challenged Visitors

Facilities for the physically challenged are improving in Geneva. Multi-level stores and shopping malls usually have lifts and specially fitted toilets. Many larger restaurants also have special facilities but this is a detail you should confirm when making your reservation.

### Meeting the Challenge

*These hotels have specially adapted rooms and facilities for the physically challenged: Crowne Plaza and Mövenpick near the airport, and the Noga Hilton, Epsom Manotel, Royal Manotel, du Midi and Calvy in the city centre.*

Some public toilets are specially adapted for wheelchair use (there is one near the flower clock). At most road crossings the pavements slope down to allow wheelchair access, although public transport remains fairly inaccessible. However, there are special transport services for the physically challenged (see Taxi Companies, [p.32]). You'll have no trouble finding special parking places for the physically challenged, although be sure to display an official sticker on your car or you'll be heavily fined. These stickers ('macaron handicapé) are available free of charge from the Brigade du Traffic (27 Boulevard Helvétique, 022 327 6627) on presentation of a medical certificate.

Geneva International Airport does have some special facilities for the physically challenged, but some additional assistance will probably be required (see Meet and Greet, [p.19]).

## Dress Code

The dress code in Geneva is informal and almost anything goes. Clothes that are especially provocative or unusual are likely to attract attention and stares, just like anywhere else. For restaurants, bars and nightclubs the dress code will depend on the rules of each particular establishment, and you'll probably find that jeans are not acceptable in the more upmarket places. For work and business, those who hold positions in upper management will most likely have to adhere to a fairly strict dress code, but for middle and lower management work attire is quite casual. At many of the outdoor swimming pools women sunbathe topless without turning too many heads.

## Dos and Don'ts

You should make the most of all that Geneva has to offer during your stay, but as with any travel destination you should respect the local customs and obey the law. Basic common sense should keep you out of trouble. The Swiss are an orderly bunch and disapprove of people breaking the law or bucking the system, so even if there are no uniformed police officers around while you are doing something naughty you may find yourself being reported by a diligent member of the public. Similarly, if you are being a noisy neighbour the Swiss people in your building are likely to call the police rather than knock on your door and ask you to keep it down.

There are a few Swiss rituals surrounding eating and drinking that you should remember so as not to offend anyone. It is considered rude to take even the smallest sip of your drink before you have clinked glasses and wished each other 'santé' (good health). It is very important to keep eye contact as you do this and in German speaking parts of Switzerland it is also customary to say the person's name. At lunch or dinner, don't tuck in until you've wished everyone at your table 'bon appétit' (good appetite).

Graffiti – don't!

## Safety

Geneva is considered to be one of the safest cities in Europe but there are still pickpockets and criminals so you should remain vigilant. Keep your valuables and important travel documents locked in your hotel room or in the hotel safe. In crowds, be discreet with your money and wallet and don't carry large amounts of cash with you. Handbags are one of the most common targets.

Pedestrians have right of way on pedestrian crossings but accidents have happened in the past, so on pedestrian crossings without lights, be certain that a car is actually stopping for you before you step out onto the crossing.

The level of driving in Geneva is quite high, although drivers can be quite aggressive, especially in rush hour traffic. Therefore it is best to drive defensively, especially when changing lanes.

Whether you're driving or walking, check carefully for oncoming trams, buses and bicycles

## Police

Geneva's police officers are generally helpful and some of them speak at least one other language (usually English or German). Their Website (www.geneve.ch/police) gives information on preventing crimes and maximising the safety of children, women and the elderly. You can also find information on what measures to take if you are the victim of a crime or accident. Unfortunately, information on this Website is in French.

### Police Hotline

*If you are a victim of or witness to of any kind of aggression, report it to the police by calling 112 or 117, or go to the nearest police station.*

### Lost/Stolen Property

If you have had anything stolen, whether from your pocket, your car or your hotel room, report the theft immediately to the nearest police station, giving as many details as possible.

If you lose something at Geneva International Airport you can either contact Jet Aviation (022 717 80 61) or Swissport Geneva (022 799 33 35). Outside the airport, the cantonal lost and found office ('Objets Trouvés') is located at Rue des Glacis de Rive, 5 and is open from 07:30 to 16:00. Their Website (www.geneve.ch/objets_trouves) suggests the steps you should take if you lose or find an item, and all information is given in English and French.

## Swiss Tourist Info Abroad

Although Switzerland Tourism does have offices overseas, they have a free international phone line for all bookings and information (00800 100 200 29/30 or from USA and Canada: 011 800 100 200 29/30). Their Website is packed with information on how to organise your trip and provides addresses of Switzerland Tourism offices in different countries. Visit www.myswitzerland.com.

## Places to Stay

Geneva offers a variety of accommodation options from hotels, hotel apartments, youth and other budget hostels to country inns and farm guesthouses. The tourist information office ('Genève-Tourisme') operates an accommodation reservation service for Geneva and its surrounding countryside. You can contact them by phone (022 909 7020), fax (022 909 7021) or email (reservation@geneve-tourisme.ch). Alternatively, just make your reservations online at www.geneve-tourisme.ch.

## Hotels

Geneva has over 130 hotels, with more popping up all the time. In general even the Geneva hotels that are not members of the Swiss Hotel Association still adhere to the Association's classifications and standards.

More than two thirds of visitors come to Geneva for business purposes and as a result, many hotels cater to business travellers, concentrating on facilities such as computer and fax connectivity, conference and meeting facilities, and business services. It can be pretty difficult to find an available room during major exhibitions and seminars. Check the list of major events [p.45] so that you can plan your travel time accordingly. For more details on big events and their exact dates visit the Genève-Tourisme Website (see above).

General Info

Places to Stay

The Mandarin Oriental Hotel

## Five Star Hotels

### Crowne Plaza Genève     Map Ref ➜ 2-C4

Opposite the airport, this fairly recent and modern hotel offers 500 rooms that are fully equipped for the business traveller, with extensive facilities for conferences and special events. It also has fitness and wellness centres with a gym, swimming pool, jacuzzi, sauna and steam baths.

### Hôtel d'Angleterre     Map Ref ➜ 13-E2

A charming and elegant hotel built in 1872 with fabulous views of the lake, Jet d'Eau and Mont-Blanc. The restaurant's acclaimed chef proposes an international menu to suit all tastes. The 45 rooms and suites are classically and luxuriously decorated, and also fully equipped with all the necessities. Additional amenities are available for business travellers on request.

### Hôtel Les Armures     Map Ref ➜ 13-E4

Located in the heart of Geneva's Old Town, the hotel's building is steeped in history and the 28 rooms are luxuriously decorated in a style pertaining to its traditions and past – all amenities are provided. A restaurant located within offers many typical Swiss specialities, and if you don't know what to do with a pot of melted cheese, they'll be happy to teach you!

### Hôtel Beau-Rivage     Map Ref ➜ 13-E2

Founded in 1865 by the Mayer family, this elegant and distinctive hotel overlooks the lake and has a beautiful atrium. Recently restored, the atrium reveals Pompeian frescoes that originally decorated the walls when the hotel first opened. The rooms are beautifully decorated in classic and period styles with fully equipped bathrooms and Internet access.

### Hôtel des Bergues     Map Ref ➜ 13-E3

This luxurious haven of tranquility in the centre of Geneva has 93 historical suites, fully equipped and decorated in classical and romantic, French and English style, most with genuine period furniture. Its restaurant, the Chat-Botté, is an internationally acclaimed gourmet restaurant.

### Hôtel de la Cigogne     Map Ref ➜ 13-E4

Just a couple of minutes' stroll from Geneva's designer shops, the Old Town and the lake, this turn-of-the century residence combines the classic and the modern, and exudes a special charm as well as individuality and originality. A stylish glass roof restaurant offers gourmet cuisine and an exceptional wine list. Babysitting facilities are also available.

### Hôtel de la Paix     Map Ref ➜ 13-E2

Overlooking the lake and mountains, this distinguished hotel opened in 1865 and boasts a gourmet restaurant. The décor is opulent but discreet, and tastefully combines classical and modern styles. Rooms either face the lake or look over a quiet square and some of them have high speed Internet access.

### Hôtel Président Wilson     Map Ref ➜ 5-E3

The hotel is situated between the centre and the international organisations. A magnificent terrace faces the lake and the Mont-Blanc with an outdoor seawater pool and a restaurant-grill in the summer. The fitness centre and sauna are open all year round . Rooms have been luxuriously refurbished with modern amenities and Internet access.

Hotel Beau-Rivage

### Hôtel Le Richemond Map Ref ➜ 13-E2

With refined and varied décor combining tradition and innovation, Le Jardin restaurant has a striking art deco setting. It is open from breakfast to dinner, and the garden pavilion restaurant is an especially enchanting setting for a meal or a beverage any time of the day. Other hotel amenities include a fitness area, Internet access in all rooms and babysitting services.

### InterContinental Map Ref ➜ 5-D2

The main advantage of this hotel is its location, within walking distance of most international and UN organisations. It has an outdoor swimming pool open from May to September, a gym with the latest equipment, sauna, jacuzzi, steam bath and a beauty salon/barber. Most importantly, it has fantastic views of the city.

### La Réserve Hotel and Spa Map Ref ➜ 2-E2

Set in four hectares of park 5 km from Geneva and 3 km from the airport, the focus of this newly refurbished hotel is on tranquillity and wellbeing. Marble mosaics, black granite, exotic woods and photos of faraway places have been combined to produce a unique atmosphere. Amenities include indoor and outdoor pools, fitness areas, sauna, tennis courts and a range of beauty and wellness treatments. Special weekend prices are also available.

### Mandarin Oriental Map Ref ➜ 13-D3

Reputed for its two restaurants Café Rafael and Le Neptune, the latter has been rated by both Michelin and Gault Milaut. This hotel overlooks the Rhône river and the rooms are modern and bright. It has a fully equipped fitness centre with sauna and steam baths, and is an excellent starting point for a jog in the woods along the river.

### Mövenpick Hotel & Casino Map Ref ➜ 5-A2

This is mainly a business hotel with extensive conferencing and banqueting facilities and services, including a business corner with free Internet access. It hosts several restaurants, bars, cafés and a casino, as well as a fully equipped fitness centre with a sauna and jacuzzi.

### Noga Hilton Map Ref ➜ 13-E2

Among the relatively modern lakefront hotels opposite the Jet d'Eau, the Noga-Hilton's rooms are contemporary and luxurious with marble bathrooms and modern facilities. There are four restaurants, one of which has a large terrace with a lovely view over the lake. The hotel has extensive conferencing amenities with the latest audiovisual equipment, and a business corner with PC's and high speed Internet access.

Noga Hilton

### Swissôtel Métropole Map Ref ➜ 13-E4

The Métropole was built in 1854 on the city's ancient fortifications. Located just across from the Jardin Anglais and in the centre of the main business and shopping districts, this elegant, luxurious, completely renovated and modernised hotel offers a range of amenities including fitness areas and Internet access in rooms.

Swissôtel Métropole

## Hotels

### Five Star

| Five Star | Location | Phone | Map | Double (SFr) | Email |
|---|---|---|---|---|---|
| Hôtel Beau Rivage | Pâquis | 022 716 66 66 | 13-E2 | 590 | info@beau-rivage.ch |
| Crowne Plaza | Le Grand Saconnex | 022 747 02 02 | 2-C4 | 395 | sales@cpgeneva.ch |
| Hôtel d'Angleterre | Pâquis | 022 906 55 55 | 13-E2 | 520 | angleterre@rchmail.com |
| Hôtel de la Cigogne | Town Centre | 022 818 40 40 | 13-E4 | 445 | cigogne@bluewin.ch |
| Hôtel de la Paix | Pâquis | 022 909 60 00 | 13-E2 | 450 | reservations@hoteldelapaix.ch |
| Hôtel des Bergues | St Gervais | 022 908 70 00 | 13-E3 | 725 | info@hoteldesbergues.com |
| Intercontinental | Le Petit Saconnex | 022 919 39 39 | 5-D2 | 370 | geneva@interconti.com |
| La Réserve Hotel & Spa | Bellevue | 022 959 59 59 | 2-E2 | 670 | reservations@lareserve.ch |
| Hôtel le Richemond | Pâquis | 022 715 70 00 | 13-E2 | 790 | reservations@richemond.ch |
| Hôtel les Armures | Town Centre | 022 310 91 72 | 13-E4 | 505 | armures@span.ch |
| Mandarin Oriental | Rhône/lake | 022 909 00 00 | 13-D3 | 610 | mogva-reservations@mohg.com |
| Mövenpick | Cointrin | 022 798 75 75 | 5-A2 | 420 | hotel.geneva@moevenpick.com |
| Noga-Hilton | Pâquis | 022 908 90 81 | 13-E2 | 565 | gvahitwsal@hilton.com |
| President Wilson | St Gervais | 022 906 66 66 | 13-E1 | 520 | resa@hotelpwilson.com |
| Swissôtel Métropole | Town Centre | 022 318 32 00 | 13-E4 | 650 | reservations.geneva@swissotel.com |

### Four Star

| Four Star | Location | Phone | Map | Double (SFr) | Email |
|---|---|---|---|---|---|
| Ambassador | St Gervais | 022 908 05 30 | 13-D3 | 230 | info@hotel-ambassador.ch |
| Auteuil Manotel | Pâquis | 022 544 22 22 | 13-D1 | 327 | auteuil@manotel.com |
| Bristol | St Gervais | 022 716 57 00 | 13-E3 | 425 | bristol@bristol.ch |
| Century Best Western | Villereuse | 022 592 88 88 | 14-A1 | 238 | hotelcentury@bluewin.ch |
| Churchill | Les Eaux-Vives | 022 591 88 88 | 14-B3 | 258 | hotelchurchill@bluewin.ch |
| Cornavin | Les Grottes | 022 716 12 12 | 13-D2 | 277 | cornavin@fhotels.ch |
| Hôtel d'Allèves | St Gervais | 022 732 15 30 | 13-D3 | 235 | – |
| Hôtel de Berne | Pâquis | 022 715 46 00 | 13-E2 | 550 | hoteldeberne@bernehotel.ch |
| Hôtel de la Vendée | Lancy | 022 792 04 11 | 8-C2 | 260 | info@vendee.ch |
| Hôtel Diplomate | Villereuse | 022 592 87 87 | 6-A4 | 238 | hoteldiplomate@bluewin.ch |
| Hôtel Du Midi | St Gervais | 022 544 15 00 | 13-D3 | 195 | info@hotel-du-midi.ch |
| Epsom Manotel | Pâquis | 022 544 66 66 | 13-E1 | 354 | epsom@manotel.com |
| Hôtel Grand-Pré | Moillebeau | 022 918 11 11 | 5-D3 | 325 | reservation@grandpre.ch |
| Hôtel Le Montbrillant | Les Grottes | 022 733 77 84 | 13-D2 | 200 | contact@montbrillant.ch |
| Melia Rex Boutique | Moillebeau | 022 544 74 74 | 5-D3 | 267 | – |
| NH Geneva Airport | Meyrin | 022 989 90 00 | 4-E1 | 195 | nhgeneva.airport@nh-hotels.ch |
| Novotel | Ferney Voltaire | 022 909 90 00 | 2-A3 | 280 | H3133@accor-hotels.com |
| Ramada Park | Pâquis | 022 710 30 00 | 13-E2 | 280 | info@ramadaparkhotel.ch |
| Royal Manotel | Pâquis | 022 906 14 14 | 13-D1 | 354 | royal@manotel.com |
| Sofitel | St Gervais | 022 908 80 80 | 13-D3 | 490 | H1322@accor-hotels.com |
| Tiffany | La Coulouvrenière | 022 708 16 16 | 13-C4 | 320 | info@hotel-tiffany.ch |
| Warwick | Pâquis | 022 716 80 00 | 13-D2 | 345 | sales.geneva@warwickhotels.com |

### Three Star

| Three Star | Location | Phone | Map | Double (SFr) | Email |
|---|---|---|---|---|---|
| Adriatica | Les Philosophes | 022 703 53 83 | 15-E2 | 250 | reservation@hotel-adriatica.com |
| Ascot Manotel | Pâquis | 022 544 38 38 | 13-E1 | 259 | ascot@manotel.com |
| Astoria | Les Grottes | 022 544 52 52 | 13-D2 | 195 | hotel@astoria-geneve.ch |
| Balzac | Pâquis | 022 731 01 60 | 13-E1 | 175 | info@hotel-balzac.ch |
| Calvy | Villereuse | 022 700 27 27 | 6-A4 | 140 | calvy@bluewin.ch |
| Capitole | Les Grottes | 022 909 86 26 | 13-D2 | 169 | info@hotelcapitole.ch |
| Carlton | Pâquis | 022 908 68 50 | 13-E1 | 180 | carlton_gva@swissonline.ch |
| Chantilly Manotel | Pâquis | 022 544 40 40 | 13-E1 | 276 | chantilly@manotel.com |
| Hôtel Comédie | Plainpalais | 022 322 23 24 | 15-D1 | 180 | info@hotel-comedie.ch |
| Hôtel des Alpes | Les Grottes | 022 731 22 00 | 13-D2 | 195 | hotel.alpes@bluewin.ch |
| Edelweiss Manotel | Pâquis | 022 544 51 51 | 13-E1 | 276 | edelweiss@manotel.com |
| Eden | Sécheron | 022 716 37 00 | 5-E2 | 220 | eden@eden.ch |
| Excelsior | St. Gervais | 022 732 09 45 | 13-D2 | 190 | excelsior@geneva-link.ch |
| Hermitage | Town Centre | 022 310 30 24 | 13-E4 | 198 | hotelhermitage@bluewin.ch |

## Hotels

| Three Star | Location | Phone | Map | Double (SFr) | Email |
|---|---|---|---|---|---|
| J.J.Rousseau | St Gervais | 022 731 55 70 | 13-D3 | 180 | rousseau@freesurf.ch |
| Hôtel le Cerf-Volant | Cointrin | 022 798 07 57 | 5-B1 | 170 | info@cerfvolant.ch |
| Hôtel le Grenil | Les Savoises | 022 328 30 55 | 13-C4 | 150 | resa@grenil.ch |
| Hôtel les Nations | Moillebeau | 022 748 08 08 | 5-D3 | 195 | info@hotel-les-nations.com |
| Hôtel Moderne | Les Grottes | 022 732 81 00 | 13-D2 | 190 | info@hotelmoderne.ch |
| Mon Repos | Sécheron | 022 909 39 09 | 5-E2 | 235 | reservations@hmrge.ch |
| Montana | Les Grottes | 022 732 08 40 | 13-D2 | 160 | hotel.montana@span.ch |
| Phoenix | Cointrin | 022 710 03 03 | 5-B1 | 135 | info@hotel-phoenix.ch |
| Ramada Encore | Carouge | 022 309 50 00 | 8-C3 | 220 | geneve.encore@ramada-treff.ch |
| Sagitta | Villereuse | 022 786 33 61 | 6-A4 | 199 | sagitta@span.ch |
| Saint James | Central | 022 849 91 00 | na | 185 | stjames@gic.ch |
| Hôtel Suisse | Les Grottes | 022 732 66 30 | 13-D2 | 230 | reservation@hotel-suisse.ch |
| Touring-Balance | Town Centre | 022 818 62 62 | 13-E4 | 270 | touringbalance@bluewin.ch |
| Trente-Trois | Meyrin | 022 710 40 60 | 5-B1 | 150 | hotel33@bluewin.ch |
| Windsor | Pâquis | 022 731 71 30 | 13-D2 | 150 | contact@hotel-windsor.ch |

| Two Star | | | | | |
|---|---|---|---|---|---|
| Hôtel Aida | Les Philosophes | 022 320 12 66 | 15-D2 | 130 | hotel.aida.geneva@bluewin.ch |
| Hôtel Bel'Espérance | Town Centre | 022 818 37 37 | 13-E4 | 140 | belesp@swi.salvationarmy.org |
| Hôtel Bernina | Les Grottes | 022 908 49 50 | 13-D2 | 160 | info@bernina-geneve.ch |
| Hôtel Central | Town Centre | 022 818 81 00 | 13-D4 | 100 | info@hotelcentral.ch |
| Hôtel de Genève (ex Rio) | St Gervais | 022 732 32 64 | 13-C3 | 125 | hotelrio@vtx.ch |
| Ibis Airport | Cointrin | 022 710 95 00 | 5-B1 | 119 | – |
| Hôtel les Tourelles | St Gervais | 022 732 44 23 | 13-D3 | 130 | destourelles@compuserve.com |
| Hôtel Lido | St Gervais | 022 731 55 30 | 13-D2 | 150 | info@hotel-lido.ch |
| Hôtel Pax | Villereuse | 022 787 50 70 | 6-A4 | 125 | direction@hotel-pax-geneva.ch |
| Savoy | St Gervais | 022 906 47 00 | 13-D2 | 120 | – |

| One Star | | | | | |
|---|---|---|---|---|---|
| Caroline | Carouge | 022 343 36 60 | 15-C3 | 100 | – |
| City Hostel (backpack) | Pâquis | 022 901 15 00 | 13-E1 | 80 | info@cityhostel.ch |
| Esmeralda | Carouge | 022 343 96 98 | 15-C3 | 81 | – |
| Luserna | Moillebeau | 022 345 45 45 | 5-C3 | 98 | info@hotel-luserna.ch |
| Quatre-Nations | Pâquis | 022 732 02 24 | 13-D2 | 75 | – |
| Saint-Gervais | St Gervais | 022 732 45 72 | 13-D3 | 105 | – |

| Country Inns | | | | | |
|---|---|---|---|---|---|
| Auberge de Confignon | Confignon/6km | 022 757 19 44 | 8-A4 | 220 | – |
| Auberge d'Hermance | Hermance/14km | 022 751 13 68 | 3-B1 | 210 | info@hotel-hermance.ch |
| Auberge Port Gitana | Bellevue/6km | 022 774 31 48 | 2-D2 | 190 | portgitana@gve.ch |
| Bellerive | Bellerive/8km | 022 752 12 82 | 3-E3 | 115 | g.calendret@worldonline.ch |
| De Vilette | Thônex/6km | 022 789 04 70 | 9-C2 | 160 | – |
| Domaine de Chateauvieux | Satigny/9km | 022 753 15 11 | 4-C3 | 195 | info@chateauvieux.ch |
| La Coudre B&B | Céligny/17km | 022 960 83 60 | na | 180 | vivimar@deckpoint.ch |
| La Donzelle | La Plaine/14km | 022 754 12 15 | na | 130 | – |
| Le Manoir | Collonge/10km | 022 752 21 50 | 3-D3 | 150 | – |
| Le Relais de Céligny | Céligny/21km | 022 776 60 61 | na | 180 | relais.de.celigny@bluewin.ch |

### Note

*Note: The above prices are for standard double rooms. Several hotels offer a special discount rate for weekends if requested.*

*For more one or two star hotels, contact Geneva's information and hotel reservation centre, Genève-Tourisme (909 70 20) or reserve online through their Website: www.geneve-tourisme.ch.*

Many of the top end hotels are located on the shores of Lac Léman, offering beautiful views. All city centre hotels are within walking distance of the main shopping areas, restaurants and the lakeside. Hotels near the airport have less charm, and it will take you 10 to 15 minutes by taxi to reach the city centre and all its attractions. On the plus side though, these hotels are usually within walking distance of Palexpo (the huge exhibition hall near the airport). Larger hotels often have a regular airport shuttle service, so check when you make your reservation. If you're looking for reasonably priced hotel accommodation, you could try going just over the border – here you'll find pleasant rooms at cheaper rates, particularly at hotels such as the Hôtel Formule 1 (www.hotelformule1.com).

## Hotel Apartments

Several hotel apartments ('résidences') offer furnished accommodation on a daily, weekly or monthly basis. Apart from being cheaper than hotels (only slightly, in some cases), they allow more independence and feel more homely than a hotel room. They are also more practical for accommodating families. Studios and apartments usually come fully furnished, including bed linen, towels and kitchenette equipment. Prices vary considerably, but you can expect to pay anything between SFr 100 and SFr 400 per day for a studio (or a monthly rate of SFr 1,800 – SFr 5,000); and between SFr 250 and SFr 550 per day for an apartment with one or more bedrooms (or a monthly rate of SFr 5,400 – SFr 10,500).

The most central résidences are Lafitte (Pâquis), Long-Champ and Mont-Blanc (close to Cornavin Railway Station), Sagitta and Saint James (near Rive) and Cité-Verdaine (Old Town). The

Residences Studio-House Acacias and Dizerens are also within very easy access of the centre, whilst Grand Saconnex is located near the airport/Palexpo. Villette is quite far from the centre in the more rural commune of Thônex.

## Hostels

Hostels are popular with travellers on a budget. The City Hostel Geneva offers 24 hour access, daily movies in English, PCs with Internet access and a laundry service. Prices per night range from SFr 28 for dormitory accommodation, to SFr 63 for a single room with TV. All rooms are non smoking. The Youth Hostel on Rue Rothschild has self catering facilities, a laundromat, leisure rooms, a library and a self service restaurant. A bed for the night will cost SFr 26 in a dorm and SFr 85 for a double room with a shower and WC. (This is the members' rate; nonmembers will have to pay an extra SFr 6 per person). Both the City Hostel and the Youth Hostel are located in the popular Pâquis district, and are within walking distance of Cornavin Railway Station.

The Home St Pierre Hostel in the Old Town is for women only and has self catering facilities, a roof terrace overlooking the lake, a laundry service, and two living rooms with television. Dormitory accommodation will cost about SFr 24 per night, and a single room will cost about SFr 46. If you're planning a long stay the monthly rate for a single room is around SFr 700.

### Youth Hostels

| City Hostel | 022 901 15 00 | www.cityhostel.ch |
| Home St Pierre | 022 310 37 07 | www.homestpierre.ch |
| Youth Hostel | 022 732 62 60 | www.yh-geneva.ch |

### Hotel Apartments

| | Phone | Map | Studio (weekly) | Suite (weekly) | Apartment (weekly) | e-mail |
|---|---|---|---|---|---|---|
| Acacias Résidence de Villette | 022 789 04 70 | 9-C2 | 560 | – | – | – |
| Résidence Cité-Verdaine | 022 312 01 20 | 13-E4 | 660-1,200 | 1,500-1,800 | – | – |
| Résidence Dizerens | 022 809 55 11 | 15-D2 | 600-1,500 | 1,500-2,200 | – | hotel.dizerens@swissonline.ch |
| Résidence du Grand Saconnex | 022 710 27 57 | 2-C4 | 693-1,134 | – | – | rgs@fishey.ch |
| Résidence Lafitte | 022 908 02 00 | 13-E2 | 1005-1,660 | 1,500-1,900 | – | residence.lafitte@span.ch |
| Résidence de Longchamp | 022 716 48 48 | 5-E3 | 973-1,393 | – | – | longchamp@span.ch |
| Résidence Mont-Blanc | 022 716 40 00 | 13-E2 | 1,610-1,925 | – | 3,010-5,600 | residence.mont-blanc @span.ch |
| Résidence Sagitta | 022 786 33 61 | 14-A4 | 875 | 1,190 | 1,470 | sagitta@span.ch |
| Résidence Saint-James | 022 849 91 00 | 14-A4 | 1,015-1,295 | 1,750-3,150 | – | stjames@gic.ch |
| Résidence Studio House | 022 304 03 00 | 15-C2 | 595-980 | | | studiohouse@bluewin.ch |

Note: In most cases the prices vary depending on the number of persons occupying a studio, suite or apartment.

## Camping

There are several campsites on the outskirts of Geneva, most of which are quite far from the city centre but reachable with a bit of a walk and public transport. The Camping Cantonal du Val de l'Allondon is situated in a quiet, protected natural area surrounded by vineyards, forests and charming villages. The campsite at Pointe à la Bise is located by the lakeside and has a full array of amenities and facilities. It is also the easiest to access from the centre (fairly manageable cycling distance).

## Getting Around

Even with an excellent public transport network and efforts to limit the use of personal vehicles for environmental reasons, cars are still a popular mode of transport in Geneva. For those who just can't stand the frustration, congestion and road rage involved in driving, or afford the rising costs of petrol and parking, it is quite possible to get wherever you need to be without a car. The easiest ways to get around in the centre of Geneva are walking, cycling or public transport. There is a vast network of trams and buses, as well as boats (the 'Mouettes Genevoises') in the summer months. If you do prefer to drive the road network is good, but with roads constantly being dug up to lay new tramlines, and many lanes being reserved for buses and taxis, traffic congestion is on the increase.

### Colour Change

*As you cross the border into France the colours of signposts change – green signs indicate main roads, while blue signs indicate motorways.*

The roads are fairly well signposted. Green signs are used to indicate motorways, blue signs indicate main roads and white signs are used for secondary roads and different areas of the city. Hotels are indicated by smaller signs with a yellow background, which are placed under other road signs at crossroads (but you have to get up quite close before you can read them, by which time, if you're driving, you usually discover that you're in the wrong traffic lane!) Brown signs show places of interest.

Geneva is relatively easy to navigate especially if you rely on the prominent landmarks, like the mountains and the lake, to get your bearings. Take time to familiarise yourself with the area, using a map, before setting out. Basically, the city is divided into 'rive gauche' (Left Bank) on the south side of the lake and river, and 'rive droite' (Right Bank) to the north. The main bridge for crossing the lake by car is the Pont du Mont-Blanc. The next two bridges (to the west) are for pedestrians and cyclists only. The other two road bridges are the Pont de l'Ile and Pont de la Coulouvrenière. The city is divided into districts ('quartiers'), such as Eaux-Vives and the Old Town on rive gauche and Pâquis, St Jean and Cornavin on rive droite. On the outskirts of the city are Carouge to the south, Lancy to the west and Petit-Saconnex, Grand-Saconnex, Vernier, Meyrin and the airport (Cointrin) to the north. If you want to head east on the north bank, follow signs to Lausanne, and to travel east on the south bank, follow signs to Evian. In Geneva, every road, path or passageway has a name that is usually well indicated at each end by a small blue sign.

A motorway runs around the outskirts of Geneva. The speed limit on this section of the motorway is 100 km/h, and it is liberally dotted with speed traps. You have been warned!

Unireso is a joint tariff community covering the whole of the Canton of Geneva. It combines travel by CFF (rail), SMGN (lake boat operators) and the TPG (buses and trams). Tickets must be purchased before boarding from the vending machines located at each stop. SFr 2.60 buys you a ticket valid for one hour of travel through two zones (the town centre and the adjoining communes). Methods of payment include coins, the CASH chip on Swiss bank cards or the 'Carte @ Bonus' (SFr 20, 30 or 50), which offers discounted travel. See also Buses & Trams [p.32].

### Campsites

| Name | Location | Map | Tel. | Opening period | e-mail |
|------|----------|-----|------|----------------|--------|
| ACCS-Auto Camping et Caravaning Club de Suisse | Peissy | 4-A3 | 022 753 16 17 | – | – |
| Camping Cantonal du Val de l'Allondon | Satigny | 4-A2 | 022 753 15 15 | April to end October | camp.allondon@bluewin.ch |
| Camping du Bois-De-Bay | Satigny | 4-A2 | 022 341 05 05 | All year | – |
| Camping d'Hermance | Hermance | 3-E1 | 022 751 14 83 | April to end September | – |
| TCS Pointe à la Bise | Vésenaz | 3-D3 | 022 752 12 96 | April to mid October | camping.geneve@tcs.ch |

## Car

Traffic congestion is the curse of any modern city and Geneva is no exception! There is an abundance of traffic lights, each letting just a few cars through at a time. Don't be tempted to sneak through as the light turns red though – many traffic lights are fitted with little cameras that will catch you in the act.

### Driving Habits & Regulations

In general, driving standards in Geneva are quite high although you'll find your fair share of rogue drivers who push in and lane hop. The daily rush hour, and Friday and Saturday nights, tend to be the most stressful driving times. Driving is on the right hand side.

> **Traffic Accidents**
>
> If you witness a traffic violation or accident, you can report it to the police by calling the toll free number 117.

You have to wear a seat belt at all times in a car, whether you are sitting in the front or back seat. Children under the age of seven are not allowed to sit in the front, unless they have a suitably adapted seat and belt. Children between the ages of seven and twelve must wear a seatbelt appropriate for their size.

It is your responsibility to be aware of other important driving regulations, such as having to switch headlights on in tunnels, carrying a warning triangle in case of breakdowns, and displaying the proper parking disk (see Parking [p.31]). To drive on motorways you must display a 'vignette' (a sticker showing the calendar year, e.g. 05) on the windscreen of your car. The vignette costs SFr 40 and can be purchased from customs offices, post offices and garages. It is non-transferable, and only valid for that calendar year, so even if you buy one in November you will have to buy a new one for the new year. There is a grace period until the 31st January but come early February the police are usually out in force to fine drivers not displaying valid vignettes. The fine is SFr 100.

If you plan to drive on any of the mountainous routes during winter you will need to carry snow chains for your wheels. Snowploughs usually manage to clear snowfall quite quickly but it can take a while for them to clear large areas, by which time several more centimetres of snow can fall.

### Speed Limits

The speed limit in built up areas is 50 km/h, and in some residential areas it's as low as 30 km/h. On the main roads, outside of built up areas, it is 80 km/h and on motorways, 120 km/h, unless otherwise indicated. Speed limits are clearly indicated on road signs and there are frequent speed traps. Fortunately, the speed traps are pretty hard to miss – look out for one and a half metre high grey boxes (some are cunningly disguised in black and white cowprint or as blocks of cheese!)

### Driving Licence

Any foreigner over 18 years of age, with a valid international driving licence, can drive in Geneva. Third party insurance is obligatory. If you are moving to Geneva you have one year to change your driving licence to a Swiss one, or take a Swiss driving test. For more information on this and the procedures involved, see Driving Licences on [p.30, 52].

### Accidents

If you are involved in a traffic accident you can complete an official accident form and have both parties sign on it. In the event of a serious accident or disagreement, do not move your vehicle. Instead, call the traffic police (022 307 9111) and stay by your car until they arrive.

### Non Drivers

At pedestrian crossings where there are no traffic lights, pedestrians have the right of way. By law, drivers are obliged to stop to allow pedestrians to cross the road. In general, Geneva's pedestrians are a careful bunch who respect the rules of traffic lights and road crossings.

> **Driving & Alcohol**
>
> The maximum tolerance of alcohol in the blood (when driving) is 0.5% or 50 mg per 1000 ml of blood. With too many deaths and accidents being caused by drivers under the influence, the police have started cracking down on drinking and driving in Geneva. So if you're going to be consuming alcohol it is definitely best to stick to public transport or call a taxi.

> **No Mobile When Mobile**
>
> The use of mobile phones whilst driving is forbidden and, if you're caught, the fine is SFr 100.

As more and more people ditch their cars and travel around on their bicycles, Geneva's network of cycle paths is getting bigger. In many cases these are simply demarcated on the road by a dotted yellow line. Remember to watch out for cyclists when you are turning into another road.

Apart from the pedestrians and cyclists, keep a look out for people on scooters and mopeds – as frustrating as it can be watching them zip through the gaps in a traffic jam, remember to afford them the same courtesy as you would any other road user!

## Parking

Apart from the purpose built (and expensive!) car parks, parking spaces in town are like gold dust. If you are lucky enough to find a space make sure you know how long you're permitted to stay there – all parking spaces have a panel indicating particular parking restrictions. Places marked in white have time limits, with the time allowed indicated on a panel, and a 'pay and display' metre nearby. You can park in blue spaces at no charge for one and a half hours between 08:00 and 19:00, but it is obligatory to display a disk on the inside of your windscreen indicating time of arrival. This disk is available from Fondation des Parkings, Carrefour de l'Etoile 1, CH-1211 Geneva (022 827 4490) or from any police station. There are several underground car parks, and these are convenient but quite expensive. Alternatively you can make use of the various park and ride ('Parkez et Roulez') areas on the outskirts of the city, and ride public transport into the city centre. Parking violations will get you a hefty SFr 140 fine, so don't be lazy!

## Petrol/Gas Stations

There are plenty of petrol stations all over the city, either run or franchised by various companies such as Shell, BP, Migrol, Elf, AGIP and Total. Petrol in Switzerland has been cheaper than in other European countries, mainly because of lower taxes. However, that will change with the introduction of the $CO_2$ tax, which is added to the price of petrol. The aim is to discourage people from using their personal vehicles and opt for public transport instead. Petrol prices vary throughout Switzerland but as a rough guide, expect to pay around SFr 1.43 for a litre of unleaded fuel.

Many petrol stations have a mini market, some have a car wash, and most have 24 hour service

with machines that take bank notes (usually SFr 10 and SFr 20 notes) and credit cards.

## Car Hire

Most car rental companies are near the centre of town. The main ones however, also have offices in the arrivals hall of the airport. Prices vary so you need to shop around, but to give you an approximate idea, the rate for the smallest category of car is around SFr 150 a day and larger cars, around SFr 200 to SFr 290 a day. As a general rule: the longer the rental period, the lower the daily rate.

The most popular car hire company is EasyCar.com, which is part of the easyJet group. EasyCar offers the best rates in town, starting at approximately SFr 80 per day. Bookings can only be made online, and cars must be picked up and dropped off at the airport. Visit www.easycar.com.

| Car Rental Agencies | |
|---|---|
| Autolocation Léman | 022 732 01 43 |
| Avis | 022 731 90 00 |
| Budget Rent a Car | 022 717 86 75 |
| EasyCar.com | www.easycar.com |
| Elite Rent a Car | 022 909 87 87 |
| Elite Chauffeured Services | 022 909 87 72 |
| Europcar Amag Services | 022 732 52 52 |
| Europcar Chauffeur Drive | 022 798 11 85 |
| GL Geneva Limousine | 022 719 85 60 |
| Imperial Car Services | 022 738 36 10 |
| Prestige Rent a Car & Limousine | 022 731 26 00 |
| Privilege Limousine | 022 738 33 66 |
| Sixt Rent a Car | 022 732 90 90 |

## Taxi

Taxis in Geneva can be ordered by phone, hailed in the street or found at one of the 60 taxi stands in town. There are usually lots of taxis at the railway station (Cornavin) and on the arrivals level at the airport.

A taxi from the airport to the city centre costs anywhere between SFr 28 to SFr 33, depending on the density of traffic, the time and the number of passengers. A supplement may be charged for baggage but service and taxes are included, although it is usual to round up the amount to the nearest franc.

The base charge is SFr 6.30 plus SFr 2.90 per kilometre. The charge per kilometre goes up to SFr 3.50 at night, on Sundays and public holidays, outside the canton or if there are four or more passengers. Waiting time is SFr 55 per hour and each piece of luggage, or animal, will be charged an extra SFr 1.50. These tariffs are approved by the municipal police but are subject to change. In case of any difficulty or dispute, just note the registration number of the taxi and ask for a receipt.

| Taxi Companies | |
| --- | --- |
| AA Taxi Cab | 022 320 20 20 |
| Coopérative Taxis | 022 320 22 02 |
| Taxi des Bergues | 022 732 30 32 |
| Taxi-phone | 022 331 41 33 |

| Transport Services for the Disabled: | |
| --- | --- |
| Aloha | 022 321 12 21 |
| Paramedica | 022 348 53 15 |
| Transport One | 079 776 26 17 |
| Transport Handicap | 022 794 52 52 |

## Bus and Tram

The TPG (Transports Publics Genevois) operates an extensive bus and tram network throughout the canton. The service is constantly being expanded, including the installation of new tramlines (hence, lots of roadworks). At every bus and tram stop you will find timetables as well as maps covering the entire network. The public transport system is safe, clean, efficient and cheap, and is used by people of all ages and social status, especially for getting around the city centre. Buses and trams run from about 06:00 to 24:00, depending on the service. On Friday and Saturday nights several destinations are covered by the TPG's Noctambus service, which operates throughout the night. There are bus stops for all the Noctambus routes at Cornavin Railway Station, Rive and Place Bel-Air. However, Noctambus buses are few and far between, and if you miss one you could find yourself waiting for at least an hour for the next one so it is best to check the times and routes in advance. There is a single fare of SFr 3 per person for all Noctambus routes, though monthly passes are also accepted. Payment should be made to the driver.

Fares must be paid at the vending machines, found at each stop, before boarding. You will need the exact amount in coins as the machines do not give change. You can also buy prepaid discount cards (Carte @ Bonus) from newsagents (SFr 20, 30 or 50) that give you a discount on the first ticket. Every time you use your card to purchase a ticket the remaining credit is indicated. If the remaining credit is less than the price of another ticket, don't throw away the card because you can still purchase a SFr 2.60 ticket even if you have only SFr 0.20 credit left on your card. The Carte @ Bonus is not rechargeable.

Tickets cost between SFr 2 and SFr 6.40 depending on the duration of validity (30 – 90 minutes) and number of zones covered. All options are clearly indicated on the vending machines. Children and retired persons travel at reduced rates but for dogs the full fare must be paid.

Day passes can also be purchased at these machines. They cost between SFr 8 and SFr 13, depending on the number of zones you intend to cover. Monthly passes are available from the TPG office at Cornavin for SFr 100 for a transferable pass, or SFr 70 for a nominative one (requires a passport size photograph).

There is no systematic checking of tickets in the buses and trams. However, groups of controllers hop on and off buses (not necessarily at bus stops) throughout the day and night in groups of sometimes six controllers at a time, so there really is no escape! Anyone caught without a valid ticket will be made to buy one and also fined SFr 60.

If you wish to travel further by bus (including organised excursions), there is a coach station that is just a five minutes walk in the direction of the lake from Cornavin Railway Station. All inter city connections and organised excursions leave from here.

## Train

Switzerland has an extensive railway network that is clean, safe and reliable. From Geneva Cornavin you will find connections to other Swiss cities, such as Bern, Zurich or Lugano, as well as to mountain resorts, such as Zermatt or Champéry (in the vast Portes du Soleil ski area). If you're looking to head further, you will

> ### Airport Buses & Trains
>
> *The number 10 bus connects the centre of town to the airport. Alternatively, all trains that leave from the airport stop at Cornavin in the centre. Although trains are faster (seven minutes), they are less frequent than buses. Tickets for trains and buses to the centre cost SFr 2.60 and are valid for one hour of travel in the city, including changes.*

> ### TPG Website
>
> *Check out the TPG Website (www.tpg.ch) for detailed information on the public transport network, including Notambus.*

find connections to all corners of Europe, including Berlin, Brussels, Paris, South of France, Italy or Spain. A travel agency at Cornavin (Railtours) offers a choice of package tours that combine the train journey and hotel stay, while also making all the reservations for you.

If you plan to make a few train journeys it is worthwhile subscribing to a half price concession or discount card ('abonnement'). In some cases you can also get half price fares on boats and cable cars or other modes of transport. It costs SFr 150 for a year, which may seem a lot, but after a couple of long journeys you'll find yourself saving quite a bit of money.

## Air

Geneva's central location in Europe makes it easily accessible, and most European destinations are between one and three hours away. Over 40 airlines fly out of Geneva and 66 international destinations are linked directly.

> ### Pennywise Travel
>
> *Stretch your Swiss Franc. Did you know that you can get discounts on short stays? Check out the Swiss Federal Railways Website (www.cff.ch) for more information.*

The airport handles almost 7.5 million passengers a year and was recently extended, but still only has one terminal and not much space left for further expansion. All the usual services are offered, such as car rental, banks, shops and duty free on departure. A train station adjacent to the airport links Geneva with the rest of Switzerland.

Geneva airport is very close to the French border and you can even access the airport from the French side (at Ferney Voltaire). If you enter the airport on the Swiss side and are flying somewhere in France, you have to go through customs before checking in (look for signs saying 'France' at check in level).

| Airlines | |
|---|---|
| Aeroflot | 022 909 27 70 |
| Air Canada | 0848 24 72 26 |
| Air France | 022 827 87 87 |
| Air India | 022 732 06 60 |
| Air Portugal | 0848 800 704 |
| Alitalia | 022 799 40 09 |
| American Airlines | 01 654 52 56 |
| Austrian Airlines | 01 286 80 88 |
| Bmibaby | 0900 00 13 00 |
| British Airways | 0848 80 10 10 |
| EasyJet | 0848 888 222 |
| Etihad | 022 906 90 42 |
| Finnair | 022 906 10 15 |
| Iberia | 0844 845 003 |
| KLM | 0900 359 556 |
| Lufthansa | 022 929 51 51 |
| Olympic Airlines | 022 319 64 70 |
| Qantas | 0848 888 747 |
| SAS | 022 929 79 79 |
| Swiss | 0848 852 000 |
| United Airlines | 01 212 47 17 |

## Boat

Other Options → Lake Cruises [p.127]

During the summer months (April to October) the passenger ferries 'Mouettes Genevoises' operate a regular service crossing the lake. As part of the

View over the Rhône

SFr 10 ~ € 6

Unireso, the same ticket can be used for the ferries as for the trams and buses. They also organise lake and river cruises.

From early April to mid September, several other companies offer a variety of cruises on the lake that last anywhere between 45 minutes to half a day. You can also combine a cruise up to the other side of the lake and return by train.

For a boat trip with a little more excitement try rafting down the Arve river. If you wish to stop and take a dip in the lake, renting a pedal boat or a small motorboat is a better option.

## Walking

Walking is actively encouraged in Geneva. The main shopping street is pedestrian, apart from buses and trams, and you can safely walk to virtually anywhere in the city. The tourist authorities (Genève-Tourisme) have introduced a series of suggested walking routes, dotted with places of interest and tourist attractions. There are many dedicated footpaths and walking tracks, both within the city and in the surrounding countryside. Along the lakeside is a particularly popular walk, especially during the weekends and warm summer evenings, with lots of icecream stands along the way! Free copies of walking routes are available from the tourism information arcade on the Pont de la Machine.

## Biking

Geneva boasts an extensive network of cycle lanes and signposted itineraries. You can cover a lot more ground on a bike than on foot, so it's a healthy and ecological way of discovering the sights and appreciating the lovely scenery of Geneva and its surrounding countryside. Just a short bike ride from the city will find you in the countryside amongst the vineyards, forests, fields and charming villages, many of which have an in or tavern ('auberge') where you can stop for lunch or refreshments.

All privately owned bicycles have to have third party liability insurance. Bike owners must display a sticker ('vignette'), which indicates they have paid the grand insurance sum of SFr 6 per year. These vignettes can be bought from the post office.

Bikes can be borrowed free of charge for the day from several locations, such as Place de Montbrillant, Bains des Pâquis, Place du Rhône and Plaine de Plainpalais. These are open seven days a week from May to October, but close on Sundays during the winter months (November to April). To rent a bike all you need is a valid identity card and a cash deposit of SFr 50. Bikes must be returned on the same day. Place de Monbrillant offers rentals for longer periods at a very reasonable price.

The environmental organisation, ATE, has produced a cycle map for the canton of Geneva. You can find it in bookshops for SFr 26.80. Alternatively, pick up free maps and itineraries from the tourism information centre on the Pont de la Machine. If you wish to venture further, log on to www.cycling-in-switzerland.ch and browse the nine official cycle routes that run through the different parts of Switzerland. One particular 309 km route starts in Andermatt and follows the Rhône all the way to Geneva, taking you through breathtaking Alpine scenery.

General Info

Getting Around

## Money

Credit cards are widely accepted in Geneva and throughout Switzerland, although some restaurants and shops may refuse credit cards for small amounts. Foreign currencies and traveller's cheques can be exchanged in banks, exchange offices and hotels (a passport or other form of official identification is required for traveller's cheques). Some shops, restaurants and hotels accept Euros but will usually give change in Swiss Francs.

Cheques are not widely used in Switzerland and are slow and expensive to cash. Household bills and other invoices are often paid through the post office, although electronic banking is becoming increasingly widespread.

## Local Currency

The monetary unit is the Swiss Franc (SFr), which is divided into 100 centimes (cts). Notes come in denominations of SFr 10, SFr 20, SFr 50, SFr 100, SFr 200, SFr 1,000. Coin denominations are 5 cts, 10 cts, 20 cts, 50 cts, SFr 1, SFr 2 and SFr 5.

The Swiss Franc is not pegged to any other currency, not even the Euro.

## Banks

There are over 200 banks in Geneva, which roughly works out at an average of one bank for every 2,000 inhabitants. Nearly half of these banks are foreign and nine are private. As one would expect from a city famous for its banking industry, all sorts of commercial and personal banking services are available. There is no exchange control, so transfers can be made very easily and the Swiss Franc is freely convertible. The recent clamp down on money laundering has made it more difficult to open a bank account, especially for non residents. Banks are usually open Mondays to Fridays from 08:30 to 16:30, but remain closed on Saturdays, Sundays and public holidays.

### Exchange Rates

| Source | 1 unit FC = x SFr | SFr 1 = x FC |
|---|---|---|
| Argentina | 0.39 | 2.56 |
| Australia | 0.91 | 1.11 |
| Bahamas | 1.14 | 0.87 |
| Bermuda | 1.14 | 0.87 |
| Canada | 0.97 | 1.02 |
| Cayman Islands | 1.40 | 0.72 |
| Cyprus | 2.61 | 0.38 |
| Czech Republic | 0.49 | 20.55 |
| Denmark | 0.20 | 4.92 |
| Egypt | 0.18 | 5.44 |
| Euro | 1.51 | 0.66 |
| Gambia | 0.04 | 25.71 |
| Gibraltar | 2.15 | 0.46 |
| Hong Kong | 0.15 | 6.79 |
| Hungary | 0.01 | 162.26 |
| Iceland | 0.02 | 57.60 |
| India | 0.30 | 39.36 |
| Israel | 0.26 | 3.82 |
| Japan | 0.01 | 89.56 |
| Jordan | 1.61 | 0.62 |
| Kenya | 0.01 | 70.96 |
| Kuwait | 3.88 | 0.26 |
| Malaysia | 0.30 | 3.32 |
| Malta | 3.49 | 0.29 |
| Mexico | 0.10 | 9.84 |
| New Zealand | 0.82 | 1.22 |
| Norway | 0.19 | 5.38 |
| Oman | 2.97 | 0.34 |
| Pakistan | 0.19 | 52.11 |
| Poland | 0.36 | 2.79 |
| Qatar | 0.31 | 3.18 |
| Russia | 0.04 | 24.71 |
| Saudi Arabia | 0.31 | 3.27 |
| Singapore | 0.70 | 1.43 |
| South Africa | 0.19 | 5.14 |
| Sri Lanka | 0.01 | 91.76 |
| Sweden | 0.17 | 5.91 |
| Taiwan | 0.04 | 28.15 |
| Thailand | 0.03 | 34.54 |
| UK | 2.15 | 0.46 |
| United Arab Emirates | 0.31 | 3.21 |
| USA | 1.14 | 0.87 |

### Main Banks

| | |
|---|---|
| ABN Amro | 022 819 77 77 |
| American Express | 022 319 08 08 |
| Arab Bank (Switzerland) | 022 715 12 11 |
| Bank of America | 022 318 69 38 |
| Bank of New York Intermaritime Bank | 022 906 89 89 |
| Banque Cantonale de Genève (BCGE) | 022 317 27 27 |
| Banque de Commerce et de Placements | 022 909 19 19 |
| Banque Multi-Commerciale | 022 817 88 33 |
| Banque Raiffeisen | 022 879 11 00 |
| Barclays Bank | 022 819 51 11 |
| BNP Paribas | 022 787 71 11 |
| Citibank | 022 317 51 11 |
| Commerzbank | 022 316 61 00 |
| Crédit Agricole Indosuez | 022 319 91 91 |
| Crédit Suisse | 022 391 21 11 |
| Crédt Lyonnais | 022 705 66 66 |
| Deutsche Bank | 022 739 01 11 |
| HSBC Republic Bank | 022 705 55 55 |
| ING | 022 787 11 11 |
| UBS | 022 375 75 75 |

For a detailed listing of banks with their corresponding Websites, visit www.geneva-central.com.

## ATMs

Most banks operate ATMs (Automatic Teller Machines), as does the post office, and they accept most major credit cards. You will find ATMs all around town, outside banks and post offices, and in shopping malls. The exchange rate used varies and may or may not be more favourable than exchange centres, but for small amounts, the difference will be minimal and, in any case, it is a lot less hassle than changing traveller's cheques. At some ATMs, you can also withdraw Euros.

## Money Exchanges

There are several money exchanges around the city centre and the airport. Their exchange rates vary, but they generally offer better rates than banks and are much cheaper than hotels. All money exchanges have different opening hours, but the one at Cornavin railway station and the UBS at the airport are open from 06:45 – 21:00, seven days a week. The Change Dorcière (at the coach station) is also open seven days a week, from 07:30 – 20:30 (it closes an hour earlier on Saturdays and Sundays). Change Cité is closed on Sundays, and Change GFC is closed on Saturday afternoons and Sundays.

| Exchange Centres | | |
| --- | --- | --- |
| Change Cité | Rue du Mont-Blanc, 21 | 022 901 15 15 |
| Change G.F.C. | Rue des Pâquis, 12 | 022 732 41 31 |
| Change Dorcière | Place Dorcière | 022 731 10 88 |
| Gare Cornavin | Place Cornavin | 051 225 14 71 |
| UBS Geneva Airport | Airport (arrivals) | 022 306 14 88 |

## Credit Cards

Most shops, hotels and restaurants accept the major credit cards (American Express, Diners Club, Eurocard/Mastercard and Visa). Some small shops and restaurants may be reluctant to take credit cards for small amounts (eg, less than SFr 50).

## Tipping

Taxes and service charges are included in the bill in hotels, restaurants, taxi fares etc, so tips are not required. However, they may be justified for good service, in which case the amount is discretionary. In taxis, it is common to round up to the nearest franc, while in restaurants, up to ten percent is acceptable.

## Media & Communications

### Newspapers/Magazines

The main local daily newspapers are *Le Courrier*, *Le Temps*, the *Tribune de Genève* and *Le Matin*. There are no English dailies, although the *Tribune de Genève* now offers a regular section in English. Among monthlies, *Swiss News* is the English language newspaper.

There are several local magazines in English. *GEM* (Geneva's English Speaking Magazine) is a monthly aimed at integrating expatriates into the Geneva community. *Swiss Style* covers a variety of topics related to the whole of Switzerland. A number of clubs and UN organisations publish in-house magazines that are in English.

You can browse a selection of foreign newspapers and magazines, in English (and several other languages), at newsagents, but you'll find the price to be quite a bit more expensive than back home. It seems that newsagents have a monopoly on newspapers and magazines as you won't find them anywhere else (with the exception of *GHI* – a free weekly distributed to all the households). A few local newspapers have self service boxes spread over town. You're expected to pay the correct amount though, before you can help yourself to a paper.

### Further Reading

Genève-Tourisme publishes a number of guides and leaflets on what's happening in Geneva, including shows, events, museums, exhibitions, sporting events, sports clubs, restaurants and nightlife. *Genève Agenda* is a free weekly brochure published by Genève-Tourisme with all the latest information on the hip and happening events for the week.

Visitors will find a variety of books and travel guides on Switzerland or Geneva in local bookstores, from coffee table books to those dealing with specific aspects, such as Swiss culture, fauna and flora, hiking etc. Lonely Planet produces both general guidebooks and walking guides, while others deal specifically with activities for families with children (eg,

*Know It All Parents*). Several authors have published books on Swiss culture (eg, *Culture Shock! A Guide to Customs & Etiquette in Switzerland*, and *Beyond Chocolate*) but not only do these tend to be more relevant to the German speaking parts, they also include many generalisations that are a little over the top and need to be taken with a pinch of salt, although they do make fun reading.

Bookshops selling English books include Payot (Rue Chantepoulet 5), Fnac (Rive and Balexert shopping mall), and Off the Shelf (Boulevard Georges Favon 15). Point de Repère (Rue de Monthoux 13) stocks books dealing specifically with family issues, religious education and spiritual healing, while at Ellipse (Rue Rousseau 14), you will find anything relating to computers and business.

## Post & Courier Services

SwissPost is the sole provider of postal services in Switzerland but there are also numerous courier companies that operate both locally and internationally. SwissPost has joined forces with TNT to provide express courier services.

First class letters to local addresses are usually delivered the following working day, as long as they are deposited at a post office by 16:00 (or before last pick-up time in a post box). Delivery of second class letters may take two to three days. First class letters to Europe take three to five days; to the rest of the world, they can take seven to ten days, depending on the country.

Yellow post boxes for outgoing mail can be found at post offices and all around Geneva. Pick up times are sometimes quite early in the day (these are indicated on the box).

Stamps can be bought from post offices as well as some shops that sell cards or postcards; you can also acquire stamps from machines outside post offices. First class stamps for postcards and letters up to 20 grams within Switzerland cost SFr 1, to Europe they cost SFr 1.30, and to the rest of the world, SFr 1.80.

### Courier Companies

| | |
|---|---|
| Adeo Motocourrier (local) | 022 341 2026 |
| DHL | 0848 711 711 |
| Federal Express (FedEx) | 0800 12 38 00 |
| TNT SwissPost | 0800 55 55 55 |
| United Parcel Service (UPS) | 0800 55 88 33 |
| World Courier | 022 827 3060 |

## Radio

Geneva has a number of commercial radio stations, most of which broadcast in French. There are two English stations.

The main English radio station in Geneva is WRG FM (88.4 FM), which broadcasts 24 hours a day, seven days a week. They regularly feature interviews with members of the local community, quizzes, special reports, local news (as well as the BBC world news every hour on the hour during the day and in the evenings), traffic information, and a wide variety of music from the latest pop to classical and jazz. The schedule can be viewed on their Website (www.wrgfm.com). You can also listen online. Another English speaking radio station that broadcasts from just over the border in France is Radio 74 (88.8 FM).

The main French speaking radio stations broadcasting out of Geneva are Europe 2 (90.1 FM), Nostalgie (105 FM), NRJ (103.6 FM), One FM (107 FM), Radio Cité (92.2 FM), Radio Lac (91.8, 93 and 95.6 FM) and Radio Suisse Romande, which has several stations (La Première – 94.9 FM, Espace 2 – 101.7 FM, Couleur 3 – 104.4 FM and Option Musique – 90.8 FM).

Old Town fountain

## Television/Satellite TV

The Swiss television channels are broadcast in French, German and Italian, but for some films and soaps you can opt for the original, undubbed version. Euronews broadcasts some of its

# Ten kilos or ten tons, DHL moves the Middle East.

**With DHL's Road Express,** you can now transport all your light or heavy goods across the region with total peace of mind and reliability from the world's leading provider of customised logistics solutions. Call us now toll free on 800 4004.

*WE MOVE THE WORLD* ≡**_DHL_**≡

programmes in English. You can also pick up several French channels in Geneva if your TV is both PAL and SECAM compatible.

Many places now have cable and/or satellite, which provide channels from all over the world and immediately expand viewing choice.

Urban reflections

## Telephones

### Telephone Codes

*The code is an important part of the telephone number when dialling a number in Switzerland. Even if you are calling a Geneva number from Geneva, the code (022) is included. If you are dialling from outside of Switzerland, you add the international code (+41) but drop the zero from the Geneva code (22). So, you would dial +41 22 999 99 99. The code for mobile phones varies depending on the provider, but the same applies; include the code if you are in Switzerland, but drop the zero for international calls.*

National and international telecommunications are excellent. Although the telecommunications market was liberalised in Switzerland in January 1998, Swisscom is still the only company that can provide a landline connection. Once you have your connection however, you can subscribe to the services of other telecommunications providers (eg, Sunrise and Tele2) whose rates are considerably cheaper than Swisscom.

Public pay phones are available throughout Geneva. Some still accept coins but more often than not you'll need a phone card (PTT Taxcards). These can be purchased from post offices and newsagents and are more suitable for local and national calls. If you want to make international phone calls, a cheaper option is to purchase special discount phone cards.

Mobile phones are used extensively in Geneva and the exchange of short messages using mobile phones (SMS) is something of a national pastime, especially amongst the younger generations. Coverage and GSM international roaming is very good, except perhaps at the tops of mountain peaks! Unlike landlines, you can obtain a mobile telephone number from several providers, including Swisscom, Orange, Sunrise and Tele2. Most phone shops (see Mobile Phone Providers on [p.70]) display comparative rates.

If you need a mobile telephone number in Geneva but are not a resident, the Natel Easy is a pay as you go system which does not require you to have a fixed address or residence permit (but you will have to produce ID). You can simply buy a SIM card and use it in your own phone, or purchase a package that includes a SIM card and mobile phone; calls will be charged at the local rate, which varies depending on the provider.

### Phone Shops

| | |
|---|---|
| ECS The Phone House | 022 317 97 47 |
| FUST | 022 817 03 80 |
| Orange | 022 810 37 90 |
| Rentaphone (mobiles, faxes) | 022 717 82 63 |
| Telefon Corner | 022 716 47 20 |
| Sunrise Center | 0800 333 777 |
| Swisscom Shop | 0800 800 800 |
| Swisscom Mobile Shop | 022 797 74 73 |

## Internet

The Internet is widely used in Geneva. A growing number of people have home computers with fast Internet connections, such as ADSL, which allows unlimited connection time for a fixed monthly fee. Wireless Internet connection was also introduced recently. Several companies, such as Bluewin, Cortex and Sunrise provide Internet connections.

Internet cafés can be found all around town. The Internet Café de la Gare (in Cornavin railway station, next to Citydisc) has 40 PCs and is open seven days a week from 09:30 to 22:00. They are well stocked with the regular services, such as English language software, webcams, Netmeeting and Microsoft Office. They also have printing, photocopying and fax options.

# The benchmark for Geneva

Geneva's English-speaking Magazine (GEM)

Monthly news, culture and society.

Available at all amazingly good newsagents, bars and cafes

www.**gem**.ch

## Internet Cafés

| | |
|---|---|
| Charly's Multimedia Check Point | 022 901 13 13 |
| Cyber-Café | 022 320 74 55 |
| Internet Café de la Gare | 022 731 51 87 |
| Lan-Zone | 022 329 10 28 |
| Nath-Soft | 022 797 26 04 |
| Speed Net Café | 022 731 67 47 |

## Websites

There are numerous Internet sites with information on Geneva and Switzerland. Many official government departments and services have their own site and some allow official forms to be downloaded and printed. The following table lists the sites that we found to be useful, relevant and informative. However, if you have any suggestions or know of any Websites that are not listed but worth mentioning, please let us know and we'll make sure they are included in the next edition!

## Geneva Annual Events

There are numerous annual events in Geneva and its surrounding areas, some of which have a long history and are firmly rooted in tradition. The events listed below are regular fixtures that mark the seasons. In March, people flock to the annual motor show and May brings the chance to sample the first wine from the previous year's harvest. Throughout the summer, there are regattas on the lake, music festivals and fêtes. With autumn, the cows come down from their summer pastures in mountain villages like St-Cergue; then the commemoration of the Escalade and the pre-Christmas period bring their own enchanting and amusing festivities. Whatever the time of year, there's always something to look forward to in Geneva.

### American Independence Day (July)

This is the biggest American Independence Day celebration outside the USA, with concerts, stands and fireworks. It is held on the vast sports grounds of Bout-du-Monde (near Champel/Carouge).

### Bâtie Festival (September)

This is a two week festival, held in a huge country park and featuring concerts, theatre and dance, as well as food stands and bars. At weekends the dancing continues into the early hours of the morning.

### Bol d'Or (June)

This boating festival takes place on a Saturday morning in mid June, when around 600 boats set sail from Geneva and race to the other end of the lake and back. Some of the competitors are professionals, some are just in it for fun.

### Caribana Festival (Crans-sur-Nyon) (June)

A 3-day music festival with an eclectic programme of music from all over the world. The festival takes place at the small port of Crans near Nyon, just along the lake from Geneva. On the Sunday afternoon they have a special programme of events for mini-festival goers, with face-painting and entertainers.

### Caves Ouvertes (May)

For one weekend a year Geneva's wine producers open their doors to allow visitors (and hopefully buyers) to come and taste the newly bottled wines from the previous autumn's harvest.

### Christmas Open Air Skating (November to January)

From November to January an open air skating rink is set up on Place du Rhône. You can rent your skates and enjoy a selection of mulled wine and tasty Christmas treats.

### Christmas Swimming Cup (December)

This annual swimming competition is for the very brave only – it takes place in mid December in the lake (between the Jardin Anglais and Quai General Guisan) when water temperatures are around four or five degrees, and air temperatures can be as low as minus ten!

### Christmas Tree Festival (December)

This original event features numerous Christmas trees that have been uniquely decorated by a selection of talented artists. The trees are on display around Geneva's lakeside.

### CineLac (July-August)

During this film festival, a different film is shown each night on a huge outdoor cinema screen. The screen is erected by the lakeside near the Parc des Eaux-Vives. Tickets can be bought in advance (if you want to avoid the queues), and programmes are available from Genève-Tourisme.

### Course de l'Escalade (December)

This popular annual road race features hundreds of runners and walkers, regardless of age or

## Websites

### Business / Industry

| | |
|---|---|
| www.ccig.ch | Geneva's Chamber of Commerce and Industry |
| www.economiesuisse.ch | Umbrella organization for the Swiss economy |
| www.gva.ch | Geneva International Airport |
| www.osec.ch | Information on doing business in and with Switzerland |
| www.palexpo.ch | Geneva's largest international convention centre |
| www.swissbanking.org | Swiss Banking Association |

### Culture / Leisure / Events

| | |
|---|---|
| www.batie.ch | Music festival in La Bâtie country park (September) |
| www.boldor.ch | Bol d'Or sailing race (June) |
| www.caribana.ch | Caribana festival in Crans sur Nyon (June) |
| www.cinelac.ch | Switzerland's biggest outdoor cinema (July and August) |
| www.concours-hippique.ch | Geneva's international show jumping show |
| www.escalade.ch | The official site for the Escalade Race |
| www.fasnacht.ch | A guide to Basel's carnival |
| www.fetedelamusique.ch | Music festival throughout the city of Geneva (June) |
| www.fetesdegeneve.ch | Geneva's annual Fêtes de Genève (August) |
| www.knie.ch | Knie Circus (Geneva: late August/early September) |
| www.montreuxjazz.com | Montreux Jazz Festival |
| www.paleo.ch | Palèo Festival in Nyon (July) |
| www.pro-helvetia.ch | Organisation for the promotion of Swiss Culture |
| www.salon-auto.ch | International Motor Show (March) |

### Embassies / Visa Information

| | |
|---|---|
| www.eda.admin.ch | Department of Foreign Affairs, list of Swiss Representations |
| www.etrangers.ch | Visa requirements and information on residency permits |

### Geneva Information

| | |
|---|---|
| www.cagi.ch | Website of the International Geneva Welcome Centre |
| www.cityexpat.com | A guide for expats living in Geneva and Neighbouring France |
| www.geneve-tourisme.ch | General tourist information for Geneva |
| www.geneve-central.ch | Links to hotels, businesses, services, associations, etc. |
| www.geneve.ch/police/ | Geneva Police |
| www.geneve.ch | Geneva's official website with links to various departments |
| www.newtogeneva.com | Information on living in Geneva |
| www.tpg.ch | Geneva's public transport network |
| www.wrgfm.com | Local English-speaking radio station |
| www.xpatxchange.ch | A one-stop site for English speaking expats in Geneva |

### Swiss Information

| | |
|---|---|
| www.admin.ch | Links to all Swiss Federal Authorities |
| www.cff.ch | Information and online booking for the Swiss railways |
| www.chocolat.ch/chocosuisse.htm | All you ever wanted to know about chocolate |
| www.directories.ch | Online telephone directory for the whole of Switzerland |
| www.europa.admin.ch | Information on the Swiss-EU bilateral agreements |
| www.myswitzerland.com | Information, travel, news, and events relating to Switzerland |
| www.statistique.admin.ch | Swiss Federal Statistical Office |
| www.swisspolitics.org | All you ever wanted to know about Swiss politics |
| www.switzerland-in-sight.ch | Swiss information and communication platform |
| www.tdg.ch | Tribune de Genève (local newspaper with English corner) |

fitness level. They make their way around the Old Town (some in fancy dress), while onlookers cheer them on and keep warm with a feast of sausages and wine.

The beauty of seasons changing

### Escalade Parade (December)

This very special day commemorates the foiled attack on Geneva by the Savoyards in 1602. People dressed in 17th Century costume take to the streets to mark this historical event, while children earn extra pocket money by singing the commemorative song in restaurants and at people's homes.

### Fête de la Musique (June)

This music festival takes place during one weekend in June, and features free concerts in various musical styles such as rock, pop, jazz and classical. The full programme can be downloaded from the Internet, or found in the Tribune de Genève a few days before the event.

### Fête des Vendanges (September)

The grape harvest festival in the tiny village of Russin attracts over 10,000 visitors, both locals and tourists. Visitors can enjoy the freshly pressed grape juice ('moût'), as well as local cuisine, wines, concerts and parades.

### Fêtes de Genève (August)

A 10-day festival around Geneva's lakeside with loads of amusements, shows, concerts, food stands with specialities from all over the world, parades, stalls selling arts and crafts, a 'tropical village' and lots more. Don't miss the spectacular fireworks on the second Saturday of the festival.

### International Christmas Market (December)

From late November, Place de la Fusterie is occupied by mini-châlets selling a variety of arts and crafts with lots of original ideas for all those Christmas presents you need (or don't need). There are also stands selling food and mulled wine.

### International Horse Show – World Cup (December)

This four day international event attracts tens of thousands of visitors each year who come to see the biggest names in equestrian sport demonstrate their talents and compete in a variety of disciplines such as jumping, dressage and harnessing, at World Cup level.

### International Motor Show (March)

Visitors from all over the world come to view the latest sleek and shiny cars at this exhibition. Manufacturers unveil their newest commercial models, as well as vintage cars and futuristic non commercial designs that will leave any car fan drooling.

### Knie Circus (September)

This is Switzerland's most prestigious circus, held on the Plaine de Plainpalais in early September. As a sideline, you can also visit their zoo, which contains domestic and exotic animals, including a rhinoceros.

### Montreux Jazz Festival (July)

This world famous jazz festival has featured many great artists over the years. The festival now includes blues, pop and rock performances, and is visited by nearly 200,000 music fans annually.

### Paléo Festival (Nyon) (July)

This superbly festive music event stretches over six days and features performances by big names and up and coming artists on multiple stages. Apart from enjoying the music, visitors can wander freely around the grounds, sampling cuisines from all over the world at the various food stands. Tickets sell out early, so book in advance!

## Summer Concerts (July-August)

Throughout July and August free concerts are given in the Old Town and in the Parc La Grange. Whether you prefer pop, jazz, world music or classical, you'll find a performance to suit your tastes. You can pick up a programme from Genève-Tourisme.

## Swiss National Day (August)

This nationwide celebration features patriotic speeches by local personalities and passionate renditions of the Swiss national anthem. In Geneva, the festivities are held in the Parc des Bastions, but most communes and villages also have their own fêtes, featuring bonfires, fireworks, sausages, soup and wine.

## Yodelling Festival (June)

Now you can't get much more Swiss than this in terms of entertainment. On the Friday and Saturday yodellers compete by performing in the different cafés and restaurants of Carouge whilst patrons enjoy a meal. On Sunday the judges make their decisions and hand out the prizes.

## Main Annual Events – 2005

### January
| 01 – 30 | Christmas Ice-Skating Rink |
| | Place de Rhône |

### February
| 17 – 19 | Geneva Carnival |
| | Old Town |

### March
| 3 – 13 | 75th International Motor Show |
| | Geneva Palexpo |

### April
| 27 – 31 | Geneva Intl. Fair for Books, Press and Multimedia |
| | Geneva Palexpo |

### May
| 8 | Geneva Marathon |
| | Geneva |
| 28 | Hope Festival |
| | Stade du Bout-du-Monde |

### June
| 9 – 12 | Caribana Festival |
| | Crans-sur-Nyon (Vaud) |
| 11 – 12 | Bol d'or |
| | La Nautique – Le Bouveret and return |
| 17 – 19 | Music Festival |
| | City Centre and Villages |
| 21 | Rose Competition |
| | La Grange Left Bank |

### July
| 1 – 16 | Montreux Jazz Festival |
| | Montreux |
| 4 | American Independence Day |
| | Stade du Bout-du-Monde |
| 19 – 24 | Paléo Festival (Nyon) |

### August
| 1 | Swiss National Day |
| | Parc des Bastions |
| 26 – 31 | Knie Circus |
| | Plaine de Plainpalais |

### September
| 1 – 16 | Knie Circus |
| | Plaine de Plainpalais |
| 2 – 4 | Vogue de Carouge |
| | Carouge |
| 17 – 18 | Fête des Vendanges (Grape Festival) |
| | Russin |

### November
| 19 – 30 | Christmas Ice Skating Rink |
| | Place du Rhône |
| 26 – 30 | Christmas Circus |
| | Plaine de Plainpalais |
| 26 | Christmas Tree Festival |
| | City Centre |
| 28 | International Christmas Market begins |
| | Place de la Fusterie |

### December
| 1 – 31 | Christmas Circus |
| | Plaine de Plainpalais |
| 1 – 31 | Christmas Ice-Skating Rink |
| | Place du Rhône |
| 2 – 3 | 20th International Supercross Geneva |
| | Geneva Palexpo |
| 2 – 9 | Trees & Lights Festival |
| | City Centre |
| 3 | The 'Escalade' Run |
| | Old Town |
| 8 – 11 | CSI-W Geneva Intl. Horse Show Jumping Competition |
| | Geneva Palexpo |
| 11 – 12 | The 'Escalade' Celebration |
| | Vielle-ville |
| 11 | Coupe de Noel |
| | Jardin Anglais |

# Take it easy!

**GPA** watches over your security 24/7.

- Installation of alarm systems
- Video surveillance
- Call-out team
- 24/7 service
- 24/7 alarm receiving centre

| | |
|---|---|
| Telephone | +41 22 707 94 00 |
| Fax | +41 22 707 94 94 |
| Internet | www.gpa.ch |
| E-mail | securite@gpa.ch |

## GPA GUARDIAN PROTECTION SA®

Geneva I Nyon I Lausanne I Fribourg I St Moritz

# New Residents

**EXPLORER**

# New Residents



### MUST HAVE

*In order to get your residence permit in Geneva, you have to get compulsory health insurance. The advantage is that if you have a medical mishap, you are covered. The disadvantage is that it is an added expense, but it is one that all Genevans have to accept. You can choose various degrees of cover, from comprehensive (expensive!) to basic, but the insurance provider must be a company that is approved by the authorities – almost all of these 'approved' providers are Swiss companies, so your existing international health cover may not be sufficient.*

### MUST GO

*To French lessons! Even if you know hundreds of English speaking people in Geneva and never have to converse in French, it will be to your great advantage to learn some basics of the language in order to make the most of the city. Your company may offer this to you as part of your work package, but if not, refer to [p.XXX] to find a language school that suits you. Once you've got your tongue around French, you could go on to learn Italian, or Spanish, or Arabic, or Swahili.......*

## Overview

If you've just packed up and relocated to Geneva, congratulations! In a recent Mercer International Worldwide Quality of Life Survey, Geneva was the top scoring city (along with Zurich). When it comes to factors like health and safety, public services, transport, schooling, and economic and environmental issues, Geneva is the place to be. Add to that the city's picturesque location on the shores of Lac Léman, the breathtaking views of the Swiss Alps, and the geographical convenience of being at the crossroads of Europe, and by now you should be feeling pretty good about your recent move.

Nearly half of Geneva's population is made up of expats and foreigners, and some statistics have estimated that only one out of every two workers is Swiss! Not only does this make for a vibrant and diverse culture, it also ensures that English is commonly spoken and widely understood. Learning to speak French, however, will undoubtedly help you make the most of the city.

Bureaucracy is alive and well in Geneva, and is probably one of the few things that lacks the famous Swiss precision. However, while you're standing in your tenth queue of the day, wondering what can go wrong next, just remember that although things may take a little longer here, they get done eventually.

Although at times being a newcomer in Geneva can be confusing or frustrating, the information that follows is a thorough guide to the ins and outs of settling in.

## In the Beginning...

### Customs

If you are not an EU national, the first step to acquiring residency is to enter the country on a valid visa. The original entry visa documentation must be presented to airport immigration upon your arrival, and your passport will be stamped. For more information on what type of visa is most suitable for the purposes of your visit, and how you can apply for it, visit the Website of the Swiss Federal Office of Immigration, Integration and Emigration (IMES) at www.foreigners.ch.

When you arrive in Switzerland you must bring an inventory of everything you wish to import. You are not required to pay value added tax (VAT) on any item that you have used for more than six months. You should fill in form 18.44 to request duty free import for these items; any new items will be charged at 7.6%, and itemised invoices must be shown.

### Residents' Control

Within eight days of your arrival in Geneva, and before starting work, you must register yourself at the Cantonal Population Office ('Office Cantonal de la Population') in order to finalise your permit status. Among the questions on the registration form is a box asking you to list your religion. Note that if you tick this box you may have to pay church tax ('impôt de culte'). As the Swiss constitution upholds freedom of religion and belief, you are not required to pay church tax unless you are a member of an official church. For more information on where to find the Office Cantonal de la Population, refer to the 'Important Addresses' table on [p.88].

### Embassy Registration

Most countries represented in Switzerland have their embassies in Bern, with consulates in Geneva. It is recommended that you inform your embassy or consulate of your arrival, so that they can add your name to their citizens' register. Not only is this an important security measure, but it is also a useful way to start networking as many embassies organise regular or seasonal events for expats.

### International Geneva Welcome Centre

The International Geneva Welcome Centre should be one of your first ports of call – it offers practical assistance and advice for newcomers on topics such as schooling, housing, health and employment. On the third Thursday of every month they host the 'Happy Hour', an informal meeting where newcomers can meet members of the local community. The Centre is based in an old villa just behind Place des Nations (see 'Important Addresses' on [p.88])

### Essential Documents

The bureaucratic hurdles of moving to a new city can be tiring and frustrating, and the last thing you want is to have stood in a queue for hours, only to be told you are lacking some vital document and that you should come back tomorrow! The following list shows the basic set of documents that you simply should not leave home without when you're heading off to a government department. Any additional documents will be referred to in the appropriate paragraph.

- Original passport
- Employment contract (if you have one)
- Police statement indicating that you do not have a criminal record
- Birth certificate
- Passport-sized photographs

You will be asked for countless photographs over the next few months. Usually two are required for each procedure, but it is always worth taking more. The same goes for documents – if there is even the remotest possibility that you will need a certain document, take it! You could save yourself a lifetime of waiting in unnecessary queues. The Office Cantonal de la Population has a very handy check desk on the ground floor, where your documents will be examined to see if they are complete before you start your inevitably long wait to register. Take a good book or magazine with you too.

## Documents

### Entry Visa

To enter Switzerland, your passport must be valid for at least six months. Depending on your nationality, you may also require a visa. Citizens of the European Union (EU) need not apply for a Swiss visa before entering the country. For certain other nationalities, the obligation to get a visa can be waived if the stay in Switzerland is for less than three months, and is not for work purposes. In some cases, people holding a valid Schengen visa (a visa valid for 15 EU countries), don't need a separate Swiss visa. To determine whether you require a visa, consult the Swiss embassy in your country of residence, or visit the IMES Website at www.foreigners.ch.

Should you require a visa, make certain that you submit the application to the Swiss embassy or consulate in your home country well in advance – it can take as little as 24 hours to process a visa, but it could take as long as three weeks.

When you arrive in Switzerland, the customs office may request proof that you can support yourself financially for the duration of your stay (around SFr 100 per day). If possible, take a recent bank statement or payslip with you, as proof of solvency.

### Host Guarantee Certificate

As part of the visa application process, you may be required to produce a 'Host Guarantee Certificate'. This is a signed declaration from a friend or associate in Switzerland, stating that they will bear the costs of your stay, and any healthcare costs you incur. The host need not be Swiss, but they must have a valid permit of residence, and since they can be liable for expenses of up to SFr 20,000 if anything goes wrong during your stay, they should probably be a very good friend! There are special short term insurance policies available for 'hosts', to cover any costs they incur on your behalf. Once the certificate is signed, your host should send it to the Office Cantonal de la Population.

### Tourist Visa Validity

After a period of three months, foreign tourists are required to leave Switzerland for a period of at least one month before returning on another visa. The stay must not exceed a total of six months out of every 12. If for any reason you need to extend your stay past three months without leaving Switzerland, you should apply to the Office Cantonal de la Population. For more information refer to General Information [p.18].

## Work Permit/Residence

All foreigners must have a permit to be able to work in Geneva. The permit system is complex and depends largely on factors such as nationality and duration of stay. Certain categories of permits are 'canton specific', so you may not be free to live in a different canton to where you work, nor may you be able to change jobs for a stipulated time. A basic

> **Bilateral Swiss EU Agreement on the Free Movement of Persons**
>
> *Introduced on 1 July 2002, this is the legal basis for examining applications for residency and work permits for Europeans and EFTA nationals. During a 12 year transition period there will be changes to the procedures and conditions for obtaining work permits. Five years into the agreement, it will no longer be necessary for Europeans to have a permit.*

rundown of the permit system follows, but for more detailed information you can contact the Office Cantonal de la Population.

### Permit Application Conditions

The most important step in applying for a permit is having a valid job offer or 'gainful employment'. This includes those who are self employed or employed, full or part time, and either on a permanent or temporary basis. Companies have to meet stringent requirements before they offer employment to a foreigner – they must first prove that they have done their best to hire a Swiss national or a foreigner already holding a permit.

## Types of Permit

**Temporary Residence Permit (Type B):** This permit is the most common type, issued to people who have a work contract of at least one year. It is renewed annually, although for EU citizens it only needs to be renewed every five years. It is canton specific.

**Permanent Residence Permit (Type C):** The C permit is issued to EU citizens who have lived and worked in Geneva for five years, and to other nationalities who have lived and worked there for ten years. It is also issued to foreigners who have been married to a Swiss national for five years. C permit holders are free to change jobs or live in a different canton to where they are employed.

**Border Commuter Permit (Type G):** The G permit does not include residential rights in Switzerland; it is a work permit for those who are employed in Geneva, but who live across the border in neighbouring France. To qualify, you must have been resident in France for at least six months. The permit is renewed annually and cannot be converted to a type B permit.

**Short Term Residence Permit (Type L):** The L permit is a short term residency permit for non EU citizens and is valid for up to one year.

## Spouses/Children

If you have a type B or type C permit, your spouse is entitled to live and work in Geneva, and will be granted residency as a dependant. If you are not married, your partner does not have any residency rights. Children under 18 years old are included on their parents' permit.

## Students

Foreigners who come to Geneva for study purposes should apply for a type B permit. The education establishment you are enrolled with will provide you with a certificate, which should then be presented to the Office Cantonal de la Population as part of your permit application.

## Applying for a Permit

Your employer, or their representative (a lawyer), should apply for your permit in writing. If you are self employed or unemployed, you have to apply in person. Application forms can be obtained from the Office Cantonal de la Population. Permit applications can take several months to process, but the average time is three months. Once your employer has taken all the necessary steps, you will be issued with your 'Livret pour Etrangers', which you should carry with you at all times. This small booklet is proof that you are authorised to live and work in Geneva.

## Documents

The documents you will need are:

- Photocopy of ID
- 2 passport photos
- Report from medical insurance company (see Health Insurance [p.72])
- Recent bank statement
- Completed application form
- The fee (SFr 75)

If you are self employed, you will also need to submit a 'letter of motivation', a copy of your CV, your certificates or diplomas, and your business plan.

## Medical Check Up

Depending on your country of origin, you may need to have a medical examination when you enter Switzerland. Citizens of the EU, USA, Australia, Canada and New Zealand, as well as holders of diplomatic passports and employees of international governmental organisations, are exempt from this provision. The check up consists of a chest x-ray to identify any signs of tuberculosis, and should be done within five days of arrival in Switzerland.

## Health Insurance

Health insurance is compulsory in Switzerland, and it is an expense that you just have to accept. This compulsory insurance covers illness, accidents, maternity care and in some cases even dental care. If you have existing international health insurance, you should check whether your insurance company is included on the list of providers that has been approved by the Swiss authorities. A full list of authorised health insurance providers can be obtained from the Health Insurance Bureau (Service de L'assurance Maladie). See the 'Important Addresses' table for details [p.88]. For more information on healthcare in Switzerland, see the 'Health' section [p.72].

## Exemptions

Some categories of employee (such as representatives of foreign states and officials of international organisations) are exempt from mandatory health insurance. These exemptions are purely job related, and do not depend on your country of origin.

## Renewal of a Permit

You should apply to renew your permit three months before expiry. You will need a photocopy of your previous permit, one passport photo, and the relevant application form. The cost is SFr 75.

## Certificates & Licences

## Driving Licences

While it may be easy and enjoyable to walk from one place to another in Geneva, it is also a great place to get behind the steering wheel and explore the city and its surroundings. Outside the city the roads offer spectacular views of the Alps, and the narrow twists and turns of the Alpine passes will make you feel like you're driving in a luxury car advert.

Tight parking

The legal age for driving in Geneva is 18. All foreigners need to apply for a Swiss driving licence within 12 months of their arrival in Switzerland. People from the EU, USA and certain other countries can exchange their valid national licence for a Swiss one. If you are not from one of the exempt countries, or your existing licence is not valid, you will have to take the Swiss driving test ('Course de Contrôle'), which is notoriously rigorous and expensive.

To change your existing licence to a Swiss one, you need to go to the Service des Automobiles et de la Navigation du Canton de Genève, which is located on the outskirts of the town centre (see Important Addresses, [p.88]). Before you go, you will need to get an eye test done with an approved optician, who will sign the relevant section of your application form.

Once you have submitted your application (either by hand or by registered post), you should receive your licence about two weeks later. It is valid for life.

### Driving Licence Documents

- Completed application form
- Original drivers' licence
- Eye test results (should have been done within the previous six months)
- Two colour passport photos
- Residency permit
- SFr 200

Diplomats and other VIPs benefiting from judicial immunity do not need to change their licence to a Swiss one. However, if your licence is in a language other than French, German, Italian or English, you are advised to exchange your national licence for an international licence. The international licence will only be valid up to the expiry date of your national licence, and has a limit of three years. To obtain an international driving licence in this category, you need to present a legitimisation card (from your organisation) or your residency permit, attestation from your organisation proving that you live in Geneva, one passport photo and SFr 40.

### Driving Test

If you do have to take a driving test in Switzerland, bon courage. It is a long and arduous process, and it is not light on your pocket! The first step is to sign up with a driving school. The Federation Romande des Ecoles de Conduite (based in Lausanne) can assist you with finding an English speaking instructor (see Important Addresses, [p.88]). Alternatively, you could contact one of the following driving schools.

| Driving Schools | |
|---|---|
| Auto-école des Eaux-Vives | 022 786 48 58 |
| Auto-école Rue du Lyon | 079 203 36 13 |
| École de Conduite EUROPA | 022 321 45 45 |

The cost per driving lesson is approximately SFr 85 and lessons last around 50 minutes. There is also a one off payment of approximately SFr 70, for insurance. Your driving instructor will issue you with a learner licence ('permis d'élève conducteur'), which is valid for two years. During this time you will be allowed to drive, provided you are accompanied at all times by a licensed driver and you display the 'L' plate (a white 'L' on a blue background). The fee for the learner licence is SFr 295, which includes the theory exam and up to three attempts at the practical exam (just in case you don't pass the first time!). Your instructor will also give you a theory book and a road traffic book, both of which are available in English and which should be in the car with you whenever you drive. It is also compulsory to take a ten hour first aid course, either with your driving instructor or with an approved institute or motoring organisation.

You will also have to take a road traffic course, which your instructor will enrol you on. The next step is to take the theory exam, followed by the practical road test. Once you're licensed to drive, there are other road safety courses that you may find useful; in particular the anti-skid course (see Transportation section, [p.82]).

## Birth Certificates & Registration

All births should be registered within three days at the registry office of the district ('commune') where the birth took place. This is usually done by the hospital, but if the baby was born at home or in a different canton to where you live, you will have to register the birth yourself. To get a birth certificate, you need to submit the family register ('livret de famille') or marriage certificate, the parents' passports and residence permits, and a fee of SFr 25. You also need to fill in the relevant form at the Civil Registrar's Office (Office de L'Etat Civil – see Important Addresses, [p.88]).

## Marriage Certificates & Registration

The path of true love never runs smooth, as the saying goes, and this is certainly true when it comes to the process of getting married in Switzerland! Regardless of whether you want a church service or not, you need to apply for a marriage certificate at the registry office in the district where you live, or where the wedding will be held. It is accepted that both the soon-to-be bride and groom should be active participants in the preparations for marriage, to ensure that they

are responsible for what they are doing. For this reason it is necessary to go in person (either separately or together) to the registry office, which will provide all necessary information both orally and in writing. The documents required may vary according to your district, as may the necessary preconditions for marriage and the consequences (for example, in some districts it may be compulsory for the woman to take the man's name, or at least hyphenate it after her maiden name).

The next step is for the happy couple to collect all relevant documents and make a request to the registry office for permission to marry. You'll need to attend an appointment and fill in a form, in the presence of the registrar, confirming that you are free to marry and requesting that preparations for the marriage go ahead.

Having been thoroughly vetted, you will then receive written notification of approval of your marriage, and when the ceremony can take place. A marriage can be celebrated not less than ten days and not more than three months after such notice has been given.

The official marriage ceremony takes place in the registry office and you must be accompanied by your principal witnesses. At the end of the ceremony you receive a 'livret de famille', a marriage deed, and a marriage certificate which costs SFr 25. Even if you have planned a church wedding, you have to get married at the registry office first, before proceeding with your religious ceremony.

In the case of divorce, a woman must wait between six months and a year before she can go back to using her maiden name, and she is required by Swiss marriage law to wait 300 days before remarrying. There is no such stipulation for men.

## Death Certificates & Registration

In the unhappy event of the death of a family member, friend or relative, the first step is to call a doctor immediately to issue a doctor's report. The death must then be registered with the Civil Registrar's Office in the district where the death occurred. If the death took place in a hospital or institution, the management will take care of this for you. If the death occurred at home, the spouse, closest living relatives or witness are responsible.

The death certificate will only be issued to the person who declares the death. It costs SFr 25 and can be obtained by post, fax or e-mail from the Civil Registrar's Office.

### The documents you will need are:

- the deceased's passport or ID card
- the deceased's residence permit
- the doctor's report

The doctor who issues the report will give you a list of the three funeral parlours ('Pompes Funèbres') in Geneva, of which two are private. The third, Pompes Funebres de la Ville de Genève, is run by the state (see Important Addresses, [p.88]). This is a public service, and if you live in the commune of Geneva you are entitled to a free coffin and transportation of the corpse. All three funeral parlours will take care of all the formalities, from the registry office to the burial.

## Work

### Working in Geneva

Geneva is full of foreign workers, many of whom are employed by international organisations such as the UN, CERN, and other NGOs and government missions. However, some of the world's largest companies, in various industries, have also set up operations in Geneva. In the IT sector, IBM has its European microelectronics headquarters in the city, and other IT multinationals such as Sun Microsystems, Oracle Software, Hewlett Packard and Dell have a presence here as well. In the FMCG sector, both Gillette and Proctor & Gamble have large operations in Geneva. Then of course there are the thriving 'typically Swiss' industries such as watch making and banking. Each sector is highly individual and operated with precision and attention to detail. However, although the Swiss pride themselves on efficiency, this is rarely at the expense of home life, and work is not normally allowed to encroach upon personal time.

That said, if you work for a Swiss company (as opposed to an international company with an office in Geneva), you may find the atmosphere more reserved than you are used to. As a general rule the Swiss do not mix business with pleasure, and therefore there may not be much in the way of rowdy after-work drinks sessions with your colleagues.

It may not be necessary to speak fluent French in order for you to get a job here, especially if you work for an international company and your colleagues speak English. If you are required to improve your French, very often the company will invest in language classes for you.

### Working Hours

If you're the type of person who struggles to get out of bed for a job that starts at 09:00, you'd better form a close relationship with your alarm clock! In order to make the most of their free time in the afternoons and evenings many Swiss employees start the day earlier than usual, and it is not uncommon to find people at their desks from 07:00. But the early start pays off later, when you'll have plenty of time to enjoy late afternoon and evening activities.

The Swiss lunch hour is an institution, and you won't find many people munching a furtive sandwich at their desk. After 11:30, people stop working and go out for lunch.

On the whole though, the Swiss are among the hardest working people in the world, and the average working week is around 40 – 42 hours.

Annual leave is usually 20 days. Public holidays include those for Federation Day (1st August) and for Christian religious events. Geneva also has its very own public holiday, the 'Jeûne Genevois', which falls in the third week of September on a Thursday. It is normal practice to 'faire le pont' (make a bridge) by taking the Friday off as well, making for a nice long weekend!

> **All Work and No Play...**
>
> *Folks gather on summer evenings at La Terasse, a casual bar by the Bains des Pâquis.*
>
> *On Thursday, late afternoon, people head straight from the office to Soleil Rouge, a Spanish wine bar at the start of Bd. Helvétique.*
>
> *Sindy parties are a legend in Geneva. Look out for the afterwork parties, beach parties, fancy dress parties and the Christmas ball. The Sindy team have recently been organising Salsa lessons. For information on Sindy events, see www.sindy.ch.*

### Finding Work

The easiest way to find work in Geneva is to be recruited internationally. Many Geneva-based companies look for English speaking, internationally trained experts, and therefore their hunting grounds are the job markets of English speaking countries. Many positions are also recruited through international agencies.

If you see a job vacancy advertised for Geneva, don't be surprised to find no mention of the proposed salary. The Swiss are pretty discreet, and remuneration will vary drastically depending on experience and even age (older people are paid higher salaries, even if they have the same qualifications as a younger candidate).

If you arrive in Geneva with the intention of finding work, make sure you bring your networking skills with you, as this is the best way to start job hunting. Your first point of contact should be the local business groups (see Business Groups and Contacts, [57]).

The International Geneva Welcome Centre

Alternatively you can scout the local papers for job vacancies, or advertise your own profile. The *Tribune de Genève* has an employment section on Wednesdays (or you can visit their Website at www.annonces.ch/emploi). On Fridays, *Le Temps* has a jobs section, although this is mainly for executive positions and it is not Geneva-specific. See also *Tout l'Emploi*, which is published on Wednesdays and which has a Website at www.Tout l'Emploi.ch.

In addition to the newspapers, there are a few Websites advertising job vacancies. If you are interested in joining one of the international organisations, you can usually get their vacancy listings directly from their Websites.

One way of finding employment fairly rapidly is by teaching your mother tongue as a foreign language at one of the international language schools. (See Education [p.78])

## Recruitment Agencies

If you're the shy, retiring type and networking is not for you, you could always send your CV off to a recruitment agency that will introduce you to suitable companies. In general, recruitment agencies do not actively seek jobs for you, but they may have opportunities that match your criteria, and if that's the case they will forward your details to their client.

## Main Recruitment Agencies

| | | |
|---|---|---|
| Adecco | 022 718 44 90 | www.adecco.ch |
| Curriculum SA | 022 708 01 20 | www.curriculum.ch |
| Jobup | 022 700 45 50 | www.jobup.ch |
| Manpower SA | 022 908 21 21 | www.manpower.ch |

## Applying for a Job

The local practice for job applications is to send a complete dossier, including copies of your certificates and references, with your CV. A CV of two pages is acceptable, although it will not count against you if your CV is longer and more detailed. If you are not selected for a position, your dossier will be returned to you as it is illegal for companies to keep candidates' records without their express permission. If you want the company to keep your CV on file for future opportunities, you should indicate this in your covering letter.

### e-Job Hunting

www.espace-emploi.ch lists a range of jobs in general categories; www.medienjobs.ch specialises in vacancies in the media and communications sectors and www.topjobs.ch lists managerial and executive positions.

## Employment Contracts

You should insist on a written employment contract, and know exactly what is in the contract before you sign it. It should contain basic details such as your job title, salary, leave entitlement, working hours, probation period, notice period and the date of commencement. In addition, it should list your duties and responsibilities, which department you will be working in and who you will be reporting to, and any special employment conditions (such as health fund, confidentiality agreements, etc.). There will also be a clause stating that employment is subject to the granting of the necessary permit by Swiss authorities.

Before you sign, you should also consider factors such as:

- Whether the salary is sufficient in relation to the cost of living in Geneva, how often it is likely to be reviewed, and whether it includes a bonus or 13th cheque.
- What deductions will be made from your salary – the contract will give the gross salary, but this is usually subject to deductions such as AVS (pension and surviving dependants' insurance),

AI (unemployment insurance), LPP (a retirement scheme), and LAA (accident insurance). Your employer will also deduct income tax.

- Whether the company will pay all or part of your relocation expenses, both at the time of joining and also at the end of your contract if you return to your home country.

Once you are satisfied with the conditions of your contract (you can request a verbal or written translation if it is in French), the usual practice is to initial each page to show that you have read all the terms and are in acceptance.

## Labour Law

If you have a question relating to your rights at work, you can contact the SIT Employment Syndicate (Syndicat Interprofessionnel de Travailleuses et Travailleurs). They can advise you on work contracts, problems with employers, dismissals or unemployment. They are situated in the Old Town, and are open on weekdays. (See Important Addresses [p.88])

## Financial & Legal Affairs

## Banks

Now that you're living and working in Geneva, you too can be privy to the intrigue and glamour of having your very own 'Swiss bank account'. While in the past the untouchable secrecy of account numbers made Swiss banks a safe haven for 'hot' money, there has been a dramatic clamp-down in recent years on money laundering and other financial crimes. Even so, Switzerland remains the global home of private banking. However, unless you have a couple of million lying around, the private banks will not show much interest, and if you just need somewhere to deposit your salary every month, you'll have to make do with one of the retail banks.

Both Migros and Coop have lower banking charges and higher interest rates than other high street banks. BCGE also has relatively low bank

charges with branches everywhere. You can also open an account with the post office; visit the Website www.postfinance.ch.

Banks issue the usual credit cards. There is also the debit card (this used to be the EC card but it is now known as the Maestro card). The debit card is issued by the bank, and you can use it to pay for various services and items. The card also has an embedded CASH chip, which can be recharged with credit of up to SFr 300 and used to pay for things like parking, phone calls, public transport, etc. Chequebooks are not used in Switzerland.

### Cost of Living

| Entrance Fees/Club Memberships/Covers | |
|---|---|
| Cinema | SFr 13 – 17 |
| Museum | SFr 8 – 10 |
| Nightclub | Usually free or can be from SFr 10 – 25 (includes first drink) |

| Sports | |
|---|---|
| Gym (Holmes Place) | SFr 165/month |
| Pedalo (one hour) | SFr 15 |
| Sailing (one hour) | SFr 45 – 70 |
| Windsurfing (one hour) | SFr 20 |

| Telephone calls | |
|---|---|
| One minute to land line 08.00 – 17.00 | SFr 0.08 |
| One minute to land line 17.00 – 08.00 or Saturday and Sunday | SFr 0.04 |
| One minute to mobile 08.00 – 17.00 | SFr 0.55 |
| One minute to mobile 17.00 – 08.00 or Saturday and Sunday | SFr 0.45 |

When it comes to bill payment, Switzerland has a system of bill slips ('Bulletin de Versement'). Every bill received by post will have one of these attached. There are several methods of payment. At the post office you can pay cash, and you will be given the stamped invoice stub. This is your only record of payment. Alternatively you can use e-banking. E-banking is easier than standing in queues for the counter, and since most banks charge a small fee for counter transactions, it is cheaper too. E-banking can be done from home or the office using the Internet, or some banks provide a machine called a multimat. The multimat scans the bill and deducts the amount from your

### Banks

| Banque Coop | Pl. Longemalle 6–8 | 1204 Geneva | 022 818 44 44 | www.bankcoop.ch |
|---|---|---|---|---|
| Banque Migros | Rue Pierre-Fatio 15 | 1204 Geneva | 022 707 12 12 | www.migrosbank.ch |
| Banque Raiffeisen | Pl. Charles David 11 | 1290 Versoix | 022 950 98 60 | www.raiffeisen.ch |
| Credit Suisse Private Banking | Pl. Bel-Air 2 | 1204 Geneva | 022 393 21 11 | www.credit-suisse.com |
| UBS SA | Rue du Rhône 8 | 1204 Geneva | 022 375 75 75 | www.ubs.com |

account. You can make a printout of payment, and it will appear on your monthly statement. With some banks e-banking is free and with others the fee is around 30 centimes per transaction.

If you do not pay your bills in the required time (usually one month but it is stated on the invoice) you will receive a reminder. The new amount will be a few francs higher. If a second reminder is sent and ignored, the standard procedure is that your debt will be sent to the Debt Office ('Office des Poursuites et Faillites' – see Important Addresses, [p.88]). Thereafter, you have to pay the outstanding bill to them, plus a handling charge of around SFr 70, depending on the amount owed.

## Financial Planning

Geneva is a major financial centre and although the private banks cater to the very wealthy, there are schemes available to those with more modest financial means. Adequate financial planning for the future is always sensible, and especially so if you are an expat. Many people accepting an expatriate position do so for some degree of financial gain, so it is worth saving a little bit extra in a safe place. If you are working for one of the international organisations in Geneva, it is very important to save wisely, given that these organisations do not normally cover you for unemployment benefit or loss of earnings, nor do they participate in Swiss pension schemes.

Stay away from long term investment plans if you are on a short term contract. Once you have had a chance to settle down in Geneva and feel you want to stay a while, you may want to diversify your investments. It is widely accepted that the following financial precautions are ideal: an emergency cash buffer (between three and six months' salary), retirement income, property and personal and family protection (life and medical insurance). Should you choose to consult a financial planner, stick to major international companies. If you need assistance with your financial planning, you could enlist the services of an accountancy firm ('ficuiare'). The following firms offer services in English:

| Accountancy Firms | |
|---|---|
| BFB | 022 311 36 44 |
| Curtis and Company (including US tax services) | 022 329 53 26 |
| Orion Investments and Trust Ltd | 022 732 48 05 |
| STG Asset Management | 022 710 74 00 |

## Taxation

Value added tax (VAT) is included in the price of all goods and services in Geneva. The good news is that compared to most EU countries, Swiss VAT is lower. (Currently 2.4% on food and drinks, 3.6% on hotels, and 7.6% on anything else).

Income tax is also comparatively low, and the average rate is 15 – 35%, depending on income. If you work for an international organisation, you may not have to pay income tax at all. Your company will usually make specific arrangements to deduct your income tax directly from your salary. If you are self employed, you will have to do your taxes yourself. The deadline for the fiscal year is 31st March.

The amount of tax you pay depends on the canton you live in, as well as on other factors, such as whether you are married or single. There are also various types of tax: cantonal tax, community tax, federal tax, fire service tax and church tax . Federal tax makes up about 20% of your tax bill, with the remaining 80% made up from cantonal, community, fire and church taxes.

If you need help filling in your tax returns, you can contact SIT (Syndicat Interprofessionnel de Travailleuses, see Important Addresses [p.88]), or online at www.estv.admin.ch.

All expats should find out from their home countries if they are required to pay any income tax there.

## Business Groups & Contacts

The following groups are useful for networking and making business contacts. They also run events or hold talks on matters helpful to foreigners working in Geneva.

| Business Groups & Contacts | |
|---|---|
| American Int'l Women's Club | 022 736 01 20 |
| British Swiss Chamber of Commerce | 031 301 14 73 |
| Career Women's Forum | 022 340 00 63 |
| First Tuesday (Business Networking) | 022 733 84 01 |
| Geneva's English-speaking Magazine | www.gem.ch |
| SIT (Syndicat Interprofessionnel de Travailleuses et Travailleurs) | 022 818 03 00 |
| Swiss American Chamber of Commerce | 022 738 72 55 |

## Legal Issues

Swiss law operates on a three tier system of confederation, canton and commune. Switzerland is said to be a model of democracy, and this is certainly reflected in the legal system, where a petition with 100,000 signatures can be enough to amend the constitutional law. Requesting a referendum requires just 50,000 signatures!

Crime rates are pretty low in Switzerland, and if you do have a brush with the law it is more likely to be on an administrative level, rather than criminal. To apply for a permit, for example, you will need the signature of a notary ('notaire'). If you have an enquiry and are not sure who to address it to, the Chamber of Notaries will see you without an appointment for a nominal fee (around SFr 50). See Important Addresses on [p.88].

If you do break the law, it is recommended that you contact your local embassy. Depending on the infraction, you may be fined, or if it is a serious matter you will appear before the Tribunal where court proceedings are conducted in French.

The following lawyers advertise their services in English:

Etude Oberson, specialising mainly in taxation law (www.oberson.ch), James A. Tidmarsh, specialising in international commercial law (www.tidmarsh.ch), and Ziegler Poncet and Grumbach, specialising in press freedom (www.praetor.ch). Other lawyers can be found in the table below, or for a full list, see www.notaires-geneve-cng.ch.

## Housing

### Housing in Geneva

Most people living in Geneva live in apartments that they don't actually own. This is even the case if their families have lived there for years. Some say Geneva is on the brink of a housing crisis, as there are too many people and not enough apartments. It can be helpful to keep your ear to the ground, in case a friend of a friend knows someone who might be vacating their apartment. Sometimes the Human Resources department of your company will offer assistance with your search, and many companies have noticeboards where people leaving town post their details.

Once you manage to find somewhere to call home, however, you'll find the renting system straightforward and well organised. Most apartment blocks have a guardian ('concierge') who is a good point of contact for minor maintenance and who cleans the stairwell. Almost all apartment buildings have a communal laundry room ('buanderie'), which is usually located in the basement. In some buildings you may not have to pay to use the washing machines, although it may be included in the rent. In others, you will have to pay per wash, using either coins, cards or tokens (usually available from the concierge). You'll find that your building has a specific system when it comes to using the laundry – in some buildings you can wash your clothes whenever the machines are free, but in others you may have to slot into a strict rota system where you will not be allowed to use the laundry unless it is your turn. If you have your own washing machine make sure that you are allowed to install it into your apartment. On the other hand, if you don't own a washing machine and don't intend to buy one, then make sure your apartment building has a communal laundry, because external laundromats are few and far between.

Every apartment has its own storeroom, use of which is included in the rent. If it is in the cellar it is called the 'cave', although in older buildings it may be in the attic ('grenier'). It is extremely useful to have a separate storage area for your skis! Check where your cave is and that you have the key for it.

Modern buildings come equipped with a nuclear bunker in the cellar. Occasionally the sirens are tested in town, which is a very eerie feeling. If your building does not have one, in the event of a nuclear attack, there will be trained people on hand to direct you to safety.

Don't assume that your rent includes a parking space, so check before you sign the lease whether parking is available and covered by the rent. You might have to pay extra for using a

## Lawyers

| | | | | |
|---|---|---|---|---|
| **Aubert Yves** | Bd. Georges Favon, 14 | 1204 Geneva | 022 809 67 10 | aubert.rosset@safemail.ch |
| **Bonnefous Patrick** | Pl. du Molard, 11 | 1211 Geneva | 022 311 46 66 | info@pbg-not.ch |
| **Christ Jean-Rodolphe** | Rue Toepffer, 5 | 1206 Geneva | 022 703 53 00 | etude@necnot.ch |
| **Ducret Jean-Luc** | Rue de Candolle, 26 | 1205 Geneva | 022 320 22 66 | jlducret@swisnot.ch |
| **Girard Caroline** | Rue du Rhône, 29 | 1204 Geneva | 022 318 44 00 | etude@wicht-christen.ch |
| **Keller Denis** | Cours de Rive, 4 | 1211 Geneva | 022 311 29 11 | keller_glaser@swissonline.ch |
| **Pictet Marc** | Rue de Rive, 4 | 1211 Geneva | 022 311 91 88 | info@pictet-eardley-not.ch |
| **Terrier Didier** | Rue de Candolle, 2 | 1205 Genève | 022 322 12 12 | etude@bernasconi-terrier.ch |

Geneva housing options

garage or parking space – this is usually about SFr 150 per month.

Check also the pet policy in your building – many apartment blocks have a strict 'no pets' policy, so your beloved Fido may not be welcome.

### House Hunting Tips

*There are some free publications which are delivered to all mailboxes in town containing information about renting or buying property. These are: Geneva Home Informations, GHI (www.ghi.ch), Extension, Tout l'Immobilier (www.toutimmo.ch) and Immorama (www.immorama.ch).*

*Local papers also publish property pages. On Mondays see 24 Heures which publishes Léman Express. On Tuesdays the Tribune de Genève publishes real estate ads and on Wednesdays Le Temps has a property section.*

*Otherwise, supermarkets have bulletin boards where notices are posted for apartments to rent.*

*For a list of Real Estate Agents, see Real Estate Agents Table [p.63]*

## Real Estate Glossary

It is important to remember that in Geneva, apartments are described according to the number of rooms ('pièces') they have, including the kitchen. (In other areas of Switzerland, including neighbouring Vaud, kitchens are not counted as a 'pièce'). So in Geneva, a one bedroom apartment with a living room and a kitchen would be called a three room ('trois pièces') apartment. 1/2 piéces refers to a separate dining room or bigger lounge.

### Housing Abbreviations

| | |
|---|---|
| **Balcon/Terasse** | *balcony/terrace* |
| **Ch.** | *rooms ('chambre') or bedrooms* |
| **Charges comprises** | *hot water and other heating costs included in rent.* |
| **Cheminée** | *fireplace* |
| **Cuisine agencée** | *The kitchen is equipped with an oven, but not necessarily a fridge.* |
| **Libre** | *free from* |
| **Loyer mens** | *monthly rent* |
| **Meublé** | *furnished* |
| **r-d-c** | *ground floor ('rez de chausée')* |
| **Renovée** | *renovated* |
| **Séjour** | *living room ('salle de séjour')* |
| **Sdb** | *bathroom ('salle de bains')* |

## Purchasing a Home

If you resent shovelling all your lovely money into your landlord's pocket every month, you could consider buying your own home. The housing market in Geneva is stable and properties are well built. The laws surrounding property buying vary according to canton, but in Geneva the process is relatively straightforward. If you have a B type permit, you can only buy property in the same canton where you work, and your house must be your main place of residence – the law prohibits you from renting out your own house. Therefore, it is advisable to buy a house only once you are sure you want to stay in Geneva for a while, as if you leave, you may have to sell. For C permit holders, the law is less restrictive. You can buy property outside the canton, and it is not necessary for the property to be your main residence.

If you are an employee of an international organisation, you will have to apply to the Federal Office (the Swiss Agency for the Environment, Forests and Landscape) in Bern for permission to buy property. Such permission is nearly always granted. See Important Addresses on [p.88].

Once you have decided to buy, and have found your ideal home, you put in an offer which is submitted (usually by the real estate agency) to the property owner. A ten percent deposit should be given to the lawyer overseeing the purchase. The agency may recommend a suitable lawyer; alternatively refer to Lawyers on [p.58].

The lawyer will prepare a contract ('l'acte') for both parties to sign. On the day of signing, you are required to pay the balance of the deposit.

## Mortgages

By Geneva standards, the mortgage rate ('Taux Hypothécaire') is currently quite low and fairly steady – the ideal time to buy! The mortgage rate stands at around 3.7% (depending on various factors). In Geneva (unlike some other European cities) the length of the mortgage can extend beyond 20 years, but obviously this will depend on your personal circumstances. You'll be able to get more details from your bank.

## Renting a Home

If you think that renting a home is all about 'first come, first served' or 'the early bird catches the worm', you may find the rental procedure in Geneva a bit strange. Basically there is an initial 'viewing period', when everybody who wants to view the property can do so. Then if you're interested, you can put in an offer and submit the necessary documents to the letting agency. Nearly all rented accommodation in Geneva is done through a letting agency, even if owned by a private landlord, to maintain discretion. The documents you will probably have to give the letting agent include:

- a copy of your residency permit
- a copy of a recent pay slip
- a copy of your work contract
- a police record from your previous country
- a declaration from the Debt Office (Office des Poursuites et Faillites) to attest that you are not in debt (see Important Addresses, [p.88])

Then the landlord looks through all the applications and decides who is the most appropriate tenant (oh, the suspense!). If you are the lucky one, you will then be informed of the decision.

## Rent Disputes

Good luck with getting the letting agency on your side if you think that the rent for your apartment is unfair – their interests are firmly with the landlord. But there is an organisation that represents tenants' rights, called ASLOCA (022 716 18 00). You have to become a member, which costs SFr 50, but as a member you will receive free legal advice (further correspondence is then paid for on an 'as and when' basis). If you

sign a housing contract and subsequently find it is scandalously overpriced, all is not lost – it is still possible to negotiate successfully for fair rent, since a signed rental contract is not binding. Phew!

## The Lease

The lease agreement ('le bail') is signed in triplicate and you, your landlord and the letting agency each get a copy. In general, you sign up for between three and five years, with no notice period in the first year, and three months' notice period during each subsequent year. With the current housing shortage, however, you should have no problem find someone to sub-let your apartment if you have to break the lease.

### Don't be a Nightmare Neighbour!

There are laws in Switzerland governing good neighbourly behaviour:

- No flushing of toilets after 22:00
- No running a bath after 22:00
- No hanging washing outside
- No washing your car in the street on a Sunday

These laws are very often ignored, however. Genevans tend to keep to themselves, and in most cases don't even know who their neighbours are!

Once you sign the contract, the letting agent will require three months' rent as a security deposit. This money will be set up in a special (low interest) account, and will be released only when you vacate

View over a residential area

the property and the letting agent confirms everything is in order.

Rent is usually paid on the first of the month, one month in advance.

It is common practice to have a little plaque bearing your name on your letterbox (by the building's main entrance), and also on your front door. Your landlord or letting agent will help you order the plaques, for which there may be a small charge (usually around SFr 30).

## Main Accommodation Options

### Apartment/Villa Sharing

It is unusual for people in Geneva to share an apartment. Out of the main town, you'll find villas a bit more common, and some of these are divided into apartments.

### Standard Apartments

Most people live in apartments. Apartments are usually rented without furniture – a furnished apartment ('appartement meublé') will have higher rent. With unfurnished apartments, you'll often find that all traces of previous inhabitation have been removed – including the light fittings, so it's a good idea to unpack your screwdriver before anything else.

### Villas

Private villas are very pricey, to rent or to buy. You'll find some gorgeous villas by the lake, but these usually belong to the rich and famous!

### Hotel Apartments

Your company may put you up in a hotel apartment when you first arrive, as a stop-gap while you search for your new home. The advantages are that these apartments are fully furnished, supplied with clean bedding and towels, and they have a small kitchen equipped with utensils and appliances. However, they cost almost twice the monthly rent of a standard apartment. Refer to Hotel Residences in General Information [p.28].

## Youth Hostels

If your budget is limited, or you prefer a youthful environment where you can mingle informally with other newcomers, there is a choice of hostels. The main youth hostel is located near the train station. The Foyer St-Justin is near the cathedral and has one of the best roof terraces in town (and one of the longest waiting lists).

| Monthly Rent | | | |
|---|---|---|---|
| Rooms | Apartments | Hotel Apartments | Villas |
| Studio | 1000 | 1800 | na |
| 2 | 1200 – 1500 | 2500 | na |
| 3 | 1500 – 1700 | na | na |
| 4 | 1700 – 2000 | na | na |
| 5 | 2350 – 3500 | na | na |
| 6 | na | na | 4500 |
| 8 | na | na | 13000 |

Note: All prices in SFr per calendar month

## Residential Areas

The main residential areas of Geneva are:

**Old Town** – The quaint Old Town has a lot of charm, a great atmosphere, and it is nice and close to the centre of town. On the downside, it was built when there were fewer cars around, so there is not much in the way of parking spaces or garages. Also, it is not uncommon for buildings to have no central heating, and the use of electric or gas heaters means higher bills.

**Jonction** – This is where the Arve from Chamonix flows into the Rhône from the lake, and the glacial waters mix into the river in a distinctive shade of cloudy blue. The areas of Jonction closer to the

| Youth Hostels | | | | |
|---|---|---|---|---|
| | Address | Tel No. | Website | Email |
| Cite Universitaire | Av. Miremont, 46 1211 Geneva | 022 839 22 22 | na | na |
| Centre St-Boniface | Av. Du Mail, 14 1205 Geneva | 022 322 26 00 | www.cstb.ch | accueil@cstb.ch |
| City Hostel Geneva | Rue Ferrier, 2 1202 Geneva | 022 901 15 00 | www.cityhostel.ch | info@cityhostel.ch |
| Foyer St-Justin | Rue du Prieuré, 15–17 1202 Geneva | 022 731 11 35 | na | na |
| Youth Hostel | Rue Rothschild, 30 1202 Geneva | 022 732 62 60 | www.yh-geneva.ch | booking@yh-geneva.ch |

river are pretty, and further down stream there is a low cost housing project.

**Plainpalais** – The high density of bars, restaurants and shops in Plainpalais makes it a vibrant place to live.

**Pâquis** – This area has some lovely apartments on the lakeside, and there are loads of bars and cafés which make it lively, even on Sundays when the rest of Geneva is like a ghost town. Its location in front of Cornavin train station where most of the hotels are situated means that you'll be living in close proximity to the city's red light district. The Rue de Lausanne is an up and coming area which has really opened up as a result of the number 13 tram route.

**Champel** – Located behind the Old Town. With Parc Bertrand situated in the middle of this area, the streets near the park are quiet and residential. The main through roads are Route de Florissant and Route de Malagnou (which leads onto the Autoroute Blanche to Chamonix) are busy, with supermarkets and traffic, and the residences are mostly high-rise.

**Servette** – This area behind Cornavin train station is very convenient for getting to work for employees of the UN, IBM and some other international organisations.

There'll be one along in a minute...

**Eaux-Vives** – The area of town on the Rive Gauche (Left Bank) up to the Parc La Grange. It's a cosmopolitan part of town where little shops and bistros are plentiful and the proximity to the lake is a bonus.

**Chêne-Bourg** – The advantages of being slightly outside town are that you are closer to the countryside! As the name suggests (a 'chêne' is an oak tree) this district is leafy and is close to the Arve river and Carouge.

**Carouge** – A separate town from Geneva, although close and serviced by trams and buses. It was originally part of Savoy and is built in Sicilian style. Buildings are smaller and the area has a friendly atmosphere, with cute continental cafés and good restaurants.

## Other Rental Costs

Your monthly rent will usually include hot water charges, including heating (if this is the case, your lease will stipulate 'charges comprises'). Electricity and gas are billed by SIG (Services Industrielles de Genève) and you have the option of regular energy or green energy (which is slightly more expensive) when you sign the contract. (See the Utilities section, [p.67])

To open a telephone contract as a foreigner, Swisscom ask for a SFr 500 deposit, which is refunded when you leave. (See the Utilities section, [p.67])

You might have to pay to use the washing machine in your building. (See Housing in Geneva, [p.58])

Parking places may be charged additionally. (See Housing in Geneva, [p.58])

| Real Estate Agents | |
| --- | --- |
| Brolliet | www.brolliet.ch |
| CGI Immobilier | www.cgi.ch |
| Comptoir Genevois Immobilier | www.comptoir-immo.ch |
| Moser Vernet | www.moservernet.ch |
| Naef | www.naef.ch |
| Société Privée de Gérance | www.spg.ch |

**Note:** For a full list of registered estate agents in Geneva, contact the Société des Régisseurs de Genève (022 715 02 20).

## Moving Services

The following removal companies are based in Geneva. If you wish to use an international removal firm, try Pickfords International or Allied

Van Lines. If you live in the UK, Luker Brothers, based in Reading, have a Geneva service that runs twice a week.

## Moving Services

| Moving Services | |
|---|---|
| Allied International | 022 593 58 80 |
| Harsch | 022 300 43 00 |
| Intertransport | 022 827 70 10 |
| Tammaro | 022 798 32 24 |

## Relocation Experts

Relocation experts offer a range of services to help you settle into your new life in Geneva as quickly as possible. Practical help ranges from finding accommodation or schools for your children to connecting a telephone or information on medical care. In addition, they will often offer advice on the way of life in the city, helping people to establish a new life as quickly and as smoothly as possible.

## Furnishing Accommodation

IKEA is the mecca of those who have recently moved here. Situated on the main road towards Lausanne at Aubonne, it is easily accessible by car or train. If you're worried about how you'll bring all your flat-packed furniture back on the train, relax – you can pay to have it delivered to your apartment (particularly useful if you live on the top floor in a building with no lift!). IKEA also offers a van rental service.

If you don't fancy assembling all your own furniture you can pay IKEA to do it for you. Or, you could always try to buy some items from people who are leaving town. Check the noticeboard at your office or in the supermarkets. You can also check the classifieds section of the *Tribune de Genève,* or the classified ads on the WRG radio station Website (www.wrgfm.com).

The Old Town boasts many antiques and interior design shops, catering to all tastes from abstract to over the top to zen.

## Second-hand Goods

Flea markets, antiques fairs and bric a brac all fall under the term 'broccante'. There are festivals of broccante in Switzerland and nearby France where you can rummage to your hearts content; check the local press for details (see Markets [p.163]). The Salvation Army has a warehouse for rummaging in. Emmaüs is another charity place where people donate furniture and you can make some surprising finds. Note though that you will have to arrange your own transport for any pieces of furniture.

**Salvation Army:** Route de Chêne 18 – 20; 1207 Genève. 022 736 15 80

> *Opening hours: 08:30 – 12:00 14:00 – 18.30 Tues, Thur, Fri; 08:30 – 17.00 Sat all day, Wed afternoons only*

**Emmaüs:** Route de Drize 5, Rondeau de Carouge, CH 1227 Carouge. 022 342 39 59

> *Opening hours: 13.30 – 17.30 Mon – Fri; 09:00 – 17:30 Sat*

Flag of peace

## Household Appliances

High street and department stores selling household appliances (such as Interdiscount, Globus and Manor) may not be able to give knowledgeable advice on various items, nor might they have a large range. You'll be better off heading for the shopping malls if you want maximum choice. The main ones are M-Parc La Praille, Migros in the shopping centre Balexert, or The Media Markt superstore in Meyrin (see Shopping [p.144]). Alternatively you can do your shopping over the border in France, where the hypermarkets sell a range of items at competitive prices. Take note of customs regulations though – you should declare any goods at the border and pay the necessary VAT as you re-enter Switzerland.

## Household Insurance

Although you are required by law to insure your house, the basic coverage is not expensive (around SFr 250 per year). This will cover you for fire and theft, but not necessarily for items which get damaged outside the house. If you move house, you don't need to change your insurance. Just remember to notify them of your change of address, and they will transfer the coverage.

| Household Insurance | |
| --- | --- |
| Allianz Suisse | www.allianz-suisse.ch |
| Bâloise | www.baloise.ch |
| Coop Assurance | www.coop.ch |
| Generali | www.generali.ch |
| Helvetia Patria | www.helvetiapatria.ch |
| La Genevoise | www.genevoise.ch |
| La Mobilière | www.lamobiliere.ch |
| La Suisse | www.lasuisse.ch |
| Winterthur | www.winterthur.ch |

## Laundry Services

Not washing your dirty laundry in public takes on a whole new meaning in Switzerland, where you will find hardly any self service laundromats! You will perhaps have a laundry room in your building, (see Housing in Geneva [p.58]), and the concierge may even offer to do your washing (but this shouldn't be taken for granted!). Laundry services ('pressing') and dry cleaning services ('nettoyage à sec'), are plentiful. The major chain is called Cinq à Sec and has branches in most areas. There are other family run establishments, but do not expect them to do anything in a hurry. Three working days is the usual minimum requirement.

Dry cleaning prices are high:

- Shirt SFr 7.50
- Trousers SFr 10
- Skirt SFr 11
- Jacket SFr 13.30

One kilo of laundry washing is around SFr 25.

## Domestic Help

In Geneva there is a relatively large population of illegal immigrants, particularly from Latin America, who depend on cleaning for their livelihood. It is up to you to decide if you want to employ someone illegally, but if you do, and you are caught, you will be heavily fined. There is no shortage of notices in supermarkets and newsagents offering domestic service; you can expect to pay SFr 20 – 25 per hour for a cleaning lady, and more if you use a company. The following companies offer professional handy help:

| Domestic Help Agencies | |
| --- | --- |
| All Net Service | 022 344 19 39 |
| Cleaning Service | 022 733 07 33 |
| Cogenet | 022 342 02 40 |
| Net Inter | 022 797 23 50 |
| Omniservices | 022 328 24 80 |
| Star Services | 022 798 08 55 |

## Pets

### Bringing Your Pet to Geneva

Lots of people in Geneva have cats and dogs, and it is relatively straightforward to bring your pets here from your home country. Before you leave, ask your vet for an International Health Certificate, declaring that your pet has been vaccinated against rabies and certifying that it was in good health at the time of vaccination. The vaccination must have been given not less than 30 days and not more than one

Housing development in Lignon

year before you arrive in Geneva. If your pet is under five months old and being imported from Europe (excluding Turkey), Australia, New Zealand or the USA, then you do not need the rabies vaccination but you still need to produce a vet's certificate confirming the age and good health of the animal.

Birds need a special import licence, which you can get from the Customs and Excise authorities in your home country. Your bird will have to stay in quarantine until the authorities are satisfied that it doesn't have parrot fever. Rabbits will have to stay in quarantine for 15 days, and must also be vaccinated against rabies.

Bear in mind that many apartment buildings do not allow dogs, although keeping a cat is usually okay.

### Pet Services

| | | |
|---|---|---|
| **Animaux Services** | 078 734 10 35 | Grooming, walking, feeding |
| **Chemin d'akita** | 022 757 51 62 | Animal psychology |
| **Chatterie des Curieux** | 022 756 14 02 | Cattery |
| **La Vigie** | 022 732 41 17 | Kennel |
| **Of Liberty** | 022 756 16 60 | Boarding, English spoken |

## Taking Your Pet Home

The regulations for exporting your pet depend on the laws of the country to which you are moving. Your local vet or the airline you are travelling with can inform you of the specific regulations pertaining to your destination, such as quarantine rules and vaccination certificates. Check with the relevant authorities well in advance.

Fountain in the Old Town

## Cats & Dogs

### Vaccination

After your dog is six months old, it should be vaccinated against rabies every two years. There is also a recommended (but not compulsory) vaccination against distemper. Cats are not required to have the rabies vaccination, but it is recommended that you do it anyway, especially if your cat likes to wander around outside the house.

### Licence

You must have a licence for your dog once it is six months old. In Geneva, it is also necessary for the dog to have a microchip inserted just under the skin on the neck – this microchip contains information about your dog and can be read like a barcode. Your vet will fill in all your (and your dog's) details on the identity form, and send a copy to ANIS (the Animal Identity Service in Bern), keep a copy for his/her records, and give one copy to you. Once you have received this form from the vet, you should call your household insurance company to notify them that you have a dog – they will send you another form.

You then need to present both forms, along with the animal's rabies vaccination certificate, to the District Mayor's office ('La Mairie'). They will issue a small aluminium tag, inscribed with the year, licence number and canton, which should be attached to your dog's collar and worn at all times. The total cost for the microchip and licence is SFr 79. It is not necessary to get your cat licensed.

> **Help!**
>
> If you see an animal that looks lost or injured, during the day you can call a vet. For advice on the 24 hour vet on duty, call 0900 83 83 43 evenings, weekends and holidays.
>
> If you feel an animal is being ill treated or if you find a stray, call the SGPA, the Société Genevoise Pour la Protection des Animaux, (022 757 13 23).

> **La Fouine**
>
> If you see a long thin animal a little smaller than a cat, particularly at night time, it is likely that it is a stone marten ("Fouine" in French). These animals are very shy and cute, but they cause havoc in car engines as they like to chew the rubber insulating tubes and connections. They do not venture into town but are very common in suburban and rural areas.

### General Advice

Kennels tend to get booked up early, so if you are going on holiday without your pet, you should book it in early. As an alternative, you could try one of the home pet-sitting services available.

Dogs must be kept on a lead everywhere except special areas of parks where they are allowed to run free. Some parks and gardens provide free plastic bags for picking up your dog's 'oopsies'.

Dogs require half-price tickets when travelling on public transport and are permitted in most bars and restaurants. In general, you will not be able to take your dog into shops where food is sold, but these usually have hooks outside where you can tie your dog up.

### Veterinary Clinics

| | |
|---|---|
| Cabinet Vétérinaire de Frontenex | 022 719 10 10 |
| Cabinet Vétérinaire de St Jean | 022 340 27 27 |
| Diane Cuenoud et Corinne Ritter | 022 736 44 00 |

## Utilities & Services

### Electricity & Water

The sole provider of electricity, water and sewerage is Services Industriels de Genève (SIG) (see Important Addresses [p.88]). The service is excellent and disruption is rare. When you first move into your new apartment, your landlord or the letting agency may take the necessary measures to get you registered to receive gas, water and electricity in your home – this will save you the bother of having to do it yourself. You will be billed for these services quarterly.

### Electricity

Geneva's electricity supply is produced by hydraulics and provided solely by SIG. There are several types of electricity supply, including:

**SIG Vitale Bleu:** This is the least expensive, and will cost around SFr 45 per month (average estimate for a couple living together);

**SIG Vitale Jaune:** This is slightly more expensive (by about SFr 5 per month), and is energy that is produced only in Geneva;

**SIG Vitale Vert:** This 'green' energy supply costs around SFr 59 per month, and helps develop ecological energies of the future.

The Swiss are big on renewable energy, and SIG claims that 56% of the energy it provides is renewable.

Socket type is generally standard European two pin, yet some plugs or sockets have the third pin.

Adaptors are widely available at any grocery or hardware store. Electricity is 220 volts AC, 10 amps maximum with a frequency of 50 hertz (Hz).

### Water

The quality of tap water in Geneva passes the most stringent tests in the world and is very high quality, so no need to buy a water purifier. Most of the water comes from the lake. There have been problems with phosphates in the water, but these occurred a long time ago and the situation has since improved.

Drinking water

### Gas

Gas is not available in all buildings. If you require activation of a mains gas connection, you should call SIG on 022 420 75 50. If you need to buy a gas grill stove, you can try the main dealers, or see if there are any good second-hand ones available (see Second-hand Goods, [p.156]). To purchase bottled gas for a gas grill stove, the following companies sell bottled gas and gas appliances and provide installation.

### Gas Suppliers

| | |
|---|---|
| AGA SA | 0844 800 300 |
| Carbagas | 022 343 71 50 |
| Pangas | 022 989 39 00 |

### Rubbish Disposal and Recycling

Household waste can be disposed of in the bins provided in your building. Geneva has an intricate system of collecting different types of rubbish. There are certain days of the week or month when

New Residents

Utilities & Services

items can be left outside your home for removal. For example, paper and cardboard are left out on Tuesday night and collected early Wednesday morning, or furniture and large household items are collected twice a month (the date depends on which neighbourhood you live in). You can get a calendar of rubbish collection in your area from your local post office, and you will receive updates through the post several times a year. There are steep fines (SFr 100) for leaving rubbish out a day early. Alternatively, you can visit the State of Geneva's Website for further information on rubbish collection in your area. This site also gives information on where to find the nearest recycling points for the following items. The address of the Website (in French) is www.geneve.ch/dechets.

- Glass should be recycled at bottle banks. These are large plastic containers, colour coded for different colours of glass.
- Clothes can be recycled in clothes boxes ('les boîtes à fringues'), which are yellow.
- Aluminium cans and tins should be crushed and placed in the blue metallic recycling box.
- Used batteries should be taken to your local supermarket, where there is a special recycling box.

If you have items of refuse you wish to dispose of yourself, they can be taken to Espace Récupération du Site de Chatillon (see Important Addresses, [p.88]). Any other queries about refuse disposal can be addressed to the Service Inf-eau-déchets (DIAE) (see Important Addresses, [p.88]).

## Telephone

The national telecommunications company, Swisscom, has a near monopoly on telecommunications, as they are the only company that can supply you with a telephone line.

### Landline Phones

The first step in getting your home phone connected is to buy a handset and get a Swisscom number. The easiest way to do this is to go to an independent local phone dealer, who can advise you on a suitable handset and contact Swisscom on your behalf to get your phone connected. This process is usually done pretty swiftly, since they have access to the local technicians' network. They will provide you with all the relevant forms, and if you have bought your handset from them they will usually do the installation for free.

If you prefer a bit of a challenge, you can try to do it yourself. Call Swisscom (0800 800 800) to request a line. They will then send you a contract through the post, which you should sign and return. The next step is to buy or rent a handset, either from a Swisscom shop or from any telephone dealer. There are two Swisscom shops in Geneva, one in Centre Commercial Balexert, and the other on Rue Ami Lullin, 4. Once you have your handset, you need to supply Swisscom with your address and a copy of your permit, and pay the one off line connection fee (SFr 43). Foreigners who do not have a C type permit will also have to pay a deposit of SFr 500. It will take around two to three days to have your line connected.

Line rental will cost you SFr 25 per month – this is a fixed amount which must be paid monthly. If you do not pay your bill, you will be sent a first reminder after ten days, and a second reminder ten days after that. If both reminders are ignored, then your line will be disconnected, and you will have to pay a reconnection fee of SFr 40.

### Telephone Calls

Once you've got your line connected, you can either have your call billing done directly through Swisscom or through a service provider (e.g. Sunrise, Tele2 or Cablecom).

Swisscom calls to landlines cost SFr 0.08 during peak times, and SFr 0.04 off peak. Calls to mobile phones cost SFr 0.55 peak and SFr 0.45 off peak. Long distance calls are cheaper after 19:00 and at weekends. Different billing options are available, such as fixed prices for frequently dialled numbers. You will be billed monthly, at the end of the month.

Sunrise, offers a competitive billing system – the more calls you make, the greater your discount will be. There is a small connection charge (SFr 0.03) for each call, and then the rates per minute are SFr 0.069 during peak hours and SFr 0.035 off peak. You are billed monthly, one month in arrears, and bills are itemised. You can contact the Sunrise information centre on 0800 707 707, or visit their Website at www.sunrise.ch.

### Mobile Phones

Most people in Geneva have mobile phones, and some no longer even bother to get landlines. Mobile phone service providers offer an ever increasing range of services and special offers. It is possible to use the GSM network in Geneva.

SFr 10 ~ € 6

1st Edition | GENEVA EXPLORER

Bin there, done that!

## Mobile Phone Providers

| | |
|---|---|
| **Orange** | 022 810 37 90 |
| Rue du Rhône, 17 | |
| **Sunrise** | 022 555 21 11 |
| Av. Louis-Casaï, 84 | |
| **Swisscom Mobile Shop** | 022 797 74 73 |
| Rue du Mont-Blanc, 19 | |

### Non Resident

If you are a visitor to Geneva, or you are waiting for your permit to be approved, you can buy a SIM card for prepaid calls from the main dealers. In the past you could register for a prepaid telephone number without providing proof of identification; now however you will have to produce ID. The SIM card costs around SFr 49, which includes SFr 20 worth of talk time. Recharge cards are available from most newsagents.

### Resident

Once you have your permit to live and work in Geneva, you can apply for a mobile phone contract. You can fill in the relevant application form where you buy your handset, or with one of the service providers (either Swisscom, Orange or Sunrise). You will be required to produce your passport and residence permit. You may be required to produce a guarantee of employment or even pay a deposit. The contract duration will be either for one or two years.

Swisscom Mobile offers various contract options, ranging from paying no monthly fee (but then your calls are more expensive), to paying a monthly fee of SFr 25 with cheaper calls. With the second option, the various rates per minute are: SFr 0.59 peak, SFr 0.40 off peak, SFr 0.20 evenings and weekends. International calls (to UK or France) cost SFr 0.60 and sending an SMS costs SFr 0.20. For more information on Swisscom and its range of services, visit their Website at www.swisscom-mobile.ch.

Orange offers various contracts, including one with a monthly fee of SFr 30, which includes 30 minutes of free talk time. Sending a text message costs between SFr 0.15 and SFr 0.25.

Sunrise offers services ranging from SFr 0.65 per minute with a monthly fee of SFr 12 per month, or SFr 0.40 per minute paying SFr 80 per month.

### Bill Payment

Bills ('factures') are sent monthly and should be paid within the month. If payment is not received, a reminder bill will be sent, which will include the fee for the reminder letter (a few francs at most). If payment is still not received, a second and final reminder is sent, subsequent to which your service will be suspended. Reconnection is very costly and can be up to SFr 1,500, depending on the size of your original bill.

### Missing Mobile

Mobile theft is not common in Geneva, and most people feel safe leaving their phones out on tables in cafés and restaurants. If your phone does go missing, call your service provider immediately to suspend the line.

## Internet

Both Swisscom and Sunrise can hook you up to the information superhighway. You can access the Internet from any standard telephone line (using a modem at a speed of 56 Kbps). Alternatively, if you feel the need for speed, you can apply for an ISDN line (64 Kbps) or an ADSL line (128 Kbps). With ADSL, your connection is open 24 hours a day and you pay no further charges, but for standard line and ISDN connections you pay an additional user charge.

Swisscom offers a standard connection called 'Highway' that costs SFr 0.70 per hour off peak and SFr 2.80 peak. You can pay your connection fee either in monthly instalments of SFr 16.90 or as a yearly lump sum of SFr 169. The cost for ADSL varies according to connection speed, ranging from SFr 49 per month for ADSL 600 to SFr 99 per month for ADSL 2400. The special modem must be purchased separately and costs around SFr 100. For more information, consult the Swisscom Website or call their helpdesk (0848 844 884).

Sunrise offers preferential rates to existing Sunrise customers of SFr 2.20 per hour (peak rate) or SFr 0.60 (off peak). If you are not a Sunrise customer, you will be charged slightly more. The Sunrise ADSL service costs from SFr 49 per month for ADSL 600, to SFr 98 per month for ADSL 2400. With Sunrise, you get a free modem, and there is no initial charge.

### Dial and Surf

Both Swisscom and Sunrise have numbers you can use to access the Internet without registering for an Internet connection:

**Swisscom Freeway**

Dial 10741 0840 840 222

Connection costs from SFr 0.70 – 2.80 per hour

**Sunrise Freesurf**

Dial 0840 555 555

Connection costs SFr 0.60 – 2.20 per hour

## Internet Cafés

Internet cafés are found all over town, with new ones opening up all the time. For a listing of cafés, see [p.42] eCafés are getting up to speed with LAN connectivity, so you can take your laptop and connect to the Internet with WiFi.

## Postal Services

Switzerland has an excellent postal service and first class national post arrives the following day. The stamp prices vary according to the weight and size of the letter, so if you're saving pennies, fold A4 documents in half and use an A5 envelope. Post boxes are yellow and most of them issue stamps. Key in the value of the stamp you require and the number of stamps you need, insert the coins and follow the instructions on the machine.

## Television (Local Channels)

If you were thinking of bringing your TV with you to Geneva, think again – there is a different transmission standard in Switzerland, and TV sets from other countries may not work. Bad news if you've just bought a brand new telly, but at least it's one less thing to pack! So, shortly after you arrive you'll be doing the rounds at TV shops, and one important feature you should consider is getting a TV with teletext – this will allow you to have subtitles on foreign language programmes and films.

It is mandatory to have a TV licence ('concession'), which costs SFr 264 per year and is payable quarterly. An organisation called 'Billag' supplies licences, and you can call them (0844 834 834) or visit their Website (www.billag.ch) for more information.

The licence funds the TV channels you receive in Geneva, which are TSR 1, TSR 2 and Léman Bleu Télévision. Most TV sets will also be able to receive TF 1, France 2 and France 3 (all French channels).

Virtually all Geneva buildings have cable TV. The connection is via a socket that connects to your TV aerial. Geneva's cable network (Telegeneve – 0844 822 123) offers around 30 channels in various languages. English language channels include CNN, BBC World, and BBC Prime. Depending on what channels are provided, cable TV costs between SFr 10 and SFr 40 per month. Check with your landlord, as the cable could be included in your apartment's monthly costs. If not, it is billed annually. Additional channels are available through monthly subscription, but for this you need a decoder (available at most electrical shops).

## Satellite

If you can't live without your favourite programmes from back home, and the choice available on cable is unsatisfactory, you may want to consider satellite TV. You'll have to check first whether your building has a suitable satellite dish. If it doesn't, make sure that you have permission to install one. Buildings in the Old Town, for example, may not allow you to do so.

| Satellite Main Dealers | |
|---|---|
| Patrick TV | 022 796 26 85 |
| Sat-Antenne Lauber | 022 779 09 69 |
| Spot-Vision SA | 022 348 11 48 |

### Pay TV Satellite Channels

These are channels that require payment for installation and equipment such as the decoder, dish, etc., followed by a viewing subscription for the channels you want to watch. Generally, subscriptions can be paid monthly, quarterly or annually. Take your time making the right choice because if your selection is not available in Geneva, you can subscribe from the UK.

### Free to Air Satellite Channels

Once you've got your dish and decoder installed, these channels can be watched free of charge.

### Equipment

Equipment can be bought from main dealers in your home country (eg the UK for BSkyB), from dealers in Geneva or from electrical shops. Dealers will usually perform the installation.

## Health

## General Medical Care

The standard of medical care is excellent in Geneva. The cantonal Hospital, HUG (Hôpital Universitaire de Genève) has several national experts in various areas of medicine. Doctors are generally sympathetic and quick to offer remedies on prescription. The Swiss pharmaceutical industry is a source of national pride.

## Health Insurance

It is mandatory to be covered by a recognised Swiss health insurance provider. (See Health Insurance, [p.51]). This insurance covers the costs of medical consultations, in-patient stays and some prescription medicines. Standard insurance policies don't usually cover dental treatment. You will pay a monthly sum, or premium, to the insurance company to cover initial costs. Medical bills are reimbursed after you have spent a base sum or 'franchise'. The minimum franchise went up in 2004 to SFr 300. If you pay a low monthly premium, your franchise will be higher and you will have to pay more of your medical bills before you are reimbursed. For more information, you can contact Geneva's Health Insurance Bureau (see Important Addresses on [p.88]), or visit the website www.assurance-info.com.

### Health Insurance Companies

| | |
|---|---|
| Allianz Suisse | www.allianz-suisse.ch |
| Assura | www.assura.ch |
| Bâloise | www.baloise.ch |
| Generali | www.generali.ch |
| Helvetia Patria | www.helvetiapatria.ch |
| Intras | www.intras.ch |
| La Genevoise | www.genevoise.ch |
| La Suisse | www.lasuisse.ch |

Old Town at night

## 24 Hour Pharmacies

The standard opening hours of pharmacies are from 08:30 to 18:00, Monday to Saturday. Some pharmacies are open 24 hours a day on a rota system, so it is worth calling ahead to check whether or not your usual pharmacy is open.

Many pharmacies keep all your details on record, making it easier to issue repeat prescriptions. Pharmacies usually charge a small fee (around SFr 10) for issuing prescriptive drugs to first time customers, so it is advisable to use the same pharmacy every time you need a prescription filled.

### Pharmacies

| | | |
|---|---|---|
| Pharmacie Dancet | Rue Dancet, 3 | 022 329 05 38 |
| Pharmacie Floreal | Av Pictet-de-Rochemont, 17 | 022 736 88 27 |
| Pharmacie SunStore | Rue de Lausanne | 022 738 55 95 |
| Pharmacie Voltaire | Rue Voltaire, 30 | 022 344 73 80 |

### Hospitals

| | |
|---|---|
| Hôpital Cantonal | 022 372 33 11 |
| Hôpital Cantonal Paediatrics | 022 372 33 11 |

### Diagnostics

| | |
|---|---|
| Acacias | 022 342 54 55 |
| Carouge | 022 309 45 45 |
| Cornavin | 022 731 21 20 |
| Eaux-Vives | 022 735 55 50 |
| Meyrin | 022 780 08 11 |

### Private Centres/Clinics

| | |
|---|---|
| Clinique Belmont | 022 735 78 11 |
| Clinique de la Coline | 022 346 34 22 |
| Hopital de la Tour | 022 719 61 11 |

### Dermatologists

| | |
|---|---|
| Chemin du Beau Soleil | 022 346 69 62 |
| Dermatologie Hopitaux | 022 372 94 52 |
| P. Chavaz | 022 700 67 84 |
| Skinpulse | 022 329 70 00 |

## Maternity

Childbirth usually takes place in hospital, although you can also arrange to have a home birth, if preferred. Your husband is encouraged to play an active part in the birth. The costs of having a baby will depend on where you go, what insurance you have and how long you've been on your current insurance scheme. If you do have to

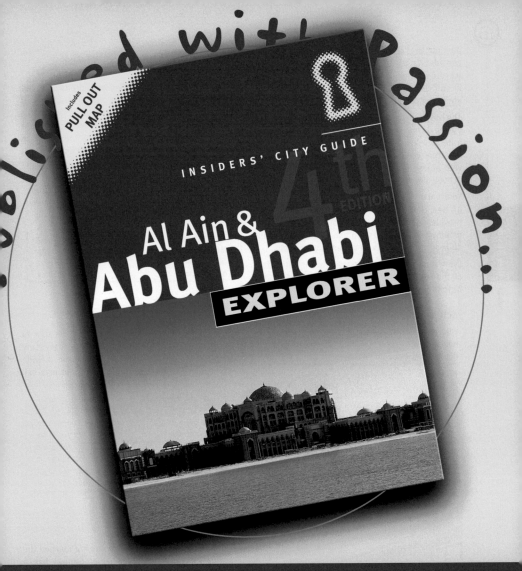

*published with passion...*

Includes
PULL OUT
MAP

INSIDERS' CITY GUIDE

4th EDITION

Al Ain &
Abu Dhabi
EXPLORER

# The Authoritative Guidebook on Abu Dhabi & Al Ain

Capitalising on all things cultural and cool in our capital, the 4th edition of the **Abu Dhabi Explorer** is packed with more than a few excuses to improve your get up and go. Let's just say with this book, life's a walk in the park, or a stroll down Abu Dhabi's Corniche.

- General information & UAE overview
- Resident tips & advice
- 250 independent restaurant, bar & cafe reviews
- Exploring - museums, heritage, parks & beaches
- Shopping - what to buy and where to buy it
- Activities - sports, leisure, clubs & kids
- 36 fully referenced photographic maps

*Passionately Publishing...*

**Phone** (971 4) 335 3520 • **Fax** (971 4) 335 3529 • **Email** Info@Explorer-Publishing.com

**Insiders' City Guides** • Photography Books • Activity Guidebooks • Commissioned Publications • Distribution

**EXPLORER**

www.Explorer-Publishing.com

pay all the costs yourself, you may want to consider having the baby in your home country (if you are entitled to free treatment there and you are in sufficiently good health to travel by the end of your pregnancy).

The hospital stay after giving birth is relatively long (seven days). Once you take your new baby home, a nurse will visit you a few days later to check the health of you and your baby and offer assistance with breastfeeding (if required). Breastfeeding is actively encouraged in Switzerland.

Your baby should be insured before three months of age, so you should notify your insurance provider of the birth. You should also keep your employer informed, as you may qualify for a 'child allowance', which will be added to your salary.

Every birth should be registered within three days at the registry office of the commune where the birth took place (see [p.53]).

### Ante/Post Natal Care

| | |
|---|---|
| Clinique Générale Beaulieu | 022 839 55 55 |
| Hôpital de la Tour | 022 719 61 11 |
| Hôpitaux Universitaires de Genève | 022 372 33 11 |

### Gynaecology & Obstetrics

| | |
|---|---|
| Beau Soleil | 022 346 59 09 |
| Blaise Bourrit | 022 786 25 86 |
| Christian Berli | 022 347 62 22 |
| Gabriel de Candolle | 022 781 53 80 |
| Pierre Rapin | 022 789 51 56 |
| Stephan Burgener | 022 736 49 00 |

Hôpital Beau-Séjour

## Dentists/Orthodontists

The cost of dental care in Geneva is pretty high, but you get what you pay for as the standard of dentistry is excellent. Most basic insurance packages do not cover the costs of dentistry, except for emergency dental treatment following an accident. It should be easy enough to find a dentist who speaks English well enough – your friends or colleagues may know of someone.

### Private Dentists/Orthodonstists

| | |
|---|---|
| Adent Clinique Dentaire Privée | 022 700 81 00 |
| Cabinet Honegger | 022 329 27 43 |
| JJ Demartines | 022 310 05 62 |
| Mario Bernhard | 022 320 31 22 |
| Michel Epars | 022 320 85 24 |
| MM Hanutz | 022 329 27 43 |

## Opticians

Geneva has many opticians who will be able to carry out eye tests and sell you the necessary glasses or contact lenses. Most have a wide selection of frames to choose from, and also sell sunglasses. See also Eyewear [p.148].

### Opticians

| | |
|---|---|
| Berdoz Optic | 022 320 71 20 |
| Cuttat Optique | 022 755 50 59 |
| Grand Optical | 022 818 42 00 |
| Optic 2000 | 022 340 37 97 |
| Perret Opticiens | 022 342 17 42 |
| Voirol Optique | 022 328 56 86 |

## Alternative Therapies

Although alternative medicine has not reached the status of conventional medicine, Geneva has a good range of alternative therapies to choose from. You'll probably find that word of mouth is the most trustworthy way to find a suitable practitioner. The following are some of the treatments offered and the main practitioners in Geneva.

### Acupressure/Acupuncture

These are two of the oldest healing methods in the world. Acupressure is a system where manual pressure is applied by the practitioner at specific points along the body's energy lines, whereas acupuncture employs needles or a laser beam to stimulate various points corresponding to vital organs.

## Acupressure/Acupuncture

| | |
|---|---|
| Barbara Vesely | 022 789 00 01 |
| China Import | 022 789 27 10 |
| Helene Cormon | 078 678 1911 |
| Institut Yuying | 022 736 30 36 |
| Jaccqueline Berset | 079 507 3460 |

## Homeopathy

Homeopathy uses natural remedies to help with both physical and emotional problems, and can also strengthen the body's immune system. Cures come in small vials of tiny tablets. The Homberger homeopathy range is widely available in pharmacies, and the pharmacist will often be able to advise you on which homeopathy treatment to take.

### Homeopathy

| | |
|---|---|
| AC Roll Piguet | 022 320 63 10 |
| Crêts de Champel | 022 346 85 58 |
| Homberger | 022 310 45 33 |
| Tour | 022 798 10 90 |

## Reflexology/Massage Therapy

Reflexology is a science based on the premise that zones and reflex areas in the feet and hands correspond to all parts and systems of the body. Pressure applied to these reflex areas can result in stress reduction and improved health.

### Reflexology/Massage Therapy

| | |
|---|---|
| Centre de Santé | 022 908 33 33 |
| Ceres | 022 774 39 00 |
| FA Curchod | 022 321 06 60 |
| N Clerc-Rey | 022 738 20 48 |
| P Charpentier | 022 785 72 50 |

## Back Treatment

Having back problems can not only prevent you from performing daily tasks, but without treatment, permanent damage can occur. Fortunately Geneva has a range of back specialists. Chiropractic and osteopathic treatments concentrate on manipulating the skeleton in a non-intrusive manner, to improve the functioning of the nervous system and the flow of blood to the body. Chiropractic is based on the manipulative treatment of misalignments in the joints, especially those of the spinal column, while osteopathy involves the manipulation and massage of the skeleton and musculature. Craniosacral therapy aims to relieve pain and tension by gently manipulating the skull to balance the craniosacral rhythm. Pilates is said to be the safest form of neuromuscular reconditioning and back strengthening available.

### Back Treatment

| | |
|---|---|
| Association des Chiropracticiens du Canton de Genève | 022 830 17 30 |
| Cabinet Bernet Robert | 022 329 58 49 |
| Cabinet CB Illi | 022 346 47 33 |
| Centre de Physiothérapie | 022 301 44 40 |
| Centre de Physiothéraphie (Carouge) | 022 342 62 96 |
| Christiane Amito Berger | 022 736 11 47 |
| Kilinkenbergh | 022 329 32 55 |

## Mental Health

Culture shock and homesickness can lead to depression and other mental health problems among people who have recently relocated to a foreign country. Even the most resilient of personalities can be affected by feelings of frustration and alienation, and this can be compounded by the fact that your trusted friends and family members seem to be a world away. Geneva is home to a whole host of mental health professionals who are trained to help you with any problems you might be facing. There are several English speaking therapists in town, so language need not be a barrier. If appropriate, consult your doctor who will be able to recommend someone to suit your requirements.

### Psychology

| | |
|---|---|
| Carmen Religieux | 022 734 67 74 |
| Helene Rey Ruf (hypnosis & sophrology) | 079 217 57 13 |
| Jean Loup Muller | 022 779 17 19 |
| Pierre Scheidegger | 022 329 31 22 |
| Pierre Zwicky | 022 786 11 24 |
| Simone Kish (English speaking) | 022 735 97 22 |
| Ursula d'Arcis (English speaking) | 022 786 30 06 |
| Xenia Heinze (English speaking) | 022 910 22 22 |

### Psychiatry

| | |
|---|---|
| Unité d'Urgence Psychiatrique des Hôpitaux Universitaires de Genève | 022 372 38 62 |

## Support Groups

### Help on the Web

To help you to find the doctor you require, the Website www.docteur.ch lists all categories of health professionals in Geneva.

When you move away from home, you leave behind a support network of friends and family that has taken you a lifetime to establish. It is a scary thought that you may not have anyone trustworthy to talk to as you experience personal milestones (such as pregnancy) or trying times (such as if you are ending a relationship, battling addictive behaviour or you become ill). Everybody needs to talk, and the following groups offer community assistance to those who do not wish to face their problems alone.

- The Samaritans (143 or 022 328 28 28). 'La main tendue' (the outreaching hand) for anyone who needs to talk
- Rape Help (022 345 20 20).
- English Cancer Support Group (021 825 45 62). www.ecsg.ch
- Group Sida Genève (022 700 15 00). Support for those whose lives are affected by HIV/AIDS. www.groupesida.ch
- Alcoholics Anonymous (0848 848846)

## Education

If you're moving to Geneva with children, you can rest assured that the Swiss education system is excellent. However, you will have to make the decision about whether you send your children to the local state school, or invest in private education. Children are given places in state schools according to the area in which they live, so you may want to keep this in mind – if there is a school you have heard of and you want your children to go there, it may be worth checking out the accommodation available in that area.

The school system in Switzerland is generally more disciplined than your child may be used to in their home country. The hours are quite demanding, and there is usually lots of homework.

School terms run from September to December, January to March and April to June. Hours are usually from 08:00 to 12:00 and 14:00 to 18:00. There are no lessons on Wednesday afternoons, but some schools have Saturday morning classes, although there is talk of this being phased out.

Compulsory schooling for children begins from age six or seven, and four to six year olds can go to pre-school, although this is optional. State schools do not generally teach in English, although the younger your child is when you arrive in Geneva, the less of a problem this will be. Parents whose children attend local schools are offered French lessons, so they can keep up! For more information, call Ecole des Parents du Cycle D'orientation (022 791 78 11). If your child is showing difficulties in adapting to a foreign language, you may want to consider enrolling him/her in a private international school, where English is the language of instruction. To register your child at a school, you need to provide a valid residency permit and a health insurance certificate.

## Nursery & Pre-School

Crèches in Geneva are in great demand, so the best advice is to book your child in early. Crèches accept young children up to the age of around four. They are open all day and lunch is usually provided.

Kindergarten (jardin d'enfants) is for children aged three to four, and is usually open several half days per week, with the aim of children attending regularly. Nursery school (garderie) is for children aged 18 months to two years. Pre-school is for children aged four to six years. For a complete list of addresses of nurseries and pre-schools, you can call the Bureau d'Information Petite Enfance (BIPE). See Important Addresses on [p.88].

| Nurseries & Pre-Schools | |
|---|---|
| Crèche A Carfagni Pâquis | 022 732 51 43 |
| Ecole La Découverte | 022 733 54 33 |
| Ecole Montessori – Nation | 022 738 81 80 |
| La Maison des Enfants | 022 733 44 26 |
| The Bell One World Nursery School | 022 740 21 93 |

| Private Primary/Secondary Schools | | |
|---|---|---|
| Collège du Léman, Versoix | 022 775 55 55 | www.cdl.ch |
| Geneva English School, Genthod (primary only) | 022 755 18 55 | www.geneva-english-school.ch |
| Institut Le Rosey | 022 822 5500 | www.rosey.ch |
| Lycée International, Ferney-Voltaire | +33 4 50 40 00 00 | www.lyferney.net |
| The International School, Grande Boissière | 022 787 24 00 | www.ecolint.ch |

# Summer Camps

## Rolle and Gstaad, Switzerland

# 2005-2006

# A school for Life !

LE ROSEY

Established 1880

The educational balance provided by Le Rosey comes from a conscientious and professional team. The campuses and facilities together consititute an exceptional setting. And after leaving Le Rosey the Association of Former Roséens (AIAR) offers the advantages of a powerful worldwide network.

All Roséens are educated to become global citizens and key players on the world stage after their university studies. In the course of their education particular attention is paid to their intellectual development, knowledge of languages and artistic potential. Discipline, self-respect, life within an international community, and the chance to take on responsibilities all contribute to personal character building. While regular participation in our sports programmes and demanding expeditions guarantee a healthy mind in a healthy body and a fighting spirit.

# www.rosey.ch

## Primary & Secondary School

Primary school is for children aged six to eleven years old. Secondary school is for children from the age of eleven upwards, and is obligatory up to the age of 15 years. An intricate grading system applies, so the marks your child gets in the final year of primary school will affect which secondary school they go to, which will in turn affect the tertiary education options open to them. This system of pigeon-holing is tough, but if you feel your child has been graded incorrectly, you can request an entrance exam for a different secondary school. Some schools are changing their approach and now have classrooms full of children of varying abilities, rather than putting all the clever-clogs in one class, and all the underachievers in another!

To enrol your child at your local state school, you should telephone 022 327 24 12 for primary education, and 022 791 78 11 for secondary education.

The cost of private education varies according to the age of the child, but ranges between SFr 8,000 and SFr 16,000 per year.

A Geneva school

### Universities – Private

| European University | www.euruni.edu |
| College Int'l Brillantmont | www.brillantmont.ch |
| Int'l University in Geneva | www.iun.ch |
| Webster University | www.webster.ch |

## University & Higher Education

The high standard of universities and tertiary education in Geneva, particularly in the fields of international law and politics, is the reason why thousands of international students choose to study here. Among expats, some university age children choose to return to their home countries, but for those who wish to stay in Geneva, there is a good choice of institutions and curriculums.

*Fees: Higher academic institutions charge around SFr 1,200 per year.*

## Special Needs Education

If your child has special learning needs, they should have an assessment by a medical professional who can then suggest an appropriate institution. For more information you can contact Service Médico Pédagogique, Bd. Saint-Georges 16–18 (022 327 43 91).

In general, Switzerland is very supportive of those with special needs, and there is a variety of community groups for sport and entertainment.

## Learning French

Even if your friends and colleagues all speak good English, learning French will undoubtedly enrich your time in Geneva. Some companies offer French language lessons to their international employees, but if yours doesn't then there are many language schools who will be able to help. It may be quicker to have lessons with a private tutor, although this will be more expensive.

The internationally recognised 'Alliance Française' is the most well known certificate in French language, and most of the language schools will offer it. Some associations, such as the UN Women's Guild (022 917 33 86) and the Geneva Foundation (022 749 10 40), offer French classes to their members.

### Universities – Public

| Institut Universitaire d'Hautes Etudes du Développement | 022 906 59 40 | www.unige.ch/iued/new/ |
| Institut Universitaire de Hautes Etudes Internationales | 022 908 57 00 | http://heiwww.unige.ch/ |
| Université de Genève | 022 705 71 11 | www.unige.ch |

## Transportation

A car is certainly not a necessity for getting around in Geneva, and with the limited parking spaces and traffic jams, it can often be a hindrance. Fortunately the public transport system is efficient and user friendly. Cycling is a popular way of getting around, and once you're in the centre of town you can pretty much walk from place to place. A car does come in handy though, especially when you want to escape to the countryside and up into the mountains.

### Vehicle Leasing

To hire a car you should be over 21 and produce your driver's licence and passport. It is often cheaper to hire a car in France – there is a French side to the airport (the entrance is through French Customs) where there are several major car hire companies. If you do this, you should know that the car may not come with the compulsory Swiss highway tax sticker, and you should buy this when crossing over to Switzerland. If you are self employed, it is worthwhile to lease a car rather than buy, as you can deduct the entire cost for tax purposes.

During winter, hired cars are usually equipped with snow tyres and chains, but you should check on this, particularly if you are going to a ski resort.

| Vehicle Leasing Agents | |
|---|---|
| Avis | 022 929 03 30 |
| Budget | 0844 844 700 |
| Hertz | 022 731 12 00 |
| Sixt | 022 732 90 90 |

### Buying a Vehicle

If you do decide to buy a car the good news is that cars are generally less expensive in Switzerland than in some other European countries, and petrol is cheaper too.

### New Vehicles

The new car market is bustling in Geneva as cars older than five years are often seen as being past their prime! If you do buy a brand new car, make sure that you bargain with the dealer – they have been known to offer discounts of five or even ten percent, but only when asked. Every new car has to undergo a thorough test ('examen') to check that it is in proper working order before you drive it out of the showroom. This test will be arranged by the garage where you bought

the car. Don't forget to sort out your insurance before you get behind the wheel – see [p.84].

### Used Vehicles

The Swiss preference for new cars means that you can find some real gems on the used car market, and cars older than five years are pretty cheap. Buying a second hand car is quite straightforward and the paperwork is minimal. Just be sure to check that the car you are buying has not been involved in an accident, that it has a full service history, the registration documents match the chassis number, and that any import duty on the car has been paid.

| Car Dealers | | |
|---|---|---|
| **New Cars** | | |
| Autos Evasion | Porsche | 022 823 26 04 |
| BBG Garage | Renault | 022 735 08 33 |
| BBG Garage | Volkswagen | 022 735 08 33 |
| DB Automobiles | Porsche | 022 771 30 23 |
| DB Automobiles | Audi | 022 771 30 23 |
| DB Automobiles | Volkswagen | 022 771 30 23 |
| Garage Alain Favrod | Toyota | 022 346 25 00 |
| Garage Caveng | Infinity | 022 349 3050 |
| Garage Caveng | Nissan | 022 349 3050 |
| Garage Central Cully | Peugeot | 021 799 5560 |
| Garage du Plateau | Opel | 022 792 15 70 |
| Garage Grand Lancy | Volkswagen | 022 794 34 73 |
| Garage Grand Lancy | Audi | 022 794 34 73 |
| Garage Grand Lancy | Porsche | 022 794 34 73 |
| Perly Automobiles | Daewoo | 022 771 10 06 |
| Perroud | Ford | 022 796 71 22 |
| **Used Cars** | | |
| Auto Maxi | | 022 792 99 77 |
| BCH | | 022 794 89 39 |
| Bernard | | 022 885 06 60 |
| Cars Kamal | | 079 611 4575 |
| Gato Autos | | 022 792 62 22 |
| Jaillat | | 022 788 87 20 |
| Marthe | | 079 204 0342 |

### Ownership Transfer

In Geneva number plates follow the driver, not the car, so if you get a new car you will have to change the plates, which will cost you SFr 95. You should go to the Service des Automobiles et de la Navigation (see Important Addresses, [p.88]), with your proof of ID.

### Vehicle Import

If you are importing a car, it is your duty to inform Customs on arrival. You will have to complete a form, show the relevant papers (invoice, driver's licence, ID, proof of car's origin) and pay the necessary tax and import duty (this will depend on

how long you have owned the car). Customs will inform the Service des Automobiles, who will then send you forms which you should complete in order to get Swiss licence plates. Imported cars should be fitted with a catalyser to reduce pollution – most EU and US cars will already meet this requirement.

If your car is less than six months old, you must provide documents confirming the value of the vehicle and its country of origin. Import duty is calculated on weight and engine size, and 7.6% VAT of the car's cost. If your car is older than six months, you are exempt from paying customs duty and VAT for two years. Your foreign licence plate is valid for one year. To check if your car requires a control test, contact the Technical Control Sector (022 342 2280).

Cars and motorcycles imported from Europe can be brought in tax free, as long as proof of origin is presented.

## Vehicle Insurance

Car insurance is expensive, although your foreign no claims bonus is usually valid. Some insurance companies charge different rates for foreigners, but some don't, so shop around! It's worthwhile to get at least three quotes, as prices can vary. Check also whether the company will offer a short term policy with a three month notice period. Insurance relates to the vehicle rather than to the driver, so it doesn't matter who was driving your car at the time of an accident.

Before you can register your car or get your licence plates, your insurance must be in place. Insurance is mandatory, but there are various options available, including third party liability insurance (which is compulsory), full cover and restricted cover.

Take your pick and hop on!

## Registering A Vehicle

In Switzerland, your licence plates belong to you at your registered address, and not to the car. The cost for registration and licence plates is SFr 135, and the plaque for Geneva is GE. If you own two cars but only use one at a time, then you can just transfer your licence plates from one car to another.

Great plate!

Personnel of permanent missions and international organisations are eligible for CD ('Corps Diplomatique') licence plates. In general, only the owner of a vehicle registered with CD licence plates is authorised to drive that vehicle, although family members may be allowed to do so. If you are going to be resident in Geneva for less than three months, you can get temporary Z plates for your car.

In addition to licence plates, your car must have a car permit ('carte grise'). This permit acts as a ledger, indicating when it has been tested, if it has ever been in an accident, etc. It costs SFr 45 to get your permit, which is available from the Service des Automobiles (see Important Addresses, [p.88]).

Before your Swiss plates and road permit ('permis de circulation') are issued, your car must undergo a roadworthiness test (also called a 'technical control'). If the car is more than ten years old, a control is required at the time of registration (the cost of the test is included in the registration fee). Cars older than five years have to pass a technical inspection similar to the UK MOT. This should be done every two or three years, depending on the age of the car. If you are importing a car, it is a good idea to have TCS (Touring Club Suisse) or ACS (Automobile Club

New Residents

Transportation

Suisse) perform the technical control, as they will be able to advise you on what modifications need to be made to your vehicle (if any). Certain dubious garages may see an unsuspecting expat and suggest unnecessary modifications. The cost for the technical control is SFr 60. For more information, and to make an appointment for your inspection, contact the Service des Automobiles (see Important Addresses, [p.88]).

Road tax is calculated at between SFr 12 and SFr 15 per 100kg, depending on the cubic capacity of the engine and the weight unity. Depending on engine size, a medium sized car will cost between SFr 300 and SFr 700 per year. When you register your car at the Service des Automobiles, the road tax bill is sent with your car registration papers. A refund is available if you leave the country within the paid year. If you own two cars and transfer the plates, you only need pay road tax for the car with the largest engine (the most expensive!).

To use the motorway, you must have a vignette displayed on the left hand side or top centre of your windscreen. It costs SFr 40 and is valid for one year. You can buy it at border crossings, post offices and service stations.

Every two years your car will have to have an emissions test ('test anti-pollution'), unless it is an old car, in which case this test should be done annually. You have to display a green and white sticker on the side window of your car, showing the month and year that the test is next due. The test certificate should be kept in your car. The inspections are carried out by the Service des Automobiles (see Important Addresses, [p.88]), and the cost is SFr 75.

## The Process

To register your car you should go to the Service des Automobiles et de la Navigation in Carouge (see Important Addresses, [p.88]). You will need to take the following documents:

- Your driving licence
- Your residence permit
- A certificate of residence (available from your community office)
- Certificate of insurance
- Original legitimisation card
- Attestation of technical control
- If the car is imported, form 13.20A from Customs
- SFr 150

## Traffic Fines & Offences

Being a bad driver is costly in Geneva! If you are caught driving on the motorway without displaying the necessary vignette, you will be fined SFr 100. Driving through a red light will result in a fine of SFr 70 or more, and bad parking can get you a fine of SFr 70 – 200.

| Speed Limits | |
| --- | --- |
| Town | 50 km/h |
| Open road | 80 km/h |
| Motorway | 120 km/h |

Drinking and driving is heavily fined – if you are caught driving while over the legal limit, the fine could reach several thousand francs AND you could lose your licence. From January 2005, the maximum tolerated amount of alcohol in the blood will be 0.5 mg/l, which translates to one unit of alcohol (one glass of beer or wine/one measure of spirits) every two hours. A new law allows police to breathalyse you, even if there is no visible evidence that you have been drinking, so expect more random checks.

Traffic fines and tickets are issued by the Service des Agents de Ville et du Domaine Public (see Important Addresses, [p.88]).

If you can't resist pushing the pedal to the floor on open roads, just be warned that speeding can result in some pretty hefty fines. Radar traps are common,

Obey the sign.....or get a fine!

SFr 10 ~ € 6

although not very well disguised (look out for the square 'cow' on Rue de Lausanne approaching the highway!). Fines start at around a few hundred francs, and can go up to well over a thousand. In extreme cases you could even face a jail sentence.

If you're caught speeding 30 km or more over the limit, your licence will be withdrawn and you'll have to pay a heavy fine (this can be up to 20% of your monthly salary, depending on how fast you were going).

Speeding fines are sent out by the traffic brigade ('Service des Contraventions'), and you can contact them on 022 327 66 20. If your licence is withdrawn as a result of a traffic violation, you should contact the Bureau des Autos (see Important Addresses, [p.88]).

## Breakdowns

If your car breaks down you will need to call a road recovery service ('service de dépannage'). Whether or not you are a member of TCS, they have a good network of road recovery vehicles and are usually first on the scene. Members receive the service free but nonmembers will have to pay for repairing or towing. The cost depends on how far away the vehicle is, and whether it is day or night or during the weekend. Recovery of your vehicle, whether it means roadside repair or towing to the nearest garage, costs between SFr 174 and SFr 250 for nonmembers.

## Traffic Accidents

In the unfortunate event of a traffic accident, you should call the police on 117. All drivers involved in the accident should write a report of what happened and sign it for insurance purposes. The police can help you do this. The report should then be filed with your insurance company. In any case, be sure to take the licence plate numbers and contact details of all involved.

### Recovery Services

| Recovery Services | |
| --- | --- |
| Aubertinaz | 022 771 27 80 |
| Automobile Club Suisse (ACS) | 022 342 22 33 |
| Emil Frey | 022 308 53 08 |
| RL Forfait Depannage | 022 733 00 80 |
| Road Assistance | 140 |
| TCS (Touring Club Suisse) | 0844 888 111 |

## Repairs

Whether you require repairs to body work ('carrosserie') or to the engine ('méchanique'), it is advisable to get your car repaired at a garage where they specialise in your brand of car, as they are most likely to have the spare parts.

Lac Léman...part of everyday life

New Residents

Transportation

## Important Addresses

| French Name | English Name | Street Address |
| --- | --- | --- |
| Office Cantonal de la Population | Cantonal Population Office | Rue David-Dufour 1-3, CP 51, CH1211, Genève 8 |
| Centre d'Accueil Genève Internationale | International Geneva Welcome Centre | Villa 'La Pastorale', 106 Route de Ferney, 1211, Geneva 20 |
| Service de L'Assurance Maladie | Health Insurance Bureau | Route e Frontenex 62, CH-1211 Geneva |
| Office Cantonal des Etrangers | Cantonal Office for Foreigners | Rue David-Dufour 3, CH1211, Genève 8 |
| Service des Automobiles et de la Navigation du Canton de Genève | Automobiles and Navigation Service of the Canton of Geneva | Rte De Veyrier 86, CH-1227, Carouge |
| Fédération Romande des Ecoles de Conduite | French-speaking federation of Driving Schools | Av. De Provence 10, 1000 Lausanne |
| Office de l'Etat Civil | Civil Registrar's Office | Rue de la Mairie, 37, CH-1211, Genève 6 |
| Pompes Funèbres de la Ville de Genève | Geneva Funeral and Cemetery Services | Rue du Vieux-Marché, 4 CH-1207, Genève |
| Syndicat Interprofessionnel de Travailleuses et Travailleurs (SIT) | Interprofessional Union of Workers | Rue des Chaudronniers, 16 CP-3287, Genève 3 |
| Office des Poursuites et Faillites | Office of Continuations and Bankruptcies | Rue de l'Hôtel de Ville, 11 CH-1211 Geneva |
| Permanance de la Chambre des Notaires de Genève | Association of Notaries of Geneva | Rue Verdaine, 13, CH-1204, Geneva |
| Office Fédéral de l'Environnement, des Forêts et du Paysage | Swiss Agency for the Environment, Forests and Landscape | CH-3003, Bern |
| Services Industriels de Genève (SIG) | Industrial Services of Geneva | Pont de la Machine, 1 |
| Espace Récupération du Site de Chatillon | Chatillon Space Recuperation Waste Recycling Area | Route d'Aïre-La-Ville, CH-1233 Bernex |
| Service Inf-eau-déchets (DIAE) | Waste and Water Services | Rue David-Dufour, 1, Case Postale 206, 1211 Genève 8 |
| Bureau d'Information Petite Enfance | Infant Information Office | Rue du Cendrier, 8, CH-1201, Genève |
| Bureau des Autos | Automobile Bureau | Route de Veyrier, 86, Carouge |
| Service des Contraventions | Parking Ticket Service | Bd. Helvétique |
| Service des Agents de Ville et du Domaine Public | Service of City Agents and Public Domain | Bd. Helvétique, 29, CH-1211 Geneva |

Geneva....as seen from the cathedral

| Phone | Office Hours | Web/mail |
|---|---|---|
| 022 327 44 11 | Mon – Fri: 09:00 – 15:30 | www.geneve.ch/ocp |
| 022 918 02 70 | Mon – Thu: 10:00 – 12:30, 16:00 – 17:30. Fri: 10:00 – 12:30 | www.cagi.ch |
| 022 327 65 30 | Mon – Fri: 08:00 – 19:00. Sat: 08:30 – 12:00 | www.geneve.ch/social/assurance/welcome |
| 022 327 48 88 | Mon – Fri: 09:00 – 15:30 | etrangers.ocp@etat.ge.ch |
| 022 388 30 30 | Mon – Fri: 07:30 – 16:00 | www.geneve.ch/san |
| 021 625 90 30 | na | info@frec.ch |
| 022 418 66 50 | Mon – Fri: 09:00 – 11:15, 14:00 – 16:00 | etat-civil@ville-ge.ch |
| 022 418 60 00 | na | na |
| 022 818 03 00 | Mon – Thu: 09:00 – 12:00; 14:00 – 18:00. Fri: 09:00 – 12:00; 14:00 – 17:00 | www.sit-syndicat.ch |
| 022 327 28 34 | na | www.geneve.ch/opf |
| 022 781 08 28 | 10:00 – 19:00 | www.notaires-geneve-cng.ch |
| 031 322 93 11 | na | na |
| 022 420 75 50 | Mon – Fri: 09:00 – 18:00 | www.sig-ge.ch |
| 022 727 05 22 | Mon – Fri: 14:30 – 19:30. Weekends: 09:30 – 17:00 | na |
| 022 327 47 11 | na | www.geneve.ch/ |
| 022 321 22 23 | Mon – Fri: 13:00 – 17:45 | www.ville-ge.ch/dpt5/enfance/bipe_f.php |
| 022 343 02 00 | na | na |
| 022 327 66 20 | na | na |
| 022 418 61 01 | na | http://www.adp.ville-ge.ch/ |

# World class quality to catch your eye

When it comes to printing, our expertise speaks for itself.

**EMIRATES PRINTING PRESS (L.L.C.)**

 ISO 9001 Registered | ISO 14001 Registered
*The Quality Advantage*

P.O.Box 5106, Al Quoz, Dubai, United Arab Emirates
Tel:+971 4 347 5550/347 5544, Fax:+971 4 347 5959
Email: eppdubai@emirates.net.ae, www.eppdubai.com

**EMIRATES PRINTING PRESS (UK) LTD.**
European Sales office :
4 High Street, Burnham, Buckinghamshire SL1 7JH
United Kingdom,Tel:01628 668884, Fax: 01628 660703
Email: eppeurope@aol.com, www.eppdubai.com

 sappi *Printer of the Year*  CiB Aw 200

# Exploring

# Exploring

**MUST KNOW**

Geneva is known as the gateway of Europe, because it is so easy to get from there to a whole host of fascinating places. You're within easy driving distance from major cities such as Frankfurt, Luxembourg, Milan, Munich, Paris and Nice. Plus it has its own international airport, if you wish to go further afield. Or if you choose to stay in Switzerland, there are plenty of mountains to climb and rivers to cross before you'll have the chance to get bored.

**MUST GO**

Geneva is home to an astounding number of museums and art galleries, and not just the kind housing dusty old artefacts either. You can learn all about the history and manufacturing of ceramics (Ariana Museum), the horrors and heroes of war (International Red Cross & Red Crescent Museum), and the meticulous precision of watch making (Patek Philippe Museum). Art is an important part of Geneva life, and you'll find it virtually everywhere you go, from art museums to state sponsored and more exclusive art galleries. And check out the 'graffiti' in some parts of town - a different kind of art, but art nonetheless!

**MUST SEE**

Geneva residents put the beautiful Lac Léman to good use throughout the year. There are a number of beaches and beach parks along the coastline of the lake, which are particularly popular during summer (although don't miss the Turkish Baths at Bains de Pâquis in winter). You can take to the water for a coastal cruise, ideal for daytrips. Or you can join the thousands of Genevans who use the lake for various watersports, including sailing, waterskiing and even scuba diving.

**MUST DO**

Climb the 157 steps of the north tower of St. Pierre Cathedral, and once you've caught your breath you'll have the most amazing view of Geneva and the lake. Of additional interest are Clèmence, the six ton bell, and the stark décor of the cathedral, reflecting the Reformist austerity which was ushered in back in the 16th Century. The other sightseeing necessity is Geneva's famous Jet d'Eau, which at a height of 140 metres, is the tallest fountain in the world. To reach that height, an incredible seven tons of water is shot into the air at a speed of around 200 km/h!

Table of Contents

Exploring

## Exploring

If you were to rank the best cities in the world Geneva would be a serious contender for the crown. Situated in the heart of Europe, Geneva is an international melting pot, weaving together the best of cultures from around the world. Geneva's worldview is evident in every corner of the city, from the colourful red light district filled with kebab shops and hookah lounges to the monolithic banking district where international bankers can step out of their front doors to spend their money on the latest designer fashions. Geneva is rather like a crossroads where people meet – delegates at the United Nations, business leaders, students, refugees, sports enthusiasts, artists and leaders of science – all in the familiar streets of this eclectic city.

This cacophony of cultures and subcultures is reflected in the geography as well as the physical character of Geneva. The city is situated at the foot of the Alps where Lac Léman meets the mouth of the Rhône River on the border of Switzerland and France. The town itself incorporates a charming mix of modern and old architecture – dating back thousands of years when Geneva was a major seat of the Roman Empire. In addition, these classic and modern elements are beautifully incorporated into nature, evident by the hundreds of parks that have earned Geneva the nickname 'city of parks'. All this makes exploring Geneva the best of both worlds – there is always something familiar, but always enough of the new to keep things interesting.

Geneva is best explored on foot. Almost every major attraction in the town centre can be reached within a 20 minute walk. The rest is made easily accessible by a highly efficient and convenient public transportation system that lives up to all Swiss expectations. The city is primarily divided into two sections by the lake and the river. The 'Left Bank' (eastern) is crowned by the old walled city built atop the highest hill in Geneva and overlooking the much more modern town centre filled with the shiny spoils of capitalism. The 'Right Bank' (western) is a cauldron of ethnic neighbourhoods and home to the headquarters of many international organisations, including the United Nations and the Red Cross. Towards the city limits Geneva quickly transforms from metropolis into countryside, with numerous farms and forests set in the rolling landscape. Beyond Geneva sit many quaint villages inviting exploration, each with their own old world charm.

This section of the book is designed to help newcomers to Geneva navigate the city, and spark a journey of rediscovery for veteran residents. A comprehensive overview of the main areas of the city has been provided, including the 'not to be missed' highlights of each area.

**Geneva Areas**

**Exploring**

On the waterfront

## Geneva – Main Areas

### City Centre & Beyond

The streets along Geneva's central shopping district are filled with enough bright shiny objects to lure even the most reluctant shoppers. They may not be paved with gold but it often feels that way, with cases exhibiting some of the most renowned jewellery on the planet. Along Rue de Rive, it becomes increasingly difficult to determine what came first – the clothes or the accessories? The street resembles a fashion runway with a daily parade of Geneva's most beautiful people on the prowl for the latest designer threads. Everyday is Christmas on the Rue, so be sure to pack your credit cards before you go.

The royal entrance to the main shopping street is through the 'Passage des Lions' just beyond Pont de la Machine. Two huge stone lions loyally guard the passage.

Geneva by night

The passage exits into the heart of Geneva's banking district. Every major bank in Geneva has its headquarters here, where money flows like the Rhône. Needless to say you should have no problem finding an ATM before hitting the shops.

Heading east, The Confédération Centre Shopping Mall marks the beginning of the shopping district. Across the street from the mall the Fusterie Temple is a bastion of modesty amid the carnage of commerce. The Baroque was the first temple dedicated solely to Calvinist worship (in 1715) and is easily identified by its curved design and bell turret. A great time to visit Place de la Fusterie is during the annual Christmas Market that begins in November and runs through to Christmas. The market showcases the works of local craftsmen and features a mouth watering array of yuletide feasts.

Place de la Fusterie is traditionally one of the sites for the International Christmas Tree Festival. The festival, which began in 1999, transforms trees throughout the city into urban works of art. Every tree is different and includes spectacular lights.

Next door at Place du Rhône, from November to February an ice rink, sponsored by Geneva Tourism, completes the holiday scene with rosy cheeked skaters gliding beside the Rhône River. The rink attracts over 30,000 visitors annually and is open everyday from 10:00 to 21:00. Skates can be rented at SFr 3 for children and SFr 6 for adults.

Across the street from Fusterie, at Place des Trois Perdrix, is the city library, squeezed back off the street by the fussy elbows of commerce. The library is six storeys tall and is a valuable, yet largely undiscovered, resource.

### Area Highlights

The cliché 'shop till you drop' could well have been invented by a seasoned Geneva shopper. Be sure to look up and appreciate the unique architecture and façades along the street.

**Malbuisson Passage Clock**

This clock, designed by Edouard Wirth in 1962, pays homage to the Escalade. The clock sounds every hour when 13 chariots and 42 bronze figures emerge to dance to 16 chiming bells.

**L'Alhambar**

This popular nightspot at Rue de la Rôtisserie, 10 is a chic and welcoming club with great music. It also happens to serve Sunday brunch and hosts a popular film festival in its adjoining theatre.

Opposite the library, to the north, is Place du Molard. The plaza is shadowed by the Molard Tower, a 14th century remnant of the wall that once stood there. The top of the tower is pointed in the shape of a soldier's helmet with a clock in the middle. The tower itself is decorated with paintings portraying scenes from the middle ages. In the centre of the square is a fountain that is surrounded by buzzing outdoor cafés.

From Molard you can hit the stores, theatres and food stands all the way to Rond Point de Rive, where the pace slows down. The next street, Boulevard Helvétique, is home to a farmers' market every Tuesday and Saturday beginning at 08:00.

The Russian Church

From Helvétique, the gold cupolas of the Russian Church on Rue Rodolphe-Toepffer are visible in all their glory. The church was built between 1863 and 1866 by orthodox Russians living in the city, and is a Byzantine masterpiece. The interior is filled with eye catching icons that greatly contrast the drab furnishings of most other Geneva churches. The area around the church, known as Les Tranchées, quickly grew into one of the most pre-eminent neighbourhoods in Geneva. Taking inspiration from the church, the façades of the townhouses are dramatic and angular, unlike anywhere else in Geneva.

To the north is another distinctive district, the lakeside suburb of Eaux-Vives. The Eaux-Vives Train Station, behind Route de Chêne, marks the end of the main strip. The station is the main departure point for nearby cities such as Annemasse and Annecy.

## International District

Geneva is home to over 190 international organisations and world bodies. Most are located around the grounds of the Palais des Nations, and the ideal starting point for any tour around this area is the giant 'Broken Chair' sculpture. This 12 metre high, three legged chair was erected in 1997 by Handicap International, an organisation dedicated to helping landmine victims around the world.

From the Place des Nations, the next logical step is the European headquarters of the United Nations. The Palais des Nations was established in 1946 in Ariana Park. The lake front property was donated by the Revilliod de Rive family on the condition that peacocks must always roam free on the grounds. The peacocks still greet visitors today and are fitting tribute to the pomp and circumstance inside the Palais. For a glimpse inside, take one of the guided tours offered daily for SFr 8.50. The Palais is filled with interesting art and sculpture donations from member states. The highlight of the tour is the council chamber, decorated by José Maria Sert in 1934, with gold murals depicting the human struggle for peace throughout history. Other stops on the tour include the bronze Armillary Sphere, the symbol of the United Nations on the palace grounds, and the Grand Assembly Hall, where the delegates of the member states meet and debate the issues of the day. If you're lucky you may even get to witness some of the proceedings in action.

Whether you're an enthusiast of glass and ceramics or not, the grounds around Ariana Museum, just west of the UN, are still worth a chunk of your exploring time. The museum is housed in a neo-Baroque mansion and admission to all exhibits is free. The intricate glass and pottery works are delicate yet boldly beautiful.

Across the street is the International Committee of the Red Cross and the International Red Cross & Red Crescent Museum – a must see for any visitor. The entrance to the museum is marked with a sculpture titled 'The Human Effort', depicting several blindfolded stone figures that represent the ongoing struggle for human rights worldwide. The museum is a sobering testimony to the history of this organisation, which has provided aid to victims of almost every major war fought over the last 100 years. The museum itself is very interactive and well organised. One section is dedicated to the founder of the Red Cross, Henry Dunant, whose efforts resulted in

## Geneva Visitor's Check List

The following is a list of recommended sights and activities. In Geneva, you can't walk in a straight line without running into something cultural, artistic or historical, so don't be afraid to get out and make your own special finds. Just make sure you tell us about them!

Geneva can accommodate the pace of any traveller. On the lake, you can jet along on a wakeboard, glide along on a sailing boat, or remain totally immobile as you laze under the sun along the shore. You can also party until the early hours, or get a good night's sleep so you can wake up early for a stroll in the countryside. Wherever you go, just remember to relax and enjoy the scenery along the way.

### The Lake [p.198]

Stroll along the promenades around the lake, join the local Genevois soaking up the sun at Bains des Pâquis, relax in one of the parks and watch the sailing boats drift by. You can have a coffee or an icecream at one of the many cafés or food stands, and if you have time, a one or two hour boat cruise around the lake is a good option.

### The Old Town [p.100]

Wander along the cobbled streets and pop into one of the many boutiques tucked away in the charming alleyways, but be prepared to fight temptation. If you do end up spending too much, stop by Saint Pierre Cathedral and repent! Alternatively, check out the best panoramic view of Geneva from the Cathedral tower.

### The United Nations [p.95]

Take a tour of the United Nations or one of the surrounding museums, including the Red Cross Museum or the Ariana Museum. Wander the grounds of the various world organisations in the international district. Have a power lunch at one the excellent restaurants in the area that serve the diplomatic elite.

### The Salève [p.111]

This mini mountain is a quick and easy escape to the countryside. Ride the cable car to the top and enjoy the breathtaking views of the city below and the Alps in the distance. If you're really adventurous, sign up for a tandem parasail or paraglide flight for a birds eye view of the city.

### Carouge [p.108, 164]

Hop on one of the trams or walk across the bridge to Geneva's Savoy sister city filled with interesting cafés and boutiques. Enjoy the contrasting laidback qualities of the area and don't be afraid to engage one of the artisans in a friendly conversation. Hang around after hours in one of the jazz clubs for a full Carougeois experience.

### Out of Geneva [p.129]

Take an excursion to one of the surrounding mountain towns around the lake or up in the Alps. In wintertime catch one of the daily ski buses up to one of the world class resorts located within an hours drive and practice your snow plough!

### Parc des Bastions [p.120]

Marvel at the stirring statues along Reformation Wall as you wander down a tree lined promenade that was once a botanical garden. Stop at the life sized chess board to try your hand against one of the locals, or just offer encouragement as you relax at the nearby pavilion café.

### Place Neuve [p.102]

Head to the centre of Genevois culture at Place Neuve just outside the Old Town wall. Put on your fanciest duds for an evening performance at one of the grand theatres surrounding the square. Even if you don't understand the language the beautiful architecture and extravagant productions should keep you entertained.

### Plainpalais Flea Market [p.163]

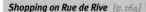

Experience the wonders of the flea market at Plainpalais every Wednesday and Saturday from 08:00 to 17:00. Whether you're looking for a nice pair of slightly used socks or an antique chair once owned by Napoleon's cousin's brother-in-law's barber, you'll most likely find it here.

### Pâquis [p.164]

Enjoy the true international character of Geneva's daily life in the city's own, loosely labelled, red light district. Try one of the ethnic restaurants for a taste of Africa, Asia or the Middle East. Shop at one of the unique boutiques in the area, unlike any other in Geneva, and enjoy the friendly atmosphere of local bars and cafés.

### Shopping on Rue de Rive [p.164]

Try not to fog up the windows as you count the zeros on price tags along Geneva's most famous shopping street. The street sparkles with designer names and extravagant jewellery. Relax at one of the surrounding cafés and watch Geneva's elite as they power walk between the banks and shops lining the street.

### Schtrumpfs Building [p.107]

Conceptualised by three cutting edge architects who set out to break all the traditional rules of the craft. The result, located at Rue Louis-Favre, 23-29 is a housing complex like no other, whose residents happily embrace the title of "Smurfs".

### Take a Bike Ride [p.176]

Free bike rentals are available throughout the city. Hop on a cruiser and ride by the lake or through the surrounding countryside. You will find a number of car free paths throughout the city and beyond for easy travel. For a workout, climb the hills of the Old Town or the Salève.

### Wine Tasting [p.128]

Geneva is surrounded by some of the best wine country in all of Switzerland. It produces some excellent whites and noteworthy reds, including Gamaret. Wines aged in oak casks are especially good. The wineries are often beautifully situated with mountain and lake views that are well worth toasting.

### Football Match [p.179]

Experience Europe's greatest passion at one of the many professional venues in and around Geneva. The Meyrin Football Club is the most popular and attracts dedicated fans to its new stadium, completed in 2003. The stadium is also home to large concerts throughout the summer months.

### Place du Bourg-de-Four [p.6]

Located in Geneva's oldest town square, Bourg-de-Four remains a hub of activity and a popular meeting spot. The square, surrounded by classic medieval buildings, is home to some of the best bistros and outdoor cafés in the city.

### Picnic in the Park [p.120]

Almost a quarter of Geneva's land is covered by public parks. Many are the grounds of former estates from Geneva's aristocratic past. The Parc des Eaux-Vives on the Left Bank is Geneva's largest and just one of many peaceful havens embedded in the city's landscape.

### Rafting L'Arve River [p.110]

This river joins the Rhône at La Jonction on the south side of the city and provides a quick outlet for adventure, guaranteeing to thrill and delight rafters of all levels. The excitement of the rapids and waterfalls is complemented by the lush scenery along the river.

the signing of the first Geneva Convention in 1864 and started Geneva on the path to becoming an international capital.

The area around the Palais des Nations and the International Red Cross Museum is a who's who of international offices, most of which are not open to the public. In this list is the WHO (otherwise known as the World Health Organisation) on Ave Appia, and its stated mission is to promote complete physical, mental and social wellbeing throughout the world. The gym inside this office is testimony to a healthy attitude and well worth checking out.

International Red Cross / Red Crescent

Also located nearby is the towering International Telecommunications Union, the World Council of Churches and the International Workers Union. The information centre at the World Intellectual Property Organisation (34 Chemin des Colombettes) is open on weekdays and welcomes visitors to view permanent and temporary exhibitions. The building itself is a architectural marvel designed to reflect the organisation's purpose. Just down the street is the welcome centre and memorial for the UN High Commissioner

for Refugees. The centre was originally one of Switzerland's first service stations, designed by pioneering Geneva architect, Maurice Braillard. A huge concrete roof sits atop a sleek glass rotunda that still evokes images of the old petrol station. The final organisation of note, the World Meteorological Organisation (near the Botanical Gardens), is housed in a modern building constructed with a double façade, which takes advantage of insulation effects and natural lighting, and is constructed from environmentally friendly materials.

If you get tired of the highly charged atmosphere around the Place des Nations you can always retreat to one of the surrounding cafés or nearby parks. The Château de Penthes in Parc de L'Impératrice, behind the Palais des Nations, is a lovely 14th century château, now home to the Museum of the Swiss Abroad. The grounds of the William Rappard Centre offer a similar escape. The centre, named after the founder of several international organisations in Geneva, is set in a picturesque wooded estate with many walking trails to explore.

## Lakefront, The

The dividing yet magnetic heart of the city is the lake. Every view from Geneva's picturesque lakefront is like a living postcard. Tree lined promenades pave the way for strollers as they meander, gazing out on the surrounding mountains or the sailing boats dotting Lac Léman. From the far bank you can over look the city but still be very much part of it.

The centrepiece of the lakefront is the Jet d'Eau, the world's tallest water fountain, shooting some 500 litres of water per second, 140 metres into the air. The fountain, originally constructed in 1881 as a 'liquid monument' to Geneva's revolutionary Coulouvrenière Hydraulic Factory, now stands as a symbolic beacon of the 'world's biggest little city'.

### The Right Bank

The northern city limits of the western lakefront are bounded by a magnificently manicured botanical garden and conservatory, which offers visitors the opportunity to relax and learn about horticulture, indigenous animals and environmental protection issues. Immediately beyond the botanical garden are four more interconnected parks. Each park (Barton, the Perle du Lac, Moynier and Mon-Repos) was once an estate donated to, and now tended by, the city. The old estate mansions are home to various public works including the Museum of the History of Sciences in the Pompeiian decorated Villa Bartholoni and the Centre for Humanitarian Dialog, which is housed in the old Phillippe de Plantamour mansion. The grounds also feature a symphony of different trees and flowers that compete for attention with the lovely lake views. The beautiful integration of architecture and nature make it easy to see why Le Corbusier once called this area the 'Promised Land'. Le Corbusier's utopian vision lives on today and is enjoyed by thousands of lounging citizens and visitors every day.

Continuing south, the Wilson and Mont-Blanc Promenades connect the outlying parks to the heart of the city. The various sculptures, flowerbeds and walkways are the result of a competition held in 1915 to beautify the shoreline. This bank is host to a number of seasonal markets and festivals, and is a popular area for inline skaters, cyclists and strolling pedestrians alike. For those low on energy and short on wheels, the Pâquis Express mini train operates from March to November, shuttling riders between the various sites along the Right Bank.

The street running parallel to the promenades is lined with some of Geneva's most majestic buildings including the Palais Wilson, the original home of the League of Nations in 1920 and now the home office of the United Nations High Commissioner for Human Rights. A few blocks beyond is the Brunswick Monument – a mausoleum that is the resting place of one of Geneva's early benefactors, Charles d'Este-Guelph. The monument sits in Alps Square, so named because it is considered the best vantage point in the city to view the Mont-Blanc – the tallest mountain in western Europe (at 4807 metres).

Along the Right Bank you will find plenty of opportunities for water activities. Be it boat cruises, water skiing or sailing there is an array of excursions and rentals available for every type of enthusiast. No less than five different boat companies offer lake cruises ranging from one hour tours to four-hour dinner cruises. Several marinas in the Port of Pâquis rent small motorboats, sailboats or paddleboats throughout the year. By far the most popular 'water' activity, however, is lounging at the Bains de Pâquis – Geneva's own version of the French Riviera. The large jetty, constructed in 1932, is a prime spot for swimming and people watching. During the warmer months the concrete beach is riddled with the bikini clad, cosmopolitan elite. In winter, the indoor-outdoor sauna and Turkish bath facilities offer the utmost in luxury.

### Area Highlights

*Walk along the promenades surrounding Geneva's world famous lakefront. Enjoy the lake and mountain views from a lakeside park or café. Hop onboard one of the many tour boats for a memorable and relaxing experience.*

#### d'Ile Rousseau

*Named after the Genevan philosopher, Jean-Jacques Rousseau, this small garden island in the centre of the Rhône features a statue of its namesake and a romantic open air restaurant with a 360 degree view of the city.*

## Crossing Over

Swimming is generally frowned upon (and cold!), but there are numerous bridges or crossing points from the Right Bank to the Left. All the crossings are free and offer unique and inviting views of the lakefront area. The first (and busiest) is the Mont-Blanc Bridge, averaging 80,000 vehicle crossings per day. Far more pleasant for pedestrians, is to pass under the Mont-Blanc bridge via the Barge du Mont-Blanc and cross the river via one of the two following pedestrian bridges; Pont des Bergues, from where you can access the d'Ile Rousseau, or the Pont de la Machine, home to the Geneva Tourist Office. The next bridge along is the Pont de L'Ile. This bridge spans a small island containing a large quay wall that is a popular lunch spot for sharing one's lunch with Geneva's most shameless beggars – the swans – no doubt hungry from battling the swift currents of the Rhône all day. The island was once the site of a large fortress. All that remains today is the old castle tower, known as La Tour de l'Ile. Around the tower are several cafés and galleries, including the 'Art Centre on the Island' at 1 Place de L'Ile, dedicated to showcasing the work of local art students. Finally, the Coulouvrenière Bridge is anchored to the Bâtiment des Forces Motrices – Geneva's first hydroelectric power plant, built in 1886, which is currently home to a 985 seat opera house. The stone opera house resembles a floating train station with stunning high arched windows and classical statues perched on the roof.

Geneva – Main Areas

Exploring

## The Left Bank

Though not as popular as the Right Bank, the eastern waterfront offers just as many sights and activities. When crossing the Mont-Blanc Bridge, the first attraction encountered on the Left Bank is the famous 'Flower Clock' at the edge of the Jardin Anglais. The huge clock, a monument to Geneva's watch making industry since 1955, is redesigned every season with up to 7,000 flowers. The Jardin Anglais features a number of fountains, including a huge bronze monument to the Nymph of Springs created by the Parisian sculptor, Alexis André.

The Gustave-Ador Promenade is a long tree lined boulevard, host to many marinas and mooring docks. Most of Geneva's sailing clubs can be found along this shore, including the Société Nautique de Genève (SNG), official home to America's Cup champions Alinghi. The cup itself is on display in the club for public viewing, at least until 2007, when Alinghi will defend the title. Most of the sailing clubs sponsor regattas for the more advanced sailors and offer lessons for beginners.

The famous Geneva landmark, the Jet d'Eau, is at the end of a pier that juts out from the Gustave-Ador Promenade. Stand too close and you'll get soaked!

Wandering down the promenade the Eaux-Vives neighbourhood, with its wide open green spaces, showcases the 1930's city planning philosophy of socialist architect, Maurice Braillard. Braillard's vision culminates in two gigantic parks on the waterfront – Parc La Grange, featuring three rose gardens, and the Parc des Eaux-Vives with its rhododendrons (a gift from the Netherlands following World War II).

Not to be outdone by the Bains des Pâquis, Genève-Plage (or beach) sits at the outskirts of the Left Bank. This 'beach' is actually a huge water park complex complete with an Olympic size pool, waterslides, a playground and a snack bar. For most who attend the Plage, the lake is merely a backdrop for a more modern form of relaxation.

## Old Town, The

Just as the fountain beckons people to the lakefront, so too does Saint Pierre Cathedral, visible from every part of the city centre, calling visitors to brave the steep slopes and explore the many hidden passages of the old town. This area is located on the Left Bank just four blocks south of the lake near the city centre and the cathedral, in accordance with a common European tradition, is the highest point of the city. For SFr 3, you can

climb an additional 157 steps to the top of the north tower for the ultimate panorama. The cathedral is an excellent starting point for any tour of the Old Town.

The cobbled streets of the Old Town

One of Geneva's most important archaeological sites lies just underneath the Cathedral. Although construction of the cathedral didn't begin until 1160 AD, its location has been a site of worship from as far back as 350 AD. The area is divided into eleven different excavation zones. Most interesting are the remnants of a Romanesque church buried in the foundations, dating back to 1000 AD.

Above ground, the courtyard in front of Saint Pierre is the scene of one of Geneva's most enduring traditions. L'Escalade, held each year on 11 December, marks Geneva's successful defence against the surprise attack mounted by the Duke of Savoy and his mercenaries, in 1602. The event is celebrated each year with a torch lit parade. The procession culminates in a huge bonfire in front of Saint Pierre Cathedral.

Next door to the cathedral is a small 15th century chapel known as the Calvin Auditory, named after Jean Calvin who once taught theology in the chapel. Despite its size, the Gothic style chapel is a beautiful complement to the austere cathedral.

Just below the cathedral, to the north, is Place de la Madeleine, named for the temple on the west side of the square that was once an important Reformation site and admired for its lavish stained glass windows. The square is better

# Life's a Journey... Take a Guide

Ain't no mountain high enough (even the Hajar) or riverbed wide enough (even Wadi Bani Khalid) to keep us from bringing this book to you. From Arabian charm to the call of the wilderness, get ready to explore. It's Oman, it's breathtaking and it's time you bought this book!

Passionately Publishing...

known today for its wooden carousel and outdoor market.

Two streets over, on Rue Théodore-de-Bèze, is Calvin College – the oldest school building in Geneva, established by Jean Calvin in 1559. Up the hill from the college is the comprehensive Museum of Art and History (Geneva's largest museum) situated along the picturesque Promenade de L'Observatoire.

### Area Highlights

*Explore and discover the maze like passageways of the Old Town. Dive down one of the side streets, resembling Harry Potter's Diagon Alley, to find your own Nimbus 2000 or other unique trinket.*

#### The Grand Rue

*The central street in the Old Town is filled with trendy boutiques that are museums in their own right. Also, the many cafés offer a historic and attractive ambience where you can relax with friends.*

#### Terrasse d' Aubigné

*Tucked behind the cathedral, this little known terrace is a tranquil oasis with intimate views of the corridor streets below. There is not much space in this secret gem so travel light.*

At the end of Rue Etienne-Dumont is the oldest public square in Geneva, which has been a marketplace since Roman times. Place Bourg-de-Four is a lively place filled with modish bistros, cafés and boutiques. The 18th century fountain in front of the Palais de Justice is a popular meeting spot. During the summer months, the square is blocked off to all traffic to make way for the avalanche of chairs that spill out onto the streets from the surrounding establishments.

Down Rue de l'Hôtel-de-Ville is the Town Hall, which is home to Geneva's parliament. A ramp starting from the entrance and running to the third floor was once used by officials on horseback who wished to ride rather than walk up to the main hall. The building has been the site of many important meetings, including the first Geneva Convention.

Just across the street is the Old Arsenal, still protected by five antique artillery cannons that once lined the city walls. The old munitions depot is now the State Archives. In the archway are three mosaic frescoes by Alexandre Cingria (1949), including one illustrating Julius Caesar's arrival to the city.

Around the corner on Rue du Puits-Saint-Pierre is the oldest private house in Geneva – Maison Tavel. The house presents an accurate representation of daily life in Geneva through the ages. Switzerland's largest relief map is housed in the attic, a scale floor model of Geneva circa 1850, when it was still surrounded by walls – the old, Old Town.

## Place Neuve

The centre of high culture in Geneva is undoubtedly found at Place Neuve just behind the Old Town. The wide boulevards and ornate monuments give the area a Parisian feel, especially at night when the various venues are lit up. The best way to approach the square is from Rampe de la Treille that leads from the Old Town down the only remaining rampart wall from the old city. The promenade is lined with chestnut trees and the world's longest wooden bench, which provides more than enough room to sit and admire Parc des Bastions and Place Neuve spreading out below.

View over Place Neuve

The central roundabout at Place Neuve is adorned with a triumphant statue of General Henri Dufour – a military hero who helped found the Red Cross and was the first person to map Switzerland. Around the General's statue sit the major houses of fine art in Geneva, including the Grand Opera House, the Conservatory of Music, Victoria Hall and the Rath Museum, each an architectural delight. The Grand Theatre (www.geneveopera.ch) is a replica of the Garnier Opera House in Paris. The original façade burned down in 1951 after a rehearsal of Wagner's 'Walkyrie', which involved a live ring of fire that got out of hand. The building has since been restored with even more ornamentation. The 19th century Conservatory of Music sports a splendid Byzantine edifice decorated with stone muses. The lights of the classical music hall are reflected in the facing fountain, which maintains the symmetry of the overall presentation. Nearby, Victoria Hall (Rue

Saint Pierre Cathedral

Général-Dufour,14), named after England's Queen Victoria, was constructed in 1894 to be a worthy venue for the Queen's own brass band, 'Harmonie Nautique'. The interior features intricate Rococo style woodcarvings spreading like vines from the floor and through the balconies – enough visual stimulation to keep you awake through even the most slumber-some sonatas. If you do drift off, the resplendent ceiling is a good enough reason for your head dropping back! Finally, the Rath Museum is Geneva's oldest, resembling a religious temple and housing numerous exhibitions throughout the year.

When the theatre crowds let out, most hang around in one of the glowing street cafés or take a stroll through Parc des Bastions on the south side of Place Neuve. The park, formerly a botanical garden, is a budding refuge of green spaces skirted by tree lined walkways. The north side of the park is bounded by the 100 metre 'Reformation Wall.' The wall commemorates the four giants of the Reformation: Guillaume Farel, Jean Calvin, Théodore de Bèze and John Knox, who are immortalised in statue beneath the motto, 'After the Darkness, Light'. Other carvings along the wall depict significant events throughout the history of Protestantism.

After the Darkness, Light

Opposite the Wall is the University of Geneva, founded by Jean Calvin in the 16th Century. The pavilion restaurant at the entrance of the park is a popular spot for students. Adjacent to the restaurant is a field of life size chessboards that attracts retirees, happy to sit and watch or teach the youngsters a thing or two about the game.

One block off the park is Boulevard des Philosophes, a hip street with alternative shops and high concept cafés, such as La Sixième Heure (6 Place des Philosophes). Next door is Arts Vivendi, a unique interior design shop featuring objects constructed by local artists, from recycled material. The theatre hall Comédie de Genève, up the street, presents challenging interpretations of classic dramas with periodic productions in English. The 'Rhino' building on the corner of Boulevard des Philosophes and Boulevard de la Tour is easily identified by a large red horn protruding from the corner of the building. The Rhino is a communal squat containing illegal, though tolerated, occupants who help run the Bistr'ok bar and music venue on the ground floor.

---

### Area Highlights

**Chess in Parc des Bastions**

*Near the main entrance to Parc des Bastions is a field of life size chessboards where you can attempt check mate, or leave it to the seasoned players to show you how it's done.*

**The Rhino Building**

*Easily identified by a large red horn protruding from the building, this communal squat at the corner of Boulevard des Philosophes and Boulevard de la Tour is home to the Bistr'ok bar, a popular music venue on the ground floor.*

---

## Plainpalais & Vicinity

In the heart of Geneva is a diamond shaped no man's land called Plaine de Plainpalais, which overflows with a wonderful chaos that is not present elsewhere in the city. At the top of the diamond is a huge skate park constantly filled with kids in baggy jeans The biggest draw is the flea market that runs (officially) from 08:00 to 17:00, Wednesdays and Saturdays. This is where the locals pawn off anything from old records, to antique pipes to paint cans. Also on the Plaine is an amusement park, football field and performance area. Plaine de Plainpalais has also been home to visiting productions such as Cirque du Soleil.

Around Plaine de Plainpalais is the greatest assortment of cafés in Geneva. Cave Valaisanne, Café Cuba and Café Remor, all at Place du Cirque, are café haunts with outdoor seating, where a quick cup of coffee can easily turn into a lazy afternoon. Sitcom fans would want to visit Central Perk (6 Ave du Mail), which is a replica of the coffee shop from the set of *Friends*. Highly recommended is the Café at Place de la Synagogue. It's entirely shaded by trees and sits in front one of the oldest synagogues in the city.

On the cultural menu, the special of the day in Plainpalais is Musée d'Art Moderne et Contemporain (Museum of Modern Art) or MAMCO. The museum is housed in an old warehouse at Rue des Vieux-Grenadiers, 10 and is among Geneva's most compelling. The industrial qualities of the facility are used to enhance the museum's collection of visual and conceptual artworks, dating back to the 1960s. The collection and layout are constantly updated with new works, including some from the nearby art school at the Centre d'Art Contemporain. Many of the surrounding warehouses and buildings contain lofts and design studios, where the next modern masterpieces are in progress. Artmis, or 'Friends of Art,' north of Boulevard de Saint Georges, is a gated artist's compound covering four square blocks. Every building is covered with layers of graffiti. The collective studios and galleries stage weekly exhibitions and performances open to the public.

Place Neuve

The theatres around Plainpalais and neighbouring Jonction are the antithesis of the high brow venues at Place Neuve. The Arditi-Wilsdorf Auditorium at 1 Ave du Mail is a 1950s cinema designed by Marc-Joseph Saugey. It was targeted for destruction in 1980, but was rescued by a determined group of citizens who came together to preserve the unique structure, characterised by its suspended balconies and maze of orange entrance ramps. Next door is Geneva's own Moulin Rouge, complete with a neon red windmill and cabaret performances nightly. North of Plaine de Plainpalais, L'Usine (The Factory)

at Place des Volontaires and the Palladium at Rue du Stand,3 are two alternative music venues with performances ranging from 'electro dark' to vomit rock. A host of other warehouses in the vicinity sponsor concerts throughout the week. Keep your eyes open for posters splattered like wallpaper throughout the area, or contact the International Social Syndicate 'Sindy' (www.sindy.com) for more information. The group, comprised of Geneva based English speaking professionals, is always out for a good time and stages regular parties throughout the year.

### Area Highlights

#### 'Friends of Art' Artists' Compound

*North of Boulevard de Saint Georges is a gated artists' compound covering four square blocks called Artmis. The collective studios and galleries stage weekly exhibitions and performances, which are open to the public.*

#### Skate Park at Plaine de Plainpalais

*Get a feel for the alternative flavour of the area by visiting this park at the northern tip of the Plaine. This huge concrete and iron jungle is constantly filled with talented skaters from the MTV generation.*

To the south of the warehouse district, on Boulevard de Saint Georges, is the Plainpalais Cemetery – resting place of such greats as Jean Calvin, Argentinean author Jorge Luis Borges and inventor Sir Humphry Davy. The cemetery is now reserved for dignitaries. Sergio Vieira de Mello, the late UN High Commissioner for Human rights who died while serving in Iraq, was laid to rest here on August 29, 2003.

To the east of the cemetery is the area known as Jonction, extending from the point where the Rhône and the Arve rivers meet. Jonction was primarily an industrial area, powered by nearby hydraulic turbines until the early 20th century. Today the area is mostly residential with some industry remaining. A popular local activity in the summertime is jumping from the Sous-Terre Bridge into the Rhône river. For information about other local goings on, visit the Maison de Quartier at 18 Ave Sainte-Clotilde. The Maison de Quartier is a cantonal sponsored establishment whose charter is to promote cultural activities in the neighbourhood and provide other services, such as day care, art classes or just a place to throw a party. Most neighbourhoods in Geneva have their own version of the Maison de Quartier. For other centres around Geneva, log on to www.fase.ch.

Geneva – Main Areas

Exploring

## Train Station & Vicinity

Gare Cornavin is most visitors' first stop in Geneva and makes for a memorable experience. The station is an hive of international activity and marks a great starting point from which to explore the city.

Directly in front of the train station, at Place Cornavin, is the Notre Dame Church. The church, built between 1852 and 1857, is one of the few Catholic parishes in Geneva. Constructed out of sandstone in classic Gothic style, the church has valiantly withstood the tides of modernity which have flooded the rest of the area, and still remains a peaceful island amidst the stream of activity swirling around it.

The train station

Stretching southeast from the church is Rue du Mont-Blanc – a pedestrian boulevard full of souvenir shops and street cafés. Street musicians can be found performing here, come rain or shine. To the right, facing the lake, is the Saint Gervais quarter, formerly home to watchmakers, jewellers and goldsmiths. The guilds have since moved to Hong Kong and been replaced by shopping centres. However, the Gothic temple at Rue du Temple, across from the Gallery of Contemporary Image, is a well preserved token of the old neighbourhood.

Rue du Temple turns into Rue Voltaire after passing the railway tracks. The Voltaire Institute and Museum, in the nearby Parc des Délices (Park of Delights), is an elegant estate with well manicured grounds.

If you take a right at the Pont de Délices onto Ave des Tilleuls and walk three blocks, you will find Maurice Braillard's socialistic masterpiece, 'The Circular House'. This towering hemicycle is known as the 'Coliseum' to locals because of the semi-circular turrets that surround the building.

## Pâquis

Forget the United Nations, the true international heart of Geneva beats just outside the door of Gare Cornavin in Geneva's red light district, where a world bazaar of unofficial delegates parade the streets with the tune of 'It's a Small World After All' faintly playing in the distance. Pâquis is filled with a cosmopolitan mix of nationalities. Careful though, as the quarter can be a bit dodgy at two in the morning on a Saturday night, but in general, the district is a subtle red and definitely not to be missed.

The best way to explore Pâquis is to get lost and wander the side streets until you find something unexpected. The local ethnic restaurants are authentic and reasonably priced, attracting even Geneva's most well-to-do residents looking to try something new. The Rue de Berne is famous for its kebab shops, exuding mysterious aromas of the east. Edelweiss, at Place de la Navigation, is a tourist fondue favourite featuring live traditional Swiss music every night. The atmosphere is a bit cheesy, but after all, it is a fondue restaurant! You can't go wrong with any of the African restaurants in the area, and Thai food is abundant too. For more upscale fare, check out the Asian fusion cuisine at Comptoir on Rue de Richemont. The sleek glass and steel décor is a bastion of modernity amidst the generally earthier textures of Pâquis.

Afterwards, you can stop at one of the Egyptian hookah lounges further down the street or check out one of the many bars and cafés in the area. The AMR Jazz School on Rue des Alpes is perhaps the most famous hot spot in Pâquis, offering live concerts most nights – many by former and current students of the school. Tuesday nights are reserved for free jam sessions when anyone with an instrument and some soul can join in the mix and help jam the night away. AMR also organises several jazz festivals throughout the year. Another live music option is the little known Tcherga's on Rue de la Navigation – a Turkish bar with live 'gypsy' music at weekends. The 5 Portes Café on Rue de Zurich and the Café Art's on Rue des Pâquis are classic bohemian hangouts, ideal for both amateur and seasoned 'people watchers'. Mr. Pickwick's and Les Brasseurs, both on Rue de Lausanne, attract boisterous English speaking crowds almost every night of the week. Before the bars close, hit the Magneto bar on Rue de Monthoux or Club Cactus on Rue Chaponnière to bump and grind to the spins of local DJs. You can also dance on Saturday nights in the school gym of the Sale du Môle at one of the Latin connection's sponsored parties – a great late night option if not a little like going to the prom!

For those with a taste for the racier side of life, Pâquis' seedy underbelly is not hard to uncover – just follow the trail of neon lights and net stockings through any dark doorway from where you can hear muffled dance music, be it a Saturday night or Sunday afternoon. Prostitution is legal in the brothels around the Rue de Berne and the working girls even charge 6.5% VAT.

Another major Pâquis attraction, similar to many other parts of Geneva, is the shopping. The Pâquis, however, is exceptional in that you can manage to find something both unique and affordable in one of the many boutiques and shops packed into the quarter. Many stores offer second hand goods in excellent condition. Clothes are perhaps the main shopping staple in the area, and you can find outrageous threads on just about any street.

A number of interesting bookshops and speciality stores account for Pâquis' more intellectual offerings. The Bookworm on Rue Sismondi is owned by a friendly Bostonian offering a reasonable collection of second hand books and five day movie rentals for SFr 5. The American Library (www.amlib.ch) is housed in an English speaking church at Rue de Monthoux, 3 just opposite the Noga Hilton Hotel, and is a relaxing place to browse or borrow (SFr 100 per membership). The Arab bookshop on Rue de Fribourg has translated versions of work by Arab authors and texts in English. Next door to it is the surreal American Café – an Arab owned pool hall with cheap Internet access and the Al Jazeera channel on television.

Though you probably wouldn't guess, there are several churches in Pâquis. The most significant is the Holy Trinity Church at Rue de Lausanne, 69. The church, completed in 1993, is a perfect sphere 20 metres in diameter and covered in pink granite. Inside it is a small chapel and gallery connected by a floating staircase. The church is open daily.

A church in Pâquis

## Les Grottes

Situated behind the train station at Cornavin is one of Geneva's most interesting yet untapped areas. Les Grottes is home to a progressive mix of small business owners, squatters and artists who inhabit Geneva's most architecturally interesting district. Even the not so interesting buildings and warehouses are simply urban camouflage to the labyrinth of bars, dance clubs and galleries that lie just a scratch below the surface.

### Area Highlights

**Hookah Lounges**

*Indulge in an Arab tradition by taking a puff at a Middle Eastern café. Master the art of blowing rings from a hookah as you lounge on an Oriental rug or pillow.*

**Holy Trinity Church**

*A small chapel and gallery are encased in this modern church at Rue de Lausanne,69 . It is a perfect sphere, 20 metres in diameter and covered in pink granite. Open daily.*

The most famous of Les Grottes' treasures is the Schtrumpfs located at Rue Louis-Favre, 23 – 29. This housing complex is the amalgamation of the work of three architects who created a building with seemingly no straight lines or any sense of order. Gaudi is the only identifiable influence in the colourful mix mosaics, bricks, twisting stairways, iron protrusions and scattered

Exploring   Geneva – Other Areas

windows. The building reflects the eclectic nature of its inhabitants who proudly refer to themselves as 'Smurfs'.

The open area behind the Schtrumpfs, at Place des Grottes, hosts a farmers' market every Thursday afternoon from 14:00 to 20:00.

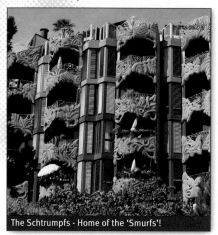

The Schtrumpfs - Home of the 'Smurfs'!

Make your way down Rue de la Faucille to Cropettes Park to enjoy one of the summertime concerts or plays performed near the crescent shaped pond in the centre of the park. The park also adjoins the Beaulieu Park estate where Napoleon stayed in 1800 while planning his conquest of Italy.

### Fondue versus Raclette

*Fondue is the most famous Swiss meal. However, another delicious, though often overlooked, traditional dairy delight is raclette. Raclette, derived from the French word meaning 'to scrape', involves scraping melted cheese over potatoes, pickles, meats, or just about anything else that you fancy.*

A series of former estates, converted into post war housing projects, pave the way along Rue de Montbrillant all the way to the International District.

## Geneva – Other Areas

### Carouge

Just beyond Geneva, across the Arve River, is the town of Carouge – an artisan paradise filled with boutiques, cafés and theatres and characterised by a laid back, open spirit. The city was founded in the late 1700s by Victor-Amedee III, King of Savoy and Sardinia, who wanted to create a Catholic economic counter balance to Geneva (which was already one of the wealthiest cities in the region at that time). Architects from Northern Italy and Southern France were brought in to transform the city into a modern Mediterranean style masterpiece. The town's design and layout have often been compared to the old town of Nice, France. The original city plans can still be viewed at the Carouge town hall in the Hôtel de Ville.

From its inception Carouge blossomed as a trading centre, welcoming Freemasons, Protestants, Catholics and Jews, and fostering an atmosphere of tolerance that prevails even today. The city also attracted those wishing to escape the puritanical confines of Geneva for a more relaxed environment. The result was the proliferation of over 150 bars and cafés, and an influx of all types of artisans. Over 200 years later, Carouge remains a Mecca for craftsmen and designers, and is commonly referred to as the 'Greenwich Village of Geneva'.

There are two main entry points into Carouge from Geneva. The Pont de la Fontenette enters at the Jewish cemetery where, until 1852, Jews exiled from Geneva were buried. The path into town passes along the river through the 'Noie-tes-puces' ('Drown Your Fleas') Park before entering Promenade des Orpailleurs ('Gold Panners Walk') where gold seekers once mined the Arve.

The Pont de Carouge, built on Napoleon's initiative and competed in 1811, has withstood the test of time, including Austrian assaults in 1814 and bombing by Royal Air Force pilots in 1940, who mistakenly thought that they were flying over Italy! The bridge was, at one point, widened to make room for the 'American train' connecting Geneva and Carouge.

The bridge enters Carouge at the Place de L'Octroi, where city officials controlled passage into the city and collected taxes. Café Bois Populaire still houses the old scales and wooden weighing floor once used to measure goods. The scales now serve as interesting perches for patrons to set their drinks on. Just beyond is the Café des Négociants, where merchants and traders gathered to haggle over prices. The café has been transformed into a trendier abode from its sawdust floor days but retains the commercial character of Carouge.

Turning left at Place d'Armes into the heart of the city, down Rue Saint Victor, you pass along the main shopping street filled with florists, carpenters, clockmakers, furniture shops, galleries, clothing stores, and a few shops that can't quite be defined. Many of the boutiques contain a studio where you can watch the artisans at work.

Carouge Flags

Further along on the left, is Place du Temple – home to the first protestant church in Carouge. It is easily distinguished by its elaborate woodcarvings that have been whittled by a single eccentric priest, and the illustrative stained glass windows telling stories of local citizens. The next square, Place du Marché, is the heart of the city, complete with beautiful flowing fountains that help make this the most appealing outdoor marketplace in Geneva. At the east end of the square is Rue Vautier, home to Carouge's hippest nightspots, most notably, Le Chat Noir (The Black Cat) jazz and nightclub at Rue Vautier, 13.

Heading south, Rue Vautier turns into Rue Ancienne, the only curved road in Carouge. This road is the original road built by the Romans, and was therefore left out of the grid system. Rue Ancienne is another excellent artisan shopping street. Do try to gain access to one of the 'secret' gardens hidden behind most storefronts and residences throughout Carouge.

## Shopping

*Switzerland is known for its army knives, chocolate and watches, but for a truly unique souvenir, head to one of the local flea markets that take place on the weekends in parks and squares around town. Carouge is another great option, filled with interesting products made by local artisans at prices well below Geneva's city centre.*

Rue Ancienne leads to the Place du Rondeau at the head of Boulevard des Promenades. The spacious promenade connects with Place de Sardaigne, which is the locale of the Carouge Museum and Cottier Park. Opposite the park are the modern Carouge Towers fronted by a pair of fountains. These mark the location of the moat that used to surround the city. The cascading fountains were designed by Slobodan Vassiljevic and are even used by some as a communal shower in the summer!

## Cologny

Just past Parc des Eaux-Vives, the winding Rampe de Cologny leads you to the self named 'Beverly Hills of Geneva.' The suburb on the hill is the original gated community with estates surrounded by walls reminiscent of those that once encircled Geneva. Instead of persecuted Protestants, the walls now serve to protect some of Geneva's most exclusive residents, including Petula Clark and Isabelle Adjani. The Villa Deodati, on 9 Chemin de Ruth, is perhaps the most famous mansion of all, and was home to Milton and Lord Byron at various times. The Maison Champuis, overlooking the lake in the district of Montalegre, was the summerhouse of Mary Shelley who got the idea for her book *Frankenstein* from a dream she had after observing an electrical storm over the lake from her bedroom. The village itself makes for a pleasant stroll or bike ride with many wooded and farmland areas throughout. Just try not to strain your neck while peering over any fences!

For a dose of culture, hit the Bibliotheca Boderiana on Route de Guignard. The library is only open on Thursday afternoons and the first Tuesday of each month, or you could make an appointment. The collection is the largest amongst private libraries in Switzerland, with over 160,000 works, including the oldest surviving text of the Gospel of St John and the original copy of the Gutenberg Bible.

## Gy

Thirty minutes from Geneva, east of Hermance, is the agricultural community of Gy. The family oriented Merlinge Farm in Gy can be reached by bus via the TPG line A. This working farm is open from March to November for an entry fee of SFr 4 (adults) and SFr 2.40 (children). Entertainment and activities include a gigantic 4.5 km maize maze, a petting zoo, a restaurant, and several seasonal gardens and fruit trees for the picking. A mini train shuttles guest around the farm, but cannot help you if you get lost in the maze.

## Arve River, The

Although the lake is Geneva's main aquatic attraction, the Arve River, which divides Geneva from Carouge, is quite literally a gold mine of activities and natural beauty. The river was once a popular spot for gold panners, up until the 1900s. Since then the 9 km stretch from La Jonction to the Swiss-French border has been developed into an eco friendly waterway banked by numerous sports facilities and promenades, and is the perfect place for a stroll.

Starting at La Jonction where the Arve meets the Rhône, La Jonction pier was originally built to keep the tumultuous currents of the river from damaging the machinery of the Bâtiment power plant. Those same currents are now the reason the river is such a popular destination for kayaking and rafting enthusiasts.

Continuing down the river, on the right, you will find the twin tanks of La Parfumerie. The tanks, once used for perfume production by the Geneva based Firmenich Company, are now home to one of Geneva's most hip and alternative hotspots, where DJ's spin late into the night and the beautiful crowd congregates.

Next come the Queue d'Arve Sports Centre and the Vernets Sports Centre. In the Queue d'Arve, you will find a cycle track, a hockey rink, climbing walls, and bowling and skittle alleys. The Vernets Sports Centre is home to the world's first indoor Olympic sized pool, and the site of numerous nail-biting curling world championships!

On the opposite side of the river sits the Cantonal Arsenal. The building is significant in that it served as the barracks from which army recruits were dispatched on 9 November 1932, to disperse a demonstration taking place at the City Hall of Plainpalais. A scuffle ensued and the recruits fired on the crowd, resulting in 13 dead and about 70 wounded. The event is commemorated every first of May (Worker's Day) at a nearby monument in Plainpalais.

Next door to this is the Mail university building – one of the largest university buildings in Switzerland and well worth a visit for its incredible glass ceiling atrium. Just beyond is another school, the Hugo-de-Senger School, where the Geneva Puppet Theatre performs on the 'Little Stage' founded by Marcelle Moynier in 1930.

The Arve River

Further down, you will find yourself walking along the banks in Carouge before arriving at the Champel Baths, which can be easily identified by the 1877 neo-Gothic Tower of Champel. The actual baths have since been replaced by a housing complex, but were once part of Europe's largest hydrotherapeutic compound, complete with Turkish baths prescribed to cure everything from sterility to depression. Across the river, on the Right Bank, is the much more modern Fontenette aquatic facility, which boasts one of the most popular water slides in the canton. Next comes the Bout-du-Monde Sports Centre that once served as a quarantine site for Jewish refugees during World War II and now features facilities for football, tennis, fencing, archery and frisbee. The final sports complex on the river, the Vessy Sports Centre, just beyond the avant-garde Vessy Bridge, is huge, with 25 grassy hectares for rugby, baseball, aeronautics and more.

The Pont du Val d'Arve passes by Beaver Island – a lovely plot in the middle of the river where Rober Hainard helped reintroduce beavers to Geneva in 1972, after a 200 year absence due to over trapping. Today, the beavers are alive and well throughout the waterways of the Arve. Another natural area, Bois de Pins (or Pine Woods), sits at the crook of the river in Veyrier and contains a footpath that leads into the Salève.

The final landmarks before the border are the Pont de Sierne and the Sierne Estate. Both once housed manufacturing stations until a fire in 1859 destroyed the area. However, the landscape was actually blessed by this accident,

as today, the green areas around the estate offer a natural and serene escape that is only minutes from the city centre.

## Meyrin

Meyrin was originally conceived in the 1950s as a satellite city to remedy the ever present housing shortage in Geneva. The city, bordering the airport, was designed with open spaces and community in mind. Although many of the buildings look a little drab and repetitive they have actually been carefully arranged to provide residents with views of the surrounding landscape, and provide convenient access to shopping and city services in Meyrin's central complex. The Forum Meyrin is a dynamic theatre and arts space that is a focal point for the community.

Meyrin is perhaps best known for being home to the largest laboratory for particle physics in Europe, the European Center for Nuclear Research (CERN), which can be reached via Bus 9. The laboratory is one of the most internationally renowned facilities with scientists from over eighty countries in residence. Even more impressive is the fact that the laboratory contains the world's largest particle accelerator with a circumference of 27 km, buried 100 metres below the surface. The lab is also famous for being the birthplace of the World Wide Web. Free tours (lasting three hours) are available from Monday to Saturday at 09:00 and 14:00. Call 022 767 84 84 for more details, or log on to www.cern.ch/public.

## Salève

The Salève is the closest mountain to the city, providing a year round backdrop and a convenient escape from the daily hustle and bustle for Geneva's citizens. The Salève is only a 20 minute bus ride from the town centre. Buses 8, 44 and 45 all terminate at convenient drop off points within walking distance of the mountain. Don't forget your passport, as the Salève actually sits across the French border.

Even though the Salève is merely a hill in comparison with the Alps beyond, it provides a wealth of activities and opportunities for day trippers. Hiking is perhaps the most popular activity. Ascending the Salève can take two to five hours, depending on your fitness level and the route. Many of the routes pass through small, isolated communities offering an idyllic portrait of mountain life. The routes also trek through a variety of natural and geographical layers including forests, rock cliffs and farmland. A route that could be of particular interest is the one from Croix de Rozon, which passes through a series of natural caves, known as the Grotte d'Orjobet. The path is also dotted with a series of informative signboards relating the different geological phenomena viewable along the way.

The summit of the Salève is the real reward, with sweeping vistas of Geneva and Mont-Blanc. For those looking for a short cut to the top, the Téléphérique Cable Car (74100 Etrembières – France; +33 450 39 86 86) offers round trip gondola rides from April to September, excluding Sundays. The cost is SFr 16 for adults and SFr 8.70 for children. The top of the Salève is a popular picnic spot with many open grassy knolls to lay out a spread and enjoy the view. The Café Table d'Orientation is another option, sitting over the vertical face of the summit. It serves a full French menu on its open air terraces.

During the summer paragliders flock to the Salève to experience a real bird's eye view of the area. The Salève has two launch pads and is famous for steady winds. If you wish, for €80, you can experience this thrill for yourself with a tandem ride, by contacting the Ecole de Parapente du Salève on +33 450 39 71 59, or log on to www.paretente-saleve.com.

## Geneva – Neighbouring France

## Annemasse

Annemasse is the first town across the French border, situated between the Salève and Voirons mountains. Although Annemasse is in Geneva's backyard, it retains its own distinctly French vibe. The town is perhaps the healthiest in France. Like water in Evian, the air quality in Annemasse is a major selling point for tourism offices. The people here seem to be in constant motion, whether cycling, hiking or kayaking, and a number of gymnasiums and pools scattered throughout the city sustain citizens when the weather is uncooperative. A very popular sport in Annemasse is skydiving. The aeronautical club on Rue de Thonon runs a parachuting school and club with a full membership roster.

The town itself has ten different parks, many of which are connected by trails. The Iris Garden along the Arve is particularly beautiful. Parc

Eugene Maitre has 50 different types of maple trees and a life size chessboard. Place de la Libération is the main shopping street with an outdoor market every Tuesday and Friday. The gigantic Annemasse Casino, at 2 Ave de l'Europe, is a popular nightspot, both for gambling and dancing. It seems that no one in Annemasse cooks, as the small town has over 150 restaurants that are always buzzing with people in the evenings.

Annemasse is part of a tourist conglomerate that incorporates the five surrounding villages of Gaillard, Ambilly, Ville-La-Grand, Etrembières and Vetraz-Monthoux. These villages jointly sponsor regular events such as a Christmas concert and the annual Artists' Exposition.

## Pays de Gex (St.Genis/Gex/Ferney/Divonne)

At the foot of the Jura Mountains, 15 km north of Geneva, is Pays de Gex. This region is famous throughout Switzerland for its thermal waters, known to help cure fatigue, insomnia and various other ailments. Since the springs' discovery in 1848, the area has become a top resort destination. The 19th century Château de Divonne set the luxurious tone and still remains one of the most popular hotels in the area. All of the villages contain the necessary resort trappings, including golf courses, health spas, boutique shopping and casinos. The public Espace Paul Vidart on Ave des Thermes is open to day trippers.

## St-Julien-en-Genevois

This French town, 10 km south of Geneva, is in a pleasant rural area that has endured a long and embattled history due to its strategic location in the Rhône Valley. St.-Julien-en-Genevois was the primary outpost for Savoy during its conflict with Geneva, and has exchanged hands more frequently than a Swiss Franc note. Following the Treaty of 1603, the city was successively occupied by the King of France, Spain, Austria, Sardinia and finally France again in 1860. The ruins of the Castle of Ternier, dating back to the 13th century, attest the withering effects of conflict on the town, but also the fortitude of its citizens. The town centre is currently undergoing an urban renewal project to help revitalise the commercial area. The biggest draw here is the annual Apple Festival in October.

### Images of Geneva

*Breathtaking mountain vistas mirrored in the crystal clear waters of the lake, the cobbled streets of the Old Town contrasted against the bustling modernity of one of the world's business capitals; Geneva is a treasure trove of beautiful views. Images of Geneva is a stunning collection of photographs of both the familiar and undiscovered sights of this remarkable city.*

## Museums, Heritage & Culture

### Art Galleries

Other options → Art [p.137]

Art is so prevalent throughout Geneva that in some places you could easily overlook it. Parks, public buildings, museums and shops are full of interesting artwork, thanks to the generous and appreciative nature of the city. Geneva itself

View of the Salève

contains more than 75 art galleries, ranging from the immense state sponsored galleries, such as the Art and History Museum, to the smaller boutique galleries featuring perhaps just one or two artists. Although it is impossible to cover them all, below is a list of some of the .most dynamic and progressive galleries fuelling Geneva's art scene today.

## Art Centre on the Island

Location ➜ Pl. de l'Ile · Town Centre     **022 312 12 30**
Hours ➜ Various
Web/email ➜ na     Map Ref ➜ 13-C3

The Art Centre and the adjoining Centre of Contemporary Applied Arts are housed in a former market anchored in the middle of the Rhône River. The gallery celebrates the energy of young, local artists and is a working studio devoted to Geneva artists of every medium, and gives new artists the chance to display their work in public, often for the first time. Many of the exhibitors are present during the weekends and available to discuss their work, or perhaps even a fair sale price.

## Centre for Contemporary Art Geneva

Location ➜ Rue des Vieux Grenadiers 10     **022 329 18 42**
Hours ➜ 11:00 – 18:00
Web/email ➜ www.centre.ch     Map Ref ➜ 13-C4

Housed in an old industrial factory the Centre for Contemporary Art Geneva is somewhat of a factory itself as it has been churning out modern works by local artists since 1974. It also produces some of the most acclaimed names in the modern art world, including Tony Oursler, Pipilotti Rist and Kiki Smith. As well as being housed in the same building as MAMCO it shares the same philosophy; to produce and present important works from local artists that are designed to challenge the public's notions of art and society.

## Centre for Contemporary Edition

Location ➜ Rue Saint-Léger 18 · Chambésy     **022 310 51 70**
Hours ➜ 15:00 – 19:00
Web/email ➜ edition@vtx.ch     Map Ref ➜ 13-D4

This centre focuses on print media, such as books, lithographs and other creative works related to publication. It contains an exhibition area as well as a production wing, where print artists steadily apply their trade.

## Centre for Contemporary Images – Saint Gervais

Location ➜ Rue du Temple 5 · Town Centre     **022 908 20 00**
Hours ➜ 12:00 – 18:00
Web/email ➜ www.centreimage.ch     Map Ref ➜ 13-C3

A unique and dynamic gallery, the Centre for Contemporary Images in Saint Gervais is a media library containing one of the most vibrant and comprehensive video collections in all of Europe. The works by video artists, such as Bill Viola and Gary Hill, as well as temporary exhibitors, are on display via a handy Internet catalogue. Admission is free.

## Geneva Photography Centre

Location ➜ Rue du General Dufour 16     **022 329 28 35**
Hours ➜ 14:00 – 18:00
Web/email ➜ cenphoto@worldcom.ch     Map Ref ➜ 13-D4

This is the only photography gallery in Geneva. Despite the lack of competition, the gallery constantly strives to present original artworks that address issues on the cutting edge of social consciousness. The gallery, started in 1985 by a group of local photographers and housed in the Grütli Arts House, presents up to 15 exhibitions each year, featuring the works of both local and international artists. The gallery also hosts a number of conferences and seminars throughout the year, which are dedicated to promoting the art of photography.

## Museum of Modern & Contemporary Art (MAMCO)

Location ➜ Rue des Vieux-Grenadiers 10     **022 320 61 22**
Hours ➜ 12:00 – 18:00
Web/email ➜ www.mamco.ch     Map Ref ➜ 13-C4

Internationally renowned since its opening in 1994, MAMCO is the largest contemporary art museum in Switzerland. The museum, inspired by the work of Marcel Duchamp, housed in an old 1950's factory called 'The Vat', is a dynamic collection of private and public works spanning the last 40 years. Despite the 4,000 plus square metres of floor space and 70 different rooms, the collections in the museum are constantly rotated to make room for new exhibitions, many of which are produced next door at the Centre for Contemporary Art. The unique industrial space also allows MAMCO the flexibility to reconstruct the interior of the museum three times a year to complement current exhibitions. Admission is SFr 8.

MAMCO

## Museum of Art and History

Location → Rue Charles-Galland 2 | 022 418 26 00
Hours → 10:00 – 17:00
Web/email → http://mah.ville-ge.ch     Map Ref → 13-E4

Founded in 1910, the museum is a virtual encyclopaedia of the history of western culture. Divided into three sections, the Archaeology wing features prehistoric as well as Egyptian, Greek, and Roman relics. A Fine Arts section contains the works of Renoir, Monet, Cezanne, Van Gogh and some 400 other paintings from the Renaissance and beyond; it also includes period sculptures by Rodin, Pradier and Houdon. The Applied Arts sector houses furniture, textiles, arms and armour dating back to the middle ages. Admission is free for permanent collections and SFr 5 for temporary exhibitions. Guided tours are available by appointment.

## Rath Museum

Location → Pl. Neuve 2 · St-Léger | 022 418 33 40
Hours → 10:00 – 17:00 12:00 – 21:00
Web/email → mah.ville-ge.ch     Map Ref → 13-D4

The Rath Museum was donated by two sisters in 1826, and designed by architect Samuel Vaucher as a 'Temple of the Muses', incorporating both French and Italian elements within the design. The museum represents an important milestone as it was the first fine arts museum in Switzerland, and holds a prominent place at the seat of high culture in Geneva, at Place Neuve. The museum benefits greatly as a branch of the larger Museum of Art and History, offering ever changing international and Swiss exhibitions. Guided tours are offered on Wednesdays at 18:30. Admission prices vary according to exhibition.

## Museums – City

Other options → **Art [p.137]**

Geneva's rich history and diverse interests are well captured by more than thirty museums. The museums generally keep entry prices relatively low and have numerous temporary exhibitions throughout the year. The buildings that house the museums are often historical landmarks themselves, worthy of exploration.

Though it is hard to keep up with the dizzying calendar of events and offerings, the museums reflect the importance and influence of history on modern Geneva. You can find a museum in almost every major area of the city, interwoven into the everyday cityscape. Most of the museums are well worth a look, but beware of certain private boutique ones, which may or may not be worth the price of entry. Below is a list of the top museums in and around Geneva. Refer also to Geneva Areas [p.100] for information on activity options that also involve a visit to a museum or heritage site. Finally, it is worth mentioning that all city sponsored museums offer free admission on the first Sunday of every month.

## Ariana Museum

Location → Av. de la Paix 10 · Grand Morillon | 022 418 54 50
Hours → 10:00 – 17:00
Web/email → http://mah.ville-ge.ch     Map Ref → 5-D1

The Ariana Museum, or Swiss Museum of Ceramics and Glass, is the only museum in Switzerland that is dedicated to kiln craft. Covering seven centuries of ceramic arts with over 20,000 pieces on display, the museum contains porcelain, pottery, glass and stoneware. The museum itself, like its contents, is a work of art. Built by Gustave Revillod, it features neo-baroque and neo-classical elements. Admission is free (SFr 5 for temporary exhibits).

## Barbier-Mueller Museum

Location → Rue Jean Calvin 10 · Town Centre | 022 312 02 70
Hours → 11:00 – 17:00
Web/email → www.barbier-mueller.ch     Map Ref → 13-D4

Art from Antiquity, Africa, Asia and Oceania, is the theme of this museum, exhibiting the 7,000 piece collection of Josef Mueller. Mueller began collecting in 1907 when he spent a whole year's salary on a single painting. Mueller went on to become one of the greatest art collectors of all time. He relentlessly tracked down new art pieces

Museums, Heritage & Culture

Exploring

from around the globe and is credited with introducing tribal art from Africa, Asia and Oceania to the mainstream. Mueller died just three months before the museum's opening in the Old Town in 1977. His collection endures, and includes African masks, Indonesian jewels, and many religious artworks.

## Botanical Gardens and Conservatory

Location ➜ Ch. de l'Impératrice 1 | 022 418 51 00
Hours ➜ See timings below
Web/email ➜ www.cjb.unige.ch | Map Ref ➜ 5-E1

As the only botanical garden in the 'city of parks', this garden and conservatory has a lot to live up to. Fortunately, the gardens established by A.P. Candolle in 1817, exceed expectations. There are over 16,000 plant species on display and over 5.5 million plant samples in the conservatory that are accessible by appointment. The Gardens are divided into several areas, including an arboretum, a rock garden, a garden of scent and touch, horticultural plants, medicinal and useful plants, and an animal park. The 'Botanicum' along the lake is a family area popular for picnics and lazy Sunday afternoon strolls. Admission is free.

*Timings:* 25 Oct – 31 Mar: 09:30 – 17:00. 1 Apr – 24 Oct: 08:00 – 19:30

Botanical Gardens

## Carouge Museum

Location ➜ Pl. de Sardaigne 2 · Carouge | 022 342 33 83
Hours ➜ 14:00 – 18:00
Web/email ➜ www.carouge.ch | Map Ref ➜ 15-C4

The Carouge Museum is a bastion of cultural identity dedicated to preserving the proud Carouge district's heritage. The museum consists mainly of handmade goods and articles reflecting Carouge's artisan character throughout the past 200 years. The museum itself is a Louis XVI style home, originally built for the master watchmaker, Monsieur Montanrouge. The permanent collection, viewed only by appointment, features ceramics produced by the Carouge factory between 1810 and 1930, and the works of Marcel Noverraz. The museum produces numerous exhibitions throughout the year and is a major sponsor of the biannual International Competition of Ceramics. Admission is free.

## Ethnographic Museum of Geneva

Location ➜ Bd. Carl Vogt 65 – 67 | 022 418 45 50
Hours ➜ 14:00 – 17:00
Web/email ➜ www.ville-ge.ch/musinfo/ethg | Map Ref ➜ 15-C1

Established in 1901 by Professor Eugene, the museum relocated to a new building in 2003 which was built by the winners of an architectural contest. The museum is Geneva's own window to the world, containing over 100,000 objects from around the globe. Visitors can explore rare archaeological finds from Amazonia, South America, Tibet, Australia, Africa and Japan. The museum's Annex at Conches, is home to updated exhibitions of local artefacts, most notably the Georges Amoudruz collection of alpine heritage – the largest of its kind in the world. The Annexe is housed in an old mansion along the Arve River. Admission is free (Adults pay SFr 4.50 for temporary exhibitions).

## History of Science Museum

Location ➜ Rue de Lausanne 128 · Sécheron | 022 418 50 60
Hours ➜ 10:00 – 17:00
Web/email ➜ mah.ville-ge.ch | Map Ref ➜ 5-E2

Set in the lovely neo-classical Villa Bartholoni, in the Perle du Lac Park, the History of Science Museum is home to an interesting collection of instruments, books and paintings, as well as a working laboratory. Sciences covered include meteorology, astronomy,

Museums, Heritage & Culture

Exploring

electricity, thermodynamics and magnetism. Sundials, barometers, microscopes and other bygone instruments are all on display highlighting how far technology has come in the past 300 years. Admission is free.

## Int'l Red Cross & Red Crescent Museum

Location ➔ Av. de la Paix 17 · Grand Morillon | **022 748 95 25**
Hours ➔ 10:00 – 17:00
Web/email ➔ www.micr.org                              Map Ref ➔ 5-D1

Located just across from the Palais des Nations, this museum is highly recommended and chronicles the history and work of the Red Cross, founded in Geneva by Henry Dunant over a century ago. The museum, opened in 1988, is divided into eleven areas, each paying tribute to the various heroes of the world's first humanitarian organisation. The exhibits feature a multimedia frenzy of pictures, films, audio and computers that help to create a memorable and moving experience. Patrons should remember that the Red Cross was founded to aid victims of war and as such, many of the images presented are highly graphic in nature and do not spare viewers from the horrors of war. In addition, the museum features a current events section that helps bring to light the relevance of the Red Cross. Entrance is SFr 10, with audio guides available for an additional SFr 5.

International Red Cross & Red Crescent Museum

## International Automobile Museum

Location ➔ Voie des Traz · Le Grand-Saconnex | **022 788 84 84**
Hours ➔ 10:00 – 18:00
Web/email ➔ www.museeautomobilegeneve.ch    Map Ref ➔ 2-B4

Geneva's International Automobile Museum contains an unrivalled collection of over 400 cars, representing over a century of automotive innovation. The collection includes classic motorcycles, sports cars, trucks, prototypes, and even some concept cars that never quite made it into production. The museum also features an array of patents, drawings, sketches, designer works, petrol pumps, radiators, engines, wheels, and chassis that will delight car enthusiasts. The museum is housed in the Palexpo Exhibition Centre, which is also the site of Europe's largest annual car show. Admission is SFr 12 for adults and SFr 6 for children aged 16 and below.

## Maison Tavel

Location ➔ Rue du Puits-St-Pierre | **022 418 37 00**
Hours ➔ 10:00 – 17:00
Web/email ➔ mah.ville-ge.ch                         Map Ref ➔ 13-D4

In the heart of the Old Town is the Tavel House, Geneva's oldest residential house. Although destroyed by fire in 1334, the house was rebuilt by the noble Tavel family and later restored by the city in 1963. The house is a living time machine, exhibiting relics of daily life in Geneva since the middle ages, including furniture, tools, silver, coins and even a household guillotine. In the cellar, medieval graffiti is on display and temporary exhibits are rotated throughout the basement. The highlight of the house, however, is the famous Magnin model in the attic. The model is a scaled replica of Geneva as it was before 1850, when the city was still surrounded by walls. Admission is free. Temporary exhibits cost SFr 2.50.

## Natural History Museum

Location ➔ Rte de Malagnou 1 · Contamines | **022 418 63 00**
Hours ➔ 09:30 – 17:00
Web/email ➔ www.ville-ge.ch/musinfo/mhng    Map Ref ➔ 14-A4

The Natural History museum covers every animal, plant and mineral that is indigenous to Switzerland. Although labels are in French only, the comprehensive collection is an impressive and educational tour of Switzerland's natural history. The museum also features a number of interactive exhibits that are popular with school

You'll see all your furry friends at the Natural History Museum!

A bygone era - the Magnin Model

groups and visiting scientists alike. The highlight, however, is a zoo like exhibit of animals from around the world, where life size giraffes, alligators, lions, tigers and bears frolic in harmony. Even though the realistic exhibit at first glance may seem like the work of a master taxidermist, the animals are actually hand created models. Admission is free.

### Olympic Museum Lausanne

Location ➜ Quai D'Ouchy 1 · Lausanne     | 021 621 65 11
Hours ➜ 09:00 – 18:00
Web/email ➜ www.museum.olympic.org     Map Ref ➜ na

Less than half an hour's drive from Geneva, the Olympic Museum is an inspiring and interactive place that not only showcases the history of the games, but also captures the impact and importance of the Olympic spirit throughout history. Set in an exquisite location on the shores of Lac Léman, the museum beautifully incorporates, in its design and content, the three pillars of Olympianism ie, sport, art and culture. Exhibits include a Greek area tracing the roots of the games, memorabilia from athletes and host locations, and several audiovisual shows that let you relive some of the games' greatest moments. Admission is SFr 14 and SFr 7 for children under 19. From the museum's terraced restaurant on the top floor you can enjoy breathtaking panoramic views of the lake and the Alps beyond.

### Patek Philippe Museum

Location ➜ Rue des Vieux Grenadiers 7     | 022 807 09 10
Hours ➜ Tue – Fri 14:00 – 17:00; Sat 10:00 – 17:00
Web/email ➜ www.patekmuseum.com     Map Ref ➜ 13-C4

Dedicated to one of Geneva's oldest industries (horology), the Patek Philippe Museum holds one of the finest collections of timepieces is the world. The museum features rare antiques from around the world as well as the works of the Geneva based Patek Philippe firm, established in 1839. The museum also contains music boxes, miniature portraits, pistols and other creations that help us appreciate the passion and meticulous talents of Swiss artisans, both past and present. The collection is spread over four floors and housed in an early 20th century building, once home to a jewellery production firm. Guided tours are offered every Wednesday at 14:00. Admission is SFr 10. Under 18 enter free.

### Voltaire Institute and Museum

Location ➜ Rue des Délices 25 · Les Délices     | 022 344 71 33
Hours ➜ 14:00 – 17:00
Web/email ➜ www.ville-ge.ch/bpu     Map Ref ➜ 13-B2

'God is a comedian playing to an audience too afraid to laugh', wrote Voltaire at this estate, which he owned from 1755 to 1765. This and other quotes are on display in the estate library and museum, which contains original manuscripts, paintings, sculptures and items belonging to this philosopher. The estate is still an active centre for research on Voltaire. The best reason to visit, however, is to enjoy the estate itself. Named 'The Delights' by Voltaire, he would refer to it as 'the palace of a philosopher with the gardens of Epicurus' – a great place to relax and contemplate life.

## Parks & Beaches

### Parks

Other options ➜ Beaches [p.121]

Geneva is known as the 'City of Parks' with good reason as it has over 330 hectares of park spaces, occupying approximately 20% of the city. Within these green spaces are 40,000 trees, 428,000 plants and 40,000 rose bushes. The city has made a conscious effort to integrate parks into every new development to preserve the balance between urban development and nature. Most of the parks are old estates donated to the city. This is why the parks often contain a central mansion with a history all its own.

## Bois de la Bâtie

Location ➜ Jonction · St-Georges | na
Hours ➜ na
Web/email ➜ na                    Map Ref ➜ 15-A1

In the heart of the city, Bâtie Woods offers a refuge of wilderness amidst an urban landscape. Covering 20 hectares, the park has greatly expanded since its original development in 1874 when it was donated to the city by the Turrenttini brothers. The park is named after the Bastie-Mellie Fort that occupied the woods from 1318 to the 16th century. In the park is a pond, terraces and a small zoo that houses deer, boar, marmots, peacocks and other animals native to Switzerland. Two restaurants, also situated on the property, provide forest views. The woods are especially popular with hikers and joggers, offering several kilometres of trails and other sports facilities.

## Jardin Alpin

Location ➜ Ch. Du Jardin Alpin 7 · Meyrin | na
Hours ➜ na
Web/email ➜ na                    Map Ref ➜ 4-E1

A little known treasure, the Alpine Garden in Meyrin on the edge of town is a peaceful spot offering a lot to discover. The central area features a rose garden designed in the shape of... a rose! There is a rock garden nearby along with several other gardens

containing 3,600 different species of plants, including a pool of aquatic plants. There is a small park with ducks, chickens and goats for younger visitors, while the main villa and greenhouse exhibit various contemporary art works, including sculpture, pottery, weaves, engravings and paintings. The villa is also home to open air concerts during the summer. Admission is free for all exhibitions and events.

## Jardin Anglais

Location ➜ Quai Gustave Ador · Town Centre | na
Hours ➜ na
Web/email ➜ na                    Map Ref ➜ 14-A3

Located on the Left Bank near the Mont-Blanc Bridge and in view of the Jet d'Eau, the 'English Garden' was once panned by the Russian author Fyodor Dostoevsky for being a tourist trap with the main purpose of selling postcards. These days, you can still buy a postcard at one of the carts along the promenade but the park has since been developed, with imported trees and flowers, and numerous sculptures including the 'Monument National' – a statue of two women, 'Geneva' and 'Helvetia', representing Geneva's admission into the Swiss Federation in 1814. The centrepiece of the park is the famous flower clock, which integrates the legendary Swiss watch making precision with the timeless beauty of flowers. The clock is the largest of its kind in the world, spanning five metres. Directly behind the clock is a large bronze fountain that continuously showers the life sized spring nymphs bathing in the basin of the fountain.

Parc des Bastions - a place of natural beauty

Parks & Beaches

Exploring

## Parc des Bastions

| | |
|---|---|
| Location ➜ Place Neuve · St-Léger | na |
| Hours ➜ na | |
| Web/email ➜ na | Map Ref ➜ 13-D4 |

Just behind the Old Town, Bastions Park was once a botanical garden before its reinvention as a public park. The park still retains its garden character with towering tree lined promenades and open green areas that are especially popular with students from the neighbouring University of Geneva. The University was originally an academy founded by Jean Calvin in the 16th century. Calvin is still present, immortalised in a statue on the Reformation Wall, along with Théodore de Bèze, John Knox and Guillaume Farel. The wall is built along one of the last remnants of the old rampart walls that protected the city from attackers until the mid 1800s. The only battles going on now, however, are at the life size chess boards at the north end of the park beside the pavilion restaurant.

## Parc Bertrand

| | |
|---|---|
| Location ➜ Contamines · Nr Champel | na |
| Hours ➜ na | |
| Web/email ➜ na | Map Ref ➜ 16-A2 |

A children's favourite, Bertrand Park is full of play equipment that encourages the imagination. A giant slide in the shape of an elephant (created by sculptor Pierre Siebold) is the highlight of the play area, while a paddling pool attracts waders on hot days. At the north end of the park is a 'not so secret' vegetable garden hidden behind the stone walls of the old estate house, now a school. The park is situated in the heart of the historic Champel neighbourhood and is an important space for residents of the many tall apartment buildings that surround it. The park also has many beautiful trees and flowers and a large green space that opens towards the Salève.

## Parc des Eaux-Vives

| | |
|---|---|
| Location ➜ Quai Gustave Ador · Les Eaux-Vives | na |
| Hours ➜ na | |
| Web/email ➜ na | Map Ref ➜ 14-C2 |

Mirroring Parc la Grange, Eaux-Vives Park is a vast expanse crowned by an 18th century castle that now serves as a restaurant. Just as La Grange has its roses, Eaux-Vives has its rhododendrons – a gift from the Dutch. The park

is also home to a set of tennis courts and the Plongeon Villa that serves as the seat of the Geneva Sports Association. The association was founded in 1940 to organise the Geneva Games during the years when the border was closed and Geneva's athletes could not compete outside the country. The association now comprises sixty five different sports groups, including the Geneva Sumo Association. Many of these sports are practised and enjoyed just outside the Villa on one of the park's many open fields.

## Parc La Grange

| | |
|---|---|
| Location ➜ Quai Gustave Ador · Les Eaux-Vives | na |
| Hours ➜ na | |
| Web/email ➜ na | Map Ref ➜ 14-B3 |

As Geneva's largest park, Parc La Grange is blessed with quality as well as quantity. Encompassing 12,000 square metres of prime real estate, the park slopes gently downwards from Route de Frontenex to the lake. The mansion atop the hill is the best viewing spot and has several benches on its terraces. Next door is a horticulture centre that is open to the public, and beyond that are a number of other activity sites, including the open air Verdure Theatre where free concerts are held every Wednesday and Friday during the summer. Nearer to the lake is a well preserved set of Roman column foundations and Geneva's largest rose garden. The garden has over 200 different types of roses on display amidst a delightful Romanesque stone setting. The roses are also the main reason that Parc La Grange is the only park in Geneva to close at night.

## Parc Perle du Lac

| | |
|---|---|
| Location ➜ 126 Rue de Lausanne · Sécheron | 022 909 10 20 |
| Hours ➜ 12:00 – 14:00  19:00 – 21:30 | |
| Web/email ➜ info@perledulac.ch | Map Ref ➜ 5-E2 |

The 'Pearl of the Lake' park is a simple but profoundly beautiful space that is the perfect spot to enjoy a sunny afternoon. The grounds were once owned by Francois Bartholoni, the founder of Geneva's Conservatory of Music, and the estate is now home to the History of Science Museum. In front of the museum is a fountain and a tree lined lawn that leads to Lac Léman. The park is decorated with well manicured beds of tulips and other flowers that help make it a rare gem. The park is bordered on either side by Parc Moynier to the north and Parc Mon-Repos to the south — both beautiful in their own right.

## Beach Parks

Other options → Parks [p.118]

If you fancy a spot of seaside sunbathing and don't mind spreading out your towel on concrete, then you need not look any further than the city limits. Both the Bains des Pâquis and Genève-Plage were built in the 1930s as public baths, at a time when public hygiene was becoming a priority for all inhabitants. Both have since been renovated but still retain their community feeling and architectural integrity.

### Bains des Pâquis

Location → Quai du Mont-Blanc 30 | 022 732 29 74
Hours → 09:00 – 20:00
Web/email → www.bains-des-paquis.ch | Map Ref → 13-E2

The baths are perhaps the most quintessential Geneva spot for many visitors. The outdoor Buvette restaurant offers one of the most picturesque brunch in town with views of the Jet d'Eau and both banks. A diving platform, slides and a zip line provide amusement for enthusiastic children. Entrance is SFr 2, or SFr 70 for a summer season pass. Throughout the spring and summer entrance to concerts and festivals held on the jetty is free.

Though the baths are popular in summer, they are often overlooked in the winter months. This is a mistake. The sauna and Turkish baths offer divine relief from the winter chill for only SFr 15. Not for the shy though, the baths are nude and mixed, except on Tuesdays when they are open to females only. Massages are also available year round for the ultimate pampering experience.

### Genève-Plage

Location → Port Noir · Cologny | 022 736 24 82
Hours → 10:00 – 20:00
Web/email → www.geneve-plage.ch | Map Ref → 14-D1

Open from May to September, Genève-Plage is much more than a water park. The park has a large lakefront area with a diving platform and waterskiing launch. The park also features a water slide, wading pool, basketball and volleyball courts and a children's playground. Most visitors, however, go to swim in the heated Olympic sized pool, or relax at the terraced restaurant. The open green area in the centre of the park is a popular spot for sun worshippers. Admission is SFr 7 for adults over 16 and SFr 3.50 for those below. Student discounts and season passes are also available.

## Beaches

Other options → Parks [p.118]

Although a beach is not necessarily the first thing that comes to mind in a landlocked city, Geneva and its beaches are an exception. The combination of crystal clear waters and mountain views, all within a city setting, is a unique phenomenon that draws visitors even from coastal and island countries. Geneva is also blessed with being in the vicinity of four other pristine lakes – Lac d'Annecy, Lac du Bourget, Lac d'Aiguebellette and Lac Nantua – all sporting gorgeous shores and beaches within an hour's drive from Geneva. Below are a few recommendations, although each town around the lake has its own lakefront bathing area or beach park. The best recommendation is to get out and explore the shorelines to find your own special piece of paradise.

### Hermance Ville et Plage (Route d'Hermance)

Hermance is the closest beach to Geneva, just a few kilometres down the Left Bank. The beach is rarely crowded and is in easy cycling distance. The village itself is a charming mix of 15th century architecture with all the updated modern amenities. There is a play area for children with swing sets and a sandy beach.

### Messery (Route D25, Messery)

Just beyond Hermance, up Route D25, Messery offers a large grassy area for relaxing by the water. The actual shoreline is a bit rocky and therefore not ideal for children, however a nearby play area keeps the kids occupied. A parking area makes for easy access and a snack stand serves cold drinks and icecream.

### Lugrin (Route N5, Lugrin)

This beach, near Evian, is one of a series of beaches in the area that offer a bit of privacy and top notch lake views. The beach is screened by a line of trees and is the perfect spot to enjoy heavenly sunsets over the Jura Mountains.

## Lake d'Annecy

Lake d'Annecy is recognised for its crystal clear water and lively atmosphere. The town of Annecy is a top resort destination in France as well as a university town and is only 45 minutes by train from Geneva. The beaches are always packed at weekends in summer and there are many bars and nightclubs scattered around the shoreline. Plage Imperial is the largest beach and within close reach of the town centre. The nearby Pop Plage bar and nightclub is the place to be after the sun sets. For a more relaxing experience head out to the village of Talloires and enjoy the serene terraces and lake views. Better yet, search out one of the local spots away from the tourists for some peace and quiet.

## Lac du Bourget

Formed by a glacier that carved through the area 19,000 years ago, the 18 x 3.5 km lake is anchored by the town of Aix-les-Bains in the foothills of the Jura Mountains. The most spectacular beach here is Plage Blanche, the only white sand beach in the region. The beach is actually on an island off the coast of Brison-St-Innocent. You can rent a pedal boat or swim out to the island for some sun drenched solitude. Brison-St-Innocent, 5 km north of Aix-les Bains, is itself a worthy destination, surrounded by award winning wineries in view of the stone beach, volleyball courts and grass area. Plage Municipale in Aix-les-Bains is a commercial spot with waterslides and a large grassy area. Admission is €5. Right next door, Point Plage rents out canoes, sailing boats and other water equipment.

Lakeside park

## Lac d'Aiguebellette

On the road from Chambery to Lyon, Lac d'Aiguebellette is a relatively small lake with its own mountain climate that makes for calm waters almost all year round. This is why the lake is popular for all kinds of rowing regattas. Although there are no sandy spots, the beach near the via Ferrata de la Tete de Cheval is a taste of Lugano, Switzerland, in the Haute Savoy, with a plunging grassy hillside that stretches down to the lake – ideal for scattered sunbathers looking to meditate beside the still waters.

## Lac Nantua

Between Geneva and Bourg-en-Bresse, Lac Nantua is a beautiful small mountain lake with a gorgeous beach on the north shore. The water is deep and refreshing, fed by surrounding mountain streams. Searching out the beach is also as good a reason as any to drive on the breathtaking A40 highway through the Jura Mountains.

# Tours & Sightseeing

## City Tours – In Geneva

### Association des Guides

| | |
|---|---|
| Location → Various · Town Centre | **022 909 70 00** |
| Hours → Various | |
| Web/email → www.agtp.ch (French) | Map Ref → 13-D3 |

Geneva's guide association offers eight different urban walks led by local experts. Walks include tours of the Old Town, parks and residences, Carouge, and the International area. As walks and themes are constantly updated, check the Website for the latest information. Nature walks are also organised for areas outside the city during the non winter months.

### Genève à Pied (Geneva on Foot)

| | |
|---|---|
| Location → Various | **022 331 41 33** |
| Hours → Various | |
| Web/email → www.ville-ge.ch/plan-pietons | Map Ref → na |

The Planning Office of the City of Geneva offers eight free do it yourself pedestrian plans that map various routes of interest throughout the city. The maps are available at all tourist offices and provide detailed information about different neighbourhoods, which you can explore at your own pace. Most walks are designed to last around three hours and are very detailed identifying many key historical sites. Some of the monuments identified, can be a bit tedious for non history buffs, such as the site of the first Swiss television tower. The walks are, nonetheless, a wonderful way to rediscover the city, especially for long time residents who might think they know all there is to know about Geneva.

### Geneva Tourism Services

Location ➔ Pont de la Machine · St-Gervais    **022 909 70 00**
Hours ➔ See below
Web/email ➔ www.geneve-tourisme.ch    Map Ref ➔ 13-D2

Geneva Tourism can help you coordinate just about any tour that is offered in the city. In addition, they offer their own regular walking tours led by official guides. The 'Morning Ramble through Geneva's Old Town' departs at 10:00 from the tourist office at Pont de la Machine every Saturday throughout the year, and from Monday to Saturday from mid June to September. The tour explores the little known nooks and crannies of the Old Town and ends with a glass of local wine. The 'Geneva History and Legends' tour is filled with lively anecdotes about Geneva's most famous sites and inhabitants. The tour departs at 18:30 from the Pont de la Machine on Tuesdays and Thursdays, from June to September. The price per person for each tour is SFr 12 for adults, SFr 8 for students and seniors, and SFr 6 for children below 14. The tourist office can also organise walking tours on request, with themes such as 'Historic Geneva', 'Jean Calvin and Protestant Rome', 'Henry Dunant and the Red Cross' and 'An Introduction to Geneva's Museums'. Contact the office for individual and group rates. For those who wish to take their time, Geneva Tourism hires out headsets with an audio guided tour of the Old Town which are available for SFr 10, and a deposit of SFr 50. The walking tour lasts around two and a half hours, and covers 26 monuments and points of interest throughout historic Old Town.

*Timings: Mon 13:00 – 18:00; Tue – Fri 09:00 – 18:00; Sat 10:00 – 17:00; Closed Sun*

### Keytours SA

Location ➔ Rue de Alpes · Pâquis    **022 731 41 40**
Hours ➔ Various
Web/email ➔ www.keytours.ch    Map Ref ➔ 13-D2

Keytours is the primary excursion company for tours outside Geneva, and offers several inner city

bus tours as well. The main city tour offers a great overview of the city which includes the lakefront, the Old Town, the international district and several lakeside residences and parks. Part of the tour is via mini train along the lakefront and through the Old Town. In December, the tour ends at Fusterie Place for a stop at the International Christmas Market. Another popular tour is the combination, city and countryside tour. In addition to the city, this tour also explores the rolling hills, farms and vineyards just outside of it. The tour stops at several estates and castles, so tourists can snap photos of Geneva's romantic surroundings. Tours run daily and range from SFr 35 to SFr 68.

Geneva Tourism Services

### Mairie de Carouge

Location ➔ Pl. du Marche 14 · Carouge    **022 307 89 87**
Hours ➔ Various
Web/email ➔ www.illico-travel.ch/en/index.html    Map Ref ➔ 15-C4

Get an insider's view into the wonderful artisan world of Carouge. Tours are offered at weekends, and centre on themes such as 'Hidden Gardens', 'Legends of our Streets', and 'Craftsmen and Artists'. Tours last approximately one hour and 15 minutes, and cost SFr 10 (adults) and SFr 5 (students and children). The tours are run by Illico Business and Travel Company, which also offers year round flexible tours designed around your own particular interest, be it chocolate, feminism, literature or theatre.

## Mini-Train Tours

Location ➔ Quai Gustave Ador · Town Centre | **022 735 43 00**
Hours ➔ Various
Web/email ➔ www.lescorsaires.ch          Map Ref ➔ 13-E3

In competition with STT, Les Corsaires mini trains depart every 45 minutes from the Jardin Anglais near the Mont-Blanc bridge, and travel along the Left Bank to sites such as Parc La Grange, the Royal House and the Monument of Port Noir. Since the trains are solar powered you can ride with a clear conscience, knowing that you are helping to reduce pollution around the harbour. Rides cost SFr 7, SFr 6 and SFr 4 for adults, students and children respectively. The duration of the tour is half an hour and commentary is offered in multiple languages by a friendly voice recorded tour guide.

## STT Train Tours

Location ➔ Bd. St-Georges 36 · Les Savoises | **022 781 04 04**
Hours ➔ Daily from March – October
Web/email ➔ www.wwsa.ch          Map Ref ➔ 13-B4

STT runs three train tours. 'The Old Town' tour departs from Place du Rhône from May to October, and runs in a circuit around all the major attractions in Old Town, from Place Neuve to Saint Pierre Cathedral. The fare is SFr 8.90 for adults and SFr 5.90 for children. The 'Pâquis Express' train is a curious amusement to locals but still the best way to gain an overview of the major sites. This tour leaves every 45 minutes from Quai du Mont-Blanc on the Right Bank. Tickets cost SFr 7.90 for adults and SFr 4.90 for children. Finally, the 'Trans Eaux-Viviens' tour leaves every 45 minutes from the Jardin Anglais and explores the parks and residences of the Left Bank (SFr 7 for adults and SFr 4 for children). Special group rates are available for all tours. Tours last approximately 35 minutes and include a free brochure.

## City Tours – Out of Geneva

The Gare Routière Bus Station (at Rue de Alpes, 7 in the Square du Mont-Blanc) is the starting point for almost any excursion outside Geneva. The tours, organised by Geneva Tourism, are designed for comfort and convenience. Many of the tours are seasonal, but all offer the opportunity to sit back, relax and enjoy the view while you let someone else do the driving. See list below for more details.

## Chamonix/Mont-Blanc

Don't forget your passport for this day trip to the town of Chamonix at the foot of Mont-Blanc, the tallest mountain in Europe. The day starts at 08:30 with a 90 minute drive through the Arve Valley before arriving in Chamonix. From Chamonix, visitors may elect to ride the two stage cable car to the top of the Aiguille du Midi, providing superb views of the Chamonix Valley from 3,842 metres. Alternatively, hop on an electric rack railway to Nontenvers for a gander at the Mer de Glace glacier, measuring 7 km long by 1,200 metres wide. Nontenvers also has an ice cave, a crystal gallery and the Alpine Fauna Museum.

To infinity...and beyond!

## Diablerets/Gstaad/Gruyères

The tour begins with a drive along Lac Léman and passes through Col du Pillon before embarking on a cable car ride up to the Diablerets glacier. At the top, visitors can take a coffee break at the panoramic restaurant designed by Mario Botta or, for an additional SFr 19, go for a dog sled ride (summer only). Powered by ten Huskies, the sleds travel over the flat Tsafleuron glacier at an altitude of 3,000 metres. The return bus trip cruises through the lush Saanenland region and stops in the village of Gruyères for a cheese break!

## Grand Alpine Tour

The Grand Alpine tour heads out at 13:00 for a similar, abbreviated trip to Chamonix, followed by a return trip through the Col de la Forclaz, providing photo opportunity views of the lake.

# hello, salut, مرحبا, salve, hola, こんにちわ, comdia, grüezi ...

## Geneva, Where People Meet

An international crossroads with easy and rapid access by plane, train or car.

Hotel facilities comprising over 14,000 beds, from country inns to luxurious hotels on the lakefront.

World center for debate and conferences, seat of international organizations. Visit the United Nations Building.

Culture and art on a daily basis: museums, the Old Town, a wealth of history. Shopping, watches and jewelry.

Many excursions in the region: the mediaeval town of Gruyères, Zermatt and the Matterhorn, Chamonix and the Mont-Blanc.

Events and entertainment. The Geneva Festival with its fireworks and a wide range of concerts to suit all tastes.

In the heart of Europe, nestled between the Alps and the Jura, hugging the shores of its lake, Geneva is a year-round holiday destination, blending culture and the arts, entertainment and sports. Whatever the length of your stay, Geneva, far much more than a city, looks forward to your visit.

Geneva Tourism
18, rue du Mont-Blanc
P.O. Box 1602
CH - 1211 Geneva 1
Switzerland
Tel.: +41 22 909 70 00
Fax: +41 22 909 70 11
info@geneva-tourism.ch
www.geneva-tourism.ch

## Travel Agencies

| | |
|---|---|
| **All Travel SA** | 022 798 77 22 |
| Ch. De la Tourelle, 6 | |
| **BC Business Class** | 022 818 00 40 |
| Grand-Rue, 23 | |
| **BTA Travel SA** | 022 800 00 44 |
| Bd. Georges-Favon, 8 | |
| **BTI Kuoni Switzerland Kuoni Voyages** | 022 929 90 00 |
| Rte de Pré-Bois, 20 | |
| **Byzance Travel & Tours Sàrl** | 022 705 11 80 |
| Rue Dancet, 2 | |
| **Railtour Suisse** | 022 732 71 32 |
| Pl. de Cornavin, 7 | |
| **SST Voyages** | 022 818 63 18 |
| Quai Général-Guisan, 10 | |
| **Travelling 2000 SA** | 022 339 88 00 |
| Av. D'Aïre 93A | |
| **Wasteels Voyages SA** | 022 906 76 86 |
| Rue de Lausanne, 42 | |
| **WTA World Travel Agency SA** | 022 741 14 82 |
| Quai du Mont-Blanc, 19 | |

## Gruyères/Lavaux

If you've visited or lived in Geneva, but feel you haven't yet had a real Swiss experience, then this tour has cheese, cowbells, castles and plenty of fresh air. The tour travels to the alpine countryside of Gruyères and Lavaux, both known for their chaste beauty and breathtaking mountain views. Tours depart in the afternoon for SFr 128 per person.

## Lausanne/Montreux/Chillon

This full day, fair weather tour begins with a drive and orientation of the town of Lausanne, home to the Olympic Museum and one of the most beautiful lakeside promenades in the area. In the afternoon the tour moves to Switzerland's most famous castle, the Château de Chillon, for a guided tour. Before heading home there are stops in ritzy Montreux for some shopping and refreshments. Half day tours of (only) Chillon and Montreux are also available – a popular option in December when the Montreux Christmas market is in full swing. Half day tours depart at 1300. Tours run at SFr 128 (full day) and SFr 98 (half day) for adults.

## Bicycle Tours

Geneva is a bike friendly town. Bicycles, in fact, used to be freely available at various points around the city as a form of public transport. Although that service disappeared after bikes started disappearing off the streets, you can still rent or ride for free (with a deposit) on an advertisement laced cruiser, or alternatively, shell out for a newer model. Cycling is also an excellent way to explore the regions around the lake. You can travel on a traffic free bike path along the lake all the way to the French border. If you're really adventurous, you can circumnavigate the lake in a day or two.

### Gare Cornavin

| | |
|---|---|
| Location ➜ Gare Cornavin Luggage Office | **051 225 14 82** |
| Hours ➜ Various | |
| Web/email ➜ na | Map Ref ➜ 13-D2 |

Conveniently located, if you don't have a lot of time to check out the city. One day rentals cost SFr 22. The shop also has recommended itinerary tours for the Geneva neophyte.

### Genèv'Roule

| | |
|---|---|
| Location ➜ Pl. de Montbrillant, 17 · Les Grottes | **022 752 38 09** |
| Hours ➜ Open only from 2ndMay – 31st October | |
| Web/email ➜ www.geneveroule.ch | Map Ref ➜ 13-C2 |

Operated entirely by refugees, this friendly company offers free bikes for a deposit of SFr 50 and a valid proof of identity. You can also hire tandem bikes and other performance bikes for SFr 7 per day. The company operates from four branches around Geneva, and it is worth checking the Website regularly as opening times vary during the winter months.

### Horizon Motos

| | |
|---|---|
| Location ➜ Rue des Pâquis 22 · Pâquis | **022 732 29 90** |
| Hours ➜ Various | |
| Web/email ➜ na | Map Ref ➜ 13-E1 |

Located next to Hot Point bike shop, scooters and motorbikes are available at hourly and daily rates.

### Hot Point

| | |
|---|---|
| Location ➜ Rue de Pâquis 22 · Pâquis | **022 738 36 96** |
| Hours ➜ Various | |
| Web/email ➜ na | Map Ref ➜ 13-E1 |

Housing a sharp selection of mountain and road bikes, this is the company to go with if you want more than a leisurely glide through the city. Bike accessories and other gear are available for purchase. An experienced staff member can also advise you on where to head if you're looking for a weekend getaway to the mountains or countryside.

## Lake Cruises

No Geneva experience is complete without taking to the water on one of Europe's largest lakes. The protected shores of Lac Lèman offer smooth sailing almost year round with a plethora of options designed for anyone, from the salty sailor to the weekend booze cruiser. The cruises offer a unique perspective on Geneva and its surrounding countryside, as well as the chance to enjoy a relaxing time and wave to frolicking sailing boats as they bob in your wake.

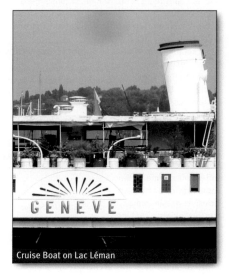
Cruise Boat on Lac Léman

### CGN Boat Company

| | |
|---|---|
| Location → Jardin Anglais · Town Centre | 022 312 52 25 |
| Hours → Various | |
| Web/email → www.cgn.ch | Map Ref → 13-E3 |

As Geneva's largest boat company, CGN has a veritable blockade on the cruising market, but with good reason. In terms of passenger capacity, the company maintains the largest fleet of paddle wheel 'Belle Epoque' vessels in the world, some of which are over 120 years old. The boats depart from four convenient departure points around the lake (Eaux-Vives, Pâquis, Jardin Anglais and Mont-Blanc). The company offers a variety of tours and programmes throughout the spring and summer months. These tours are ideal for day trips, especially to other lakefront destinations, including Hermance, Nyon, Yvoire, Thonon, Evian, Lausanne-Ouchy, Montreux and Château de

Chillon. Or you can take a cruise all the way around the Petit Lac. The most popular one is the 'Beautiful Shores of Geneva' cruise (adults, SFr 12; children, SFr 6), which departs seven times a day, paddling past major lakeside sights and providing commentary. Along with day cruises, CGN offers romantic evening, sunset and dance cruises with prime views of shoreline city lights and winking stars above – quite a lethal combination for burgeoning couples and old flames alike. Themed cruises are offered during the holidays and private cruises are available for parties from 30 to 500 people. For reservations call +41 0848 822 848

### Mouettes Genevoises

| | |
|---|---|
| Location → 8 Quai du Mont-Blanc | 022 732 29 44 |
| Hours → 07:30 – 18:00 | |
| Web/email → na | Map Ref → 13-E2 |

The cheapest and easiest way to get a water view is to take the ferry that runs between the Right and Left Banks. As part of the city transportation service (TPG), you can enjoy a ride across the city's main waterway on one of the shuttles for the price of a bus ticket. Although not ideal for those prone to seasickness, the boats are nevertheless very convenient, departing every ten minutes from five different locations around the harbour (see below). The route between Quai du Mont-Blanc and Quai Gustave Ador offers dramatic views of the Jet d'Eau that range from refreshing to soaking, depending on the direction of the wind.

***Departure Points:***

- Mouettes Genevoises
- Quai du Mont-Blanc in front of the Grand Casino
- Molard, Quai Gustave Ador
- Perle du Lac
- Parc des Eaux-Vives

### Rhône Cruises

| | |
|---|---|
| Location → Pl. de l'Ile · Town Centre | 022 732 29 44 |
| Hours → 10:00 Departure | |
| Web/email → www.swissboat.com | Map Ref → 13-D3 |

From April to October, MGN runs an unparalleled cruise down the Rhône River (one of Europe's longest at 812 km). Tickets are sold on board at the departure point (Quai des Moulins de l'Ile) an hour and a half before the cruise. Tickets can also be picked up from the MGN office in front of the Noga Hilton Hotel, 8 Quai du Mont-Blanc. Reservations are recommended as seating is limited. The cruise lasts for two hours and 45 minutes, travelling to the Verbois dam and back. Along the way you can see stunning cliffs, landscapes and mountain views. What will truly amaze you are the quaint villages, wildlife and lush flora that deck the riverbanks as soon as you pass Jonction. The price for this highly recommended cruise is SFr 22 (adult) and SFr 15 (child).

| Swiss Boat | |
|---|---|
| Location ➜ 8 Quai du Mont-Blanc | 022 732 47 47 |
| Hours ➜ Various | |
| Web/email ➜ www.swissboat.com | Map Ref ➜ 13-E2 |

Swiss Boat is designed for the tourist interested in learning a bit of history whilst cruising on the waters. Departures from Quai 7, near the Brunswick Monument, cruise by castles and famous mansions of past and current celebrities. One hour 'Mermaid' cruises and two hour 'Castle' cruises are offered at SFr 12 and SFr 20 respectively. Cruises departing from the Jardin Anglais explore the southern lakeside mansions and parks, and cost SFr 8 for 40 minutes. In addition, the company has five sail and motor boats for rent that can accommodate 30 to 100 people for a private party or event.

## Helicopter & Plane Tours

| Evolution 2 | |
|---|---|
| Location ➜ Tignes and Val d'Isère | na |
| Hours ➜ Various | |
| Web/email ➜ www.evolution2.com | Map Ref ➜ na |

For a taste of the air, Evolution 2 offers five minute discovery flights from Tignes or Val d'Isère for €30 (SFr 46.3). 35 minute flights over the Mont-Blanc are available for €195. The company also runs a light motorised mountain plane over the Mont-Blanc and la Sassière. These flights allow you to sit in the cockpit next to the pilot and marvel at the peaks below. Flights last 45 minutes and are subject to weather conditions.

| Swift Copters | |
|---|---|
| Location ➜ Geneva International Airport | 022 717 83 83 |
| Hours ➜ Various | |
| Web/email ➜ www.swiftcopters.ch | Map Ref ➜ 5-A1 |

Tour in style in your own private helicopter with Swift Copters. The company operates a fleet of ten helicopters from Geneva airport that are available for charter tours, heli-skiing, transport or, for executives tired of limousines, just to beat the traffic. Though flights cost a small fortune, you will be travelling in luxury with first class service and unforgettable views. Copter's experienced pilots know the terrain like the back of their hands and can offer many excellent itinerary recommendations.

## Ski Bus Tours

Other options ➜ Skiing [p.195]

From the Gare Routière Bus Station, ski buses depart every Saturday and Sunday during the earlier weeks of December, and daily after Christmas. The bus ticket includes a full day lift ticket to such world class destinations as Avoriaz, Chamonix, Diablerets, Les Houches, Contamines, Clusaz and Les Gets. Make sure to check with the bus station beforehand, as schedules vary according to holidays, resort openings and driving time. Ski buses provide an ideal all inclusive, hassle free day of skiing or snowboarding. The buses have a friendly atmosphere and riders often end up spending an après ski drink together. Don't forget to appreciate the scenery from your bus window either.

> **The Men in Green Jackets**
>
> *It has been said that two things are free in Geneva - newspapers and buses. This is not exactly true, as both operate on the honour system. If you do decide to take a free ride however, keep your eyes open for the 'Men in Green Jackets' who randomly board buses to check tickets. Once the door's shut, it's too late.*

## Wine Tours

Other options ➜ Alcohol [p.136]

Geneva may not be the wine capital of the world but the old canton has definitely picked up a thing or two from neighbouring France. The wine growing region on Geneva's Right Bank is the largest in Switzerland. In total, Geneva vineyards produce 13.5 million litres of wine per year. The region is perhaps best known for its white wines, but actually produces a healthy variety of guaranteed vintages from Cabernet Sauvignon to Gamay. All the vineyards around Geneva offer wine tasting and occasional events. Below are some recommended tours of wineries just outside of town. For a full list of wineries and calendar of events in the area, you can also log on to www.wine.ch/index.htm.

Pick up a bottle or two...

## La Route du Vignoble

Location → Dardagny to Lausanne  |  021 825 11 41
Hours → na
Web/email → www.routeduvignoble.ch  |  Map Ref → na

The 'Road of the Vineyard' actually runs from Dardagny, near Meyrin, all the way to Lausanne along a meandering path that winds through some of Geneva's most beautiful countryside. The road was funded by a group of over forty vineyards and country inns that came together to promote tourism and local products. The road is well marked and suitable for bikes or walking. One recommended section runs through Bourdigny to Choully, Peissy, and Russin before ending up at Dardagny.

## Parcours Dardagny

Location → Dardagny · Nr. Meyrin  |  022 746 00 18
Hours → Various
Web/email → www.balade-viticole.com  |  Map Ref → na

This is a 7 km jaunt through Geneva's wine growing history. The course is marked with signs explaining the different vines and wines. These are interspersed with quotes, history and other information about the natural bounties of the region, and the wine making process that has evolved in Geneva since Roman times. The project is the brainchild of Stephane Gros, an impassioned wine grower, who designed the course to educate and encourage new connoisseurs. Tasting is available at the main house, as are guided walks which need to be booked in advance. Highly recommended and admission is free.

## Out of the City

Other options → Weekend Breaks [p.131]

Geneva's prime location makes it an ideal base to explore the surrounding areas. The lake region is a treasure trove of lakefront promenades, each with its own take on what a mountain lakeside paradise should be. To the north are the Jura Mountains filled with lush forests and healing hot springs. Immediately south is the Haute Savoie region with its snow capped peaks, rich valleys and quaint villages.

Getting around by car is easy, although lakeside traffic in the summertime can be horrendous. The motorways in France are fast but tolls and petrol are very expensive. The mountain roads are generally in excellent condition, however, map reading can be a challenging sport, testing even the most convivial relationships. The best strategy is to follow the signs for the next town on the path towards your final destination. Even if you are lost though, chances are that you'll find something unique and memorable.

If you don't have a car, no worries. Most destinations are easily accessible by bike, city bus, train or ferry. If you plan on doing a lot of travelling it may be worth purchasing a 'Demi Tariff' card at one of the train stations, to get the best ticket deals.

Accommodation can be fairly expensive if you plan to stay overnight. Fortunately, camping around Geneva is fairly prevalent, especially in the national parks to south, where camping grounds have all the necessary amenities. Another good option is to stay in a local guesthouse; the proprietors are generally friendly and eager to share a bit of the local history or customs.

## Aix-Les-Bains

Aix-Les-Bains is a spa town situated at Lake Bourget – the largest natural lake in France. The sulphur and alum springs have been a draw since Roman times, and the Victorian village is filled with interesting Belle Epoque architecture, most notably the casino in the town centre. The town is a great base for exploring the surrounding area. Mount Revard, just behind the town, has several hiking trails, including the 'Balcons du Bourget' trail that leads to the Bourget Balcony overlooking the lake. The lake itself is surrounded by beautiful beaches, of which the most prized is the 'Plage Blanche' — a white sand beach on an island in the middle of the lake that can only be reached by boat or by swimming across. Other sites around the lake include the Martine Caves, the Abbey de Hautecombe, and the Castle of Bordeau. A good time to visit is in August during the Navigaix Celebration, featuring the largest collection of retro boats in the area. Check out www.aix-les-bains.com for specific dates.

## Annecy

Annecy, 35 km south of Geneva, is one of the most romantic cities in all of France. The resort town is situated at the north end of Lake d'Annecy along the Canal de Vasse. Annecy is commonly referred to as the 'Venice of Savoie' for the canals that run through the Old Town, although the waters are crystal turquoise blue even in the middle of the city. The Old Town is filled with cosy eateries situated alongside the canal, and there are a number of important historical sites, including the Palais de l'Isle, an old boat shaped prison situated in the heart of the Old Town. Also located there is the Renaissance inspired Saint Pierre Cathedral as well as the Museum of the Savoyard, housed in a 19th century Sardinian building, which contains costumes from the period when villages were characterised by their individual styles of dress.

What's a celebration without fireworks?

Sitting on the hill and overlooking the city is the remarkable Annecy castle, visible like a

lighthouse from every part of town. Below the castle, on the outskirts of town, is the flourishing Imperial Palace Hotel, once the seat of the Duke of Savoie. The most popular attraction in Annecy however, is the lake itself. The city surrounds the lake on three sides and is replete with lakeside promenades, beaches and activity centres. The beaches and adjoining hotels are packed all summer long so booking in advance is advisable. For details, check out http://ava.univ-savoie.fr/english/INFO_ANNECY/visite.html.

## Le Mont-Pèlerin

Le Mont-Pèlerin, just outside Lausanne, is a rural community set amongst sloping vineyards. What makes Le Mont-Pèlerin truly unique is that it is home to the Rabten Choeling Monastery — the largest Tibetan monastery in the Western hemisphere. This bright yellow and orange compound was founded by Rabten Rinpoche who escaped the Tibetan uprising against the Chinese, before being asked by the Dalai Lama to teach Buddhism to Europeans. The monastery is home to some 30 monks and 30 lay students, and is open to visitors. Weekend seminars and lectures are frequently conducted for those curious about Buddhism. For more information, log on to www.rabten.com.

> **Travelling in Switzerland**
>
> *Switzerland has the most hotels per capita in Europe. That doesn't mean that you shouldn't book ahead of time however, especially if you plan on visiting one of the mountaintop hostels or ski resorts. Hotels can be expensive, so check out one of the local auberges or family owned inns for a more affordable option.*

## Yvoire

Founded in 1306, Yvoire is a medieval city situated where Lac Léman turns from le Petit Lac into le Grand Lac. This city is perhaps the best preserved example of medieval architecture in the lake region. Lush with flowers throughout the year, there is also a beautiful port that is best approached from the water by ferry. Yvoire is also the site of the Garden of the Five Senses. This delectable labyrinth is the former garden of the Yvoire Castle and filled with hidden delights and vegetation that change with the seasons. The garden is open daily 10:00 to 19:00, from May to mid-September for €8 per person.

## Weekend Breaks

Geneva is a top vacation destination, not just because the city itself is amazing, but also because of its access to other resort locations in the Alps and beyond. The Swiss rail system is one of the most extensive in the world, making for an easy getaway to a quiet mountain town, or even to big cities, such as Paris and Milan, both just three hours away by train. If you are a resident or are planning an extensive tour, be sure to take advantage of the half tariff card and other discounts. Also keep in mind that weekends are sacred in Switzerland, so make reservations beforehand and be prepared to fight the crowds.

Once you escape the city, your options are limitless. The area surrounding Lac Lèman outside

Geneva is filled with lakeside resorts, vineyards, luxury spas and country estates. The Haute Savoie to the south contains over a hundred ski resorts within two hours' drive (Swiss children go to school on Saturdays, so that's generally the best day to go). To the east, the wonders of Switzerland unfold with inspiring peaks surrounded by lakes, farms and lush valleys. The best way to visit these nooks and crannies is on foot via the excellent trail system (you may have to step aside for a cow or two). Remember that the best places are not always in the brochures, so don't be afraid to bed down in a local auberge or family inn to experience the surprising hospitality of the German-Swiss.

For a list of places to stay, with a range of activities, prices and unique characteristics, check out the Weekend Break table [p.131].

d'Ile Rousseau

## Weekend Break Summary

| Area | Hotel | Phone | Email/Website | Rate |
|---|---|---|---|---|
| **Basel** (2 hrs) | The Art Hotel | 061 261 1010 | www.teufelkof.com | SFr 125+ |
| **Fribourg** (1 hr 30 min) | Auberge aux 4 Vents | 026 347 3600 | auberge@au4veents.ch | SFr 50-240 |
| **Gstaad** (1 hr 30 min) | Hotel Bernerhof | 033 748 8844 | www.gstaad.ch/bernerhof | SFr 250+ |
| **Kandersteg** (2 hrs 40 min) | Reudihus Hotel | 033 675 8181 | www.doldenhorn-reudihus.ch | SFr 220+ |
| **Lausanne** (45 min by train) | Beau-Rivage Palace | 021 613 3333 | www.brp.ch | SFr 250+ |
| **Lugano** (4 hrs) | Hotel du Lac | 091 986 4747 | www.dulac.ch | SFr 336-550 |
| **Montreux** (1 hr) | Montreux Palace | 021 962 1212 | www.montreux-palace.com | SFr 200+ |
| **Nyon** (30 min) | Hotel Beau-Rivage | 022 365 4141 | www.hotel-beau-rivage-nyon.ch | SFr 240+ |
| **Vevey** (30 min) | Hotel des Negociants | 021 922 7011 | www.hotelnegociants.ch | SFr 140-166 |
| **Verbier** (2 hrs) | Golf Hotel | 027 771 6515 | www.verbier.ch | SFr 180-410 |

| France | | | | |
|---|---|---|---|---|
| **Annecy** (1 hr) | Demeure de Chavoire | 33 450600438 | www.demeuredechavoire.com | € 135-265 |
| **Evian** (1 hr) | Hotel Oasis | 33 450751338 | www.oasis-hotel.com | € 50+ |
| **Les Hauteluce Savoie** (1 hr) | La Ferme du Chozal | 33 479381818 | www.lafermeduchozal.com | € 70-135 |
| **Meribel** (3 hrs) | Le Grand Coeur | 33 479086003 | www.legrandcoeur.com | SFr 230+ |
| **Megève** (1 hr) | Le Fer a Cheval | 33 450213039 | www.feracheval-megeve.com | € 128-242 |
| **Praz de Chamonix** (50 min) | Eden Hotel | 33 450531843 | www.hoteleden-chamonix.com | € 86+ |
| **St Rémy-de-Province** (3 hrs) | Mas de Cornud | 33 490923932 | mascornud@compuserve.com | € 70+ |

Exploring

Weekend Breaks

*a touch of elegance
and sensuality...*

FELINES

# Shopping

**EXPLORER**

# Shopping

## MUST GO

Across the border! It's not as extreme as it sounds – the French towns of Annemasse and Ferney Voltaire are just short drives from Geneva, and are packed with shops and supermarkets. You'll probably find that the prices in France are significantly cheaper than they are in Geneva, so you can load up your car with goodies. Just don't go over the import limits set by the Swiss customs officials, and if you do, don't get caught!

## MUST DO

Shopping in Geneva's many open air markets is a definite must for any dedicated shopper. Not only can you buy almost everything at the markets, from fresh produce to second-hand items, but the friendly atmosphere and relaxed, open air setting is (quite literally) a breath of fresh air! See [p.163] for a listing of open air markets in Geneva and its surrounding areas.

## Clothing Sizes

| Women's Clothing | | | | | | | Women's Shoes | | | | | | |
| --- | --- | --- | --- | --- | --- | --- | --- | --- | --- | --- | --- | --- | --- |
| Aust/NZ | 8 | 10 | 12 | 14 | 16 | 18 | Aust/NZ | 5 | 6 | 7 | 8 | 9 | 10 |
| Europe | 36 | 38 | 40 | 42 | 44 | 46 | Europe | 35 | 36 | 37 | 38 | 39 | 40 |
| Japan | 5 | 7 | 9 | 11 | 13 | 15 | France only | 35 | 36 | 38 | 39 | 40 | 42 |
| UK | 8 | 10 | 12 | 14 | 16 | 18 | Japan | 22 | 23 | 24 | 25 | 26 | 27 |
| USA | 6 | 8 | 10 | 12 | 14 | 16 | UK | 3.5 | 4.5 | 5.5 | 6.5 | 7.5 | 8.5 |
| | | | | | | | USA | 5 | 6 | 7 | 8 | 9 | 10 |

| Men's Clothing | | | | | | | Men's Shoes | | | | | | |
| --- | --- | --- | --- | --- | --- | --- | --- | --- | --- | --- | --- | --- | --- |
| Aust/NZ | 92 | 96 | 100 | 104 | 108 | 112 | Aust/NZ | 7 | 8 | 9 | 10 | 11 | 12 |
| Europe | 46 | 48 | 50 | 52 | 54 | 56 | Europe | 41 | 42 | 43 | 44.5 | 46 | 47 |
| Japan | S | - | M | M | - | L | Japan | 26 | 27 | 27.5 | 28 | 29 | 30 |
| UK | 35 | 36 | 37 | 38 | 39 | 40 | UK | 7 | 8 | 9 | 10 | 11 | 12 |
| USA | 35 | 36 | 37 | 38 | 39 | 40 | USA | 7.5 | 8.5 | 9.5 | 10.5 | 11.5 | 12.5 |

Measurements are approximate only; try before you buy

Table of Contents

Shopping

## Shopping

The shopping in Geneva is fabulous, although as it is a little on the expensive side you'll need plenty of cash in your pocket or space on your credit card. The multicultural society is mirrored in the broad range of items on sale, from rice cookers to rose bushes, antique jewels to world famous Swiss watches.

You can buy most of the same products that you can get back home, but the Geneva shopping scene does have its own unique quirks. For example, shopping malls are generally not the best place to shop, as many of them are rather bland and dreary inside (unlike the glitzy, gleaming malls you may be used to in your home country). However, you may find them handy on some occasions, mainly because they are climate controlled and have lots of parking space. Shopping purists will probably enjoy the Geneva street shopping a lot more. There are shops on most of the main streets. In Carouge, Pâquis and on Rue de Rhône, you'll find the more modern outlets, while the cobbled streets of the Old Town offer quaint stores in old buildings. Independent shops are still popular in Geneva, specialising in everything from art and antiques to kitchen gadgets and clothing. Or if you prefer shops that cover all bases, there are quite a few department stores that stock just about everything (many even have large grocery and speciality food stores).

Although the prices of many items may raise your eyebrows, there are also many ways to bag a bargain. Many shopping areas now feature discount stores ('solderie') selling last year's fashions at rock bottom prices. There are also several second-hand clothing shops. Then there are always the sales, which usually take place at the end of each season. Bargains are frequently found in the open air markets, and most community noticeboards list various items for sale by members of the public. WRG 88.4 FM has a Friday morning radio show called 'Garage Sale', where some real bargains can be found.

One of the major benefits of living in Geneva is that you can pop over the border to France and take advantage of cheaper shopping! The French border communities of Annemasse and Ferney Voltaire are crammed with shops, especially supermarkets, which offer goods at significantly lower prices than in Geneva.

Tram Street

### Refunds & Exchanges

Swiss refund and exchange policies are fair, and you'll have little trouble returning an unused item that you bought at full price and that you have a receipt for. The only thing you should watch out for is return time limits – some shops only accept returned items within ten days of purchase, while others give you up to 30 days to return something. Some of the smaller stores may enforce a 'exchange only' policy, so rather than a cash refund, you'll get a credit note.

If you buy an item that turns out to be faulty, you'll find the shopkeepers very helpful and accommodating. If you have a receipt, then you can get a cash refund on a faulty item, no questions asked. Even if you don't have a receipt, you'll usually get a replacement item. This applies even to perishable items, such as food or flowers, if they spoil before their expiry date.

### Consumer Rights

The federal constitution protects the rights of the consumer in Switzerland, but if you have a bad shopping experience, it is unlikely you will need to resort to legal battles. In general, Swiss shopkeepers know that the best way to keep your business is to treat you fairly and with respect, so you can look forward to good service wherever you go.

If you have any questions about a shopping experience you've had, there is a group called La Fédération Romande des Consommateurs (www.frc.ch) that provides a telephone service to answer all of your queries on consumer rights. You can call them on 0900 575 105 (Mon-Fri 09:00 – 12:30 and 13:30 – 17:00), but note that the charge for this service is SFr 2.13 per minute. Alternatively, you can email your question to permanence@frc.ch. For more details on this organisation, see their magazine *J'achète Mieux* (JAM). Other magazines highlighting various consumer rights issues are *K-Tipp* (German) and *Bon à Savoir* (French).

## Shipping

Shipping is fairly expensive. For small parcels, use any of the worldwide shipping and mailing services like DHL (www.dhl.com), FedEx (www.fedex.com) or UPS (www.ups.com). Or you can use the trusty post office, which has branches all around the town. They offer shipping at relatively economical prices for packages of up to 30 kg (for example, a 20 kg package to the UK will cost you SFr 76).

For larger items, such as furniture or cars, there are numerous moving and shipping companies who can provide a high quality shipping service (at a price!). Prices vary according to the service you require, so your quote will depend on whether you need land, ocean or air shipping, door to door, overnight or economy delivery. Refer to Moving Services in the New Residents chapter [p.63] for a list of Websites for major removal companies.

When purchasing something that you plan to have shipped, ask the shop whether they have a preferred shipping agent, as sometimes this means a reduced rate.

## How to Pay

Switzerland still has its own currency, the Swiss Franc. Although it is not part of the EU, some larger establishments may accept Euros as payment, but your change will most likely be in local currency. The smaller speciality stores, cafés and restaurants will not accept Euros, and in some cases they don't have credit card facilities, so it is always a good idea to have a nice big wad of Swiss Francs in your wallet.

You'll find ATMs in banks, major shopping malls and on high streets. It is advisable to check with your bank at home regarding which Geneva ATMs will accept your card. Money exchanges are located at various points throughout the city, at train stations and the airport. The Swiss Franc is very stable, and exchange rates are quite comparable.

## Bargaining

Trying to knock down the price of your daily purchases will probably get you nothing but a rather blank stare from the shop staff. Prices for goods are clearly marked and include sales tax, and that is what you are expected to pay.

However, you can flex your bargaining muscles when buying larger items, such as jewellery, carpets, art or cars. You can also try out your negotiating skills on private sellers, including stall owners at open air markets, but try to keep your bargain banter friendly and polite. The price of fresh produce in open air markets is usually not up for negotiation, unless you are there at the end of the day when the vendors are packing up.

## *What & Where to Buy*

While the range of shops available in Geneva is huge, the opening hours may not be as convenient as those you are used to at home. In general, shops open at 09:00 every day, Monday to Saturday. Closing times vary, with most shops closing at 18:00 or 18:30, and some offering late night shopping until 21:00. Some shops close for lunch, and in general all shops are closed on Sundays. Of course, timings may vary slightly from shop to shop, so check the entrance doors for exact hours.

In general, the service you'll get and the quality of items you can buy in Geneva are of a very high standard, but this comes at a price. You may find that to get a cheaper deal, it's better to drive over the border into neighbouring France.

## Alcohol

Other options ➜ Drinks [p.18]

In Geneva you have to be over 16 to buy wine, beer and tobacco, and over 18 to buy spirits. You can buy alcohol anywhere where food is sold, although one of the largest Swiss grocery store chains, Migros, has a strict 'no alcohol, no cigarettes' policy. Migros aside, however, alcohol is available at supermarkets, in the grocery sections of department stores, or from wholesale outlets such as Aligros (great for buying in bulk if you're having a party!). Refer to the Food section [p.136] for location details. There are also several bottle stores throughout the city, as well as small convenience stores that are open late. For top of the range wines and liqueurs, you'll find a better selection at high end wine shops such as La Cité Des Vins. Finally, there is always the option of buying duty free alcohol if you're coming through the airport, although pay attention to prices, as you may not necessarily always find the best deals there.

Why buy a bottle when you can buy a case?

## Alcohol

| | |
|---|---|
| **Haut Prestige Wines** | 022 300 31 11 |
| Rte des Jeunes, 33 bis – Carouge | |
| **La Cité Des Vins.** | 022 732 22 22 |
| Rue de Coutance, 3bis – Town Centre | |
| **Les Caves de l'Aéroport** | 022 818 12 41 |
| Geneva Int. Airport – Cointrin | |
| **Les Caves du Palais de Justice** | 022 311 40 14 |
| Place du Bourg-de-Four, 1 – Town Centre | |
| **Nicolas** | +33-4 50 43 99 16 |
| Ch. de l'Industrie, 21 | |
| **Palais des Bières** | 022 949 77 90 |
| Planète Charmilles | |
| **Retardo** | 022 700 58 70 |
| Ch. Neuf, 4 – Town Centre | |
| **Vins Nicolas Stücki** | 022 840 33 31 |
| no shop, delivery service | |
| **Wicht Caves** | 022 733 36 64 |
| Rue du Grand Pré, 48 | |

## Art

Other options → **Art Galleries [p.112]**

Judging by the staggering number of art galleries in the city, Geneva is home to many art lovers. Some art galleries exhibit pieces with a hefty price tag, although some others are a bit more welcoming to people with more normal financial means. Prices aside, the sheer variety of artistic styles available means that no matter what your tastes, you'll be able to find artwork that is right up your street. The Kashya Hildebrand Gallery showcases some exciting current artists but is neither too extravagant nor conceptual. Galleries La Cité D'art is reasonably priced and represents several artists in different mediums. Galleries Fallet is a bit more thought provoking, while Galerie Cigarini has attractive and realistic paintings and sculptures.

Carouge has many smaller galleries, easily found by exploring the area on foot. Older established art can be found in Galerie Jan Krugier. For European abstract contemporary

## Art

| | |
|---|---|
| **Center of Contemporary Art** | 022 329 18 42 |
| Rue des Vieux Grenadiers, 10 – Town Centre | |
| **Cigarini Galerie** | 022 311 29 33 |
| Rue de la Rôtisserie, 1 – Town Centre | |
| **Edward Mitterrand Galerie** | 022 800 28 48 |
| Rue des Bains, 52 – Town Centre | |
| **Evergreene** | 022 321 37 40 |
| Rue de la Coulouvrenière, 27 – 29 – Town Centre | |
| **Fallet Galleries** | 022 311 42 43 |
| Rue de la Tour-de-boel, 5 – Town Centre | |
| **Galerie Analix Forever** | 022 329 17 09 |
| Rue de l'Arquebuse, 25 – Town Centre | |
| **Ganesh Gallery** | 022 321 75 44 |
| Rue des Vieux-Grenadiers, 2 – Town Centre | |
| **Guy Bärtschi** | 022 310 00 13 |
| Rue Etienne Dumont, 2 – Town Centre | |
| **Jan Krugier Galerie** | 022 310 57 19 |
| Grand-Rue, 29 – 31 – Town Centre | |
| **Kashya Hildebrand** | 022 310 72 32 |
| Rue Etienne Dumont, 5 – Town Centre | |
| **La Cité D'art Galleries** | 022 310 28 48 |
| Grande-Rue, 8 – Town Centre | |
| **La Ligne Droite Galerie** | 022 310 86 60 |
| Rue de Saint-Leger, 28 – Town Centre | |
| **Papiers Gras Galerie** | 022 310 87 77 |
| Place de l'Ile, 1 – Town Centre | |
| **Rosa Turetsky Galleries** | 022 310 31 05 |
| Grand-Rue, 25 – Town Centre | |
| **Skopia** | 022 321 61 61 |
| Rue des Vieux-Grenadiers, 9 – Plainpalais | |
| **Sotheby's** | 022 908 48 00 |
| Quai du Mont-Blanc, 13 – Town Centre | |

**What & Where to Buy**

**Shopping**

art, Alexandre Mottier is a good option, and international abstract contemporary art can be found at Analix Forever, or Skopia. For very current abstract to minimal art, visit Galleries Rosa Turetsky or Guy Bärtschi.

For additional information, pick up *L'Art à Genève* from the Geneva information Centre or from one of the museums [p.114]. This brochure comes out every two months, and lists all the galleries and museums in the city, giving their locations and a brief description of their current exhibits.

## Art Supplies

Other options ➜ Art [p.137]

Art supplies are not always easy to come by in Geneva, despite its love of art. For crafts supplies, you can try any of the large DIY stores, such as Jumbo, the Triple M Migros and M Park, or Balexert. IKEA and some department stores often have a creative ideas section, stocking basic art, sewing and decorating supplies. Paper stores also carry a minimal range of supplies for painters, which may suffice if you're just getting started. For advanced art supplies, contact Boesner (they have a branch located between Bern and Zurich). If they don't have what you need they are happy to order it for you, and if you call them they'll send you a mail order catalogue of vast proportions!

| Art Supplies | |
|---|---|
| **Boesner** | 062 737 21 21 |
| Suhrenmattstr, 31 – Unterentfelden | |
| **Brachard** | 022 817 05 55 |
| Rue de la Corraterie, 10 – Town Centre | |
| **Loretti** | 022 311 50 17 |
| Rue de la Rôtisserie, 4 – Town Centre | |
| **Manfacture** | 022 301 35 85 |
| Rue Ancienne, 56 – Carouge | |
| **Perrier** | 022 736 94 54 |
| Bd. Helvétique , 24 – Town Centre | |

## Beach Wear

Other options ➜ Clothes [p.142]

Even though Geneva has no beach, the locals love spending their summers sunning themselves by the lakeside and swimming in the various public pools around town. However, the winters get rather chilly and there is not much call for bikinis and trunks. So, in summer you'll find beachwear in department stores, supermarkets, clothing stores, lingerie stores and just about every shop in town. But in winter you'll have to hunt much harder for that skimpy two piece, and the speciality beachwear shops should be your first stop.

| Beach Wear | |
|---|---|
| **Kykeion** | 022 786 23 86 |
| Rue des Cordiers, 4 – Town Centre | |
| **Vintage Station** | 022 732 35 53 |
| Rue Charles Cusin, 8 – Town Centre | |

## Bicycles

If you're a cycling enthusiast, you're in the right city. Bicycles are a popular mode of transport here, and most of the streets in Geneva have bike paths. Apart from the practical side of it, biking is also a huge leisure activity. If you log on to www.cycling-in-switzerland.ch, you'll find a comprehensive guide to the many facets of biking in Switzerland. It covers routes that combine trains and bike paths, cycling routes, mountain biking trails, where to rent a bike, club meetings, and includes travel reports from other cyclists. Most importantly, it translates bicycle signposts into English.

### Get a Vignette!

*If you own a bike, you have to display a vignette, renewable every year, which shows you have paid for insurance. These stickers can be purchased at the post office, train station or any Migros outlet. The police are very strict about this and you'll be stuck with an expensive fine if you are caught without your vignette.*

Bicycle shop

SFr 10 ~ € 6

If you're looking for a city bike, you'll find a variety of models in large supermarkets and sports stores. Bicycle shops deal in city, mountain and road bikes – if you're not sure which is the best for you, try a VTT ('Vehicle Tout Terrain'), an all terrain bike that is suitable for trails and paved roads. Don't forget to buy a bicycle lock, and use it! Geneva is a safe place, but if your bike is not locked up, it will get pinched sooner or later. For second-hand bikes, have a look at the Website www.rent-a-bike.ch, which has a link dedicated to these. Some shops also sell used bikes, particularly those that provide bike rentals. Alternatively you can browse around garage sales, check the community bulletin boards or tune into WRG 88.4 FM for a show called 'The Garage Sale' – there is always someone leaving Geneva, and their trusty bicycle, behind.

Serious bikers will find loads of places to offload their money on spandex shorts, lycra shirts, and the latest and greatest road and mountain bikes.

### Images of Geneva

*Breathtaking mountain vistas mirrored in the crystal clear waters of the lake, the cobbled streets of the Old Town contrasted against the bustling modernity of one of the world's business capitals; Geneva is a treasure trove of beautiful views. Images of Geneva is a stunning collection of photographs of both the familiar and undiscovered sights of this remarkable city.*

## Bicycles

| | |
|---|---|
| **BS Bikes** | 022 344 07 30 |
| Rue de Lyon, 21 – Town Centre | |
| **Cycleman** | 022 364 55 00 |
| Av. de Mont-Blanc, 16 – Gland | |
| **Veloland** | +33-4 50 84 11 80 |
| Rue Chantemerle, 2 – Ville-La-Grand, France | |

## Books

Other options → Libraries [p.215]

Curling up with a good book is one of life's simplest luxuries. Thanks to the many international inhabitants, you'll find books in almost any language on Geneva's bookshelves. English books are widely available from the book sections at Manor, Globus and Fnac, as well as at any large bookshop. You'll find technical or computer books at Elipse. Keep in mind that Geneva is pretty small

## Books

| | |
|---|---|
| **Book Worm** | 022 731 87 65 |
| Rue Sismondi, 5 – Town Centre | |
| **Elipse** | 022 909 89 89 |
| Rue Rousseau, 14 – Town Centre | |
| **Espace Voyage – Le Vent des Routes** | 022 800 33 81 |
| Rue des Bains, 50-52 – Town Centre | |
| **Fnac** | 022 979 44 44 |
| Balexert – Geneva | |
| Rue de Rive, 16 – Town Centre | 022 816 12 12 |
| **Les Recyclables** | 022 328 60 44 |
| Rue de Carouge, 53 – Town Centre | |
| **Library in English. The** | 022 732 80 97 |
| Rue de Monthoux, 3 – Town Centre | |
| **Naville** | 022 979 02 02 |
| Balexert – Geneva | |
| **Off the Shelf** | 022 311 10 90 |
| Bd. Georges Favon – Town Centre | |
| **Payot** | 022 731 89 50 |
| Chantepoulet, 5 – Town Centre | |
| **Relay** | 022 818 12 41 |
| Geneva International Airport – Cointrin | |

though, and so are its bookshops – don't expect to find any London or New York style book emporiums with a Starbucks on every floor. But you should be able to find what you're looking for, and if not then that's what the Internet is for!

If you want to borrow rather than buy, there is an English lending library at The Library. Many clubs (like the American International Women's Club) have free book exchanges for members. There is also a good second-hand bookshop called Bookworm.

Art books

The best places to buy magazines are at Naville or Relay – you'll find these at train stations, the airport, city centre and in most commercial areas. They stock a wide range of English magazines, including the high quality *Geneva's English Speaking Magazine* (GEM), which keeps you updated with all the latest news and upcoming events (see www.gem.ch).

## Camera Equipment

Other options → Electronics & Home Appliances [p.144]

It's impossible to ignore the astounding beauty of the Geneva scenery, and of course this means there are hundreds and thousands of camera enthusiasts pointing, clicking and flashing throughout the year. Most department stores and electronics shops sell entry-level cameras, both SLR and digital, and film is available almost anywhere, including grocery stores. Serious photographers will find a better range at Photo Hall, Photo Verdaine or Euro Photo, all of which have knowledgeable staff and sell top end cameras and lenses, lab equipment, and consumables such as paper and chemicals. Once you've got all the gear, it's worth meeting up with the various photography groups and clubs in the area – apart from being good company on those sunrise shooting sessions, these like minded people are a great source of advice!

| Camera Equipment | |
|---|---|
| **Center of Photography** | 022 329 28 35 |
| Rue du Général Dufour, 16 – Town Centre | |
| **Euro Photo** | 022 741 05 48 |
| Place de St Gervais – Town Centre | |
| **Photo Hall** | 022 310 14 24 |
| Rue de la Confédération , 5 – Town Centre | |
| **Sony Photo Verdaine** | 022 840 13 63 |
| Place des Eaux-Vives, 6 – Town Centre | |

## Cards & Stationery

Other options → Art Supplies [p.138]

You can usually find a small selection of English greeting cards in any bookshop, department store or supermarket. However, you may find the range a little limited compared to what you are used to – you'll find the usual birthday/anniversary/get well/thank you selection, but try finding an English card for your sister's dog's birthday or to congratulate your auntie on her successful plastic surgery and you'll have your work cut out for you!

You may also find that cards are scandalously expensive – perhaps something to stock up on during your next trip home?

If you're looking for stationery, department stores usually have a basic selection, or you could pop into one of the paper shops, such as Papier 39 (in Carouge) or Un Petit Mot.

In many of Geneva's shopping outlets, simple gift-wrapping is free. Large stores usually have tables set up all year round, equipped with scissors, tape and wrapping paper, and as Christmas approaches, virtually every store offers a gift wrapping service of some kind. To buy your own paper and gift-wrapping accessories visit any supermarket, department store, paper shop or large multi-purpose shop (like IKEA or Jumbo).

| Cards & Stationery | |
|---|---|
| **Bookbinder's Design** | 022 304 20 00 |
| La Praille Commercial Centre – Carouge | |
| **Ordning & Reda** | 022 810 10 20 |
| Rue de Rive, 20 – Town Centre | |
| **Papeterie Wolf** | 022 312 18 75 |
| Confédération Centre – Town Centre | |
| **Papier 39** | 022 342 92 22 |
| Rue St Joseph, 39 – Carouge | |
| **RSVP** | 022 979 02 02 |
| Balexert – Geneva | |
| **Un Petit Mot** | 022 752 12 33 |
| Ch. du Vieux Vésenaz, 38 – Vésenaz | |

## Carpets

If you're buying basic, everyday, functional carpets, you can get wall-to-wall carpeting at chain stores such as Carpetland, or rugs (small, large, round, rectangle, bright, faux sheepskin, etc.) for bargain prices from IKEA or DIY stores like Jumbo. But if you're splurging on an exquisite Oriental carpet, then you'll need to go to a speciality carpet shop. The shop assistants in these shops are usually very helpful and knowledgeable. What they may lack in English speaking skills they more than make up for in enthusiasm, and will happily show you carpets from all over the world in varying sizes, colours, materials and patterns. Take advantage of the 'purchase at home' option

### Rug Rules

*Shop around when buying an investment carpet – don't rush into buying one you like, only to walk into the shop next door and see one that you really love – take your time and don't make any hasty decisions.*

Shopping — What & Where to Buy

offered by many carpet shops – most will allow you to take a few rugs to your house and lay them out, so that you can see which one best suits your room. And once you've decided on one, don't forget to bargain! There is a lot of competition for your business and you should be able to knock a few francs off the asking price.

| Carpets | |
|---|---|
| **Amir Rasty** <br> Bd. Georges Favon, 30 – Town Centre | 022 321 34 77 |
| **Avakian – Tapis d'Orient** <br> Rue des Alpes, 18 – Town Centre | 022 731 61 77 |
| **Carpetland** <br> Rue de Lausanne, 45-47 – Town Centre | 022 738 77 66 |
| **Jawad** <br> Rue Verdaine, 11 – Town Centre | 022 781 02 22 |
| **Maret SA** <br> Rue de Carouge, 5 – Town Centre | 022 320 10 68 |
| **Persia** <br> Place Neuve, 2 – Town Centre | 022 321 67 66 |
| **Saint Maclou** <br> Rte de Thonon | +33 4 50 87 14 70 |

## Cars

### New Cars

Bring out the big bucks; new luxury cars in Geneva are at a premium. The stylish engines driving around this city will make your head spin. From the latest Aston Martins to Ferraris, Bentleys and Porches, you will find whatever your heart desires, as long as you can afford it. Of course if you don't have the same tastes (or the same financial resources) as James Bond, there is a large market for the regular car buyer as well. Car dealerships are spread around the city and offer comparable prices and excellent service (refer to [p.82] for a list of dealers). If possible, try to buy your new car during the International Motor Show (usually held in March each year). Carmakers spend a fortune on dazzling displays to off their latest models. Dealerships are on hand to take your order and are often doing so much business that they will offer good discounts.

### Used Cars

Once a car hits the five-year mark it is seen as being over the hill, which is happy news for second-hand car shoppers! You can normally bag a real bargain for a used car, and in most cases you'll find it has been well maintained, it has no mechanical problems, and that it was just traded in

for a newer model. For additional peace of mind, if you buy from a dealer you get a limited period warranty on the car. The largest second-hand car dealership is ROC, which may not have the lowest prices but it does have the best reputation. If you know all about cars and can easily distinguish between a good runner and a death trap, then there are bargains galore at the hundreds of smaller garages in town. You could also buy from a private seller – this is the easiest way to get a good price, but it is risky in terms of having no compensation if the engine falls out before you've driven five miles. If you do go this route, have the car checked by a neutral garage before you hand over your money – it is a small expense, but it could save you a lot of money later on.

| Cars | |
|---|---|
| **Autobritt – Rovers, MG, Jaguar & Volvo** <br> Rue Boissonnas, 15 – Carouge | 022 308 58 00 |
| **BMW** <br> Rte des Acacias, 23 – Carouge | 022 308 53 08 |
| **Jeep Chrysler** <br> Rte du Bois-des-Freres, 46 | 022 979 15 15 |
| **Mercedes-Benz** <br> Rue de Vermont, 6 – Town Centre | 022 733 37 07 |

## Chocolate

Chocolate lovers will be pleased to note that chocolate of the finest quality is readily available all over Geneva. Beautifully decorated speciality chocolate shops show off their delectable, delicious creations in shop windows, from devilish handmade truffles to the most bittersweet dark chocolate imaginable. When it's cold outside, pop into Chocolatier Auer for their world famous house

It looks almost too good to eat!

What & Where to Buy

Shopping

hot chocolate, or for a chocolate experience with a difference, visit the After the Rain Day Spa in the middle of town for a hydrating chocolate bath. For an everyday treat, just pop into your nearest supermarket for a better than average selection of chocolate – Lindt, in particular, produces a variety of bars (hazelnut, dark chocolate, raisin and almond, nougat, etc.) that are destined not to languish long in anyone's refrigerator!

### The Dark Side

*Dark Chocolate is created when a higher percentage (up to 75%) of ground cocoa is used in making the chocolate. As the percentage goes up, the sugar ratio goes down, allowing the truer, bitter, taste of the cocoa to come forward.*

## Clothes

Other options → Beach Wear [p.138]

The pages of Vogue come alive in Geneva, with many high fashion boutiques all over the city selling original designs. Rue du Rhône in the city centre is a particularly good area for fashionistas, and Carouge, the arty part of town, is the best area to buy unique pieces that will add a dash of individuality to your wardrobe. If you don't mind waiting a few months for the latest fashions, and you are on a tighter budget, you can shop at the discount stores, which often sell last season's fashions at very low prices. Department stores, such as Globus, Manor and Coop sell good quality clothing at reasonable prices, while the lowest prices are generally found at EPA, C & A, Migros and other supermarkets. Second-hand clothing is not as popular as in certain other European countries, but if you can spare an hour or two to trawl through the rails of castaways, you never know what you might find for next to nothing!

Dressed to Impress

| Clothes | |
|---|---|
| **Aigle** | 022 304 20 00 |
| La Praille Commercial Centre – Carouge | |
| **Benetton** | 022 950 86 89 |
| Chavannes Centre | |
| **Bon Génie** | 022 818 11 11 |
| Rue du Marché , 34 – Town Centre | |
| **C & A** | 022 319 06 30 |
| Rue de la Croix d'Or, 8 – Town Centre | |
| **Café Coton** | 022 970 19 00 |
| Av. Louis Casaï, 27 – Vernier | |
| Rue d'Italie – Town Centre | 022 810 15 42 |
| **Carla** | 022 312 30 05 |
| Rue du Port, 8-10 – Town Centre | |
| **Celio** | 022 304 80 00 |
| La Praille Commercial Centre – Carouge | |
| **Chanel** | 022 311 08 62 |
| Rue du Rhône, 43 – Town Centre | |
| **Christian Dior** | 022 310 62 55 |
| Rue du Rhône, 60 – Town Centre | |
| **Coop City** | 022 818 02 40 |
| Rue du Commerce, 5 – Town Centre | |
| **Cyrillus** | 022 311 35 82 |
| Rue de la Croix d'Or, 19 – Town Centre | |
| **EPA** | 022 310 61 66 |
| Rue de la Croix d'Or, 4 – Town Centre | |
| **Esprit** | 022 950 86 89 |
| Chavannes Centre | |
| **Globus** | 022 319 50 50 |
| Rue du Rhône, 48 – Town Centre | |
| **Gucci** | 022 310 84 06 |
| Rue du Rhône, 92 – Town Centre | |
| **H&M** | 022 979 02 02 |
| Balexert – Geneva | |
| **Jean & Co** | na |
| Metro Shopping Cornavin – Town Centre | |
| **Kenko Hoshi** | 022 786 00 46 |
| Rue des Photographes, 2 – Town Centre | |
| **Klima** | 022 311 38 37 |
| Rue des Chaudronniers, 4 – Town Centre | |
| **Lacoste** | 022 970 1460 |
| Balexert Shopping Mall | |
| **Le Club des Marques** | 022 738 59 08 |
| Les Cygnes – Pâquis | |
| **Levi's Store** | 022 311 52 92 |
| Confédération Centre – Town Centre | |
| **Linea Pupa** | 022 311 52 92 |
| Confédération Centre – Town Centre | |
| **Manor** | 022 950 86 89 |
| Chavannes Centre | |
| **Massimo Dutti** | 022 304 20 00 |
| La Praille Commercial Centre – Carouge | |
| **Naf Naf** | +33-4 50 43 99 88 |
| Etrembières Shopping Centre | |
| Etrembières, France | |
| **Paradigme** | 022 700 72 75 |
| Rue de la Terrassière, 2 – Town Centre | |
| **Picibi** | 022 311 33 46 |
| Rue de la Madeleine, 11 – Town Centre | |

**Rolls Royce Motor Cars Geneva**
André Chevalley SA
122 Route de Meyrin, 1216 Cointrin

## Clothes

| | |
|---|---|
| **Pimkie** | 022 304 20 00 |
| La Praille Commercial Centre – Carouge | |
| **PKZ** | 022 979 02 02 |
| Balexert – Geneva | |
| Signy Centre | 022 363 67 00 |
| **Pourquoi Pas** | 022 320 77 61 |
| Bd. du Pont d'Arve, 27 – Town Centre | |
| **Projection Privée** | 022 735 70 87 |
| Rue de la Terrassière, 15 – Town Centre | |
| **Septième Etage** | 022 310 77 70 |
| Rue du Perron, 10 – Town Centre | |
| **Tally Weijl** | 022 949 77 90 |
| Planète Charmilles | |
| **Vickyh Shop** | 022 786 17 47 |
| Rte de Frontenex, 54 – Town Centre | |
| **Volupté** | 022 300 10 12 |
| Rue Ancienne, 50 – Town Centre | |
| **Yendi** | 022 949 77 90 |
| Planète Charmilles | |
| **Zara** | 022 304 20 00 |
| La Praille Commercial Centre – Carouge | |

## Computers

Other options → Electronics & Home Appliances [p.144]

As one of the world's richer countries Geneva has the income to keep up to date with changes in technology, so no matter what gadget you're looking for you'll be able to find it here. Computer speciality shops offer comprehensive service, from advice on what model to buy to home installation if required. This will come in particularly handy if you are buying your first computer and don't have a clue what you're looking for.

Prodimex is a good starting point for brand name computers at reasonable prices. The clerks really know their stuff and can guide you through all aspects of buying a computer. Some home appliances and electronics shops have a small range

## Computers

| | |
|---|---|
| **ART Computer** | 022 795 10 00 |
| Rue de Coutance, 3 – Town Centre | |
| **Computer Shop** | 022 304 43 60 |
| Rue Ancienne, 48 – Town Centre | |
| **Dell** | na |
| Online purchases only (www.dell.com) | |
| **Generation Notebook** | 022 734 28 34 |
| Rue du Fort Barreau, 13 – Town Centre | |
| **Portable Shop, The** | 022 818 45 60 |
| Rue du Rhône, 50 – Town Centre | |
| **Prodimex** | 022 308 66 66 |
| Rte des Jeunes, 4bis – Town Centre | |
| **Top D** | 022 940 05 05 |
| Rue Gutenberg, 3 – Town Centre | |

of last year's models at very low prices. Dell has a centre in Geneva, and although you have to do all your shopping with them via their Website, the lack of a showroom translates into lower prices for you.

## Costumes

Other options → Party Accessories [p.155]

## Costumes

| | |
|---|---|
| **Au Bal Masqué** | 022 328 41 40 |
| Rue Georges Leschot, 11 – Town Centre | |
| **Beauty Flore** | 022 311 27 11 |
| Rue du Marché , 18 – Town Centre | |
| **Costumes du Théâtre du Carouge** | 022 343 44 47 |
| Rue Ancienne, 57 – Town Centre | |
| **La Gaîté** | 022 311 87 08 |
| Rue de la Rôtisserie, 13 – Town Centre | |
| **La Mascarade** | 022 311 87 08 |
| Rue des Rois, 2 – Town Centre | |

## Electronics & Home Appliances

Other options → Computers [p.144]

Electronics shops in Switzerland are well stocked and the quality of products is high. For larger kitchen appliances, interior design stores will give you the latest range of models and beautiful fittings. For the best prices, however, visit stores like Conforama. Smaller appliances are available at any of the electronic stores. Most electronic stores will sell everything from hair dryers to hand mixers, home printers, car stereos and more. Special price promotions are usually advertised well, so keep your eyes peeled. The electronics aisles of department stores and supermarkets usually have an excellent range. Overall, prices in most stores are similar, barring the sale items.

## Electronics & Home Appliances

| | |
|---|---|
| **Bang & Olufsen** | 022 732 22 42 |
| Quai du Seujet, 32 – Town Centre | |
| **Conforama** | 022 782 52 11 |
| Rue des Entreprises, 14 – Town Centre | |
| **Darty** | +33-4 50 84 24 70 |
| Rue des Esserts, 2 | |
| **Fnac** | 022 816 12 56 |
| Rue de Rive, 16 – Town Centre | |
| **Fust** | 022 950 86 89 |
| Chavannes Centre | |
| **InterDiscount** | 022 738 59 08 |
| Les Cygnes – Pâquis | |
| **Media Markt** | 022 719 80 80 |
| Ch. de Riantbosson, 15-21 | |
| **Sony Shop** | 022 840 13 64 |
| Place des Eaux Vives, 6 – Town Centre | |

Close-up view of the test winner.

RX300

COMPREHENSIVE WARRANTY
AND FREE SCHEDULED
MAINTENANCE FOR 5 YEARS OR
100,000 KM
WHICHEVER COMES FIRST.

# Overview of the test winners.

Lexus IS300/200.
The limousine with sports appeal.

Lexus IS300/200 SportCross.
The flexibly dynamic driving experience.

Lexus RX300.
The truly cultivated 4x4 offroad limousine.

Lexus GS430/300.
The benchmark in power and style.

Lexus LS430.
The new, luxurious dimension in travel.

Lexus SC430.
The coupé for convertible enthusiasts.

The globally respected «J.D. Power report» delivers impressive proof of the excellent quality for which Lexus stands. In its UK report for 2004, the rating agency ranked Lexus a peerless first in terms of customer satisfaction. And in the US J.D. Power report for 2004, consumers rated the RX300 the most reliable offroader in its class. For more details about our test winners, head for **www.lexus.ch**

Emil Frey S.A. Genève - Centre Toyota-Lexus - Rue François-Dussaud 13 - 1211 Genève 26
tél. 022 308 5 508 - fax 022 308 5 549 - E-mail: lexus.geneve@emilfrey.ch

If you want to purchase used items, check the local community bulletin boards or tune in to WRG 88.4 FM on Friday mornings at 09:00, for their program 'Garage Sale'.

## Eyewear

If your eyes are the windows to your soul, then sunglasses are the curtains! A funky, fashionable pair of sunnies is not only a way to keep the rays off your peepers, but also an important fashion statement. As the summer recedes and the dark days of winter approach don't rush to pack away your sunglasses – take them skiing! If your skills on the slopes are dire, at least you can look cool on the terrace, sipping spiked hot chocolate with your shades on.

For prescription eyeglasses, you'll find the latest frame fashions at eyewear stores. Many have in-house technicians who can even recommend lenses suitable for your eyes, although if you have a serious vision problem, it's better to see a doctor or optician.

### Eyewear

| | |
|---|---|
| **Berdoz** | 022 310 36 40 |
| Rue de Rive, 16 – Town Centre | |
| **Fielmann** | 022 544 20 20 |
| Rue de la Croix d'Or, 9 – Town Centre | |
| **Grand Optical** | 022 818 42 00 |
| Rue de Rive, 7 – Town Centre | |
| **Lindegger & Fils** | 022 735 29 11 |
| Cours de Rive, 13 – 15 – Town Centre | |
| **Philippe Pedat** | 022 320 26 30 |
| Av. De Mail, 8 – Plainpalais | |
| **Visilab** | |
| Balexert – Geneva | 022 796 40 25 |
| Chavannes Centre | 022 950 86 89 |
| Confédération Centre – Town Centre | 022 318 66 80 |
| Les Cygnes – Pâquis | 022 738 83 38 |
| Planète Charmilles | 022 949 77 50 |
| Rue Jargonnant, 3 – Town Centre | 022 786 78 10 |

## Flowers

It is strictly against the law to pick any flowers in the lush green parks of Geneva. However, fresh flowers are readily available in grocery stores and florists or the flower markets in the city. If you have a car and fancy a drive out of town, you can call in to one of the flower fields where you can pay to go in and pick your own bunch. Just look for signs saying 'Fleurs'.

Florists are common and one can be found in just about every shopping area in Geneva, each offering a different style. Fleurtoit, for example, offers beautiful traditional bouquets, while Les 5 Senses has a very modern approach to flower arranging. For a budget bouquet, visit the open air flower markets, select a few stems, and get creative!

### Flowers

| | |
|---|---|
| **Atelier Floral** | 022 784 06 03 |
| Ch. des Marais, 52 – Veyrier | |
| **Fleuriot Aéroport** | 022 818 12 41 |
| Geneva Int. Airport | |
| **Fleuriot Fleurs** | 022 310 36 55 |
| Rue de la Corraterie, 26 – Town Centre | |
| **Fleuriot Gare Cornavin** | na |
| Metro Shopping Cornavin – Town Centre | |
| **Les 5 Sens** | 022 301 28 14 |
| Place du temple, 9 – Town Centre | |
| **Les Bouquets de Marie** | 022 786 48 19 |
| Rue des Eaux-Vives, 12 – Town Centre | |
| **Vert Tendre** | 022 732 50 23 |
| Rue de Cornivan, 11 – Town Centre | |

## Food

Geneva is an international community, so there is an especially diverse selection of food items on the shelves. From naan bread and BBQ sauce to maki seaweed paper and spicy mango chutney, you'll probably be able to find your favourite items from back home. And if you can't, speak to your friendly supermarket manager, who might be able to order something especially for you. The two major Swiss supermarket chains are Migros and Coop, both with numerous stores in neighbourhoods, malls and shopping districts.

### Grocery Stores

Grocery stores are plentiful – how do you pick one? Migros and Coop have their grocery stores well spread throughout and tend to be the easiest to find. However, their hours are not always convenient. Some stores open on Sundays and after normal closing hours, but expect to pay slightly inflated prices at these outlets. If you're looking for a good deal, Denner and Pick Pay are two discount grocery stores that sell a range of items, including alcohol, but not fresh produce. They usually have (heavily advertised) weekend specials, which are a great way to stock up if you're having a party. If you are having a huge party,

## Food

| | |
|---|---|
| **A-Nam** | 022 329 49 44 |
| Bd. de St Georges, 66 – Town Centre | |
| **Afrika Food** | 022 731 36 12 |
| Rue Sismondi, 16 – Town Centre | |
| **Aligro** | 022 308 60 20 |
| Rue Francois Dussaud, 15 – Town Centre | |
| **American Market** | 022 732 32 00 |
| Rue de Neuchâtel, 3 – Town Centre | |
| **Carrefour** | 022 306 08 38 |
| Rte de Meyrin, 171 – Meyrin | |
| **Caviar House** | 022 818 12 41 |
| Geneva Int. Airport – Cointrin | |
| **Champion** | +33 4 50 40 61 23 |
| Av Voltaire, 33 | |
| – Ferney Voltaire, France | |
| **Coop** | |
| Eaux-Vives 2000 – Geneva | 022 735 17 25 |
| La Praille Commercial Centre – Carouge | 022 308 17 00 |
| Signy Centre | 022 363 67 00 |
| **Coop City** | 022 818 02 40 |
| Rue du Commerce, 5 – Town Centre | |
| **Denner** | 022 347 17 29 |
| Ch. Bizot, 4 – Town Centre | |
| **Géant** | +33 4 50 43 94 00 |
| Rue de la Résistance, 14 | |
| – Annemasse, France | |
| **Goodies – Lebanese Specialities** | +33 4 50 40 85 10 |
| Ch. sur Grosse, 2 | |
| – Ferney Voltaire, France | |
| **Indian Bazar** | 022 738 01 33 |
| Rue de la Navigation, 19 – Pâquis | |
| **Intermarché** | +33 4 50 20 60 60 |
| Rue Châlets, 148 | |
| – St Genis Pouilly, France | |
| **Jim's British Market** | +33 4 50 42 04 18 |
| Espace de l'Allondon | |
| – St Genis Pouilly, France | |
| **La Fromagerie Ursula Antonietti** | 022 731 25 05 |
| Rue Cornavin, 1 – Town Centre | |
| **Migros** | 022 738 59 08 |
| Les Cygnes – Pâquis | |
| **Pick Pay** | 022 738 59 08 |
| Les Cygnes – Pâquis | |
| **Talad Thai** | 022 732 38 86 |
| Jean Jacquet, 12-14 – Town Centre | |

Aligros sells bulk items at low prices – they have a amazing range of products, party supplies and fresh produce, plus there's lots of parking!

## Supermarkets

If you love the convenience of one-stop shopping, you'll find some good supermarkets in Geneva. Besides Migros and Coop, there is also a Carrefour, which has a huge selection of items from kitchen utensils and electrical appliances to clothes, toys, plants and groceries. They also have freshly baked bread, a cheese counter, a butcher, a cafeteria and a large wine and alcohol section (but note that Migros has a policy not to sell any alcohol or cigarettes). Supermarkets also specialise in food-to-go, and you'll get a range of pre-cooked hot meals, soups and salads. The two large department stores, Globus and Manor, have large grocery sections and speciality food shops. They are well known for their diverse selection of exotic goods and high quality fresh fish, although prices are on the high side.

## Speciality Shops

Even though many supermarkets have speciality areas in their stores, you can't beat the quality, service and selections of a speciality shop. Here they have time to spend with you, to listen to you, explain and suggest appropriate purchases as well as offer sumptuous samples. The prices are higher, but the experience is richer. Look around your neighbourhood for the speciality stores nearest you.

When only the best will do...

## Ethnic Stores

Living in a multi-cultural environment such as Geneva will give you a perfect opportunity to experiment with exotic cuisine. The international population influences many aspects of life, especially the food. There are many ethnic stores around town where you can buy ingredients from all over the world. Many of these also offer video rentals in their native language.

## Vegetarians

In Geneva, vegetarians will not have too much difficulty finding a variety of suitable foods. All the supermarkets stock fruits, vegetables, beans, rice, tofu and other non-meaty foods of all shapes and sizes. For a bit of special shopping, visit any of the bio or health food stores, especially La Maison du Tofu.

## Health Food

With cheese and bread being staples of the Swiss diet, you may think healthy eating is not a big priority. However, most supermarkets offer a selection of BIO products, which are either grown in an organic way or made using all natural ingredients. You will also find some speciality shops selling health food and related products.

| Health Food | |
| --- | --- |
| **Alna Diététique & Bio** Rue du Cornavin, 3-5 – Town Centre | 022 738 10 28 |
| **Bio Servette** Rte de Meyrin, 3 – Cointrin | 022 733 86 74 |
| **Droguerie des Alpes** Rue des Pâquis, 4 – Town Centre | 022 738 32 44 |
| **Marché de la Vie** Rue des Eaux-Vives, 25 – Town Centre | 022 735 44 34 |
| **Relais de la Nature** Place de l'Octroi, 10 – Carouge | 022 342 96 21 |

## Garden Centres

Other options → Flowers [p.148]

Gardening is a rewarding and relaxing activity, particularly when living in a country with four such distinct seasons. Geneva has a large number of garden centres that stock everything you'll need to indulge your green thumb. Speciality garden centres, such as Schilliger, are staffed with gardening experts who can answer all your questions or provide emergency assistance to your poorly plants. If you know what you're looking for, visit the large DIY centres such as M Parc where the staff may be less knowledgeable but your franc will stretch further. Some of the larger grocery stores and supermarkets stock smaller plants for home and terrace use. Across the border, France has

| Garden Centres | |
| --- | --- |
| **Botanic** Rue des Voirons (no number) – Ville-La-Grand, France | +33 4 50 37 69 03 |
| **Schilliger Garden Center** Rte Suisse, 40 – Gland | 022 354 44 44 |

some very good nurseries, but some plants and trees should not be brought back into Switzerland. The same goes for certain types of bug killers and fertilisers. To check what you can and can't bring back from France, ask a border guard or visit the Website www.douanne.admin.ch.

## Hardware & DIY

Other options → Outdoor Goods [p.155]

Clear your weekend schedule and get started on a home project. Everything you could possibly need can be found at any of the large DIY stores in and around the city where knowledgeable staff will help you locate anything, from speciality screws to heavy duty sanders. Many of the stores also have equipment for hire. The largest stores are located on the outskirts of town. Hornbach, the biggest of them all, is located half way between Lausanne and Geneva, and looks just like Home Depot. In town, you can find many neighbourhood hardware stores to purchase standard items for smaller jobs.

| Hardware & DIY | |
| --- | --- |
| **Brico Loisirs** Place de la Gare, 34 | 022 348 33 84 |
| **Bricorama** ZAC de la Chatelaine – Annemasse, France | +33 4 50 39 76 84 |
| **Coop Brico+Loisirs** Av. Gros-Chêne 14 – Onex | 022 879 05 70 |
| **Hornbach** Rte de l'Industrie, 6 – Aubonne | 021 821 02 02 |
| **Jumbo Do It Deco Garden** Chavannes Centre | 022 960 70 20 |
| Rue des Entreprises, 12 – Meyrin | 022 780 18 18 |
| **La Boite a Outils** Rue de la Résistance, 28 – Annemasse, France | +33 4 50 95 08 88 |
| **Schaffner** Rue Voltaire, 3-5 – Town Centre | 022 732 70 47 |

## Home Furnishings & Accessories

To express yourself with your living space is to make your house your home. Whether your tastes are for colourful, bohemian interiors or priceless antiques, Geneva is home to a variety of shops that will help you transform your home into a palace. Everybody's favourite superstore, IKEA, is here in force, and you'll usually find at least one IKEA piece in every home to go to. Antique stores can be found on every other corner, and smaller design shops, like Atmosphere, carry a good range of beautiful items. For the lowest prices you could try Conforama, although some of their pieces may be a bit low on quality too. Fly or IKEA stock medium to good quality items in the latest trends, and top end home boutiques obviously have some fabulous items, although the prices are sometimes shocking! Department stores carry a nice range of linen, towels, pillows, vases, candles and other home decorating items. For a unique touch, try boutiques like Schilliger or Gadgetissimo. Walking around Carouge is another way to find interesting shops, such as Du Côte de Chez Soi, with nice items to individualise your home.

Home furnishings

### Home Furnishings & Accessories

| | |
|---|---|
| **Atmosphère** | 022 310 75 75 |
| Grand-Rue, 10 – Town Centre | |
| **Conforama** | 022 782 52 11 |
| Rue des Entreprises, 14 – Meyrin | |
| **Détail** | 022 310 78 05 |
| Rue Etienne Dumont, 16 – Town Centre | |
| **Du Côté de Chez Soi** | 022 328 14 60 |
| Pl. des Augustins, 9 – Town Centre | |
| **Dunia** | 022 700 49 23 |
| Rue du Parc, 3 bis – Town Centre | |
| Rue Vautier, 45 – Town Centre | 022 343 33 31 |
| **Fly** | +33 4 50 87 27 40 |
| Rue des Deux Montagnes, 3 – Ville-La-Grand, France | |
| **Futon Design Studio** | 022 738 30 69 |
| Rue de Monthoux, 36 – Town Centre | |
| **Gadgetissimo** | 022 311 34 85 |
| Bd. Georges Favon, 15 – Town Centre | |
| **IKEA** | 0848 801 1 00 |
| Nxt to Highway – Aubonne | |
| **Interio** | 022 306 60 60 |
| Rte de Meyrin, 171 – Vernier | |
| **Interiors** | 022 310 41 35 |
| Rue Verdaine – Town Centre | |
| **Jean Jacques Favre** | 022 700 77 17 |
| Bd. Helvétique , 24 – 28 – Town Centre | |
| **La Maison** | 022 343 30 32 |
| Rue Ancienne, 49 – Town Centre | |
| **Pier Imports** | 022 363 04 54 |
| Signy Centre | |
| **Roche Bobois** | 022 311 55 40 |
| Grand Rue, 5 – Town Centre | |
| **Schilliger** | 022 304 20 00 |
| La Praille Commercial Centre – Carouge | |
| **Skeena** | +33 4 50 43 99 88 |
| Etrembières Shopping Centre – Etrembières, France | |
| **Teo Jakob Tagliabue** | 022 342 23 23 |
| Rue St Victor, 35 – Town Centre | |
| **Tip's** | 022 810 40 00 |
| Grande-Rue, 19 – Town Centre | |
| **Village** | 022 700 70 70 |
| Place des Eaux-Vives, 9 – Town Centre | |
| **Y's design** | 022 823 26 80 |
| Rue Roi Victor Amé, 10 – Town Centre | |

## Jewellery, Watches & Gold

### Jewellery

Famous worldwide for its collection of glittering jewellery, Geneva has something for every taste — all you need are the resources to acquire it. Seekers of the traditional will want to gaze at the mesmerising displays of exquisite earrings, necklaces and bracelets showcased in window displays along the fashionable Rue du Rhône. A good example is Gubelin, where you can buy stunning jewellery, loose precious stones, their own brand of superb watches, or other high quality famous brand watches. For a less expensive visit, try Orfeo by Christ, near Manor.

Geneva boasts one of the foremost designers of fabulous jewellery, Gilbert Albert, available at three locations. The works of art created in these stores may use white or yellow gold encrusted with sparkling diamonds or natural shapes of red or black coral, cabochon emeralds, rubies or sapphires, so no matter what your tastes you can be sure of picking up an eye catching piece.

In trendy Carouge, the jewellery stores tend to be more modern. Stylish necklaces and bracelets festooned with semi precious stones and designed by local artists can be found here. High quality costume jewellery has recently become more acceptable as fashion accessories for the obvious reasons of expense and security. Some people may prefer antique jewellery, such as Victorian, Arte Deco or Arte Nouveau. There are several locations where original Estate Jewellery is available that dates back to these eras.

## Jewellery, Watches & Gold

| | |
|---|---|
| **A. Collett SA** | 022 318 48 48 |
| Place du Molard, 8 – Town Centre | |
| **Audemars Piguet** | 022 731 83 87 |
| Quai du Mont-Blanc, 19 – Town Centre | |
| **Bucherer** | 022 732 72 16 |
| Rue du Mont-Blanc, 22 – Town Centre | |
| Rue du Rhône, 45 – Town Centre | 022 319 62 66 |
| **Chrono Time** | 022 311 08 55 |
| Rue de la Fontaine, 3 – Town Centre | |
| **Espace Temps** | 022 732 87 64 |
| Rue du Mont-Blanc, 13 – Town Centre | |
| **Franck Muller** | 022 818 00 30 |
| Rue de la Tour de l'Ile, 1 – Town Centre | |
| **Gallopin** | 022 716 27 16 |
| Place des Bergues, 1 – Town Centre | |
| **Gilbert Albert** | 022 311 48 33 |
| Rue de la Corraterie, 24 – Town Centre | |
| **Golyt SA** | 022 732 55 05 |
| Rue du Mont-Blanc, 17 – Town Centre | |
| **Gübelin,** | 022 310 86 55 |
| Place du Molard, 1 – Town Centre | |
| **Horlogerie de la Corraterie** | 022 310 49 53 |
| Rue de la Corraterie, 14 – Town Centre | |
| **Igor Siebold** | 022 301 29 55 |
| Rue Saint-Joseph, 8 – Town Centre | |
| **Jewels Jill Wolf** | 022 312 00 84 |
| Grand-Rue, 39 – Town Centre | |
| **Kunz SA** | 022 731 09 20 |
| Quai des Bergues, 23 – Town Centre | |
| **l'H'être** | 022 311 03 70 |
| Rue des Chaudronniers, 5 – Town Centre | |
| **Liliane Sicard** | 022 311 00 55 |
| Quai General-Guisan, 10 – Town Centre | |
| **Orfeo by Christ** | 022 312 16 30 |
| Rue de Cornavin, 6 – Town Centre | |
| **Patek Phillippe** | 022 781 24 48 |
| Rue du Rhône, 41 – Town Centre | |
| **Piaget** | 022 817 02 00 |
| Rue du Rhône, 40 – Town Centre | |
| **Purestone** | 022 731 58 68 |
| Rue de Berne, 9 – Town Centre | |
| **Swatch** | 022 900 22 10 |
| Rue du Mont-Blanc, 19 – Town Centre | |
| **Tactile** | 022 310 21 56 |
| Place du Grand-Mezel, 8 – Town Centre | |
| **Tentation Bijoux** | 022 311 63 52 |
| Rue de la Confédération , 6 – Town Centre | |
| **Vacheron Constantin** | 022 343 78 23 |
| Rue des Moulins, 1 – Town Centre | |
| **Zbinden** | 022 731 36 96 |
| Rue de Coutance, 4 – Town Centre | |

## Watches

Switzerland is home to hundreds of watchmakers and dozens of those have become world famous brands. From Swatch and Blancpain, to Tissot and Omega, you can find a Swiss watch to fit any budget. Rue du Rhône has many high-end watch shops carrying numerous brands, as well as the exclusive shops of famous watchmakers, such as Patek Phillippe, Audemars Piguet and Piaget. Place Bel Air, a short walk down the Rhône River, is home to the shop of Franck Muller. His watches range from a sturdy timepieces to a complicated works of art in gold and diamonds. Apparently, this is the only watchmaker who still allows public tours of his factory in Genthod, but a booking is necessary. For a comprehensive selection of elegant Swiss watches and jewellery, visit one of the Bucherer shops specialising in Rolex. If you would like a more reasonably priced watch, new or used, try Espace Temps. Department stores also sell a varied price range of watches and, of course, don't forget Swatch, which is available at many stores. Alternatively, visit the Swatch Store for the largest selection. Sadly, you won't necessarily pay less for a Swiss watch just because you are in Switzerland. The prices for watches run the gamut but are definitely not cheaper than in other countries. The only way possible to get a good deal in Geneva is when the Swiss Franc is low in the market.

Buy a posh watch

What & Where to Buy

Shopping

## Kids' Items

Other options → Clothes [p.142]

Your kids will have a blast in Geneva, with the lakes to swim in, the swans to feed, the mountains to climb, and the snow to play in. And you'll appreciate the safety and the huge variety of children's goods available in the shops! Kiddie Club stocks educational items, while at King Jouets it's toys, toys, toys. Turn your offspring into mini fashion statements at shops such as Baby Dior and H&M, while Kids' Planet and IKEA are the places to go for furniture. You'll find all the essentials for your (or someone else's) newborn at Babycare Orchestra, and Baby Occa's has a range of second-hand items.

### Kids' Items

| | |
|---|---|
| **Baby Dior** | 022 311 47 03 |
| Rue du Rhône, 29 – Town Centre | |
| **Baby Occas'** | 022 340 73 37 |
| Av. De Luserna 13 – Town Centre | |
| **Babycare Orchestra** | 022 731 95 74 |
| Rue Jean Jacques Rousseau, 38 – Town Centre | |
| **Franz Carl Weber** | 022 310 42 55 |
| Rue de la Croix d'Or, 12 – Town Centre | |
| **H&M** | 022 735 17 25 |
| Eaux-Vives 2000 – Geneva | |
| **Kiddie Club** | 022 736 43 92 |
| Rte de Chêne, 66 – Town Centre | |
| **Kids Planet** | 022 800 34 80 |
| Rue de Carouge, 33 – Town Centre | |
| **King Jouet** | 022 827 61 40 |
| Av. Cardinal Mermillod, 36 – Town Centre | |
| Ch. de Riantbosson, 5-9 – Cointrin | 022 989 30 00 |
| **Paquine** | 022 738 97 04 |
| Rue de Pâquis – Pâquis | |
| **Petit Bateau** | +33 4 50 37 42 48 |
| Etrembières Shopping Centre – Etrembières, France | |

Something for the kiddies

## Lingerie

Other options → Clothes [p.142]

Lingerie shops are packed with lacy, silky, sexy creations designed to raise the temperature, no matter how chilly the Geneva nights are! Prices in the high end shops might get your knickers in a twist, but department stores (and even some supermarkets) stock a range of pretty lingerie and practical underwear at more sensible prices.

### Lingerie

| | |
|---|---|
| **à Fleur de Peau** | 022 731 21 50 |
| Rue de Berne, 20 – Town Centre | |
| **A Forde de Partir Je Suis Resté Chez Moi** | 022 731 82 88 |
| Rue des Etuves, 16 – Town Centre | |
| **Beldona** | 022 810 17 10 |
| Passage de la Couronne d'Or, 82 – Town Centre | |
| **Body One** | 022 949 77 90 |
| Planète Charmilles | |
| **Estel Lingerie** | 022 311 86 20 |
| Rue du Port, 9 – Town Centre | |
| **Perosa** | 022 810 07 71 |
| Rue de la Confédération , 5 – Town Centre | |

## Luggage & Leather

### Leather

As winter approaches, you'll find an increasing range of high quality leather items on the shelves of Geneva shops. Shoes, bags, pants, coats and

### Luggage & Leather

| | |
|---|---|
| **Buzzano** | 022 796 01 41 |
| Balexert – Geneva | |
| Cours de Rive, 15 – Town Centre | 022 736 76 57 |
| Rue de la Croix d'Or, 1 – Town Centre | 022 311 56 93 |
| **Come Prima** | 022 310 77 79 |
| Rue de la Cité, 17 – Town Centre | |
| **Comptoir Des Maroquiniers** | 022 731 04 89 |
| Les Cygnes – Pâquis | |
| **Furla** | 022 312 16 88 |
| Rue du Rhône, 30 – Town Centre | |
| **Jack Cuir** | 022 731 89 15 |
| Rue de Monthoux, 40 – Town Centre | |
| **L'Antre-Peaux** | 022 342 72 25 |
| Rue Ancienne, 43 – Town Centre | |
| **Louis Vuitton** | 022 311 02 32 |
| Rue du Rhône, 31 – Town Centre | |
| **Maroquinerie** | 022 363 67 00 |
| Signy Centre | |
| **Sakapuss** | 022 320 76 74 |
| Av. de Mail, 2 – Town Centre | |
| **Valenti Cuir Distribution** | 022 741 10 30 |
| Rue de Monthoux, 21 – Town Centre | |

What & Where to Buy

Shopping

jackets are all superbly crafted from the finest leather. If you're a motorcycle enthusiast, Jack Cuir stocks a range of leather goods that will keep you warm, safe and looking smooth. Shops like à Fleur de Peau in Pâquis have a range of 'bedroom leather', if that's your bag!

### Luggage

Travel is all part and parcel of living in Geneva, so do it in style with fabulous luggage. All shopping malls have luggage shops, and department stores have luggage sections. If you're splashing out on leather luggage, visit the speciality leather shops for the best range.

### Medicine

The easiest way to locate a pharmacy is to look for a large green cross, typically accented with neon lighting. If it is closed, there will be a posting indicating where you can find your nearest open pharmacy (although pharmacies with later opening hours charge an additional fee). Pharmacists will fill your prescriptions and are particularly good at identifying the Swiss equivalent of medicines prescribed to you in your home country. English is normally spoken as a second language.

Pharmacies also stock many over the counter medicines for which you do not require prescriptions. If you're not feeling well but are not sick enough for a doctor, describe your symptoms to the pharmacist and he/she will suggest a medication. If you're getting ready to go on a trip, the pharmacist will also recommend any pills or sprays you might want to take to avoid some of the typical tourist discomforts of the area.

| Medicine | |
| --- | --- |
| **Pharmacie de la Gare** | 022 741 53 53 |
| Metro Shopping Cornavin – Town Centre | |
| **Pharmacie de la Fontenette** | 022 342 54 75 |
| Rue de la Fontenette – Town Centre | |
| **Pharmacie Principale** | 022 342 00 44 |
| Confédération Centre – Town Centre | |
| **Pharmacie Sun Store** | 022 818 12 41 |

You'll find many health, beauty and lifestyle products in most pharmacies, such as perfumes, sunscreens, special soaps and bottles. Your pharmacy can also provide you with a list of approved doctors in the area. They also serve a

special function during the fall. As the autumn brings cooler, damper weather, mushrooms begin to pop up in the wooded areas near the city. If you find any, take them to your local pharmacist who can tell you whether they are edible or poisonous.

### Music, DVD's & Videos

Large electronic stores, such as Fnac or Media Markt, have huge selections of recorded music. There is a music shop located within Globus, and Manor has its own music and video section near the electronics department. Smaller music stores tend to specialise in certain genres, so Discoclub is the place to go for jazz, while Divertimento offers a good range of classical music. Most stores allow you to listen to the music before you buy, and return policies are strict so make use of this facility.

Larger music stores carry videos and DVDs, as well as a Librairie du Cinéma. Movies are not released in theatres until they have been dubbed, so that the original and the French version can be released at the same time. This means that you can often buy the video or DVD at the same time that the movie is released in theatres. This is true of video rental shops as well. More often than not, a movie is available for hire even before it has been released in theatres. If you don't mind buying used DVDs and videos, check with your local video rental agency for good prices.

| Music, DVDs & Videos | |
| --- | --- |
| **City Disc** | 022 900 18 50 |
| Metro Shopping Cornavin – Town Centre | |
| **Discoclub** | 022 732 73 66 |
| Terreaux du Temple, 22 – Town Centre | |
| **Divertimento** | 022 310 00 00 |
| Bourg-de-Four, 4 – Town Centre | |
| **Dock Games** | 022 949 77 90 |
| Planète Charmilles | |
| **Forum** | 022 363 67 00 |
| Signy Centre | |
| **Librairie du Cinéma.** | 022 736 88 88 |
| Rue de la Terrassière, 9 – Town Centre | |
| **O'CD** | 022 328 58 28 |
| Round Point de Plainpalais, 6 – Town Centre | |
| **Plain Chant** | 022 329 54 44 |
| Rue du Stand, 40 – Town Centre | |
| **Sounds Records** | 022 328 14 11 |
| Av. du Mail – Town Centre | |
| **Stigmate – Vinyls Shop** | 022 733 71 80 |
| Rue de la Servette | |
| **Très Classic** | 022 781 57 60 |
| Rue Diorama, 16 – Town Centre | |

## Musical Instruments

Other options → Music Lessons [p.215]

Whether you're already an accomplished musician or it's something you've always wanted to try, you'll find plenty of places to buy instruments and sheet music. Some music stores have rental facilities (you can rent a piano from Knifel) and the larger shops, such as Music Arts, have practice rooms. If you are looking for an instrument for your children, their instructor should be able to tell you where to get child-sized instruments.

| Musical Instruments | |
|---|---|
| **A Bout de Souffle** | 022 740 03 85 |
| Rue de Montbrillant, 24 – Town Centre | |
| **Bernard Music** | 022 731 06 15 |
| Rue Jean Pecolat, 4 – Town Centre | |
| **Knifel** | 022 310 17 60 |
| Rue du Marché, 20 – Town Centre | |
| **La Puce à l'Oreille** | 022 328 84 47 |
| Rue Bergalone, 17 – Plainpalais | |
| **Music Arts** | 022 338 03 03 |
| Rue Voltaire, 12 – Town Centre | |
| **Vincenti Guitares – Luthers** | 022 328 99 94 |
| Bd. St-Georges, 52 – Town Centre | |

## Outdoor Goods

Other options → Hardware & DIY [p.150]

Even if you're not naturally the outdoors type, living amidst all the beautiful scenery and clean mountain air in Geneva may make a convert out of you! Hiking is a very popular activity, with many people hiking from cabin to cabin along multi-day routes. If you want to get even closer to nature you can camp outdoors. Camping stores carry loads of handy equipment for these outdoor activities, and can also advise you on various trails. Nature may be beautiful but she can also be pretty harsh at times, so never go unprepared. You can stock up on sleeping bags, tents, hiking boots and even thermal underwear (brrrr!) at any of the following stores

| Outdoor Goods | |
|---|---|
| **Athleticum** | 022 783 90 90 |
| Ch. de Riantbosson, 5-9 – Meyrin | |
| **Cactus Sports** | 022 300 30 01 |
| Rue du Pont-Neuf, 6 – Town Centre | |
| **Great Outdoor Store** | 022 840 17 57 |
| Cours de Rive, 14 – Town Centre | |
| **Peak Performance** | 022 312 34 28 |
| Rue de la Fontaine, 3 – Town Centre | |
| **Sports Aventure Geneve** | 022 321 00 48 |
| Bd. Carl-vogt, 32 – Town Centre | |

## Party Accessories

It's easy to throw a good party in Geneva as there are plenty of party supply stores. Kiddie Club has the most comprehensive selection of party supplies for children's parties. They also rent out their play space, all toys included, for a low maintenance party. If you choose to have a kids' party at your home, they have a never ending supply of party favours and decorations in various themes.

For adults' parties Aligros offers items in bulk quantities at extremely reasonable prices, including alcohol, napkins, and disposable table cloths. For standard party decorations (confetti, balloons, streamers, etc.), visit any of the shops listed in the table. Many grocery stores have ready made food items, to relieve you of some of your kitchen duties!

### The Perfect Disguise

Don't be the only sad sack not in costume at a fancy dress party! Any of the following stores can kit you out in a wide range of costumes:

- Beauty Flore 022 311 27 11
- La Gaîté 022 311 87 08
- Le Truc'store 022 329 46 28
- Costumes Du Théâtre De Carouge 022 343 44 47

The La Fiesta Absolute Show is ideal for larger parties or weddings, and they offer services such as filming the event and decorating the venue, DJ's to get the party started or the right lighting to create a perfect mood. For smaller events you can buy items such as fireworks, confetti bombs, party favours and decorations from their store.

| Party Accessories | |
|---|---|
| **Absolut Show** | 022 738 25 73 |
| Rue du Prieuré, 23 – Town Centre | |
| **Aligro** | 022 308 60 20 |
| Rue Francois Dussaud, 15 – Town Centre | |
| **Kiddie Club** | 022 736 43 92 |
| Rte de Chene, 66 – Town Centre | |
| **Pro Fêtes** | 022 757 11 22 |
| Ch. des Hutins, 31 – Confignon | |

## Perfumes & Cosmetics

With the right cosmetics you can transform yourself from a plain Jane into a gorgeous goddess. And no matter what your mood, there's a perfume to suit it. A vast range of cosmetics and perfumes are available in shops and department stores throughout the city. Some stores are strictly reserved for perfumes; others carry beauty products, perfumes and

What & Where to Buy

Shopping

cosmetics. Many large pharmacies also carry some cosmetic lines and designer perfumes.

### Perfumes & Cosmetics

| | |
|---|---|
| **Body Shop, The** <br> Chavannes Centre | 022 950 86 89 |
| **Douglas** <br> Etrembières Shopping Centre <br> – Etrembières, France | +33-4 50 43 99 88 |
| **Import Perfume** <br> Signy Centre | 022 363 67 00 |
| **Paris Parfume** <br> Rue de Rive, 2 – Town Centre | 022 311 57 35 |

## Second-Hand Items

The best place to find second-hand items, aside from antique stores, is at any of the Protestant Social Centres (CSP) or the Salvation Army. They take donations of all kinds and provide social services to those in need whilst also selling surplus items to the public. Their profits go back into the community through social services to the needy.

If you have items that you wish to donate, Geneva has many large, bright yellow bins on the sides of the road throughout the city where you can drop off your unwanted items, especially clothes. You can also call the CSP to arrange a pick up for larger items, which go mostly to benefit students.

Grocery stores always have a bulletin board stating where you can find items for sale from private citizens. Also, check at work and other community bulletin boards for miscellaneous items.

Alternatively, tune in to WRG 88.4 FM on Friday mornings at 09:00. They have a radio show called The Garage Sale, which provides a great opportunity of buying items from people, mostly expatriates, who are moving. Lastly, there is a flea market at Plainpalais on Wednesdays and Saturdays from 8:00 to 18:00.

### Second-Hand Items

| | |
|---|---|
| **Bazar Caritas** <br> Av. Louis-Bertrand, 1 | 022 792 16 34 |
| **Bric-a-brac** <br> Rue de Carouge, 53 – Town Centre | 022 708 04 36 |
| **Brocante La Renfile** <br> Ch. de la Renfile – Vernier <br> Ch.de la Cartouchiere – Plan-les-Ouates | 022 341 13 02 <br> 022 884 38 00 |
| **Cash Converters** <br> Rue de Carouge, 18 – Town Centre | 022 800 12 65 |
| **Centre Social Protestant (CSP)** <br> Rue du Môle – Pâquis | 022 731 65 41 |
| **Grand Bazar** <br> Rue de Carouge – Carouge | 022 328 02 47 |
| **Hazard Second Hand** <br> Rue de Monthoux, 34 – Town Centre | 022 731 36 59 |
| **L'arc-en-ciel** <br> Bd. Carl-Vogt – Plainpalais | 022 328 22 04 |
| **L'Aubaine** <br> Rue des Pâquis, 23 – Town Centre | 022 731 87 31 |
| **La Carouzette** <br> Rue du Carouge, 37 – Town Centre | 022 329 32 50 |
| **Les Cordiers** <br> Rue des Cordiers, 4 – Town Centre | 022 735 91 91 |
| **Paquine** <br> Rue de Pâquis – Pâquis | 022 738 97 04 |
| **Rue Des Bains** <br> Rue des Bains, 63 – Town Centre | 022 328 42 64 |

So many shops, so little time

SFr 10 ~ € 6    1ˢᵗ Edition | GENEVA EXPLORER

## Shoes

Other options → Beach Wear [p.138]

Shoes are everywhere in Geneva – high heels, platforms, strappy sandals, boots, classic and faddish – whatever your style, you'll find the shoes to fit. If you have unusually small or large feet, you might find less variety in your size. You could go to one of the many shoemakers in Geneva (such as Scarpe or Bea Novelli) to get something custom made, or try La Strada, which specialises in larger sizes. There's always the Internet – visit the Website www.bigshoedirect.co.uk, and have a few pairs delivered to your doorstep.

| Shoes | |
|---|---|
| **52 Avenue** | 022 347 49 18 |
| Rte de Florissant, 52 – Town Centre | |
| **Aeschbach** | 022 979 05 00 |
| Balexert – Geneva | |
| Cours de Rive, 17 – Town Centre | 022 840 49 10 |
| Rue de Carouge, 25 – Town Centre | 022 800 00 70 |
| Rue des Eaux-Vives, 6 – Town Centre | 022 840 49 10 |
| Rue du Rhône, 4 – Town Centre | 022 819 10 90 |
| **Bally** | 022 310 12 03 |
| Rue de Marché, 18 – Town Centre | |
| Rue du Rhône, 62 – Town Centre | 022 310 10 66 |
| **Bata** | 022 340 13 68 |
| Planète Charmilles | |
| Rue de la Croix-d'Or, 15 – Town Centre | 022 310 12 03 |
| Rue de Lausanne, 18 – Town Centre | 022 738 83 65 |
| **Daniel Bartolini** | 022 786 03 28 |
| Rue de la Terrassière, 5 – Town Centre | |
| **Dosenbach** | 022 735 17 25 |
| Eaux-Vives 2000 – Geneva | |
| Planète Charmilles | 022 940 14 20 |
| Rue de Carouge, 28 – Town Centre | 022 800 20 10 |
| Signy Centre | 022 363 67 00 |
| **Elio & Leo** | na |
| Metro Shopping Cornavin – Town Centre | |
| **JM Weston** | 022 311 86 40 |
| Rue de la Croix-d'Or, 29 – Town Centre | |
| **La Strada** | 022 342 27 33 |
| Rue Ancienne, 43 – Town Centre | |
| **La Strada Duo** | 022 786 03 28 |
| Rue de la Terrassière, 5 – Town Centre | |
| **Ochsner** | 022 732 09 10 |
| Rue de Grenus, 16 – Town Centre | |
| **Oschner Shoes** | 022 840 26 50 |
| Rue de la Terrassière, 35 – Town Centre | |
| **San Marina** | 022 311 92 27 |
| Confédération Centre – Town Centre | |
| **Shoe Box** | 022 310 10 02 |
| Rue Etienne dumont, 6 – Town Centre | |
| **Voegle** | 022 738 59 08 |
| Les Cygnes – Pâquis | |
| Planète Charmilles | 022 949 77 90 |

## Souvenirs

Classic Swiss souvenirs like chocolate, cheese, watches and Swiss army knives, make great gifts to take back home. Cheese is only a suitable gift if you have a relatively short journey, but of all the cheeses, a nicely aged Gruyère is probably the most popular choice. Chocolate always travels well, and there can't be many people in the world that wouldn't appreciate a nice big box of the finest Swiss chocs! If you're buying a Swiss Army knife, don't carry it in your hand luggage or you might have it confiscated by airport security.

Remember Geneva...

If you've fallen in love with the majestic scenery, visit any bookshop for a collection of images that can be taken home as souvenirs. The very best one (in our humble opinion, of course!) is Explorer Publishing's *Images of Geneva*. Or take your own photos – the UN buildings, the cobbled streets of the Old Town and of course the lake and mountains are all great photo opportunities. Souvenirs of the wacky, tacky variety are available in speciality souvenir shops. These include melted snowballs, calendars, cuckoo clocks, caps, cuddly toy St. Bernards, countless cow-shaped table decorations and even a can that moos when inverted! You'll find plenty of these shops all over town and at the airport.

## Souvenirs

| | |
|---|---|
| **Best of Switzerland, The** | 022 818 12 41 |
| Geneva Int. Airport – Cointrin | |
| **Bucherer** | 022 319 62 66 |
| Rue de Rhône, 45 – Town Centre | |
| **L'Ours de Berne** | 022 310 12 57 |
| Place du Port, 1 – Town Centre | |
| **Little Switzerland** | 022 731 23 69 |
| Rue du Cendrier, 28 – Town Centre | |
| **Merkur** | 022 818 12 41 |
| Geneva Int. Airport – Cointrin | |
| **Swiss Corner** | 022 731 06 84 |
| Rue des Alpes, 7 – Town Centre | |
| **Swiss Tradition** | 022 731 65 44 |
| Rue du Mont-Blanc, 17 – Town Centre | |

## Sporting Goods

The Genevois are an active bunch and take part in a surprising range of conventional and extreme sports, weather permitting. Whether you're into hiking, biking, swimming, rafting, diving, wakeboarding or skiing, you'll find almost all the gear you need at one of the sports superstores. For more technical gear, there are certain speciality stores where you can get expert advice from knowledgeable staff. Apart from selling you gear appropriate to your sport and skill level, they can put you in contact with local groups and events for your particular sport.

## Sporting Goods

| | |
|---|---|
| **Athleticum** | 022 783 90 90 |
| Ch. de Riantbosson, 5 – 9 | |
| **Decathlon** | +33 4 50 43 93 00 |
| Rue de la Résistance, 14 | |
| – Annemasse, France | |
| **Go Sport** | +33 4 50 99 11 10 |
| Centre Comm. Val Thoiry | |
| – Thoiry, France | |
| **Hofstetter Sports** | 022 818 13 11 |
| Rue de la Corraterie, 12 – 14 – Town Centre | |
| **Ochsner Sports** | 022 363 67 00 |
| Signy Centre | |
| **SportXX** | 022 979 02 02 |
| Balexert – Geneva | |
| La Praille Commercial Centre – Carouge | 022 304 20 00 |

## Tailoring

Other options → Clothes [p.142]

Mr. Ugo Presentazi is one of the few remaining clothes tailors in Geneva. Even though his English is not good, he is very charming and helpful. Most other stores will let you select fabric and a style, take your measurements and then send it off to another country to get your garments made. Atelier de Couture Longemalle and The Private Store both have garments made in Italy. Addison's (in the Confédération Centre) makes shirts and shoes. AJ Collections will make suits for both men and women, and have an extensive range of fabrics to choose from. Prices start from around SFr 790. Adam's Boutique also had a made to measure suit service for men and women, with prices starting at SFr 900 for a two piece suit.

If money is no object then a suit from Francesco Smalto is up your alley – select from half measure ('demi mesure') or full service ('couture') sewing. With half measure, you select a readymade style and fabric, and the garment is then altered to your specifications and measurements. For full service couture, a French tailor gets your measurements, makes the garment in Paris and returns with it for a fitting. Once the garment is finally finished it is sent back to Geneva. This will set you back about SFr 8,000 per suit!

## Tailoring

| | |
|---|---|
| **Adam's boutique** | 022 732 45 30 |
| Place Saint-Gervais, 3 – Town Centre | |
| **Addison** | 022 312 33 50 |
| Confédération Centre – Town Centre | |
| Rte de Florissant, 50 – Town Centre | 022 789 54 90 |
| **AJ Collections** | 022 816 37 80 |
| Rue du Marché, 12 – Town Centre | |
| **Atelier de Couture Langemalle** | 022 310 29 37 |
| Rue du Port – Town Centre | |
| **Café Coton** | 022 736 11 44 |
| Rue Louis Douchosal, 4 – Town Centre | |
| **Cotton Shop** | 022 731 60 72 |
| Rue du Cendrier, 19 – Town Centre | |
| **Francesco Smalto** | 022 818 47 27 |
| Rue du Rhône, 62 – Town Centre | |
| **Le Rouet** | 022 343 49 11 |
| place du Marché, 5 – Town Centre | |
| **McShirt Factory** | 022 300 38 17 |
| La Praille Commercial Centre – Carouge | |
| Rue Rousseau, 29 – Town Centre | 022 731 53 69 |
| **Mr. Ugo Presentazi** | 022 738 23 86 |
| Rue Winkelreid, 8 – Town Centre | |
| **Private Store, The** | 022 732 17 63 |
| Quai des Bergues, 27 – Town Centre | |
| **Retouches Desire – adjustments** | 079 721 76 65 |
| Rue Sismondi, 1 – Town Centre | |

If embroidery is your thing, The Cotton Shop has a large range of tapestry designs and thread supplies for making your own cushions and wall hangings. You can also get a range of books for ideas and help. For shirt embroidery and monogram work, you can either go to The Cotton Shop or Café Coton, which specialises in these services. For something

What & Where to Buy

Shopping

personal visit the McShirt Factory, where you can commission embroidered shirts, sweatshirts, caps, hand towels and other accessories with your own designs.

## Textiles

Other options → Carpets [p.140]

Textiles in Geneva range from reasonably priced to highly expensive – shops like IKEA and Interio have small fabric ranges at low prices, but at the opposite end of the scale Conod's, Manor, Gras or Au Manoir des Tissus have a wonderful selection of beautifully crafted textiles. You can also go further afield to Lyon (for silk) or Paris. The neighbourhood below Sacré Coeur has everything you could possibly imagine when it comes to fabrics, patterns, binding, etc. Alternatively, a few stores in the surrounding French cities and some small sewing supplies shops in Geneva may have what you're looking for. Mercerie de la Madeleine has every button you'll ever need, the Pfaff shop is a good place to buy a sewing machine and limited accessories, and the Cotton Shop has a good range of trims. What Geneva lacks is a large 'one-stop' shop for sewing enthusiasts, but fortunately everything is available online.

### Textiles

| | |
|---|---|
| **A. Gras** <br> Rue de Coutance, 5 – Town Centre | 022 732 64 64 |
| **Au Bouton Chic** <br> Signy Centre | 022 990 31 10 |
| **Au Dé d'Argent** <br> Rue de la Servette, 76 – Town Centre | 022 733 06 46 |
| **Au Manoir des Tissus** <br> Rte du Boiron, 7 – Nyon | 022 362 11 60 |
| **Conod** <br> Rue de la Fontaine, 9 – Town Centre | 022 310 11 09 |
| **Coudr'Art** <br> Bd. James-Fazy, 3 – Town Centre | 022 732 59 74 |
| **Mercerie de la Madeleine** <br> Rue de la Madeleine, 11 – Town Centre | 022 310 45 94 |
| **Mercerie Murielle Christin** <br> Place du Molard, 3 – Town Centre | 022 310 40 51 |
| **Patch World** <br> Av. Louis-Casai, 37 – Vernier | 022 796 58 07 |
| **Tissus Saint Jacques** <br> Rue de la Résistance, 33 <br> – Annemasse, France | +33 4 50 95 02 02 |

## Places to Shop

People in Geneva still do much of their shopping in the area where they reside and at individual shops. This is apparent from the lack of development and

investment in the bigger malls. The following section covers the main shopping outlets, the more common commercial centres as well as the main shopping areas in and around the city.

## Shopping Malls – Main

There are three main shopping malls in the Geneva area and a fourth in the French border town of Anemasse. All have covered parking, are climate controlled and offer a variety of stores, and within them, you will find designated food areas with various places to eat. Even though they offer convenience, malls have not become as much of a popular hangout for shoppers as the main shopping streets.

Balexert

### Centre Balexert

Location → Av. Louis-Casai · Le Grand-Saconnex | 022 979 02 02
Hours → Mon – Fri 09:00 – 19:00 Thu open until 20:00
Web/email → na                                    Map Ref → 5-B2

The largest outlet in this old but well frequented mall is, not surprisingly, the Migros supermarket. Besides carrying a good range of international grocery products, Migros also sells a very nice collection of art, office and craft supplies. Fnac too, has a fantastic electronics and home appliance store. Clothing and accessory shops cater to all ages tastes. Outlets include the Globus Men's shop for men's suits and ties, Benetton, H & M or Morgan for the teenagers, dazzling outfits at Bon Geneie and Carol for women, and satin underwear at Beldona and A Fleur de Peau for the more adventurous ladies. The gift and jewellery stores in this mall are especially eye catching, with the Gilbert Albert shop a 'must-do' on any bonafide shopaholic's list.

This mall provides the facilities to do all your errands under one roof. Drop the kids off at the daycare centre before doing your banking, booking your holiday, posting a letter, getting tickets for an upcoming event (or even the train!), getting your hair done, having your clothes altered and developing your film. In addition, the mall has some good restaurants that are even open on Sunday. These are located near the movie theatre, which happens to be one of the best in town as it has stadium seating and there are no intermissions during showings.

### Etrembières Shopping Centre

Location ➔ Ch. de L'Industrie, 21      **+33 4 50 43 99 88**
Hours ➔ Mon – Thu 09:00 – 19:00; Fri 09:00 – 21:00
Web/email ➔ na                                    Map Ref ➔ na

Located just south of Geneva (and over the French Border) in Annemasse, this shopping centre has been going strong ever since it first opened in 1994. Although not quite as big as some malls within Geneva, it is still heavily patronised simply because of the value for money that shoppers can find here. There are over a thousand covered parking spaces make it popular in bad weather. The mall houses one of the two Migros supermarkets that are situated outside of Switzerland, and you can find a much greater variety of all the French delights, such as the cheese and the pâtés that are generally hard to find in Geneva. As for clothing stores, there's Etam, Morgan and Naf Naf for the ladies, and Celio or Olly Gan for the men. Head to Nicolas for wine and spirits and Jeff de Bruges for Belgian chocolates, but don't let the border guards catch you trying to bring those back to Switzerland. Stock up on beautiful things for your baby at Petit Bateau, for your home at Skeena, or for yourself at Douglas (fresh flowers and nice perfumes). Banking, dry cleaning, shoe repairs and photo development are all services available here.

### La Praille Commercial Centre

Location ➔ Rte des Jeunes, 10 · Carouge      | 022 304 80 00
Hours ➔ Various (according to outlet)
Web/email ➔ www.la-praille.ch                       Map Ref ➔ 8-C3

M Parc-La Praille is always spoken about as one, yet is a mall with two components. M Parc is a Migros commercial centre and La Praille is the newest mall in Geneva. M Parc is a triple M Migros, meaning this is as big as it gets for the Swiss Migros store chain. All the stores in this complex are related to Migros, such as M-Electronics (electronics, appliances and books), and M-Print (an office supplies and print shop). Assortment Bricolage is the biggest garden and DIY centre in town, while Micasa has covers all your home decoration needs. Then you have the 'solderie', where they sell last season's goods at discount prices. The Migros restaurant serves up a hearty meal, while Gourmessa offers takeaways.

Across the motorway is La Praille, the newest mall in Geneva. It is full of stores, services and activities to make your life easier, such as a florist, hair salon, bank, travel agency, cleaners, film service, solarium and beauty institute. It is accessible for physically challenged shoppers, and has a huge recycling centre. Children are well looked after too – Orchestra Land is a safe, colourful, educational play area for kids and is open seven days a week.

The mall also incorporates the Harmony Fitness Centre, where you can fit in a quick aerobics class or a game of bowling. As for shops, there is something for everyone at La Praille.

### Signy Centre

Location ➔ Rue de Fléchères            | 022 363 67 00
Hours ➔ Mon – Thu 09:00 – 19:00;  Fri 9:00 – 21:00.
Web/email ➔ www.signycentre.ch                   Map Ref ➔ na

On your way to Lausanne or IKEA (whichever first takes you away from Geneva towards this direction), you'll find the Signy Centre just off the highway. With an impressive 1,200 parking spaces, it is quite hard to miss. Lots of natural light and an open central area makes for a relaxed shopping experience, and the planning and presentation is as well represented on their Website as it is in the centre. The main store is a Coop, but a large Oschner sports store is not far behind in terms of size. There are, of course, several clothing shops, gift shops and bookstores in addition to the cafés and restaurants. Other than that, services here include a bank, a dental clinic, a post office, a photo centre and the Harmony Fitness Club.

## Shopping Malls – Other

The most common type of mall in Geneva is the commercial centre, which is basically a covered strip mall that is not quite big enough to be a real mall, yet has a climate controlled environment and a decent collection of shops. However, don't expect to hear your kids requesting to be dropped off at these centres so they can meet up with friends, as there is nothing in the way of usual mall entertainment.

Shopping mall

### Centre Commercial Chavannes Centre

Location → Chavannes-de-Bogis | 022 950 86 89
Hours → Mon – Thu 09:00 – 19:00  Fri 9:00 – 21:00
Web/email → www.les-centres-magiques.ch    Map Ref → 5-A3

A quick drive out of town brings you to the Commercial Centre of Chavannes, a spacious area that lacks the city's hustle and bustle. Take your time shopping in the less crowded and more spacious aisles of the Manor grocery store. You can try on the latest styles at Benetton, Esprit or Bon Génie, or get easy assistance for any electronic appliance queries at Fust. There are many food options but if you're with kids, the Manor cafeteria is a safe bet. They'll conjure up your meals right in front of you while a large outside play area keeps the kids happily occupied. Just next door to the mall is a French furniture store called Fly, with affordable modern designs that look good but are temporary enough for the short-term expat. Other stores inside the centre include The Body Shop, H & M, Manor Sports, Mister Minit, Jean-Louis David, Naville, and Visilab. DIY Jumbo is about 100 metres down the road.

### Centre Commercial Eaux-Vives 2000

Location → Rue de la Terrassière 43 · Town Centre | 735 17 25
Hours → Mon – Wed 08:00 – 19:00  Thu 9:00 – 21:00
Web/email → na    Map Ref → 14-B4

Focusing mainly on the family, this Coop based commercial centre is packed with shops and service providers. Stop by Visilab for an eye check and glasses, pick up some pre-made meals at Le Gourmet for a delicious, easy dinner or, if you're

feeling peckish, try Edward's tasty sandwiches. A nice selection of wines can be found in the Coop, and shoes for the whole family at Dosenbach. Treat yourself to a new outfit at H & M, a new set of keys at Mister Mint and drop off your dry cleaning at Netteco. If you're ready for a vacation, drop by Helvetic Tours and book your next holiday.

### Confédération Centre Shopping Mall

Location → Rue de la Confédération | 022 311 52 92
Timings → na
Web/email → www.confederation-centre.ch    Map Ref → 13-D4

Because of its location in the middle of town, the Confédération Centre cannot provide the luxury of free parking, but on the plus side you are surrounded by shops offering all kinds of goodies, both in and out of the centre. In fact, this is the place to find the best cakes in town – just head to La Maison du Gâteau pastry shop and let your sweet tooth take over. The jewellery shops in the centre are fun and affordable, and you're bound to find a good pair of comfortable mules or stylish heels at San Marina. Hard to find Italian spices are available in abundance on the top floor at Capococcia 1899. Of course, if you're not in an 'eat and shop' mood, you could always stop by the Rex for a movie in the original version (VO) or dubbed in French (VF).

### Les Cygnes

Location → Rue de Lausanne, 16-20 · Pâquis | 022 738 59 08
Timings → na
Web/email → www.lescygnes.ch    Map Ref → 13-D2

Located in Pâquis with colourful shops on all sides, this 25 store commercial centre focuses on affordable purchases. The key tenant is an MM Migros carrying beauty products, kitchen accessories, electronic appliances, books, office supplies, toys, and even grocery items. You will find a copy service, clothing store, flower shop, solderie and more (the solderie is where last year's items are sold at a 15% to 90% discount). Aside from the Migros related stores, Bata and Voegle have shoes for any budget or outfit. InterDiscount, located near the McDonald's, fulfils all your electronic needs. Sun Store is a leading pharmacy that also sells perfumes and health products. Le Club des Marques is a menswear shop selling brand names at discount prices. Pick Pay has discounted food and wine items on offer. In one trip to Le Cygnes, you will find all you need and still have money in your pocket when you leave.

### Les Galeries at M-Aéroport

Location ➜ Geneva Int'l Airport · Cointrin | 022 818 12 41
Hours ➜ 09:00 – 20:00
Web/email ➜ www.gva.ch/fr/default.htm      Map Ref ➜ 2-C4

If you don't ski, watch movies or go to church, Sundays can be a little boring. A common activity is shopping at the airport – this may sound strange but once you get there, you'll find many other people escaping a cold, boring Sunday in the same way! This is actually one of the few places in town that is actually open on Sundays and so is very popular with people who work, as they can use their day off to shop. And the range of shops is surprising – there is a Migros grocery store, Les Caves de l'Aéroport, which sells a good selection of wines, a pharmacy, Manor department store and a Martel sweet shop. In addition, you'll find standard airport items such as Swiss souvenirs and chocolates. On the last Sunday of each month there is a small market, when the airport halls fill with artisan items. After a hard day's shopping, rest your weary feet in the Le Plein Ciel restaurant, or grab a fast food fix at Le Cockpit or Aux Bonnes Choses.

### Metro Shopping Cornavin

Location ➜ Gare CFF Cornavin · Town Centre | na
Timings ➜ na
Web/email ➜ na      Map Ref ➜ 13-D2

This mall is slightly different from usual malls in that there is no central information centre and the shops are spread out, giving the feeling of a covered street rather than a mall. The stores in and below the train station will appeal to the young and trendy. America on Sale has the latest fashions,

Claire's is perfect for affordable costume jewellery, accessories or gifts for young girls, and Maxi 15 is a unique store that carries random items for SFr 5, 10 or 15 (never more!). You can stock up on reading material at Naville, the news-stand. Yves Rocher has a range of perfumes and beauty items, while Lacoste, Jeans & Co or Manor stock some good clothing ranges. Elio & Leo have stylish boots in the winter and beautiful strappy sandals in the summer. Bon Génie Boutiques boast designer fashion, and if you want to add some spice to your weekend trip, slip into Beate Uhse Erotic Trends.

### Planète Charmilles

Location ➜ Prom.De l'Europe, 11 · Town Centre | 022 949 77 90
Hours ➜ See below
Web/email ➜ www.planete-charmilles.com      Map Ref ➜ 13-A2

This calm, quiet centre is ideal for those who like to get their shopping done in peace. Shoe lovers can find their ideal fit at Bata, Vogele or Dosenbach and Naville houses the latest magazines, which you can read while you get your hair done at Jean-Louis David. Kit out your pampered pooch or kitty at pet store Cats and Dogs, before picking up some groceries at either Migros or Pick Pay. You can get your film developed at Photo Charmilles, your clothes dry cleaned at En 5 Sec, and your caffeine fix at Coffee Land or Espresso Club. If you've had a tough day and you need some stress-busting, spend an hour or two at Dock Games arcade, or sample the range of beers at Palais des Bières (the palace of beers).

*Hours: Mon to Wed 9:00 – 19:00, Thu 9:00 – 21:00, Fri 9:00 – 19:30, Sat 9:00 – 18:00, Sun closed.*

## Department Stores

### Globus – Grand Passage

Location ➜ Rue du Rhône, 48 · Geneva, 1204 | 022 319 50 50
Timings ➜ 09:00 - 19:00  Closed Sun
Web/email ➜ na      Map Ref ➜ na

This large town centre department store is home to an impressive range of quality goods. Many designer fashion labels are represented in the clothing department, and the perfume and cosmetics section has products by all the big names you'd expect to see. Globus also sells watches and jewellery, books, electronics and home furnishings. There is a buffet restaurant and a pizzeria, and the delicatessen has a comprehensive selection of fine wines.

## Manor

Location → Rue Cornavin, 6 · 1211 Genève  
Timings → 09:00 - 19:00 Closed Sun  
Web/email → na

**022 909 46 99**

Map Ref → na

Manor is a big department store chain with outlets throughout Switzerland. With its town centre location this is a great one- stop shop with almost everything a shopper could ask for under one roof. You'll find men's, women's and children's fashion and sportswear, as well as perfume, cosmetics and home furnishings. There's also a well-stocked electronics and multimedia department. Concert and theatre tickets can be bought at Manor Ticket Corner and whilst you're here why not take care of all those little jobs – from getting a key cut to having your ice skates repaired!

## Markets

### Geneva

Does the convenience and variety of choice in the supermarkets merit the exclusive patronage of the Genevois? Is ease traded for quality; anonymous one stop shopping preferred to neighbourly conversations with individual stall vendors? The number of open air markets in and around Geneva tells us no. This is a time to say hello to old friends, catch up on the local gossip or practice your French. People here are not hurried, although the pushing and shoving of some may cause you to think otherwise. On the whole though, you can relax and enjoy the quality, variety and friendly environment.

> ### Flea Market
>
> In Plainpalais (Av. Henri-Dumant) there is a flea market on Wednesdays & Saturdays (08:00 – 15:00). They sell everything from antiques to art to junk. It's great fun to have a browse – you never know when you are going to find a treasure!

Many open air markets offer items such as fresh fruits, cheeses, flowers, baked goods, speciality soaps, dried nuts, and selected meats. Freshly ground spices, home made pasta, and delicious olives are just a few of the tempting items for sale in this convivial setting. The main markets are listed, however there are small ones that pop up all over town. They may be in front of a commercial centre, on sides of busy streets or in a large parking lot. They are not as big, but they may be closer to you and are usually full of wonderful treats waiting to be taken home.

## Open Air Markets

| Right Bank | Map Ref |
|---|---|
| **Place Grenus** (Sat) | 13-D3 |
| **Rue de Liotard** (Mon & Thu) | 5-D3 |
| **Rue de Grand-Pré** (Mon & Thu) | 5-D3 |
| **Place de la Navigation** (Tue & Fri) | 13-E2 |
| **Rue de Saint Jean** (Tue & Fri) | 13-B3 |
| **Rue des Grottes** (Thu 14:00 – 20:00) | 13-C2 |

| Left Bank | Map Ref |
|---|---|
| **Boulevard Helvétique** (Wed & Sat) | 14-A4 |
| **Pré l'Eveque** (Mon) | 14-A4 |
| **Plaine de Plainpalais** (Tue & Fri; Sun closes 18:00) | 15-D1 |
| **Place du Molard** (Daily 9:00 – 18:00) | 13-E3 |
| **Place du Marché, Carouge** (Wed & Sat) | 15-D4 |
| **Place de la Fusterie** (Thu 8:00 – 19:00) | 13-E3 |
| **Plateau de Champel** (Thu ) | 15-E1 |

Plainpalais Market

### France

Ferney-Voltaire holds a market at place Voltaire on Saturday from 8:30 to 12:00. Collonge-sous-Salève has a market at Croix-de-Rozon on Sunday from 8:00 to 12:00, but it is worth knowing that parking is difficult so your best bet is to park on the Swiss side and simply walk across the border. Make sure you know your limits on border crossing allowances. Divonne has a market in the city centre on Sundays from 08:00 to 12:00, featuring a fantastic range of exquisite items. The number of exotic peppers alone will make you want to go out and buy multiple grinders.

### Christmas Markets

Christmas markets in Geneva add to the ambience with unique gift options as well as festive decorating

ideas. Booths sell delicious treats to put you in the Christmas mood such as roasted chestnuts, fresh crêpes or mulled wine. The downtown area has a gathering of small wood stalls just after the pedestrian bridge. The area near the train station opens stands as well during this season. There are many markets advertised in other surrounding cities as well as local neighbourhood clubs which have a weekend market. One of the best Christmas markets is that in Carouge; a fantastic way to find something for those who seem to have it all and have fun at the same time. It features a great variety guaranteed to stir your Christmas ideas.

## Streets/Areas to Shop

It is more difficult to find an area of Geneva that does not offer shopping, than one that does. However, the following areas are particularly good shopping districts, packed with small galleries, jewellery shops, home décor, accessories and clothing boutiques, cafés, chocolate shops, fresh flowers, etc. Almost without exception, any street that is also a tram line is always lined with shops, so if you're out to spend just hop on a tram, keeping your eyes peeled and your purse ready!

### Carouge                    Map Ref – 15-B4

To go to Carouge is to leave Geneva. Located across the river, it seems that in crossing, you leave behind the city and enter a small community. The pace is different, mostly due to the light car traffic. A browse around this magical area is well worth it, even if you don't spend a franc. Wedding dresses of your dreams come to life at Comme Dans un Rêve. Volupté creates beautiful styles for voluptuous figures. Teo Jakob Tagliabue has wonderful contemporary items for the household and at Dunia you can buy beautiful Indonesian items for your home. Tout Feu Tout Flamme carries a range of candles, and Les 5 Sens sells floral creations that are more like works of art. If all the shopping makes you feel a bit peckish, pop into Los Tacos for handmade Mexican Food or select a freshly baked treat from Wolfisberg bakery. Many of the shops in Carouge are closed on Saturdays and Sundays.

### Plainpalais                Map Ref – 15-D1

This area borders the banking quarter, melts into Carouge and, as it is the home of the university, is frequented by students. Here you'll find galleries and museums of international acclaim such as Analix Forever, the MAMCO Museum of Modern and Contemporary Art, and the Patek Phillipe

Museum. Bars and clubs such as L'Ethno and Sip lead you right to superb restaurants like Bat Dat and Café des Bains. Gadgetissimo is full of gadgets and gifts for the person who has everything. La Truffe Noire is a café that also sells devilishly expensive culinary delights. Off The Shelf is a recently opened English bookstore and Les Voyageurs is a travel bookstore. There are also many clothing and accessories shops. La Persia is the home of the finest Oriental rugs, plus you'll find plenty of other home furnishing outlets.

### Pâquis                     Map Ref – 13-E1

The many stores that fill the streets of Pâquis are proof that this really is an area of contrasts. From unpretentious bohemian outlets to posh tea shops and shops of a decidedly adult nature, you can buy anything from oriental rugs and antiques to a rice cooker or biking leathers. Pâquis is near the lake, so it is home to some of the top hotels and some high end shops (Sotheby's office and showroom is located here). Yet just down the road you'll find ethnic grocery stores, second-hand stores and even the red light district!

### Cité or the City Centre    Map Ref – 13-E4

This area is the home of the Banking Quarter, and the main shopping street is Rue de la Corraterie. Along this street you'll find Fleuriot for fresh flowers, Gilbert Albert for jewellery creations, a few small art galleries, Le Carrousel for unique children's gifts, Hofstetter Sports, City Griffee for Italian labels at discount prices, Brachard for stationery and La Casa del Habano for cigars.

Turn the corner and you'll be on 'Tram Street'. This street is only open to trams and pedestrians, and changes names three times in ten blocks. It starts as Rue du Marché, then becomes Rue de la Croix

Piercing shop

SFr 10 ~ € 6

d'Or and Rue du Rive before it finally joins with Cours de Rive. Despite the name changes, it is lined with many great shops and department stores (C & A, EPA, Globus, DKNY, Benetton, Zara, H & M, Bally and Davidoff, to name but a few).

If you walk towards the lake from Tram Street you'll soon find yourself on the swanky Rue de Rhône, easily identifiable as many of the shops have their own doormen. It is home to the finest watch and jewellery shops, fur shops and exclusive boutiques.

A short walk up the hill from Tram Street takes you to the Old Town, a quiet world of cobbled streets, unique shops and quaint cafés. This is the place to go for hand crafted items, art galleries and antique shops, as well as old-school jewellery and watch makers.

## Outside of Geneva

### Meyrin                          Map Ref – 1-D4

This area has lots of space and many large stores just past the airport on Route de Meyrin. There is plenty of parking, so bring your car or borrow a friend's – preferably one with lots of boot space! It includes stores such as the electronics superstore Media Markt, Interio and Conforama for home décor, sports emporium Athleticum, Jumbo for DIY and garden items, a Carrefour supermarket, the home appliances store Fust and toy superstore King Jouet.

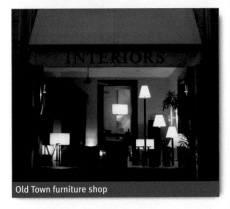
Old Town furniture shop

### Aubonne

Take the Aubonne/Allemans exit off the A1 freeway, about halfway between Lausanne and Geneva, where you'll find many large warehouse-style stores, such as furniture superstore IKEA. There is also a Nike outlet, a Hornback DIY superstore, a huge Coop supermarket that also sells DIY and garden items and Matelas Elite, a factory outlet selling mattresses. Other outlets include Pfister Meubles, Interiors and Top Tip for home décor and furnishings, and Maxi Toys for the little ones.

## In France

### Annemasse/Ville la Grand

Annemasse is known for the shopping mall Etrembières, but it also has many huge stores throughout the city and its neighbouring city Ville la Grand. There are four supermarkets; Champion, Géant, Intermarché and E.Leclerc. Other superstores include King Jouet and Maxi Toys for kids, La Halle Chaussures for shoes, Feu Vert for car accessories and Decathlon for sports goods. Veloland is for bike lovers and Botanic for those with green thumbs. Bricorama and La Boite à Outils are large DIY centres. Connexion has electronics and City-Zoo carries pet items. LP Luminaires and Keria sell lighting accessories and Quiatiss and Tissus Saint/Jacques sell textiles. No Limits is a good restaurant to stop at after a hard day's shopping, and is very family friendly.

### St Genis-Pouilly

This area is just outside of Geneva and is home to one CERN pit (the main one is in Prévessin). Here you'll find the Intermarché supermarket, Inter Sport and the Station Marché auto centre. Quel Jardin and are large garden centres and Eau & Nature meet all your spa needs. Nevada Bob's stocks anything you might need for golf. Go to Samse and La Boite à Outils for DIY items, and BUT for electronics. Perhaps the best reason to go to this shopping area is Jim's British Market, where you'll find your favourite food goodies from the UK.

### Ségny & Ferney-Voltaire

As you cross the border into Ferney-Voltaire, the small street on your right will lead you to the fabulous Good Tastes Lebanese grocery store, where you can stock up on authentic items and stop for a quick lunch. The area has three supermarkets (Ed's, Champion and Carrefour), as well as one of the biggest garden centres, Jardiland. You can find all your auto accessories at Feu Vert and DIY items at Bricorama. Sport 2000 stocks all your sporting requirements, from snowshoes to swim caps. Luminares, Casa Design, L'habitation and Home Salons are all home décor outlets. Border control is quite strict here, be aware of customs limitations.

# Activities

**EXPLORER**

# Activities

**Table of Contents**

**Activities**

---

**MUST DO**

*Switzerland is famous for its health spas, and the region around Lake Geneva has some excellent spa facilities and well being centres. Booking yourself into a spa is an essential part of life in Geneva, whether it's just for a two hour energising massage, or for a weeklong detox. Mud wraps, thermal baths, hydro massage and saunas are just some of the wonderfully indulgent treatments on offer. Go on...be good to yourself!*

---

**MUST GO**

*Head for the hills – the beautiful mountains around Geneva offer more than just a good view. Residents and visitors alike are drawn to the mountains, particularly for the extreme sports opportunities on offer. From caving and climbing, to mountain biking and skiing, people are forever out there in the fresh mountain air. Even if you're not an adrenaline junkie and would prefer a gentler mountain activity, you'll find a well organised network of hiking trails just waiting to be explored.*

The mountains and lakes in and around Geneva create an exciting natural playground and numerous alpine and aqua activities beckon. You can climb, ski, cycle, hike and snowboard until you run out of mountain, and then explore the lake with a sailing boat, waterskis or even scuba equipment! At the back of this book you'll find a collection of handy maps that should help you explore. If getting sweaty on the slopes or whizzing around on water is not for you, Geneva also offers a range of more leisurely activities, such as lakeside lounging at the beach parks or lazy, luxurious spa treatments.

Of course one of the main advantages to getting involved in an activity is the opportunity to meet new people, and this chapter lists various sporting activities and clubs that you can join. Word of mouth is often the best way to find out about clubs and organisations, so if you're interested in something that isn't listed here, ask your friends, work colleagues, or even complete strangers!

As this is the very first edition of the *Geneva Explorer*, we would welcome any comments or suggestions from you regarding what we should change or include in the next edition. Are you a member of a club, organisation or group that hasn't been listed here? If so, we need to hear from you! It doesn't matter if you are big or small, official or unofficial – just let us know who you are and what you do and we'll spread the word on your behalf, free of charge. Visit our Website (www.Explorer-Publishing.com) and fill in the Reader Response form so we know you're out there.

## Aerobics

Other options → Beach, Health & Sports Centres [p.206, 207]

### Geneva Dance Centre

Location → Rue Peillonnex, 2 · Chêne-Bourg | 022 348 49 77
Hours → Check for timings
Web/email → www.genevadancecenter.ch    Map Ref → 9-D1

Founded in 1980, the Geneva Dance Centre is primarily a school for professional ballet training, but a section is reserved for those who just want to dance for pleasure! The school has trained a number of young dancers who are now performing with some of the largest ballet companies in the world. Apart from classical ballet, the school also offers jazz dance, Pilates, mat work, body toning and conditioning, yoga and stretching classes. Open from the beginning of September through until the end of June.

## Amusement Parks

### Aquaparc

Location → Rte de la Plage · Le Bouveret | 024 482 00 00
Hours → 10:00 – 22:00   Fri-Sat 10:00 – 01:00
Web/email → www.aquaparc.ch    Map Ref → na

It's 'water water everywhere' at Aquaparc, and it's guaranteed to make a splash for children and adults alike. Nicknamed 'the Caribbean of Lake Geneva', this park is situated just over an hour outside the city. It is made up of three different 'water worlds' – Captain Kid's Land for kids; Jungle Land, which is full of exotic plants, waterfalls and six giant slides; and Paradise Land, where you can escape the thrills and relax in Turkish baths, saunas and Jacuzzis.

Ferris Wheel

### Parc du Pré-Vert de Signal de Bougy

Location → See below | 021 821 59 30
Hours → Check for timings
Web/email → signal.bougy@gmvd.migros.ch    Map Ref → na

For 30 years, this park has been providing quality entertainment for the whole family. Activities for all tastes are available, from golf and badminton, to football and volleyball, to swings, clowns and

Aerobics | Amusement Parks

Activities

even a zoo! Entrance to the park is free, and you can enjoy your lunch at one of the many picnic sites or in the self service restaurant. On major public holidays, a special programme of entertainment is arranged, including shows, musical concerts and aperitifs on the terrace.

*Location: Bougy-Villars near Rolle and Aubonne, just outside Geneva on the way to Lausanne.*

## Archery

| Noble Exercice de L'Arc | |
|---|---|
| Location → Rue Vautier bis, 9 · Carouge | **079 543 45 49** |
| Hours → See below | |
| Web/email → na | Map Ref → 15-D4 |

This club celebrated its 560th birthday in 2004 – making it Geneva's oldest club, with records dating back to the year 1444 when companies of archers protected the territory and security of lords and landowners. Nearly 600 years later, the modern day archers meet on Sunday mornings from March to November to hone their skills and socialise. This small but dedicated group is always keen to welcome new members to lead the club into its six hundredth year ... and beyond!

## Athletics

There are many athletics clubs to choose from in Geneva, since it is home to an active and healthy society. As in other countries, the clubs are fairly serious in terms of training and competing, but some do have 'amateur' sections. To find the right club for you, contact the Association Genevoise d'Athlétisme (the Geneva Athletics Association). For information on different clubs and activities, as well as details of competitions, races and their own training sessions, just log on to their Website (www.geneve-athletisme.ch).

| Stade Genève | |
|---|---|
| Location → Various · Chambésy | **022 311 23 93** |
| Hours → Check for timings | |
| Web/email → www.stadegeneve.ch | Map Ref → na |

With nearly 600 members, this is one of the largest sporting associations in Switzerland. It is renowned for its high-level runners, some of whom have even competed at Olympic and world championship level. It also has an amateur running section, which is made up of over one hundred runners of different ages and fitness levels, who meet at various times during the week. For details, check the Website or call the club directly.

## Badminton

Badminton beginners and more serious players will be able to find a club that suits them amongst the variety of clubs across the city. Many clubs offer training for nonmembers, just in case you want to improve your game before you take the plunge and join a club! To find out about other Geneva clubs, you can consult the Association Cantonale Genevoise de Badminton (the regional badminton association) who can also update you on upcoming events and how to sign up for tournaments. For further details, visit the association's Website (www.acgb.ch), which is in French, or contact them directly on 022 493 209.

| Badminton Club de Roches | |
|---|---|
| Location → Champel/Malagnou · Chambésy | **022 840 25 95** |
| Hours → See below | |
| Web/email → www.bcroches.ch | Map Ref → 2-E4 |

Roches is an extremely friendly and informal club, open to players of all levels. It was founded by four dedicated players who wanted to share their enthusiasm for the game with like-minded souls. Currently, the club has courts that are available for training three evenings per week at schools in Champel and Malagnou. As Roches is affiliated to the Geneval Cantonal Badminton Association, members can participate in specialist courses and take part in tournaments throughout the year.

*Training times: Juniors: Fri 16:00 – 18:00 (l'école de Roches); Adults: Mon 20:00 – 22:00 (l'école de Pechier) and Wed/Thu 20:00 – 22:00 (l'école de Roches).*

*Prices: A year's subscription costs SFr 200. Members can also choose to pay on a trimester basis (every four months) at SFr 80.*

| Badminton Club Geneva | |
|---|---|
| Location → Rue Francois Dussaud 12 | **022 300 36 22** |
| Hours → 12:00 – 14:00 | |
| Web/email → na | Map Ref → 15-B1 |

The Geneva Badminton Club plays at the Queue d'Arve Sports Centre, home to many international tournaments including the 2004 European Championships. Founded in 1957 and with over 200 members, the club offers training, specialist courses and access to courts for people of all ages and all levels (both rated and non rated players). Badminton courts can be hired by members or nonmembers for SFr 13 per hour. For a complete rundown of services and costs, contact the club directly or visit the Website.

*Timings: juniors' training: Wednesdays at various times; adults' training: (various depending on level); adults (members and non ranked): Thursdays 19:00 – 20:00. Specialist lessons are held at various times throughout the year, generally on Wednesdays.*

### Club du Bois-Carré

Location ➔ Ch. des Bûcherons, 14 · Veyrier | 022 784 30 06
Hours ➔ 09:00 – 22:00 Sat/Sun 09:00 – 20:00
Web/email ➔ www.boiscarre.ch          Map Ref ➔ 9-B4

Open to members and nonmembers, the Club du Bois-Carré is one of the few clubs that offer three racket sports in one club (badminton, squash and tennis). Facilities are open all year round, seven days a week. For further information on the Club du Bois-Carré, refer to Tennis [p.199].

## Basketball

There's plenty of slam-dunkin' action in Geneva, be it amongst informal teams playing each other in the park or serious league contenders. The Association Cantonale Genevoise de Basketball Amateur can provide information on clubs in your area, as well as details on tournaments and events. (Call 022 735 6700 or visit their Website at http://www.acgba.ch/). Many organisations and businesses field informal teams, taking to the courts on various evenings after work, so ask around and you might find there's a club nearer than you think. The Sports Centres section [p.171] details the basketball courts available for use.

### All American Basketball Camp

Location ➔ Stade du Bout-du-Monde | 022 340 43 94
Hours ➔ Check for timings
Web/email ➔ www.basketcamp.ch          Map Ref ➔ 9-A3

This English speaking summer camp provides the opportunity to train alongside basketball pros. The camp holds two weekly sessions on an annual basis, and is open to both girls and boys from 7 to 20 years old. There is the choice of being a day camper (SFr 400) or an overnighter (SFr 575). Check out the Website for the registration form and further details.

### International BBC

Location ➔ Av. de Trembley · Petit-Saconnex | 022 734 46 62
Hours ➔ Check for timings
Web/email ➔ na          Map Ref ➔ 5-C2

International by name, international by nature – this basketball team has around 50 members from 20 different nations! A lively and diverse group, the club comprises two men's and two women's teams which compete in the regional leagues, as well as a more informal team. Matches usually take place on a Wednesday and training is on various nights during the week. The club welcomes new members, whether serious slam-dunkers or basketball beginners.

### Nyon Basket Féminin

Location ➔ Case Postale 85, CH - 1260 · Nyon | 021 362 45 54
Hours ➔ Check for timings
Web/email ➔ www.nyonbasketfeminin.ch          Map Ref ➔ na

This one's just for the girls – the Nyon women's basketball club has teams that play in the National B League (pretty serious stuff!), but there are also teams which play for the Second League, teams for younger girls, and even a team call "The Minis" for the really little ones. A close knit club atmosphere exists, with frequent training and matches, as well as social activities like raclette evenings. Nyon is about 20 minutes from Geneva, with easy road access and good public transport links.

## Billiards

If you're a fan of potting and cueing, there are plenty of establishments around the city where you can grab a game of billiards or snooker. Most of these places have a number of tables as well as a video games area, bar, table football and more – some even house internet cafés. Games usually cost around SFr 3 – 5.

### Billard de Plainpalais

Location ➔ Plainpalais | 022 328 03 30
Hours ➔ 24 hrs
Web/email ➔ na          Map Ref ➔ 15-D1

Members can play billiards round the clock at this venue, which remains open 24 hours a day. Nonmembers can usually get a game in the afternoons. The club organises classes, training and tournaments for the discipline of French billiards, and it has five tables.

Basketball | Billiards

Activities

### Centre Carougeois

Location → Av. Cardinal-Mermillod, 36 | 022 300 21 00
Hours → 10:00 – 01:00 Fri, Sat 10:00 – 02:00
Web/email → pugliese.patrick@wanadoo.fr    Map Ref → 15-D4

This is the largest billiard hall in Geneva, with 18 billiard tables, two snooker tables, darts, a bar and a snack bar filling the 700 m2 premises. It is open seven days a week from early until late, so you should be able to rack up more than a few games. Other Billiard Clubs; America, Rue de Fribourg,3 (738 28 97) La Sphère Académie, Rue de Lausanne, 80-82 (732 36 81)

## Boules

### Boulodrome, The

Location → Queue d'Arve Sports Centre · Acacias | 022 300 10 50
Hours → Check for timings
Web/email → na    Map Ref → 15-B1

The French game of Boules is a popular pastime amongst friends in the nearby remote villages, and you can learn how to play this historical sport at The Boulodrome in the Queue d'Arve Sports Centre, Acacias. There are over 25 'pitches' for games of petanque, boules en bois and boule lyonnaise, and they can be used free of charge – all you need is at least three other willing participants. Groups and clubs are also welcome.

## Bowling

Other options → Boules [p.172]

### Bowling de Meyrin

Location → Chemin de l'Etang, 67 · Châtelaine | 022 796 05 33
Hours → Check for timings
Web/email → www.bowlingdemeyrin.ch    Map Ref → 5-B2

This popular bowling alley is a little bit special – not only can you enjoy the 12 lane bowling alley, a video games arcade and an entertainment section, but you can also order authentic Italian pizza by the metre. Run by an Italian family, the complex combines all the fun of a bowling alley with a really good restaurant that serves a full and varied menu, making this an ideal venue for special occasions or group outings. A definite 'strike'! Bookings recommended.

*Costs: Adults – SFr 8 / Children – SFr 6. Shoe rental – SFr 2*

### Bowling International de Genève

Location → La Praille Shopping Centre · Vernier| 022 301 66 63
Hours → Check for timings
Web/email → na    Map Ref → 5-A3

The largest bowling alley in Switzerland, Bowling International is a massive modern masterpiece and is open 365 days of the year. Opened in 2002, the alley has 26 bowling lanes, billiard tables, video games, table football and even a ball pool 'castle' for little ones. The alley is a fun and reasonably priced outing for the whole family, situated within the popular Praille Shopping centre.

*Costs: Weekdays: Adults – SFr 6,50 / Children, students, concessions – SFr 5. Shoe hire: SFr 2. All tickets SFr 8. Shoe hire SFr 2.*

## Boxing

### Boxing/Kick Boxing Club

Location → Thônex | 079 440 30 00
Hours → See below
Web/email → na    Map Ref → 9-D2

This club, run by personal trainer Thierry Pasche, features classes in various boxing techniques, including full contact, English boxing, kick boxing and instinct fighting, and encourages a non-violent training approach. The club, which currently has about 100 members, also runs a 'fit punching' class for ladies only – this class is non-contact, and uses punch bags and music to encourage women to get fit in a fun and friendly e n v i r o n m e n t .

*Images of Geneva*

Breathtaking mountain vistas mirrored in the crystal clear waters of the lake, the cobbled streets of the Old Town contrasted against the bustling modernity of one of the world's business capitals; Geneva is a treasure trove of beautiful views. Images of Geneva *is a stunning collection of photographs of both the familiar and undiscovered sights of this remarkable city.*

Timings: Boxing Classes: Monday and Wednesday at 17:00 and 19:00 (classes last approx. 90 mins); Fit Punching: Monday and Friday at 18:00 (classes last approx. 60 mins).

*Costs: Boxing: SFr 500 per year; Fit Punching: open to members and nonmembers in series of 10 classes, approx. SFr 11 – 14 per class.*

Activities

## Canoeing

For water babies, sports fans and nature lovers, canoeing offers the opportunity to take in superb views, get close to nature, and keep fit at the same time. With amazing rivers in the vicinity, such as Arve, Rhône and Versoix (in Swiss territory) and Dranse, Griffe, Isère and Fier (in France), canoeing enthusiasts are spoilt for choice. Clubs generally offer routes catering to various levels, ranging from gentle rides to more demanding rapid experiences. Some are even specialised for the really adventurous kayakers, offering fast and furious extreme excursions. One thing to remember is that the water in Geneva can get very cold, so go properly equipped and check with the club to ensure you have all the essentials.

Lake living

### Canoë Club de Genève

Location ➜ Pointe de la Jonction · Plainpalais  | 022 756 11 81
Hours ➜ Check for timings
Web/email ➜ www.canoe-club-geneve.ch  Map Ref ➜ 13-B4

Founded in 1935 by 26 dedicated river sports fans, this is one of the biggest and most successful canoe clubs in Switzerland. Its members have brought home five world championships, eight silver medals and over 200 Swiss championships titles. Currently the club has some 380 members, and offers lessons for beginners and experienced canoeists alike. Competitive races take place every year. More details on joining are available from the Website, or by calling the above number.

### Rafting Loisirs

Location ➜ Ch. des Marais, 52 · Veyrier  | 022 784 02 05
Hours ➜ Check for timings
Web/email ➜ www.rafting-loisirs.ch  Map Ref ➜ 12-B1

Raft? Canoe? Why choose? An excursion with Rafting Loisirs gives you the best of both worlds with its inflatable canoe and kayak rafts. The going may get a bit rough as you hit the rapids, but you're completely safe under the watchful eye of a professional instructor. Setting off from the company base in Veryier, excursions take place in Switzerland (rivers Arve, Rhône and Versoix) and France (Rivers Dranse, Griffe and Fier), and cost from SFr 70 per person.

### Rivières & Aventures

Location ➜ Château-d'Oex  | 026 924 34 23
Hours ➜ Check for timings
Web/email ➜ www.riviere-aventure.ch  Map Ref ➜ na

It may be a fair drive from Geneva, but if you fancy a change of scenery, then a canoeing or kayaking excursion with Rivières et Aventures will definitely revive your senses. Take a gentle ride down the Sarine river and lap up the fantastic natural surroundings; or test your skill with a slalom course – various levels of activity are available. No experience is needed, but you should be in good physical condition and know how to swim. And don't forget your towel and an extra pair of socks!

*Costs:* *Prices start from around SFr 70 per person; special offers available for groups and school parties.*

## Canyoning

Canyoning isn't really about exploration or discovering new scenery – it's more about having fun and going a little bit crazy. In a nutshell, canyoning is similar to caving but involves more fresh air and sunshine –canyoners crawl and climb up rugged mountainsides, and as they reach water areas, such as rapids or waterfalls, they just jump down them! Of course, the dangers of this sport need to be taken seriously – canyoning is an extremely risky activity and special equipment and a thorough knowledge of rope manoeuvres is needed. As with caving, contact clubs and associations in the area before you even think of venturing into canyoning terrain – they can offer the best advice for organised routes and courses.

Canoeing | Canyoning

Activities

### Centre Paradventure

Location ➔ Rue de la Gare
Hours ➔ Check for timings
Web/email ➔ www.swissaventure.ch

024 492 23 82

Map Ref ➔ na

Ninety minutes from Geneva, deep in the 'Diablerets' mountain area, the Centre Paradventure offers various extreme activities for adrenaline junkies. A typical canyoning adventure involves descending water chutes and sliding down natural toboggans – getting wet has never been so much fun! The company offers special guided canyoning outings, so you can enjoy the crazy canyons and appreciate the wonders of the stunning Diablerets waters in safety, either in a group or individually. For more information on canyoning and other activities, contact the club on the number above.

### Caving

Given the beautiful mountain ranges that surround Geneva, it's no surprise that caving is a popular pastime for avid explorers. However, caving ranges from being fairly safe to extremely dangerous, and even with an experienced leader it is not suitable for the casual tourist or the poorly equipped. Some of the deepest underground caves in the world can be found in the Haute Savoie region, although exploration of these is very difficult and requires extensive training. Vertical caving, horizontal caving and even 'dive' caving (a highly risky activity involving diving into pools of water in order to explore a cave) are practised in the region. You can get more information about specific routes and activities from the caving clubs in the area.

#### Caving Safely

*In order to stay safe, it is important to know the dangers of going underground and what precautions should be taken. Take at least two torches each, and enough spare batteries and bulbs. Other equipment should include a minimum of two litres of water per person, a hard hat, knee and elbow pads, long sleeved overalls to protect you from sharp rocks, a basic first aid kit, and twine to mark less obvious parts of the route. And never, ever wander off alone!*

### Société Spéléologique Genevoise

Location ➔ Av. de Châtelaine, 40
Hours ➔ See below
Web/email ➔ www.hypogees.ch

022 367 16 74

Map Ref ➔ 5-C3

This society was formed in the Blue Parakeet bar in 1931, and their principal goal has remained unchanged – exploring and mapping caves with good friends. Although the club's central activity is caving, canyoning, skiing and hiking trips are also organised from time to time. They also provide training sessions for vertical caving, and organise special outings for beginners. Interested newcomers are encouraged to attend the weekly meeting (each Thursday at 21:00), or contact the club at the above number.

### Climbing

Due to its mountainous surroundings, Geneva is an excellent starting point for climbing excursions in the nearby Jura and Salève ranges, Chamonix, the neighbouring Vaudoises Alps, and Valais, which is the furthest, yet still just an hour and a half away. If you don't mind going further, there are excellent ranges all over Switzerland and many established clubs that organise weekend (and longer) excursions at these sites. Most of the climbing activity takes place in the spring and summer months. Different routes are available to cater to all levels, from the beginner to the experienced climber. To find the one that best suits you, contact the Geneva Mountain Guides office (see Aventures Alpines, below). They'll provide you with the information you need to get started, and they can also organise excursions. Similar to climbing, the Italian activity Via Ferrata (where you climb rock faces while attached to a safety cable) is becoming increasingly popular. See Via Ferrata [p.199].

### Aventures Alpines

Location ➔ Bd. Carl-Vogt, 32 · Plainpalais
Hours ➔ Check for timings
Web/email ➔ www.aventuresalpines.ch

0840 000 841

Map Ref ➔ 15-C1

Whether you're just curious about climbing or already a dedicated professional wanting to climb a particular summit or discover a special area, Aventures Alpines can offer advice and assistance with planning. This is the legitimate office of professional mountain guides for the Léman region with representatives in Geneva and Lausanne. Apart from climbing, they also offer ski tours, hiking, rock and ice climbing, and trekking. Contact the office for a full programme of activities.

### Club Alpin Suisse

Location ➔ Avenue du Mail, 4 · Plainpalais
Hours ➔ Tue 10:00 – 13:00 Fri 15:00 – 19:00
Web/email ➔ www.cas-geneve.ch

022 321 65 48

Map Ref ➔ 13-C4

The Club Alpin Suisse brings together lovers of all mountain and adventure sports – new members are always welcome, regardless of age or experience. A wide variety of activities are organised, including climbing in the Haute Savoie, Valais, Jura and Salève regions. For more information on the club, see their website.

### Mountain Evasion

Location ➜ Parc des Sports · Les Diablerets | **024 492 12 32**
Hours ➜ Check for timings
Web/email ➜ www.mountain-evasion.ch | Map Ref ➜ na

Ninety minutes from Geneva, this Mountain Adventure Park offers every mountain activity you can imagine... and more! Climbing (specifically Via Ferrata) is just one of the many activities available. Read more about this under 'Via Ferrata' (p.199) and find out about other Mountain Evasion activities from their website.

## Cricket

It may be some time before you see the Swiss team taking home the cricket world cup, but with large numbers of expats from Britain, India, Pakistan, Sri Lanka and other cricket mad countries, this 'gentlemen's game' is growing in popularity. Many informal matches are played in Geneva's grassy parks during the summer, and cries of "Howzaaat!" can be heard well into the evenings. Several organisations field their own cricket teams for inter-company matches, and some even play in the league.

### CERN Cricket Club

Location ➜ CERN (Prévessin ground) · Meyrin | **022 767 50 39**
Hours ➜ See below
Web/email ➜ See below | Map Ref ➜ 1-C2

The CERN team participates in the Swiss Cricket Association League, and also organises friendly matches against teams from France, Germany, Italy and Spain. And it's not just for CERN employees – anyone interested in playing is encouraged to contact the club by e-mail, or simply turn up for net practice at the Prévessin site. Practice sessions

are held every Thursday between April and September, from 18:00 to 19:00.

*Website: http://club-cricket.web.cern.ch/club-cricket*

### Geneva Cricket Club

Location ➜ Rte du Bout-du-Monde, 6 | **022 700 48 83**
Hours ➜ See below
Web/email ➜ hascal2@bluewin.ch | Map Ref ➜ 9-A2

Founded in 1872, Geneva Cricket Club is the oldest in Switzerland. In a recent move, the club now has its own ground at the Bout-du-Monde stadium in Champel, which boasts first class facilities. On Friday evenings (April – October), players train for matches in the Swiss League Championship from 18:00 – 20:00. In addition, the club also plays against French and Italian clubs on a regular basis. New members are always welcome to join the club and should contact the club president Hascal Gollop on the above number or email address.

### Geneva International Cricket Club

Location ➜ Central – check with club | **079 292 96 80**
Hours ➜ Check for timings
Web/email ➜ www.gicc.ch/4520.html | Map Ref ➜ na

Founded just one year ago, this new club on the block already has a strong multinational membership with many players from cricket loving countries like India, Pakistan and Britain. The GICC was established to promote all sports in the Swiss Romande region, especially cricket. The club aims to encourage competition, improve coaching and raise the standards and the profile of cricket in Switzerland. New players, regardless of age or skill, are always welcome.

## Croquet

### CERN Croquet and Lawn Bowls Club

Location ➜ CERN · Meyrin | **022 767 57 97**
Hours ➜ See below
Web/email ➜ croquet.web.cern.ch | Map Ref ➜ 1-B4

The ancient lawn game of croquet is enjoying somewhat of a revival this summer, becoming a favourite pastime of the rich and famous. At the CERN Croquet Club, you can try it for yourself – the club is open to members and nonmembers, and boasts two excellent lawns and a well equipped clubhouse. All equipment is provided (all you need

Cricket | Croquet

Activities

is a pair of flat soled sports shoes) and coaching is offered from April onwards. The club also has an active lawn bowls section.

*Timings: Coaching classes start at the end of April; classes are in the afternoon for retirees, and at 18:00 for the working population. Match timings vary.*

*Other useful contacts: Association suisse de croquet – 022 366 47 66*

## Cycling

In the early 20th century cycling was the primary mode of transport, with the Genevois pedalling here, there and everywhere! Now Geneva is attempting to return to its biking past by promoting city cycling as an ecological and cost-effective way of getting around town and exploring the region. A network of routes equalling more than 80 km has been set up, and the city authorities have also started a scheme whereby bikes can be borrowed free of charge from various 'cycle points' around the city (see review below). Look out for the 'Vélo Love' and 'Cyclévasions' pamphlets, published by the Public Highways Department and available freely at various outlets – they contain information on recommended routes, cycle points, repairs and other practical advice. There are a number of cycling clubs in the city, and organised rides usually take place on weekends, early mornings and evenings, when the roads are quieter.

*Useful Contacts: For more information on Vélo Love or Cyclévasions, contact the city authorities on 022 418 4200, or visit their Website: www.ville-ge.ch/amenagement*

### Genève Roule

Location → Pl. de Montbrillant, 17 · Les Grottes | **022 752 38 09**
Hours → See below
Web/email → www.geneveroule.ch          Map Ref → 13-C2

Improve the health of the environment, your body and your pocket by taking a Genéve Roule ride around town. This Red Cross initiative was set up to encourage Genevois to exercise in an ecologically sound and cost effective way. Between May and October, bikes can be borrowed free of charge from various points around town. Special bikes (tandems, mountain bikes, etc) are hired out at a small fee. All you need is a valid ID document and a CHF 50 deposit, and you'll soon be pedalling your way to better health!

*Bike Points: Montbrillant, Bains des Pâquis, Place du Rhône and Plainpalais.*

*Timings: Borrowing points are open every day from 7:30 to 21:30, from May to October. Montbrillant is open on Mondays from 08:00 – 18:00, from November to April*

Cycling

### Pédale des Eaux-Vives

Location → Eaux-Vives | **022 752 38 09**
Hours → See below
Web/email → www.pev-geneve.ch          Map Ref → 14-B3

For serious bikers, this active club is definitely worth visiting. Pedalling away since 1914, the club's motto remains 'To Become Victorious', with dedicated members competing in a large range of local and international race meetings, including the Tour de Genève and the Gentlemen's Stettler Race. Training sessions and outings usually take place at weekends and on Tuesday and Thursday evenings throughout the summer. Members also meet once a month for club discussions.

### Vélo Club Lancy

Location → Av. des Communes-Réunies, 94 | **022 794 23 40**
Hours → Check for timings
Web/email → www.vclancy.ch          Map Ref → 8-C3

This well organised club was founded in 1922 and counts many Geneva and Suisse Romande champions among their members over the years. VC Lancy organises the 'Grand Prix de Lancy' cycling race, which marks the start of the Suisse Romande Cycling race season. The club also closes the season with its annual Mountain Bike and Super Cross Rally, which sees cyclists whizzing over challenging terrain in the quest for victory. New members are keenly encouraged. For juniors, contact Rémi on 079 578 5547.

# Darts

## Mr Pickwicks Pub Darts Teams

Location → Rue de Lausanne, 80 · Town Centre | **022 731 67 97**
Hours → See below
Web/email → www.mr-pickwick.com          Map Ref → na

Darts is possibly the only sport you can excel at while clutching a pint in one hand! Mr Pickwicks Pub, a favourite expat haunt, has three darts teams that compete in the Geneva Darts League with great success – the club was Swiss champion for many years, and still holds the record for number of titles won. Home and away matches take place on Tuesdays for first division and Thursdays for second division, with training sessions held on Sunday afternoons within the season, September to April.

*Other useful contacts: Geneva Darts League – 079 611 3846*

# Diving

Diving in Switzerland? But there's no sea! Luckily, Lac Léman is a popular substitute, and many clubs regularly dive there. Lake diving takes place throughout the year, and each season offers a different dive experience – winter brings chilly waters but great underwater clarity. Spring brings a host of new underwater life, including shoals of perch or the occasional unsuspecting pike! Summer sees an explosion in the growth of lake weed, confining the diver to shallow waters. And Autumn brings a halt to weed growth and is one of the best periods for exploration as the temperature and visibility are at their best. Lake diving is a popular way to get in some dive training before setting off for more exotic locations. In fact, freshwater lake diving is often tougher than sea diving in many ways – very cold water, poor visibility and weak light are all specific challenges involved in lake diving, so make sure you have properly adapted equipment and the necessary technical preparation before taking the plunge.

## Abyss

Location → Rue De La Servette, 45 · Servette | **022 733 00 08**
Hours → Check for timings
Web/email → www.abyssworld.com          Map Ref → 13-C2

Whether you're a first time diver or simply perfecting your skills, Abyss accommodates everyone. Dives take place in swimming pools, the lake or the sea, and lessons can be adapted to fit your timetable and level of expertise. The society organises training sessions as well as weekend and longer outings in diverse regions, from Geneva to the Philippines.

## Centre de Sports Sous-Marins de Genève (CSSG)

Location → Rue de Vollandes, 26 · Eaux-Vives | na
Hours → Check for timings
Web/email → www.cssg.ch          Map Ref → 14-B3

The CSSG was founded in 1956 and was one of a handful of clubs that joined to form the Swiss Sub Aquatic Sports Federation a year later. Today, the club has about 180 members in the form of divers and instructors, and most of the dives take place at Lac Léman or other nearby Swiss lakes. Standards at the club are very high and are in line with Swiss and World Federation regulations.

## Centre de Sports Sous-Marins de Morges

Location → Port du Petit-Bois 6 | **021 801 71 81**
Hours → Check for timings
Web/email → www.cssm-morges.ch          Map Ref → na

From April to September, the Morges Submarine Sports Centre organises three lake dives per week in Lac Léman at Morges (50 km outside Geneva) or at Neuchâtel. Training is given from beginner to instructor level, and the club has about 20 active members. Facilities include the centre's own boat that members have access to at all times. The centre also organises try out sessions for nonmembers. Contact the club via the above Website, or on their email address, which is info@cssm-morges.ch.

## Diving Adventures

Location → Town Centre | **022 794 48 55**
Hours → Check for timings
Web/email → www.diving-adventures.org          Map Ref → na

This diving school offers PADI courses for all skill levels, from beginner to instructor. It was founded by a group of friends who are passionate about diving, and wanted to give something back in terms of monetary support to protect the environment and develop diving first aid. Diving adventures has a group of professional and highly qualified instructors who can take you through from the basic diving techniques to the most advanced. To find out about the club and what it has to offer, you can make an appointment with an education advisor via the company's Website.

Darts | Diving

**Activities**

## Dogsledding

Dogsledding was first introduced to French fur traders by the Inuits in the 17th century in Quebec, Canada. The word 'mush' is in fact a derivative of the French word 'marche', meaning 'to go'. Dogsledding, or 'traîneau à chien' in French, migrated back to Switzerland as a means of transportation, and today it still remains a popular activity in the alpine regions. Sledding normally involves six Nordic dogs that can travel at speeds in excess of 50 km per hour, and cover up to 100 km in one day. The sport is not difficult to learn, but requires stamina. Once you know the ropes, sledding offers the opportunity to explore a whole new world of untouched alpine backcountry.

| Echaillon | |
|---|---|
| Location ➜ Ecrins Park | na |
| Hours ➜ na | |
| Web/email ➜ www.echaillon.com | Map Ref ➜ na |

Hop across the border into France and romp through Ecrins Park with your own pack of pooches for a half day or a full weekend. Weekend packages include all lodging and food, and allow you to partake in other activities, such as snowshoeing and cross country skiing.

| Evolution 2 | |
|---|---|
| Location ➜ Tignes and Val d'Isère | +33 4 79 40 09 04 |
| Hours ➜ Check for timings | |
| Web/email ➜ www.evolution2.com | Map Ref ➜ na |

Evolution 2 offers weekly outings every Thursday from Tignes and Val d'Isre resorts. You can either ride along with a guide for €25 (SFr 40) or learn to drive the pack yourself for €50 (SFr 80). A four person half day package costs €130 (SFr 200).

| La Pourvoirie | |
|---|---|
| Location ➜ Plateau du Jura | na |
| Hours ➜ Check for timings | |
| Web/email ➜ www.massifdujura.com | Map Ref ➜ na |

Experience the unique wilderness and the purest mountain air on a dogsledding trek through the heart of the Jura Mountains. The Pourvoirie site (a mountainous area including a gite, B&B rooms and a campsite) offers a range of summer and winter dogsledding activities where you can meet the Siberian Husky pack, learn how to drive a sleigh and visit the workshop where the sleighs

are constructed. Short and long treks can be organised upon request.

***Costs:*** *An all-day winter trek costs approx. €.130 per person (SFr 200)*

Nature's winter playground

## Fencing

| Escrime Florimont-Lancy | |
|---|---|
| Location ➜ Av. du Petit-Lancy, 37 · Petit-Lancy | 022 879 00 00 |
| Hours ➜ See below | |
| Web/email ➜ www.florimont.ch | Map Ref ➜ 15-E4 |

Situated within the 'Institut Florimont' school establishment, the club welcomes fencers of all ages and skill levels to practice this traditional sport in a friendly environment. Whether you aim to fence competitively or just for fun, the club offers lessons with various professional fencing masters and is affiliated to the Swiss Fencing Association (www.swiss-fencing.ch; or 061 263 3329). Members participate in the SFA's National Youth Circuit and in other national and international competitions. The recently renovated facilities now boast a new floor and lighting, worthy of the world's greatest fencers!

***Timings:*** *Tuesday and Thursday evenings (exact timings differ depending on age and level). Season runs from September – June.*

***Costs:*** *One-time entry fee: juniors – SFr 25; seniors – SFr 50. Yearly subscription fees from SFr 350 – SFr 450 (depending on age and level)*

## Fishing

Fishing is big business in Geneva – literally. Around 150 French and Swiss families currently earn their living on the water by fishing for perch, pike, trout and more, selling the majority of their catch directly to restaurants and supermarkets in the shore-side towns. The many rivers in the area also provide a plethora of excellent fishing spots for the amateur. But before you cast off, don't forget that you'll need a permit to fish in the Geneva waters. Contact the Association of Geneva Fishing Societies (AGSP) for more information on fishing in the area, permits and fishing clubs

**Useful contacts:** *AGSP, c/o Maxime Prevedello, 1233 Bernex. Tel: 022 757 6957*

## Flying

| Aéro-club de Genève | |
|---|---|
| Location ➔ Meyrin | **022 798 65 08** |
| Hours ➔ Check for timings | |
| Web/email ➔ www.aeroclub-geneve.com | Map Ref ➔ 1-E4 |

The Aéro-club de Genève is the regional branch of the Swiss Aéro-club Association. It aims to bring together (within the canton) different associations and clubs that train, develop and promote the different sporting and private aero disciplines. Definitely a good starting point for those wishing to gain information on flying lessons, flight excursions, gliding, mountain pilot navigation, ballooning or even model aircraft racing. Currently, the aero activities represented by the AéCG are the 'Groupe Vol à Moteur' (motorised flying), 'Groupe Genevoise de Vol à Voile' (gliding), 'Groupe Aérostatique Genève' (ballooning and other aerostatic disciplines), 'Groupe des pilotes de Montagne' (mountian piloting) and the 'Groupe Aéro Modelisme' (model aircraft flying). For further information regarding these clubs and additional Aéro-club activities, contact the secretariat.

## Football

If you're a budding Beckham, a veteran Vialli, a female Figo or simply an armchair Alan Shearer, there's plenty of football in Geneva to suit players and fans alike. For those wishing to show off their ball skills, the many clubs in the city cover all levels and age groups. Most international organizations and companies have at least one team who play once a week come rain or shine, so ask around! If you're more of an armchair athlete and you'd rather just shout your support, there's the nearby Servette de Genève and the further away Zurich Grasshoppers and FC Bâle, all providing quality games. After the Swiss team's participation in Euro 2004, and with Switzerland designated as co-hosts (with Austria) for the 2008 European Championships, the popularity of the beautiful game is definitely on the rise. For a detailed list of all the clubs in the area, contact the Association Cantonale Genevoise de Football (Geneva regional football association) on 022 328 2648 or check out their Website for more information at www.acgf.ch.

| Football Club du CERN | |
|---|---|
| Location ➔ CERN · Meyrin | **022 767 59 60** |
| Hours ➔ Check for timings | |
| Web/email ➔ See below | Map Ref ➔ 1-B4 |

This longstanding club has been dribbling, shooting and scoring for 35 years. The CERN team plays in the AGFC League (Association Genevoise de Football Corporative) and was promoted to League B in 2003. The club also runs an annual CERN tournament where players can get together and enter their own teams. Newcomers interested in more information about the club and its activities are encouraged to contact the club committee at the above email address. Weekly training sessions are open to everyone.

*Website: http://club-football.web.cern.ch/club-football*

| Geneva Scottish Football Club | |
|---|---|
| Location ➔ Vessy Sports Centre · Veyrier | **022 767 59 60** |
| Hours ➔ Check for timings | |
| Web/email ➔ Willie.Cameron@cern.ch | Map Ref ➔ 9-A3 |

Although not affiliated to a league, the GSFC plays about a dozen friendly matches each year against local teams from companies and football clubs in the region. The season is split into two parts – Spring (Apr – Jun) and Autumn (Sept – Oct) – and home games are usually played on Saturday mornings at Vessy sports centre. The club also has a lively social calendar for members and friends, and activities are open to interested players from all countries and cultures – not just for Scots!

Fishing | Football

**Activities**

## Servette Football Club

Location ➜ Stade de Genève · Carouge
Hours ➜ Check Website for full details
Web/email ➜ www.servettefc.ch

022 979 59 49

Map Ref ➜ 5-C3

Servette have won the Swiss championships 17 times, and a visit to the Geneva Stadium to watch them in action is a must do for all football fans. It may not be quite the same as going to the matches at your team's ground back home, but if you are missing the atmosphere of live football, it's a great way to spend a Saturday or Sunday afternoon. Tickets are available from ticket outlets or at the gates, at various prices. The stadium is situated next to the La Praille shopping mall.

## Freediving

### Dauphins Genève

Location ➜ Ch. des Floralies, 9 · Vernier
Hours ➜ Check for timings
Web/email ➜ www.dauphins.ch

022 798 34 00

Map Ref ➜ 5-B2

Freediving became popular in the 1980s thanks to the film Le Grand Bleu, which told the story of two divers, Jacques Mayol and Enzo Maiorca. Now you can recreate the Big Blue experience in Geneva by joining the freediving section of the 'Dauphins-Genève' club. This discipline is new to the club and is the only place in Switzerland where you can practice it. Beginners need to complete an eight week course that takes place every Tuesday during spring or autumn at the Varembé swimming pool. The club also organises various weekend activities.

## Frisbee

### Geneva's Flying Disk Wizards

Location ➜ Quai Capo d'Istria, 11 · Plainpalais
Hours ➜ See below
Web/email ➜ www.wizards.ch

022 328 92 92

Map Ref ➜ 15-D3

Ultimate Frisbee is an exciting, non contact team sport, enjoyed by thousands around the world. The game, a mixture of soccer, basketball, American football and netball, is played between two teams of seven players on a large rectangular pitch, using a Frisbee instead of a ball. The Flying Disk Wizards is the only Ultimate Frisbee team in the city, and encourages interested players (beginners or experts) to come along to a training session to see what it's all about.

On Sunday afternoons, the 'Golf Freak' contingent of the Geneva Flying Disk Wizards practices the unusual sport of Disk Golf – a mixture of frisbee and golf. The aim is to aim a frisbee to land in metal baskets placed around a course, in the minimum number of throws. They have helped to set up the first official 18 hole disk golf course in Switzerland, at the Evaux Sports Centre in Onex.

*Useful contacts:* World Flying Disk Federation – www.wfdf.org

*Timings:* Sun 12:00 – 16:00 & Outdoor practice (April – October), Vessy Sports Centre: Tuesdays and Thursdays, 18:30. Indoor practice (November – March), Bout du Monde Sports Centre: Tuesdays, 20:00.

## Golf

With its mountain setting and picturesque lake views, Geneva is a premier European golfing destination and many tournaments are held here annually. The Crans-sur-Sierre Golf Course in the Crans-Montana resort plays host to the Omega European Masters, which is part of the European Professional Golf Association (PGA) tour. The Evian Masters Golf course, closer to the French border, is the home to the Evian Ladies Masters. There are also many monthly local tournaments and annual competitions such as the Coupe Helvétique, Championnat de Léman, International Suisse Championship and the ASG Cup. The Swiss Golf Association (ASG) can provide amateurs and professionals with detailed information about clubs and tournaments. For further information, visit www.asg.ch or call 021 784 35 31. In addition, the Swiss Golf Network can provide useful information for budding golfers at www.swissgolfnetwork.ch.

### Evian Masters Golf Club

Location ➜ Royal Evian Resort · France
Hours ➜ Check for timings
Web/email ➜ www.royalparcevian.com

+33 4 50 26 85 00

Map Ref ➜ na

Not far from Geneva, at the foot of the French Alps, lies the Evian Masters Golf Club. The golf course is part of the Royal Evian Resort that overlooks Lake Geneva and is home to the annual PGA Evian Ladies Masters. This is a par 72, 18 hole course that's set in the heart of 60 hectares of wooded parkland. From March to November, the Evian Masters Golf Club has five types of collective programmes for adults and children corresponding to their different levels of play.

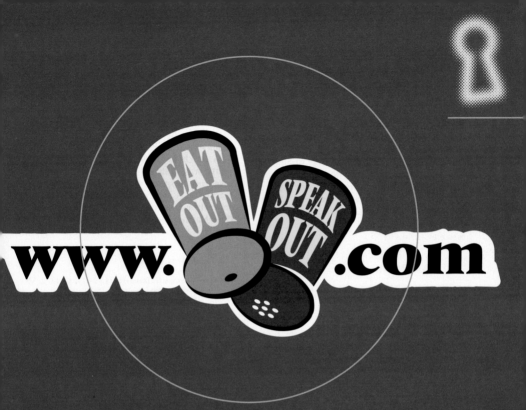

# What's Your Flavour Baby?

Fancy Yourself as a Food Critic Extraordinaire? Log On....

**Explorer Publishing** is quite proud to be a bit of a 'people's publisher'. We understand your hangovers, your need for excitement, your boredom thresholds and your desire to be heard, and we're always striving to make our publications as interactive with our loyal readership as possible. In the past, our Food Correspondent's telephone has been ringing constantly with people wanting to add their two pennies' worth to the reviews in our guidebooks.

Hence, our most ingenious solution for a satisfied diner, accurate food reporting and lower decibels in the work place, is **EAT OUT SPEAK OUT**. This Website provides the opportunity to pen down your comments, frustrations, tips and tantrums about specific dining experiences at any of the restaurants listed in our guide. Not only will we publish your thoughts online, we'll also pass on your review (anonymous, of course) to the outlet concerned and take your views into consideration for next year's edition of our guidebook.

Passionately Publishing...

## Golf Club Crans-sur-Sierre

Location → Sierre · Crans Montana | 027 485 97 97
Hours → Check for timings
Web/email → www.crans-montana.ch     Map Ref → na

It's a 200 km journey from Geneva to Crans-Montana, which is home to the Omega European Masters (part of the European PGA Tour). The golf club, nestled high above the village of Sierre in the heart of the Swiss Alps, hosts a nine and 18 hole award winning course designed by Jack Nicklaus. The courses are open from May to November, with an indoor driving range and swing analyser available all year round. Green fees are SFr 80.

## Golf Club de Bossey

Location → Château de Crevin · Bossey (Fr) | +33 4 50 43 95 50
Hours → Check for timings
Web/email → www.golfbossey.com     Map Ref → 12-B2

Set in the Salève Mountains, this 18 hole, 6,022 metre, par 71 golf course boasts spectacular views, and was designed by renowned golf course architects Robert Trent Jones. The gentle course doesn't pose too many difficulties for golfing enthusiasts, except for the 13th hole that's been nicknamed Grand Bois (Big Wood). As an interesting historical aside, Ferdinand Lasalle, the forefather of German communism, reportedly died in a duel in 1864 close to the pond near the 8th hole. Green fees are €70. Open Feb – Dec.

## Golf Club de Divonne

Location → Parc des Sports · France | +33 4 50 40 34 34
Hours → Check for timings
Web/email → www.domaine-de-divonne.com     Map Ref → na

One of Europe's most spectacular 18 hole championship golf courses, the Golf Club de Divonne is set in stunning woodland surroundings. Built in 1931, the course has a scratch score of 72 over a total playing distance of 6,030 meters. Numerous landscape architects from Nakowski in the 20s, to Harradine in 1963, have contributed to the design and enhancement of the course. Green fees range from €48 – 80. Residents of the Grand Hôtel in the Domaine de Divonne get a 50% discount on green fees. Open mid March – mid December.

## Golf Club de Genève

Location → Rte de la Capite, 70 · Cologny | 022 735 75 40
Hours → Check for timings
Web/email → secretariat@golfgeneve.ch     Map Ref → 6-D2

With beautiful lakeside and mountain views, the Golf Club de Genève offers fantastic surroundings within easy to drive distances from the city. Open from March to December, this 18 hole, par 72 course was designed by Robert Trent Jones and covers nearly 6,300 metres. There is also an indoor practice range and the club is open to nonmembers on weekday mornings. Green fees start at SFr 100. Open March – December.

## Golf Club de la Valserine

Location → Monts Jura Ski Resort · France | +33 4 50 41 31 56
Hours → Check for timings
Web/email → www.monts-jura.com     Map Ref → na

Nestled in the Valserine Valley, the natural environment of the Haut-Jura mountain range provides superb scenery and is a great place for hiking, fauna and flora discovery and golf. At the Valserine Golf Club in Mijoux, you'll find a certified nine hole, par 35 course that's over 2,800 metres in length. There are practice pitch and putting greens, training bunkers and a driving range. The club, built to follow the natural relief of the Jura landscape, is open from May to November (weather permitting) and is open to everyone without a handicap at attractive prices.

## Golf Club de Maison Blanche

Location → Naz-Dessous · France | +33 4 50 42 44 42
Hours → Check for timings
Web/email → gmb2@wanadoo.fr     Map Ref → na

The Golf Club de Maison Blanche was originally owned by Formula One aces Alain Prost and Jean Alesi. Situated 20 minutes outside Geneva, the club boasts a nine and 18 hole course. The 18 hole course is open during the week for members and nonmembers, but is reserved for members on weekends. A bar and restaurant are available for all golfers, but the swimming pool and leisure area are members only zones. Green fees are €80 for 18 holes and €35 for nine holes.

Golf

Activities

### Golf Club du Domaine Impérial

Location ➜ Villa Prangins· Gland | 022 999 06 00
Hours ➜ Check for timings
Web/email ➜ golf_domaine_imperial@bluewin.ch    Map Ref ➜ na

The Golf Club du Domaine Impérial is the only Pete Dye course in Europe and is listed as one of the top 50 European courses. The 18 hole course features tree lined fairways on the first nine holes, and the fourth hole, considered to be a Pete Dye signature hole, has been ranked as one of the best par fives in the world.    Nonmembers are welcome from Tuesday to Friday, and green fees range from SFr 75 to SFr 150.

## Handball

### Handball Club Nyon

Location ➜ Rocher · Nyon | na
Hours ➜ Check for timings
Web/email ➜ www.hbcnyon.ch    Map Ref ➜ na

Nyon Handball club is one of the largest sporting teams in the city.  With its three active teams (two men's, one women's), its two junior teams and its handball school, the Rocher club brings together some 100 players.  Well situated in the region and playing a major role in the 'West' regional championships (Vaud-Valais-Genève – Fribourg), this club led by Daniel Gerber goes from strength to strength.

### Lancy Handball

Location ➜ Various locations · Petit-Lancy | 078 620 74 05
Hours ➜ See below
Web/email ➜ www.lancyhandball.ch    Map Ref ➜ na

Lancy Handball club is made up of 32 members spread over three teams.  The senior team (H4) plays in the league and holds two training sessions per week (one 'purely handball' session and one 'purely physical' session).   The two junior teams (M17 and M15) also train twice weekly.  Matches usually take place on Saturdays and Wednesdays.

*Timings: Seniors: Mon, 19:30 – 21:30 / Thurs, 18:30 – 20:00 (new sports hall in the Petit-Lancy school) Juniors (M17): Mon, 17:30 – 19:30 (Petit-Lancy school sports hall) / Weds, 18:00 – 20:00 (Mechanic school Sports hall) Juniors (M15): Weds, 18:00 – 20:00 (Mechanic school Sports hall) / Thurs, 18:00 – 20:00 (CEPTA sports hall)*

## Hang Gliding

Other options ➜ Flying [p.179]

Harnessing the wind

### Centre de Vol Libre Genève

Location ➜ Rte de Bossey Troinex · Troinex | 022 784 10 99
Hours ➜ Check for timings
Web/email ➜ www.club-des-sports.ch/cvlg    Map Ref ➜ 11-A1

Hang gliding, delta plane, paragliding – the Geneva hang gliding club has everything you need to take to the skies. With more than 500 members in the city, the club uses three take off points on the Salève mountainside, and operates in cooperation with the French Salève hang gliding club. The club has two landing points and a clubhouse equipped with a kitchen and terrace. The delta and paragliding school, Centre Genève Vol Libre, is a vital part of the club where you can learn all there is to know about flying under the vigilant eye of experienced instructors. For all information about the school and available courses, call 022 784 38 08.

## Hashing

Sometimes described as 'drinking clubs with a running problem', the Hash House Harriers is a worldwide family of social running clubs. It all started in Kuala Lumpur in 1938, and they are now the largest running organisation in the world with

Handball | Hashing

Activities

about 1,600 chapter members scattered over 180 countries. Hashing consists of following a course laid out by a couple of hares (members of the group who lay out a trail with flour or chalk). Running, jogging or walking is acceptable; it's all about fun!

**Geneva Hash House Harriers**

| | |
|---|---|
| Location → Various locations | na |
| Hours → See below | |
| Web/email → www.genevahhh.com | Map Ref → na |

The Harriers is a social running group for men and women. The club is made up of two groups of hashers – the Léman Geneva Hash House Harriers (LGH3) and the Swiss France Hash House Harriettes (CHFH3). LGH3 run every Monday evening at 19:00 and on the second Sunday of every month, while CHFH3 run every Wednesday evening at 19.00. Both clubs meet at various locations in Geneva and sometimes go into parts of France. To subscribe to the Geneva HHH mailing list, send a blank email to geneva-hhh-subscribe@yahoogroups.com.

**Oops!**

*Did we miss anything out? If you have any thoughts, ideas or comments for us to include in the Activities section, drop us a line. If your club or organisation isn't in here, let us know and we'll shout your name from the rooftops (or at least include your details in our next edition). Visit www.Explorer-Publishing.com and say whatever's on your mind... we're listening!*

## Hiking

Switzerland has long been considered the hiking playground of Europe with its network of hiking trails and amazing mountain scenery. Whether it's the Jura, Alps or Salève, there are many well organised hiking routes to choose from. One of the classic hiking adventures is the Haute Route, a demanding high-level traverse between the mountain towns of Chamonix (France) and Zermatt (Switzerland). The Haute Route has become known as one of the most spectacular and challenging hikes in the Alps because it includes ten of the twelve highest peaks in western Europe, including the Matterhorn and Monte Rosa. For serious hikers there is also Mont-Blanc, one of the world's landmark hiking treks, which features incredible mountain landscapes, glaciers and peaks. For less experienced hikers there is a large variety of smaller, more relaxed hikes to enjoy.

If you go down to the woods today.....

**Association Genevoise Des Amis Du Salève**

| | |
|---|---|
| Location → Veyrier-Douane · Veyrier | 022 796 41 33 |
| Hours → Meet on Sun 10:00 | |
| Web/email → www.dj-web.ch/rando-geneve | Map Ref → 9-B4 |

Discover the Salève Mountains for free. Every Sunday, hikers and nature lovers meet at 10:00 at the foot of the Salève for a day of fresh air and exercise. Led by an experienced hike leader from the Association Genevoise des Amis du Salève, you'll be taken on routes with varying levels of difficulty. Hikes usually last between five and eight hours and you will need to bring your own hiking boots, raincoats, passport, money, food and water.

**International Ski Club (SCIG)**

| | |
|---|---|
| Location → Ch. Eugène Rigot · Petit-Saconnex | 022 301 25 08 |
| Hours → See below | |
| Web/email → tony.woodfield@bluewin.ch | Map Ref → 5-E2 |

Between April and October the SCIG organises up to 100 outings, for beginners and advanced hikers, to a wide variety of destinations across the Salève, Jura and Alps mountain ranges. The club provides an international and friendly environment that allows people to discover the beautiful region

Hiking

Activities

while keeping fit at the same time. In winter months, the skis come out and the club remains active. Hikes range from easy to very difficult and may require mountaineering or climbing experience in some instances. Club meetings take place on Thursdays from 18:00 – 19:00.

## Hockey

Other options → Ice Hockey [p.187]

### Black Boys Hockey Club

Location → Bout-du-Monde stadium | 022 798 78 23
Hours → See below
Web/email → www.blackboyshockey.ch     Map Ref → 9-A3

Founded in 1933, the Black Boys Hockey Club plays hockey at the highest level in Switzerland (National Premier League). The club also has a women's team and a growing juniors section. The club welcomes newcomers and encourages people from all over the world to start playing. The various teams train throughout the week and matches are usually played on weekends or mid-week. During the outdoor season, the club trains at the Richemont Stadium (rue de Frontenex), and at the Bout-du-Monde stadium during the indoor season.

*Timings: First and second teams: Mon 19:30 – 21:15 / Wed 19:30 – 21:15; Women's team : Wed 19:15 – 21:15; Juniors' B team : Wed 17:30 – 19:00 / Fri 17:30 – 19:00; Juniors' C team : Wed 16:30 – 18:00 / Fri 17:30 – 19:00; Juniors' D team : Wed 16:00 – 17:00*

### Unihockey Club de Genève

Location → Petit-Lancy | 022 787 89 74
Hours → Check for timings
Web/email → na     Map Ref → 8-C2

Unihockey is a team sport played in a hall with three or five players and a goalie. It's very similar to ice hockey, but played with a plastic puck. In Geneva, unihockey is growing in popularity with two organisations looking after the development of the sport: the Geneva Unihockey Club and the Geneva Unihockey School that trains and educates people about the game. Those interested in playing competitively can join the club, where they have a variety of teams for men, women, veterans and juniors.

### Urania Genève Sports Hockey (UGSHC)

Location → See locations below | 022 782 49 50
Hours → Check for timings
Web/email → www.ugshc.ch     Map Ref → na

UGSHC's goal is to build the profile of hockey in communities and schools. Currently they only cater for young people, and all members are aged between five and 15 years old. Although the club does not field a senior team at the moment, it hopes to be able to form an adults' first team in a few years. The outdoor season takes place at Richemont Stadium, Versoix Sports Centre and Pinchat school, while the indoor season venues are Bois-Gourmand School and Bout-du-Monde Sports Centre.

## Horse Riding

The Genevois woodlands are ideal for horse riding excursions. Riders join walkers and mountain bikers along the Jussy woodlands on the French border. From Presinge to the Cormaches woods, passing through Echanex, Monniaz or the forest house, the clay and woodchip paths allow you to discover the Geneva countryside. Between Chavanne-des-Bois, Sauverny, Collex-Bossey, Versoix and Genthod, the Versoix woodlands are full of pathways that cross Versoix, encircle the Richelieu pond lands and pass through biological reserves. Geneva also hosts of a number of international and national meetings including the annual CSI-W international show jumping competition that brings together the best riders in the world. The event, Concours Hippique International de Genève, takes place at the world's biggest indoor equestrian arena.

### CERN Horseriding club

Location → CERN · Meyrin | 022 767 21 23
Hours → Check for timings
Web/email → See below     Map Ref → 1-B4

The CERN riding club is a group of horse enthusiasts who practice all levels of riding and come together to share their love of the activity. The club focuses on dressage, show jumping and trekking excursions, and can also provide information on other riding schools in the Geneva area. The yearly subscription fee includes insurance to cover your horse (hired or owned) throughout Europe, and discounts at other riding clubs.

*Website: http://j.home.cern.ch/j/jouhet/www/CHC-E*

### Cheval Pour Tous (Horses for All)

Location → Les Mosses
Hours → Check for timings
Web/email → info@cheval-pour-tous.ch
026 924 57 83
Map Ref → na

For a winter twist on horseback riding, take a skijoring tour with Cheval Pour Tous (Horses for All) located near Gstaad. This demanding sport combines equestrian skills with skiing savvy, but is manageable by most recreational enthusiasts. One popular tour follows the track known as the Col des Mosses leading to the mountain village of l'Evitaz. Contact Norbert Chabloz for an appointment.

### Ferme Equestre de Beaupré

Location → GY · France
Hours → Check for timings
Web/email → fermeequestre@bluewin.ch
022 759 14 12
Map Ref → na

This horse farm and breeding stable is located in the countryside town of Gy, France. Jean-Daniel and Sophie Burgdorfer lead excursions into the nearby Jussy woods for all levels of riders. Prices vary and tours are by appointment only. There is also a pony club on the grounds for children of ages three and up.

### Les Ecuries D'Antan

Location → Ch. de l'Epagny 1095 · Passy
Hours → Check for timings
Web/email → www.lesecuriesdantan.com
na
Map Ref → na

Gallop or mosey through the canyons and wildflower fields of the Haute Savoie backcountry while enjoying outstanding views of the Alps. Safety and fun is emphasised throughout. Guided tours are available during the summer months for €13 (SFr 20) for one hour or €30 (SFr 46) for a half day.

### Manège d'Onex

Location → Ch. des Laz, 16 · Onex
Hours → Check for timings
Web/email → www.maneges.ch
022 792 16 88
Map Ref → 8-A2

Located a few minutes from Geneva, this is both a riding school and stables for horses and ponies. From the age of seven, the club can introduce children to riding, be it for pleasure or competition. Disciplines such as dressage, jumping and trekking are taught, and the club can also assist riders of all levels with preparations for Swiss Federation equestrian exams, professional certificates, individual or group classes, workshops and riding holidays.

### Poney Club de Presinge

Location → Rte de Presinge, 137 · Presinge
Hours → Check for timings
Web/email → na
022 759 19 37
Map Ref → na

Children from the age of three can join this pony club, and take part in the 'little riders' workshop. The riding school has training for riders of all ages and levels, and helps with preparation for Swiss Federation exams, as well as providing instruction in dressage, show jumping, gymkhana and other disciplines. All classes are run by certified professionals, and are available for individuals or groups. Apart from the training, the club also offers enjoyable horseback excursions in beautiful settings.

## Hot Air Ballooning

Ballooning is a relaxing and invigorating sport that opens up the imagination. The hot air ballooning season in the Alps runs from mid June to mid October and late December through to the middle of April. Nearby Château d'Oex is famous for hosting the largest annual winter balloon festival in Europe, which takes place every year in January.

### Balloon Heaven of Gstaad

Location → Chalet aux Borsalets
Hours → Timings on request
Web/email → www.gstaadballon.ch
026 924 54 85
Map Ref → na

With over 3,000 commercial flights under his belt, you can't find a pilot more experienced than Hans Büker. Hans was the first balloonist to cross the Alps from Switzerland to Italy. He was also the first to fly commercial passengers over the Alps in 1978. Hans is a colourful character who delights clients with tales of his ballooning misadventures and meetings with world famous celebrity clients. The cost per person ranges from SFr 285 to SFr 485.

### Funk's Ballonfahrten

Location → Vordere Gasse 27 · Wolfwil
Hours → Check for timings
Web/email → www.ballonreisen.ch
062 926 22 77
Map Ref → na

Funk's has taken ballooning to new heights since the Montgolfière brothers sent their first manned Montgolfière into the air 200 years ago. Funk's is registered as a commercial airline and utilises modern equipment to ensure top safety standards. Funk's primary emphasis is on flexibility, with eight different flight packages beginning at SFr 280, and they can also arrange tailored flights for individuals or groups of up to 100 people.

### Swissraft

Location → Various locations
Hours → Check for timings
Web/email → www.swissraft.ch/en

081 911 52 50

Map Ref → na

Two hours from Geneva you can go on a real flying adventure, taking in the stunning views of the Alps and local areas like Grisson, Enhaut and Vaud. Hot air ballooning is a good way to celebrate anything from a birthday or anniversary to a product launch. One and two hour flights operate every morning (weather permitting) from various points and are headed by a certified pilot. Local flights over cantonal regions cost SFr 370 per person, while flights over the Alps cost SFr 580 per person.

## Ice Hockey

### Genève-Servette Hockey Club

Location → Vernets sports centre · Les Vernets
Hours → Check for timings
Web/email → www.geneva-hockey.ch

022 710 70 00

Map Ref → 8-D1

Ice hockey is one of the most popular sports in Switzerland and Geneva boasts one of the country's most successful teams, the Servette de Genève. Home matches take place at Vernets Sports Centre in Acacias, usually on Fridays, Saturdays or Sundays. Wonder, the club mascot, is a real eagle that swoops down to the ice just before the puck gets thrown down, earning himself a massive cheer from the fans. Tickets for games are SFr 10 – SFr 30 for children and SFr 20 – SFr 50 for adults, depending on your seating choice. More information can be obtained from www.hockeyswiss.com.

## Ice Skating

Other options → Ice Hockey [p.187]

### Centre Sportif des Vernets

Location → Rue Hans-Wilsdorf, 4-6 · Acacias
Hours → Check for timings
Web/email → na

022 418 40 00

Map Ref → 15-B2

The Vernets Sports Centre has indoor and outdoor rinks and is home to the Servette de Genève ice hockey club. The club is open to the public at

reasonable prices, and you'll often see artistic skaters performing their tricks on the ice. Once a month, depending on rink availability, a Disco on Ice is organised at the outdoor rink. The entry fee is SFr 5 for adults and SFr 2 for children. Skate hire rates are SFr 5 for adults and SFr 2 for children.

Sports centre

### Centre Sportif Sous Moulin

Location → Rte de Sous-Moulin, 39 · Thônex
Hours → Check for timings
Web/email → www.cssm.ch

022 305 00 00

Map Ref → 9-D2

This rink opened its doors in December 2000 and welcomes ice skaters and ice hockey players. It is home to the Club des Patineurs Trois-Chêne skating and ice hockey club, and they can be contacted through the main sports club. The best times to visit the rink for normal ice skating sessions are Saturday mornings and evenings when the ice is less crowded. The entrance fee is SFr 7 for adults.

### Place du Rhône – Ice Rink

Location → Place du Rhône · Town Centre
Hours → 10:00 – 22:00  Feb – Nov
Web/email → na

na

Map Ref → 13-E3

Get your skates on and head straight to the city centre's outdoor ice rink in Rhône Square. Open from February to November, the rink truly captures the seasonal spirit. Entry is free, and if you don't have your own skates, they can be hired at SFr 6 for adults and SFr 3 for children.

Ice Hockey | Ice Skating

Activities

## Jet Skiing

Jet ski use is prohibited on the lake with the exception of official competitions. Organised under the auspices of the Swiss and International Aquabike Federations, competitions operate under international and national authorities. Those interested in casual jet skiing will have to look to waters that are further away. If you'd like more information about the competitions though, the best place to inquire is at the Société Nautique de Genève. You can call them on 022 707 0505 or email hélice@nautique.org.

## Karting

### MK Circuit

| | |
|---|---|
| Location ➔ Nr Annemasse/Bonneville | +33 4 50 25 53 47 |
| Hours ➔ 10:00 – evening | |
| Web/email ➔ /www.mk-circuit.com/ | Map Ref ➔ na |

You'll find this karting centre just ten minutes away from Geneva. The karting circuit is accessible for everyone and offers a range of racing opportunities for individuals, teams, groups or corporate parties. Some competition courses are also organised, including the popular Trophée MKCircuit. The circuit is open seven days a week and prices range between €12.50 – €20 per kart. There is also a bar where you can quench your thirst.

## Laser Game

### Gotcha Entertainment

| | |
|---|---|
| Location ➔ Ch. des Batailles, 22 · Vernier | 022 341 40 00 |
| Hours ➔ 14:00 – 22:00 Wed – Sun | |
| Web/email ➔ www.paintball.ch | Map Ref ➔ 4-E2 |

Armed with a laser gun and an electronic jacket, you have to enter a laser labyrinth and shoot your friends. Part of the Gotcha Entertainment Centre (which also offers paintball), laser games are great fun for groups of friends or work colleagues. Special sessions can be organised for occasions such as birthdays, corporate events and stag and hen nights. Before or after the laser shooting competition, you can relax at the clubhouse where you'll find a bar, billiards tables, pinball machines and table football.

## Luge

Luge (sledging) is a fast and furious, family fun activity, available at all snowy slopes near you. Activity centres, such as 'Centre Paradventure' (see below), offer the sport of luge, as do a large number of ski resorts. See RailAway [p.188] for details on one day rail, and fun activities that include luge.

### Centre Paradventure

| | |
|---|---|
| Location ➔ Rue de la Gare · Les Diablerets | 024 492 23 82 |
| Hours ➔ Check for timings | |
| Web/email ➔ www.swissaventure.ch | Map Ref ➔ na |

Situated about 90 minutes away from Geneva, the Centre Paradventure offers luge facilities for large groups of friends and family. Austrian and traditional sledges will help you on your way, and daytime and night-time descents are available. For those with a fondness for good food, the Mazots restaurant offers a fondue menu for groups larger than 15 people. Reservations are recommended.

### RailAway

| | |
|---|---|
| Location ➔ See below | 0900 30 03 00 |
| Hours ➔ Check for timings | |
| Web/email ➔ www.railaway.ch/International/ | Map Ref ➔ na |

RailAway is the leisure arm of the Swiss Railway organisation and offers a large range of one day travel programmes. Luge is one of the many activities on offer, and RailAway invites you to take a grand tour on a sledge. The activity takes place on the Sparenmoos plateau where you will sled down seven kilometres of luge piste to Zweisimmen. Prices include the train fare, transfers to the luge piste by bus, and the sledge ride itself. Consult the RailAway web site for prices.

## Martial Arts

### Club d'Aikido de Meyrin

| | |
|---|---|
| Location ➔ Prom. de Vaudagne, 39 · Meyrin | 022 782 08 55 |
| Hours ➔ Check for timings | |
| Web/email ➔ www.aikidomeyrin.ch | Map Ref ➔ 1-E4 |

Aikido can be translated as the search for coordination of mental and physical energy. This is a non violent, non combat martial art that teaches students to transpose strength and energy, and train the mind to diffuse or defend itself against negative situations. The Meyrin Aikido club has been running since 1994 and its instructors have over 60 years of experience between them. Men and women of all ages and skill levels are encouraged to join this club that currently boasts a membership of over 110 juniors and 70 adults.

### Ecole de Kung-Fu de Genève

Location ➔ Avenue de Luserna, 18 · 022 734 17 30
Hours ➔ Check for timings
Web/email ➔ www.arts-martiaux.ch       Map Ref ➔ 13-A1

The Geneva Kung Fu School offers classes at three different sites in the city and has 450 members in age groups ranging from six years old upwards. For beginners, or those who want to perfect the art of kung fu (Liuhe Quan style) or Taiji Quan, there is something for everyone. Training involves combat with bare hands and instruments under the guidance of experienced masters that teach Shaolin School rigour and discipline. Each year the school takes a number of students to a special workshop in Beijing. Classes are available from Monday to Saturday, and you can contact the club directly for specific timings depending on your level and discipline.

### Judo Club de Genève

Location ➔ Rue Goetz Monin, 24 · Plainpalais · 022 321 20 03
Hours ➔ Check for timings
Web/email ➔ www.judogeneve.ch       Map Ref ➔ 15-E2

Founded in 1947, the Judo Club de Genève offers a full and varied judo ju jitsu programme, as well as aikido and t'ai chi. Judo classes take place from Monday to Friday, with aikido classes on Mondays, Wednesdays and Thursdays. For more information on t'ai chi, contact the club. The Institute has a long history of dedication and excellence, and renowned judo and aikido masters regularly visit the dojo, which is located at Rue Goetz Monin.

### Karate-Do Gojoryu Genève

Location ➔ Eaux-Vives · 079 247 22 52
Hours ➔ See below
Web/email ➔ www.karatedogojoryu.ch       Map Ref ➔ 14-B3

Karate is an art that develops courage, as well as physical and mental health. In addition to this, a person knowledgeable in this art can ably defend themselves against physical attacks without the use of weapons. The Karate-Do Gojoryu School was founded by Suriyon Jans and has a large

membership. Training takes place every evening at the Ecole du 31 Decembre from 20:00 (19:00 on Fridays). For more information, please consult the club's Website or call Sven Buschi at the number listed above.

### Keum Yong Dojang Genève

Location ➔ Rue des Lattes, 63 · Meyrin · 079 284 90 09
Hours ➔ 18:30-20:00 check days on Website
Web/email ➔ www.gold-dragon.ch       Map Ref ➔ 1-E4

Taekwondo is a combat and self defence martial art that originated in Korea and is characterised by its fast and high spinning kicks. The Keum Yong Dojang Taekwondo Club in Geneva was opened in 2000 and is identified by a golden dragon that symbolises the strength and energy that lies in all of us. The club is affiliated to the Swiss Taekwondo Academy, which is under the instruction of Grand Master Kim, president of the World Taekwondo Academy.

### Yamabushi

Location ➔ Various · Petit-Lancy · 079 479 88 13
Hours ➔ Check for timings
Web/email ➔ www.yamabushi.ch       Map Ref ➔ 8-C2

Yamabushi Martial Arts is a club that offers various martial arts and combat sports. A variety of disciplines including karate, full contact boxing, Thai boxing, ju-jitsu and jeet kune do are offered in dojos across the Geneva and nearby Vaud counties. The club offers classes to girls and boys from the age of six, and also caters for teenagers, adults and veterans. The club has many champion trainers including Carl Emery, full combat kickboxing world champion, and Swiss karate champion Jean-Pierre Baechler.

## Motor Sports

The Genevois really love their cars – the city is teeming with sleek and shiny vehicles, and motoring is a very popular pastime. The Groupement Ecuries Genevoises (GEG) is an association founded by a number of different racing teams with the aim to develop their skills, practice the sport and enjoy some competitive fun. For the past 15 years the association has organised a 'slalom' race for amateur drivers, which takes place on the Esplanade du Bureau in Carouge. The GEG also helps organise the annual Geneva Automobile Championships. For more information on GEG activities as well as individual racing

Martial Arts | Motor Sports

Activities

teams, contact the club president Joaquin Gabarron (022 787 28 87) or log on to their Website (http://web606.petrel.ch). Another useful contact for racing information is the Automobile Club de Suisse (Geneva branch – 022 342 22 33).

## Mountain Biking

Geneva is perfect for mountain biking due to the miles of hilly countryside and rocky trails. For hardcore mountain bikers there is varying terrain that ranges from woodland areas in Veyrier and Jussy to mountain routes in Salève, Jura and the Alps, but be warned that some of the routes are very challenging. There are many tracks to follow and most routes are open all year round. As with all activities that are physically demanding, you need to be sensible and well prepared. In summer, the sun can be strong and you will need ample water. During the winter months it is advisable to wear warmer clothes.

| Rafting Loisirs | |
|---|---|
| Location ➜ Ch. des Marais, 52 · Veyrier | 022 784 02 05 |
| Hours ➜ Check for timings | |
| Web/email ➜ www.rafting-loisirs.ch | Map Ref ➜ 12-B1 |

The Rafting Loisirs base in Veyrier is located close to the countryside and provides riders with varying types of routes. The activity centre offers mountain bike rallies that take place in the city itself, stopping off at cultural and historical points of interest. There is also the possibility of organising company challenges. Mountain biking is available all year round at Rafting Loisirs, and levels of physical exertion can be adapted to suit the individual or group. Prices start at SFr 70 per person, which includes the cost of hiring a bike and helmet.

## Mountaineering

While the techniques, equipment and accessibility of mountaineering have evolved, the motivations of mountaineers have remained the same – it is all about the call for discovery, the victory of mind over body, and the pursuit of new challenges. Whether you are a beginner or an experienced climber, this is a sport where your enjoyment is directly linked to the effort and enthusiasm you contribute. Geneva and its surrounding areas provide ideal terrain for all levels of mountaineer. With the Alps right on its doorstep, Geneva has an array of routes and challenges just waiting to be explored. The mountain guides at Aventures Alpines (see review below) are the best people to advise you on excursions and routes in the region, so check with them first before you take to the mountains.

| Aventures Alpines | |
|---|---|
| Location ➜ Bd. Carl-Vogt, 32 · Plainpalais | 022 321 00 48 |
| Hours ➜ Check for timings | |
| Web/email ➜ www.aventuresalpines.ch | Map Ref ➜ 15-C1 |

Founded in 1992, Aventures Alpines offers a starting point for people interested in mountaineering, as well as rock and ice climbing, ski touring and snowshoe hiking. The club offers excursions at three levels: beginner, medium and advanced, all of which offer fantastic views and varying challenges along the way. Outings range from three to four hours for beginners and six to eight hours for experienced mountaineers. There are also longer excursions available across the Alpine peaks.

Wheeeeeeeeeeeeee!

## Swiss Alpine Club

Location → Av. de Mail, 4 · La Coulouvrenière | na
Hours → Check Website for timings
Web/email → http://www.sac-cas.ch/ Map Ref → 13-C4

The Geneva branch of the Swiss Alpine Club was founded in 1865. The club's goals are to unite mountain and mountaineering lovers, and to encourage and facilitate the practice of Alpine sports, whether for competition or pleasure. Activities take place all year round, and include ski trekking, mountaineering, snow shoe excursions and hiking.

When you're a mountain goat, life rocks!

## Mudbike

### Centre Paradventure

Location → Rue de la Gare · Les Diablerets | 024 492 23 82
Hours → Check for timings
Web/email → www.swissaventure.ch Map Ref → na

Mud biking is a year round activity, and the Centre Paradventure offers a full range of excursions from easy routes (green) to challenging routes (black), where participants will descend pebbly paths,

rocky routes and even glassy glaciers on mad mud machines. Groups are accompanied by a guide and prices range depending on the level of challenge you're willing to undertake.

## Paintballing

Other options → Shooting [p.195]

### Gotcha Entertainment

Location → Ch. des Batailles, 22 · Vernier | 022 341 40 00
Hours → 14:00 – 22:00 Wed – Sun
Web/email → www.paintball.ch Map Ref → 4-E2

In paintballing, you get to live out your war games fantasies by running around an indoor course, armed with a paint gun, shooting at your 'enemies'. This fun (and messy) activity is ideal for special occasions and corporate events. When you've either won or lost the paintball war, you can relax in the clubhouse bar.

## Parachuting

### Parachutisme 74

Location → Aérodrome, Rte de Thonon | +33 4 50 92 06 50
Hours → Check for timings
Web/email → www.parachutisme74.com Map Ref → na

The 'Parachutisme 74' Club is located close to Annemasse, which is about 20 minutes outside Geneva. Situated between Lake Geneva and the Alps, the club is ideally situated for high flying and jumping expeditions. Whether you're a nervous beginner or an experienced leaper, the club has something for everyone including initiation tandem jumps with an instructor, and complete training courses that lead to solo jumps. The club opens in March and is closed during the winter months.

## Paragliding

Paragliding lets you rise above it all and enjoy a bird's eye view of Geneva. Soar over some of the most beautiful countryside in Europe, high above beautiful lakes and mountain ranges. Whether you're brave enough to go it alone, or you'd prefer the security of a tandem flight, the various clubs and schools in the area can advise you on the available options. For more information, refer to Hang Gliding [p.183].

MudBike | paragliding

**Activities**

### Centre Paradventure

Location → Rue de la Gare · Les Diablerets    **024 492 23 82**
Hours → Check for timings
Web/email → www.swissaventure.ch    Map Ref → na

Paragliding is easy to learn at Centre Paradventure where you are placed in the hands of aerial professionals. The centre is located 130 km from Geneva and offers a range of activities including canyoning, via feratta and luge. Qualified instructors will advise, prepare and train students to obtain their paragliding license. Biplane flights are also available throughout the year. This activity is, however, only suitable for people over the age of 15.

### Club de Vol Libre Genève

Location → Rte de Bossey · Troinex    **022 784 10 99**
Hours → Check for timings
Web/email → www.club-des-sports.ch/cvlg    Map Ref → 11-A1

See the review under Hang Gliding [p.183] for more details.

### Ecole de Parapente du Salève

Location → Chemin de Verdun, 167 · Veyrier    **na**
Hours → Check for timings
Web/email → www.parapente-saleve.com    Map Ref → na

For beginners, it's probably best that you discover paragliding through a tandem flight with an experienced pilot. Tandem flights are available throughout the year (depending on weather conditions) at various locations in the Haute Savoie region. For those that are ready to fly solo, the school offers a range of piloting courses from initial 'flying with your own wings' to advanced and technical long-distance and cross flights. These courses are available throughout the year, so check with the club for exact dates and times.

## Polo

Other options → Horse Riding [p.185]

### Geneva Polo Club

Location → Domaine de Veytay · Mies    **022 755 63 25**
Hours → Check for timings
Web/email → polo.club.veytay@bluewin.ch    Map Ref → na

The magnificent grounds of the Domaine de Veytay, in nearby Mies, are home to the Geneva Polo Club where many high profile meetings, such as the Maharajah Cup and the Geneva Polo Open, are held. The Open attracts spectators from all over the world and the sunny summer conditions make for a perfect day out. The Open also marks the end of the Swiss high goal polo season. The Geneva Polo Club also participates at the Swiss Championships in August.

## Rafting

With two excellent rivers running through town, and at least another 17 rivers within 100 km of the city, Geneva is an ideal location for water sports enthusiasts of all levels.

Two Rivers Meet

### Rafting Adventure Centre

Location → Quai des Vernets 8 · Les Vernets    **079 213 41 40**
Hours → Check for timings
Web/email → www.rafting.ch    Map Ref → 15-C2

The Adventure Centre offers multiple types of tours including rafting, kayaking and even 'hydro speeding', in which you are armed with a wetsuit, flippers a small raft-like 'hydro speeder' to float and bob down the river of your choice. The most popular rafting package is a half day, 12 km trip down the Arve River that plunges and crashes over six waterfalls and countless rapids. The

Polo | Rafting

Activities

Dranse River and Giffre River rafting tours both explore classical alpine river runs, famous for their beautiful scenery and big drops. Swimming is always a possibility and sometimes not even a choice! All other types of tours, including kayaking, canoeing etc, are organised on an individual basis to fit your preferred schedule and budget. One popular program is a canoe or kayak trip to the Versoix marsh, which is filled with beaver dams and water reeds. Finally, for the extremely extreme, the company organises multiple rafting trips during the year to exotic locales such as Nepal and Costa Rica.

### Rafting Loisirs

Location → Ch. des Marais, 52 · Veyrier | 022 784 02 05
Hours → Check for timings
Web/email → www.rafting-loisirs.ch | Map Ref → 12-B1

This versatile adventure company in Veyrier offers a full range of extreme activities from rafting and kayaking to mountain biking and snow-shoe excursions. Raft and kayak tours (led by professional guides) are available between May and October, and are available in various levels to suit beginners, seasoned rapid riders, and everyone in between. Certified rafting courses and summer river camps (for children) are also available. In addition to the tours, Loisirs is a full service retailer, selling a full range of rafting equipment.

### Rivières & Aventures

Location → Château-d'Oex | 026 924 34 23
Hours → Check for timings
Web/email → www.riviere-aventure.ch | Map Ref → na

Situated 90 minutes outside of Geneva, Rivières et Aventures Club organises rafting, canoeing, kayaking and other fun activities. Read more about this club in the canoeing review [p.173].

## Rollerblading & Roller Skating

The lakeside promenade is a very popular summer hangout to a growing number of enthusiastic rollerbladers. Rollerbladers who are particularly brave will also be found skating through the city, over cobbled streets in the Old Town, and even during the winter. It's an easy sport to get into – all you need to do is pop down to your nearest sports store for a pair of rollerblades, and then start working on your balance!

### Genève Rink-Hockey Club

Location → Rue Hans-Wilsdorf, 4 · Acacias | 022 418 40 00
Hours → Check for timings
Web/email → www.geneve-rhc.ch | Map Ref → 15-B2

The Geneva Rink-Hockey club has been running since 1939 and is one of the oldest clubs in Switzerland. With eight championships and nine Swiss Cup titles, the club is also one of the most successful in the country. It also boasts the largest juniors' section. The club uses the facilities at the Queue d'Arve Sports Centre.

## Rowing

### Société Nautique de Genève

Location → Port-Noir · Cologny | 022 707 05 00
Hours → Check for timings
Web/email → www.nautique.org | Map Ref → 14-E2

The rowing section of the Geneva Yacht Club was born with the founding of the club in 1872. The rowing team participates in and organises numerous competitions including the famous Tour du Lac, which at a distance of 160 km is the longest regatta in the world. The club also sends teams to regional and international regattas. The Geneva rowing scene begins in the early morning when competitors arrive to train while the lake is calm. In the afternoons, schools give rowing lessons and in the evenings, the more serious training sessions take place.

## Rugby

When you think of great rugby nations, Switzerland may languish near the bottom of the list. However, there are plenty of rugby enthusiasts in Geneva, who play in an active Suisse league. If the organisation you work for doesn't have a rugby team, you can contact one of the following rugby clubs to find out how you can join in.

### Rugby Club CERN – Meyrin – St Genis (CMS)

Location → CERN · Meyrin | +33 4 50 42 18 06
Hours → Training: Tue & Thu 19:00 – 21:00
Web/email → www.cern.ch/rugbyclub | Map Ref → 4-D1

CMS is Switzerland's oldest rugby club and is also one of the largest. It welcomes players from beginner to international level and from five years old upwards. Apart from good rugby, the club has a real expat flavour with members from France, England, Ireland, Switzerland, Italy, Spain and Australia, and a lively social atmosphere is guaranteed!

---

### Rugby Club de Hermance

Location ➜ Chens-sur-Léman · Hermance | 079 203 52 53
Hours ➜ Training – Tue & Thu 19:00 – 21:00
Web/email ➜ www.hrrc.ch     Map Ref ➜ 3-E1

---

The Hermance Rugby Club was founded in 1971 by a group of young people that wanted to play something other than football. The club grew in popularity and now has members from all over the world including Britain, Argentina, Canada and South Africa. Hermance is a hugely successful club and has won the Swiss Championship ten times over the last 12 years. Interested players are encouraged to contact the club for details on how to sign up. Based in the Marius Berthet Stadium.

## Running

With its hilly terrain, lakeside location and fantastic views, Geneva is the perfect setting for running. Even though spring and summer are obviously the more popular running seasons, it is not unusual to see the bravest of runners out and about during the chilly winter months. Clubs and informal groups meet regularly, and many international companies have their own running teams. Popular competitions include the Tour du Canton, a series of four consecutive 10 km races, which attracts thousands of runners. In December, runners young and old turn out for the annual Course de l'Escalade, a traditional race around the Old Town to commemorate the historical victory of the city of Geneva in 1602 over its neighbour, duc Charles-Emmanuel de Savoie. Additional information on running can be obtained from the Association Des Courses Hors Stade de la Région Genevoise (www.courir-ge.ch), Tour du Canton (www.courirge.ch/courses/tdc2004/accueil/index.htm) or Lausanne Marathon (www.lausanne-marathon.com).

---

### Course de l'Escalade

Location ➜ Old Town · Town Centre | 022 700 59 02
Hours ➜ See below
Web/email ➜ www.escalade.ch     Map Ref ➜ 13-E4

---

Every year on the first Saturday of December, the people of Geneva put on their running shoes and take part in the La Course de l'Escalade. The race attracts tens of thousands of runners and was designed by the Stade Genève Athletics Club to commemorate Geneva's historical victory over Charles-Emmanuel de Savoie. The course is set at various levels for different categories of runners (men, women, children and veterans) and distances range from two to nine kilometres. You can register by visiting the above Website.

## Sailing

With its vast lake and ideal summer conditions, Geneva is a wonderful location for sailing and watersports. Sailing is a very popular pastime in Geneva and many residents are members of the lakeside sailing clubs. Having a membership allows you to participate in club activities and to dock your own boat. If you're merely stopping over in Geneva, you can rent boats by the hour (or day) from a handful of quayside operators including Société Nautique de Genève (see below), Les Corsaires (33 Quai Gustave-Ador, 022 735 43 00) and Marti Marine (31 Quai du Mont-Blanc, 022 732 88 21).

Boats on the lake

## CERN Yachting Club

Location → Port Choiseul · Versoix | na
Hours → Various. Club night Thur 18:00
Web/email → http://yachting.web.cern.ch    Map Ref → 3-A2

The Yachting Club of CERN (YCC) is open to all CERN employees, as well as their families and friends. The club owns 14 sailing boats, including small dinghies, a 25 foot cruiser and a Boston-Whaler power boat. They also have several windsurfing boards. All the boats and boards are located in Port Choiseul (Versoix). The club offers sailing and windsurfing courses, enrolment for which takes place in February and March. Experienced newcomers can join the club at any time and use the boats once they've passed a basic skills test.

## Club Nautique de Versoix

Location → Port Choiseul · Ch. des Graviers | 022 755 35 00
Hours → Office open Mon – Fri 08:00 – 12:00
Web/email → www.cnv.ch    Map Ref → 3-A2

The Versoix Yacht club is located in the beautiful Port Choiseul and has three different sections – yachting, motor boating and water skiing. The yacht section is a very popular component of the club and it organises a variety of sailing courses. Interested parties should contact the club for more information on available courses for all ages and experience levels. Club teams can also participate in many of the regattas that take place in the region, including the European Junior championships that took place in 2003.

## Société Nautique de Genève

Location → Port-Noir · Cologny | 022 707 05 00
Hours → Check for timings
Web/email → www.nautique.org    Map Ref → 14-E2

The Société Nautique de Genève was established in 1872 and now has more than 3,000 members. It has four divisions that include rowing, water skiing, yachting and light yachting, (a term which is used for the smaller classes such as the 49er and 470s). The yachting and light yachting sections organise and participate in a number of regattas every year and their race schedule includes the Suisse Championship and a leg of the European Championships and World Championships.

# Shooting

Other options → Paintballing [p.191]

## Association Sportive Genevoise de Tir (ASGT)

Location → Various | 022 776 24 10
Hours → Check for timings
Web/email → sct-geneve@freesurf.ch    Map Ref → na

Shooting is fairly popular in the region, with some 15 societies making up the Geneva Sporting Association of Shooting ('Association Sportive Genevoise de Tir', or ASGT). The Association will be able to recommend the club best suited to you. A variety of shooting ranges exist, both indoors and outdoors. For a detailed listing of clubs in the region (including the English speaking ones), contact Mary Kehrli-Smith, instructor and communications representative for the Association, on the above number.

## Ball-Trap Club de Geneve

Location → Ch. des Méandres, 8 · Laconnex | 022 756 11 31
Hours → Sat 09:30 – 12:00, 13:00 – 18:00
Web/email → na    Map Ref → 10-A2

The shooting stand at this club is located near Petit Lancy, and because it is in a residential area all the guns are fitted with silencers. The club is open on Saturdays from 09:30 to 12:00, and from 13:00 to 18:00. The afternoon session is generally reserved for members, but nonmembers are welcome if they are visiting Geneva. Annual membership for the club costs SFr 200.

# Skiing & Snowboarding

Nestled between the French Alps and the Jura Mountains, Geneva is a perfect skiing destination. There are many ski stations to choose from, including Leysin, Villars and Les Diablerets in Vaud, and the Verbier, Crans and Nendaz resorts in Valais. The closest Swiss resort is in the Jura Mountains and the Monts Jura range offers slopes that are ideal for beginners. For more experienced skiers and snowboarders, the Alps are very popular and Contamines, Flaine, Morzine-Avoriaz, Argentière and Megève are highly recommended. By car, you can reach some ski resorts in under two hours from Geneva, which makes it possible to have a skiing day trip if you're staying in the city.

Shooting | Skiing & Snowboarding

Activities

## Club Alpin Suisse

Location → Av. du Mail, 4 · Plainpalais
Hours → Tue 10:00 – 13:00 Fri 15:00 – 19:00
Web/email → www.cas-geneve.ch        Map Ref → 13-C4
| 022 321 65 48

The Club Alpin Suisse brings together mountain lovers of all sporting and adventuring backgrounds, and all ages and experience levels. A wide variety of activities are on offer, including ski trekking and snow shoe excursions. For more information on the club, see the review in the Mountaineering section [p.190].

Rush hour on the slopes

## International Ski club de Genève

Location → Ch. Eugène Rigot · Petit-Saconnex
Hours → Weekly meetings Thu 18:00 – 19:30
Web/email → www.scig.ch/index.htm        Map Ref → 5-E2
| na

The International Ski Club of Geneva is mainly open to staff members of international organisations, staff in permanent missions and the diplomatic corps, as well as their families, but the Club does admit other people interested in its activities. In winter, activities include ski school (downhill and snowboard coaching), Alpine and Nordic ski lessons and snow shoe outings. When the snow melts, the club also runs a number of summer activities including hiking, rafting and biking.

## Ski Club du CERN

Location → CERN · Meyrin
Hours → See below
Web/email → http://club-ski.web.cern.ch        Map Ref → 4-D1
| 022 767 34 60

With 1,200 members, the CERN Ski Club is the largest in Geneva and offers a number of different winter activities. They specialise in skiing, snowboarding, cross country skiing and ski trekking lessons, and cater for beginners and experts. Buses usually leave from the CERN Prévessin site at 07:15 sharp, and on arrival at the ski resort you will be given your ski resort pass. From there it's off to the slopes for a lesson or free skiing.

## Ski Club Genève

Location → Various
Hours → Check for timings
Web/email → www.skiclubgeneve.ch        Map Ref → na
| 022 784 08 54

Ski Club Genève is the official club of the city and provides many different categories of entertainment for skiers, snowboarders and snow lovers of all ages and levels. For kids there is an array of activities including skiing and snowboarding training. Adults can go on various weekend and weekday outings, which can involve lessons If you are a beginner. For a slightly harder challenge, the club organises ski trekking expeditions, where you climb up a mountain with your skis, and then ski down afterwards.

## Snownex Ski and Snowboard School

Location → Ch. de la Distillerie, 2 · Bernex
Hours → Check for timings
Web/email → www.snownex.ch        Map Ref → 7-D3
| 022 727 04 00

Snownex is dynamic ski and snowboard school in Geneva that offers a wide variety of classes for beginners and experienced skiers. The club offers classes in all types of skiing and snowboarding disciplines, including freestyle, carving, snow park, boarder cross and slalom, all under the watchful eye of experienced professionals. Lessons take place every Saturday from January to March, and cost SFr 80 for the whole day including transport, ski pass and lesson. In addition to skiing and snowboarding, the company also offers wakeboarding activities at the Plage du Reposoir.

Skiing & Snowboarding

Activities

## Skwal

Invented by local Savoyard Thias Balmain, this relatively new activity mixes skiing, monoskiing and snowboarding, and allows larger sweeping turns using a long thin board. At the moment, Geneva does not house any skwal clubs or associations, but there is one near Morgins and Grand Bornaud, called the Skwal Team Franco Suisse. For more information on other teams in the region as well as the sport itself, log on to www.skwalzone.org.

## Softball

### Geneva Slow Pitch Softball League

| | |
|---|---|
| Location → Various · Bellevue | 022 767 12 26 |
| Hours → See below | |
| Web/email → http://Softball.cern.ch/GSL | Map Ref → 2-D2 |

The Geneva Slow Pitch Softball League is made up of teams from the Geneva area as well as teams from international organisations such as CERN, ILO, US Mission and the UN. League teams play matches every Sunday, from April to September, at Bucker Field between Bellvue and Collex and at Higgs Field, CERN Prévessin. For more information on the sport and the teams that participate in the league, visit the above Website.

Sports centre

## Speedboating

When living in a city that is dotted with fast cars, expensive restaurants and even more expensive tastes, it is no surprise to see fancy speedboats whipping about on the lake. If you haven't yet joined the ranks of the rich and famous, and don't own your own speedboat, don't despair! Different models are available for hire from the various yacht clubs. You do need to have a licence though. For more information, refer to Sailing [p.194].

## Squash

Other options → Beach, Health & Sports Centres [p.206, 207]

### Club du Bois-Carré

| | |
|---|---|
| Location → Ch. des Bûcherons, 14 · Veyrier | 022 784 30 06 |
| Hours → 09:00 – 22:00 Sat/Sun 09:00 – 20:00 | |
| Web/email → www.boiscarre.ch | Map Ref → 9-B4 |

Open to members and nonmembers, the Club du Bois-Carré offers three different racket sports in one club (badminton, squash, tennis) in facilities are open all year round, seven days a week. For more information on the Club du Bois-Carré, see the review in the Tennis section [p.199].

### Squash Club de Genève

| | |
|---|---|
| Location → Ch. du Joli-Bois · Chambésy | 022 758 22 07 |
| Hours → Check for timings | |
| Web/email → See below | Map Ref → 2-D3 |

Whether you're just a beginner or already a champion, the Geneva Squash Club is happy to welcome all new members. They have six quality courts available free of charge to members. For those who want to get competitive, there are four men's teams and two ladies teams registered in the national league. The club also has a mini league that gives players the opportunity to play other people of a similar standard.

*Website: http://mypage.bluewin.ch/Geneva-Squash-Club*

## Swimming

With a host of swimming pools around Geneva and the lake right on your doorstep, you'll have plenty of opportunity to use your swimming skills. For more structured year round swimming training, check out the various sports centres and clubs offering full

Skwal | Swimming

Activities

and varied programmes. If it's just a casual swim that you desire, the sports centres still oblige, as do the lakeside 'beaches' (Bains des Pâquis, Genève Plage, Baby Plage) that have special swimming areas during the summer months.

### Bains des Pâquis

Location ➜ Quai du Mont-Blanc 30    **022 732 29 74**
Hours ➜ 09:00 – 20:00
Web/email ➜ www.bains-des-paquis.ch    Map Ref ➜ 13-E2

Swimming in Lake Geneva is an experience that should not be missed. When the summer months set in you'll find mobs of people queuing to get into the Bains des Pâquis that allows people to sunbathe and swim in an area of the lake. Established in 1870, and made public in 1890, the Bains des Pâquis hasn't lost any of its appeal. In the winter months the Bains des Pâquis buildings are used as saunas and massage parlours.

Bains des Pâquis

### Dauphins Genève

Location ➜ Ch. des Floralies, 9 · Vernier    **022 798 34 00**
Hours ➜ Check for timings
Web/email ➜ www.dauphins.ch    Map Ref ➜ 5-B2

The Dauphins-Genève club focuses on promoting aquatic and sub aquatic activities in all their forms. As a member of the Dolphins, you'll have the opportunity to practice six different disciplines – scuba diving, swimming with flippers, free diving, swimming, triathlon and synchronised swimming. All the activities are monitored by professional and experienced instructors and the club has an excellent record of producing top level swimmers including Swiss national champions and members that have made European and world selections. The club also has a swimming school for babies. If you would like to become a member, visit the club Website for more information or call the above number.

### Genève Natation 1885

Location ➜ Centre Sportif des Vernets    **022 342 19 72**
Hours ➜ Check for timings
Web/email ➜ www.geneve-natation-1885.ch    Map Ref ➜ 8-D1

Genève Natation 1885 is one of the oldest swimming clubs in Switzerland and is a founder member of the Swiss Swimming Federation. The club specialises in training for swimming, diving and water polo at all levels ranging from beginner to professional, and has a full and varied training schedule. For more information on specific training times, costs and other details, contact the club office on the number above, Mondays and Thursdays from 14:00 – 18:30.

### Varembé Sports Centre

Location ➜ Varembé · Petit-Saconnex    **022 733 12 14**
Hours ➜ Check for timings
Web/email ➜ na    Map Ref ➜ 5-D2

The Varembé Sports Centre has excellent swimming facilities, including two huge indoor pools (one is 33 metres, the other is 25 metres) and a selection of diving boards (from one to five metres). Outdoors, you'll find a 25 metre pool as well as a children's area that is very popular during the summer. The centre hosts a variety of swimming, synchronised swimming and diving schools.

## Table Tennis

Table tennis (ping pong in French) is a popular summer activity with most of the beach areas and picnic spots accommodating at least one table. Some sports centres are also equipped with ping pong facilities (see Sports Centres [p.207]). If you want more than just a casual bat and are looking for serious table tennis action, a number of clubs offer coaching and tournaments. Check out Bernex Club (www.cttbernex.ch) or Espérence Table Tennis Club (www.esperance-ttc.ch).

Swimming | Table Tennis

Activities

## Tennis

With Roger Federer doing so well on the international tennis scene, Switzerland is establishing itself as a real contender on the international tennis circuit. The Allianz Swiss Open in Gstaad, held in July, is attracting growing crowds. For those who want to get a piece of the action themselves, there are numerous places in Geneva to enjoy this sport. High quality outdoor courts are readily available at most health and sports clubs. There are also a number of established tennis clubs in the city (see reviews below).

### Club du Bois-Carré

Location ➜ Ch. des Bûcherons, 14 · Veyrier  |  022 784 30 06
Hours ➜ 09:00 – 22:00 Sat/Sun 09:00 – 20:00
Web/email ➜ www.boiscarre.ch            Map Ref ➜ 9-B4

With its four badminton courts, five squash courts and 13 tennis courts (indoor and outdoor), Bois-Carré is the ideal place for racket sports fans. The facilities are excellent and allow players to train in all three disciplines. If you're competitive by nature, Bois-Carré regularly organises tournaments that are open to everyone. The club also organises a variety of other social activities throughout the year.

### Tennis Club de Genève

Location ➜ Park des Eaux-Vives · Eaux-Vives  |  022 735 53 50
Hours ➜ Check for timings
Web/email ➜ www.tc-geneve.ch            Map Ref ➜ 14-B3

The Geneva Tennis Club (with help from its sister club in Champel) has established itself as a bastion of Genevois tennis. Open from mid April to mid October, the club has a clay centre court, 16 other clay courts, four hard courts and a training wall. Players of all ages and levels are welcomed, and they should contact the club to get advice on what programme to join. The club also takes part in internal and inter-club tournaments.

### Tennis Club de Genève Champel

Location ➜ Rte de Vessy, 41 · Veyrier  |  022 784 25 66
Hours ➜ Check for timings
Web/email ➜ www.tc-geneve.ch            Map Ref ➜ 9-B3

The Champel branch of the Geneva Tennis Club is open all year round (summer season from mid April to mid September, winter season from the end of September to the end of March) and has a number of different courts. There is an indoor hall with five courts (royal slide surface), six outdoor courts (three royal slide surface, three hard courts) and a training wall. Budding tennis players are encouraged to contact the club for more information on how to join.

## Triathlon

Other options ➜ Cycling [p.176]

### Dauphins Genève

Location ➜ Ch. des Floralies, 9 · Vernier  |  022 798 34 00
Hours ➜ Check for timings
Web/email ➜ www.dauphins.ch            Map Ref ➜ 5-B2

See the review under Swimming [p.197].

### Triathlon Club de Genève

Location ➜ Various  |  022 757 49 69
Hours ➜ Check for timings
Web/email ➜ www.trigeneve.ch            Map Ref ➜ na

The Triathlon Club de Genève has been promoting the triathlon in the Geneva region by offering a wide range of training sessions to athletes of all ages and levels. The club currently has more than 200 members, along with experienced and dedicated coaches that share their knowledge with athletes. If you'd like to work more specifically on one area of the triathlon, individual coaching is available to assist athletes in the fields of swimming and running.

## Via Ferrata

Via Ferrata is a climbing sport that originated in Italy and has become quite popular in Switzerland. This activity involves following a charted course around rock faces while attached to a safety cable. There are plenty of Via Ferrata opportunities all over Switzerland and close to France. For more information, check out the official Via Ferrata Website (www.viaferrata.org), which lists areas that offer this activity. Alternatively, you can contact Mountain Adventure (Diablerets) – 024 492 1232 (www.mountain-evasion.ch), Centre Paradventure (Diablerets) – 024 492 23 82 (www.swissaventure.ch), Club Alpin Suisse – 022 321 65 48 (www.cas-geneve.ch) or Aventures Alpines – 022 321 00 48 (www.aventuresalpines.ch).

Tennis | Via Ferrata

**Activities**

## Volleyball

Whether you're a serious volleyball player or you just want to play socially, Geneva has over 25 clubs that you can join. To get advice on the club that will best suit your experience and skill level, contact the Geneva Volleyball Association by calling them on 022 736 96 11, or visit their Website at www.agbv.net.

## Wakeboarding

Because of its similarity with snowboarding, wakeboarding has become popular with today's young and hip, and the lake in Geneva provides a great place for participants to wakeboard. Wake boarding involves being pulled along by a boat, and using the waves produced to perform various tricks. Other wake sports include waterskate, hydrofoil, water-skiing and barefoot water-skiing. All these disciplines can be practised at the Wake Sport Centre (see review below).

### Snownex Ski and Snowboard School

Location ➜ Ch. de la Distillerie, 2 · Bernex
Hours ➜ Check for timings
Web/email ➜ www.snownex.ch
022 727 04 00
Map Ref ➜ 7-D3

In collaboration with the EasyWake school based at the Plage du Reposir, Snownex offers wakeboard lessons and other wake sports activities. From May to September they are open every day of the week and also offer other crazy sports such as wakeskate, waterskiing, wakesurf and floating rubber ring. Boat transportation, wakeboard or other device, isothermal wet suit, life jacket and lessons are all included in the package.

### Wake Sports Center

Location ➜ Genève-Plage · Town Centre
Hours ➜ Check for timings
Web/email ➜ www.wake.ch
079 202 38 73
Map Ref ➜ 14-D1

Whether you're new to the sport or an advanced wakeboarder, this centre offers something for everyone. If you're at a competitive level, the Wake Sport Team unites riders of a certain skill. Training sessions take place once a week and the team takes part in the Geneva and Romande Championships as well as the Swiss Tour. The Wake Sports Centre also offers other wake sports including waterskate, hydrofoil, and barefoot and conventional waterskiing.

## Water Polo

Other options ➜ Polo [p.192]

### Genève Natation 1885

Location ➜ Centre Sportif des Vernets
Hours ➜ Check for timings
Web/email ➜ www.geneve-natation-1885.ch
022 342 19 72
Map Ref ➜ 8-D1

Water polo is one of three disciplines offered at the Genève Natation 1885 Club and they have seven different teams including the Elite Team that plays in the National League B, the team for everyone that plays in League Two, the under 19 team and a women's team. The club also has a team for juniors, masters (players over 30 years old) and a veteran's team. For the younger players, there is a water polo school that works in collaboration with the swimming section.

## Water Skiing

Other options ➜ Beach Clubs [p.206]

### Club Nautique de Versoix

Location ➜ Port Choiseul · Ch. des Graviers
Hours ➜ Office open Mon – Fri 08:00 – 12:00
Web/email ➜ www.cnv.ch
022 755 35 00
Map Ref ➜ 3-A2

The waterskiing section of the Versoix Yacht club offers this exciting sport to the public at reasonable prices. The club has a loyal following of over 600 participants in Versoix, Reposoir, Meuzac, St-Symphorien and Montrevel. The club has been around for 18 years and has 11 boats. Special workshops are also organised by the club and take place in different locations. In 2003, the club welcomed female world jump and overall record holder, Elena Milakova, as an honorary member.

### Société Nautique de Genève

Location ➜ Port-Noir · Cologny
Hours ➜ Check for timings
Web/email ➜ www.nautique.org
022 707 05 00
Map Ref ➜ 14-E2

Under the direction of trainer Claude Perez, state certified instructor, the waterskiing section of the Geneva Yacht Club provides participants with the necessary material and equipment for various activities (including wakeboarding and waterskiing) as well as details of the different disciplines that can be practised on the lake (such as slalom and mini slalom). Age is not a limitation, but you should be able to swim.

### Wake Sports Center

Location → Genève-Plage · Town Centre | 079 202 38 73
Hours → Check for timings
Web/email → www.wake.ch | Map Ref → 14-D1

Wake offers a selection of waterskiing activities and lessons. For more details see Wakeboarding [p.200].

Water ski club

## Windsurfing

### CERN Yachting Club

Location → Port Choiseul · Versoix | na
Hours → Various. Club night Thu 18:00
Web/email → http://yachting.web.cern.ch | Map Ref → 3-A2

The CERN yachting club offers sailing and windsurfing courses, enrollment for which takes place in February and March. Find the full review under Sailing [p.194].

## Zorbing

### Centre Paradventure

Location → Rue de la Gare · Les Diablerets | 024 492 23 82
Hours → Check for timings
Web/email → www.swissaventure.ch | Map Ref → na

This unconventional sport hails from New Zealand. The zorb is a plastic padded ball that measures three metres in diameter. The zorbonaut climbs inside the ball and proceeds to roll around in it. Because of the plastic padding in the zorb, the zorbonaut can roll down hills and over bumps without getting hurt. Centre Paraventure in Diablerets offers zorbing as one of its many summer activities.

## Well-Being

## Beauty Salons

Geneva is full of beautiful people who can get buffed, fluffed and puffed up in one of the city's many salons. While smaller institutes offer a more personal touch, the sheer range of services and products at the larger establishments is amazing. Most gyms and fitness centres also offer certain beauty services, so you can put your body through a gruelling workout and then give it some much needed pampering! Check with individual establishments for details of their beauty services (refer to Gyms and Health Centres [p.206]).

### Holmes Place Sports and Health Club

Location → Rue de Rhône · Town Centre | 022 818 47 70
Hours → 06:30 – 22:00  Sat 09:00 – 21:00, Sun 09:00 – 20:00
Web/email → www.holmesplace.ch | Map Ref → 13-E4

The Holmes Place complex is a beauty salon that's open to both members and nonmembers. Whether it's a French manicure, relaxing massage, makeover or leg/bikini wax you're looking for, Holmes Place can accommodate you in their smart and modern surroundings. Experienced beauty therapists provide friendly and professional service, and as the salon is in a gym, you can combine your beauty treatments with a workout.

### Institut Bio-Aromatique

Location → Rue Le Corbusier, 11 · Eaux-Vives | 022 347 70 50
Hours → 09:00 – 19:00  Sat 09:00 – 14:00
Web/email → www.institut-bio-aromatique.com  Map Ref → 16-C2

Beauty treatments, cosmetic consultations and massages are offered at the Institut Bio-Aromatique.

### Institut Carita

Location → Rue de Candolle · Plainpalais | 022 329 34 62
Hours → 09:00 – 19:00  Sat 09:00 – 12:00 Sun closed
Web/email → na | Map Ref → 15-E1

Located in an old distinguished building facing the Parc des Bastions, the Institut Carita offers beauty

Well-Being

Activities

treatment out of the top drawer. Carita products have made their mark in the world of beauty for their quality and luxury status. The institute is renowned for its quality and employs two beauticians who carry out treatments using special Carita methods, and are able to offer advice for all skin types. Favourite treatments at the institute include the anti-ageing selections, which involve massages and firming cream.

## Institut Clarins

Location ➜ Passage des Lions · Eaux-Vives | na
Hours ➜ 08:00 – 20:00
Web/email ➜ www.clarins.ch                    Map Ref ➜ 13-D3

Clarins is well known for its high quality beauty products and their institute echoes this. As soon as you enter through the door you feel completely relaxed thanks to their friendly staff and beauticians that are trained to the highest level in Clarins techniques and methods. The institute offers many services including waxing, facial and body care, manicure and make-up. Guys don't have to feel left out, because there is a special range of men's products and treatments.

## Institut Rubinstein

Location ➜ Cours de Rive · Town Centre | 022 311 66 94
Hours ➜ 08:00 – 18:00
Web/email ➜ na                    Map Ref ➜ 13-E4

Many different beauty treatments await you at the Institut Rubinstein and including the Helena Rubinstein and Guinot beauty treatments. If you want banish your cellulite, the famous Cellu M6 treatment is designed to remodel your figure through a series of draining massages that consist of seaweed or paraffin body wraps. You can also have a manicure, pedicure or laser hair removal.

## Institute Amandine

Location ➜ Pl. du Temple, 7 · Carouge | 022 342 16 66
Hours ➜ Check for timings
Web/email ➜ See below                    Map Ref ➜ 15-D4

After all the wraps, massages, facial masks and waxes that one can receive at the Institute Amandine, there's no excuse for not donning your bikini and hitting the beach. The institute also offers services for men including skin and waxing treatments. The institute uses Hormeta products, which are part of a traditional Swiss skin care programme designed to keep the skin super soft and young looking.

**Website:** www.hormeta.com/pages/Revend_ch/institut_amandine

Hair salon

## La Sultane de Sabah

Location ➜ Rue de l'Athénée, 44 · Plainpalais | 022 347 44 46
Hours ➜ See below
Web/email ➜ www.lasultanedesabah.ch                    Map Ref ➜ 16-A2

The Sultane de Sabah offers clients a selection of oriental treatment methods and cosmetics. You can choose from sugar hair removal sessions, as well as facial and body treatments using exotic oils including cinnamon, honey, karate butter, perfumed salts and mint tea. Every oil has special properties depending on what you are looking for (relaxing, slimming or toning) and the aromas stay with you long after you've left the salon.

*Timings: Mon 10:00 – 18:30, Tue – Fri 09:00 – 18:30, Sat 09:00 – 15:00*

## Peggy Sage

Location ➜ Rue de Carouge, 9 · Carouge | 022 800 32 20
Hours ➜ Mon – Fri 09:00 – 18:30, Thu open late  Sun closed
Web/email ➜ See below                    Map Ref ➜ 15-D1

Peggy Sage nail varnishes are renowned for their resistance and colour range. At the Peggy Sage Institute you have a choice of various full manicure and pedicure treatments, along with relaxing spa treatments for your feet, facials and make-up care. As well as offering beauty treatments, the institute is also a training centre, focusing on the use of Peggy Sage products.

**Website:** www.centredeformationpeggysage.com

## Phylea

| | |
|---|---|
| Location → Rue Rousseau · Town Centre | 022 908 25 10 |
| Hours → Check for timings | |
| Web/email → na | Map Ref → 13-D3 |

Phylea covers all your beauty needs under one roof – you can get your hair cut, have a massage, manicure or facial, and even buy evening wear.

## Privilège

| | |
|---|---|
| Location → Ch. de la Chaumière · Grand-Lancy | 022 300 47 |
| 85 | |
| Hours → Check for timings | |
| Web/email → na | Map Ref → 8-D4 |

The Privilège Institute, based in an exquisite garden, is a relaxing beauty centre that will help you feel good about life. The institute offers facials, laser hair removal (with anaesthetic cream), weight loss programmes, full body treatments and permanent make-up application.

## Health Spas

What better way is there to get away from the pressures of work and life than a trip to a spa? The Swiss are proud of their spa and health resorts and the region around Lake Geneva is famous for its health facilities and well-being centres. The climate, long experience and high levels of specialist knowledge are the basis for this particular Swiss popularity. Health spas and internationally recognised clinics offer various treatments that have one goal in mind: harmony of the body and soul. Some Swiss resorts are steeped tradition and have been around since Roman times, and they offer time honoured and expert treatments for many health problems. In the southwest between Bern, Geneva and the Alps, you should look at visiting Yverdon-les-Bains, Schwefelberg-Bad, Lenk, Leukerbad, Breiten, Lavey-les-Bains and Saillon.

## Centre Thermal

| | |
|---|---|
| Location → Rue des Bains · Yverdon-les-Bains | 024 423 02 32 |
| Hours → Check for timings | |
| Web/email → www.thermes-yverdon.ch | Map Ref → na |

Situated on the south bank of the Lac de Neuchâtel (40 km north of Lausanne) are the ancient thermal baths of Yverdon-les-Bains, which date back to Roman times. The spa has outside pools for warm relaxation, and is equipped with jet pools, hydro massages, whirlpools, waterfalls and an aquadrome. In addition, there is also a giant Jacuzzi on the terrace, Japanese baths, saunas, hammams and a resting room. A fitness area is also available where you can join aqua gym classes.

## Domaine de Divonne

| | |
|---|---|
| Location → Av. des Thermes · Divonne (Fr) | +33 4 50 40 34 34 |
| Hours → Check for timings | |
| Web/email → www.domaine-de-divonne.com | Map Ref → na |

The Domaine de Divonne Casino, Golf and Spa Resort is situated between the Jura Mountains and faces the French Alps, and is a ten minute drive away from Geneva International Airport. The Domaine is set in a private park, just minutes away from the Divonne thermal spa baths, and has 130 deluxe rooms and suites. The spa facilities within the Domaine include a fitness centre (with Jacuzzi, sauna, steam bath and gymnastics room) and the Atelier de Beauté Anne Sémonin, where you will be pampered by professional staff offering energising massages.

## Institut Mìngmén

| | |
|---|---|
| Location → Rue de la Gare, 23 · Morges | 021 803 56 22 |
| Hours → Check for timings | |
| Web/email → www.massage-thai.net | Map Ref → na |

Here you can learn how to take care of your body and soul in accordance with age old Asian traditions. Either lie back and enjoy traditional Thai and Chinese massages and acupuncture administered by professional staff, or sign up for a class to learn how to perform massages yourself. The institute is in Morges, which is situated between Geneva and Lausanne.

## La Réserve Genève Hotel and Spa

| | |
|---|---|
| Location → Rte De Lausanne, 301 · Bellevue | 022 959 59 59 |
| Hours → Check for timings | |
| Web/email → www.lareserve.ch | Map Ref → na |

Built on the shores of Lake Geneva, La Réserve Genève Hotel and Spa is a suitable destination for business or pleasure. The spa and wellness centre offers an indoor and outdoor pool, sauna, steam bath, state of the art fitness equipment, hair salon, two tennis courts, 17 treatment rooms and a private beach. All rooms and suites have a private terrace or balcony, and all suites offer panoramic views of the lake and the surrounding Alps.

Well-Being

Activities

La Réserve Genève

### Le Grain de Vie

Location ➜ Ch. sur-Rang, 9 · Veyrier | **022 343 54 90**
Hours ➜ 09:00 – 12:30 14:00 – 19:00 Sat, 09:00 – 12:30
Web/email ➜ www.graindevie.com      Map Ref ➜ 8-E3

The macrobiotic Le Grain de Vie Centre focuses on preventative health care. Since 1980, the centre has offered a number of different classes including cooking, Yoga and Shiatsu. The art of Shiatsu is taught as a technique based on Chinese historical traditions, and is believed to prevent health problems and cure various ailments, and is recommended for convalescence. The centre also offers Shiatsu massages given by a professional masseuse. Closed on Sundays.

### Le Mirador Kempinski Resort and Spa

Location ➜ Mont-Pèlerin · | **021 925 11 11**
Hours ➜ Check for timings
Web/email ➜ www.lemirador.ch/en      Map Ref ➜ na

Relaxation is the predominate theme at Le Mirador Kempinski. The Givenchy Spa is a sanctuary of health and beauty, where the focus is on shaping, revitalising, promoting circulation, hydrating and enhancing the face and body, and achieving complete relaxation of body and mind. The spa offers care treatment through essential techniques

that relax the body and mind and revive the skin. They offer a special Day Package, which costs SFr 310 per person and includes a facial, massage treatment, body wrap and lunch.

### Valvital – Thermal Spa Baths, Divonne

Location ➜ Divonne · France | **+33 4 50 20 27 70**
Hours ➜ Check for timings
Web/email ➜ www.valvital.fr      Map Ref ➜ na

The thermal spa baths in Divonne have been around since 1848, and are said to wash away stress, worries, tiredness, insomnia and other ailments of modern life. Different thermal spa treatments are available using the spring water from the Morel source. The thermal season runs from March until November, and you should contact the baths directly to organise an assessment. As well as the healing baths, the spa includes two indoor heated mineral water swimming pools, an aqua gym and a hot tub with a Jacuzzi, massage board and powerful jet streams.

### Valvital Thermes de Thonon

Location ➜ Thonon-les-Bains · France | na
Hours ➜ 08:30 – 20:30
Web/email ➜ www.valvital.fr      Map Ref ➜ na

Spa activity at Thonon-les-Bains dates back 100 years. The diuretic and detoxifying properties of Thonon water (from the Versoie spring) are notably recognised in the treatment of dietary ailments, and the water's mineral content favours the treatment of rheumatic disorders. A programme that uses a wide range of hydrotherapy treatments including baths and showers, mud wraps, cataplasms, underwater massages and pool exercises has also been implemented. Les Thermes Spa is situated 40 km from Geneva.

## Massage

Other options ➜Beauty Salons [p.201]
Health Spas [p.203]
Gyms & Health Centres [p.206]

In the busy and bustling city of Geneva, there are a variety of massage options to help you unwind. Specific massage centres and institutes offer a variety of treatments along with massages. Most beauty institutes [p.211], gyms and health centres [p.206], and spas in the region [p.203] also offer these services.

### Centre Do

Location ➜ Merle d'Aubigné, 17 · Eaux-Vives | 022 308 13 17
Hours ➜ Check for timings
Web/email ➜ www.shiatsu-do.ch          Map Ref ➜ 14-B3

Centre Do specialises in relaxation and stress busting. Certified therapist Eric Gygax can help ease your aches and pains away using the traditional 'hands on' methods of Shiatsu. Before going for your massage, you should not eat heavily or drink alcohol, and you should wear loose clothing.

### Institut Mìngmén

Location ➜ Rue de la Gare, 23 · Morges | 021 803 56 22
Hours ➜ Check for timings
Web/email ➜ www.massage-thai.net          Map Ref ➜ na

Please see review under Health Spas [p.203].

### Le Grain de Vie

Location ➜ Ch. sur-Rang, 9 · Veyrier | 022 343 54 90
Hours ➜ 09:00 – 12:30  14:00 – 19:00  Sat, 09:00 – 12:30
Web/email ➜ www.graindevie.com          Map Ref ➜ 8-E3

Please see review under Health Spas [p.203].

### Wellness and Massage Services (WMS)

Location ➜ Rue de Lausanne, 67 | 022 738 32 92
Hours ➜ Check for timings
Web/email ➜ www.wms-services.com          Map Ref ➜ 5-E3

WMS offers onsite massage and wellness services to companies, and cater for VIP and sports events, seminars, conferences, exhibitions and product launches. Massages are all Oriental and the client remains fully clothed. Sessions last for twenty minutes, during which the client can ask questions relating to well-being. WMS is also a massage school that leads to a diploma in classical, sports and therapeutic massage, which is certified by the Swiss Massage Federation ('Fédération Suisse des Masseurs').

## Pilates

The primary aim of pilates is to stretch and strengthen the body through a series of routines based on deep breathing, relaxation and co-ordinated movements. This discipline will result in a more balanced and flexible body, and improved body alignment. Some gyms and health clubs [p.206] offer regular classes, as do certain spas [p.203] or dance studios [p.212].

### Ecole-Club Migros

Location ➜ Rue du Prince, 5 · Town Centre | 022 319 61 61
Hours ➜ Check for timings
Web/email ➜ www.ecole-club.ch          Map Ref ➜ 13-E4

Pilates is offered in packages of nine classes (the package costs SFr 145). Each class involves 50 minutes of toning and stretching, and pilates experts will guide you through the intense movements, using over 500 floor exercises, all designed to strengthen the lower body and abdomen.

### Swissbody Inc.

Location ➜ Av. Jules Crosnier, 16 · Plainpalais | 022 346 42 82
Hours ➜ Check for timings
Web/email ➜ www.swissbody.com          Map Ref ➜ 16-A1

Swissbody boasts one of the most advanced pilates studios in the world, and is equipped with machines based on Joseph Pilates' original techniques. There are classes for men and women of all ages, regardless of fitness level. Sessions are conducted on a private or semi private basis, although there is the option for group classes.

## Reiki

Reiki uses a 'universal life force energy' to emotionally cleanse, physically invigorate and leave you more focused. Unlike meditation, which can be practised at home with only basic knowledge, Reiki requires a bit more training.

### Cabinet SB

Location ➜ Versoix · Genthod | 079 651 08 76
Hours ➜ Check for timings
Web/email ➜ www.reiki-sb.com          Map Ref ➜ 3-A2

The SB Centre specialises in energetic therapy and practices Reiki as a base treatment for healing. The centre also offers Reiki teaching, designed to help interested people practice the technique at home or even at a professional level. People suffering from fatigue, stress, worry, lack of motivation or seasonal depression may find that Reiki can help them to regain balance in their lives.

Well-Being

Activities

### Centre Sivananda de Yoga Vedanta

Location → Rue des Minoteries, 1 · Plainpalais | 022 328 03 28
Hours → Check for timings
Web/email → www.sivananda.org      Map Ref → 15-D2

The Sivananda Centre offers meditation courses where attendees will receive a detailed explanation on concentration techniques and guided tutorials on the workings of meditation. The course includes an introduction to the 12 steps of meditation and the respective mantras. For more information on the Sivananda Centre, refer to the Yoga section [p.206].

### L'atelier de Reiki

Location → Collonge-Bellerive      | 022 752 35 96
Hours → Check for timings
Web/email → www.reiki-geneva.com      Map Ref → 6-C3

Reiki is a natural healing technique that originated in Tibet many thousands of years ago, and was rediscovered by Dr. Mikao Usui at the end of the last century. The Atelier de Reiki in Collonge Bellerive follows this art of healing and caring, and offers various degrees of Reiki teaching that are all given by an experienced Reiki master. Classes are provided in a beautiful mansion setting in Collonge-Bellerive.

## Yoga

In Geneva, classes in the discipline of yoga are highly popular with many health clubs now boasting classes and workshops at various levels. Many international organisations and large companies offer evening sessions. However, tying yourself up in knots doesn't come cheap – yoga classes tend to be quite pricey, starting at around SFr 20 per lesson.

### Centre Sivananda de Yoga Védanta

Location → Rue des Minoteries, 1 · Plainpalais | 022 328 03 28
Hours → Check for timings
Web/email → www.sivananda.org      Map Ref → 15-D2

The International Sivananda Yoga Védanta Centre is a non profit organisation that aims to further the teachings of Yoga and Vedanta as a means of achieving physical, mental and spiritual well being on the road to self-realisation. At the Geneva branch you can bend and stretch in a variety of courses at different levels ranging from beginners to experts. You can attend the classes free of charge on Thursdays at 20:00 or Tuesdays at 12:30, and there is no need to book.

### Ecole-Club Migros

Location → Rue du Prince, 5 · Town Centre      | 022 319 61 61
Hours → Check for timings
Web/email → www.ecole-club.ch      Map Ref → 13-E4

At Ecole-Club Migros you can experience a variety of different yoga methods that include power yoga, Hatha yoga, yoga-lates, Tibetan yoga, yoga for future mothers, and even Yoga for Oldies. Classes generally last up to an hour and with so many different classes to choose from you are guaranteed to find one that compliments your lifestyle and expertise level.

### Le Grain de Vie

Location → Ch. sur-Rang, 9 · Veyrier      | 022 343 54 90
Hours → 09:00 – 12:30  14:00 – 19:00  Sat, 09:00 – 12:30
Web/email → www.grainedevie.com      Map Ref → 8-E3

Le Grain de Vie Centre offers classes in Yoga and Shiatsu. The Yoga-Do method taught at the school uses traditional exercises to help develop mental serenity and spiritual enlightenment. Using your internal energy, varying postures and breathing, you'll be able to take your body and mind to a higher plane. Courses take place throughout the year on Mondays and Wednesdays for a minimum of five people. Costs are SFr 20 per class or SFr 180 for a ten class package.

## Beach, Health & Sports Centres

### Beach Clubs

Although beach clubs are situated on the shores of the lake, rather than the sea, the idea is the same – sun, sand (or concrete, in some cases!) and swimming.

### Health Clubs

With a multitude of classes to choose from, you can easily step, pump, body combat and aerobic your way across Geneva. Most health clubs offer members exercise classes on a regular basis. For a complete list of sessions, timings and instructors, check with the individual clubs (see the Health Clubs Table [p.208]).

SFr 10 ~ € 6      1st Edition | GENEVA EXPLORER

## Sports Centres

Geneva may be small but it is home to a surprising number of sports centres. These all weather centres offer excellent facilities and diverse activities. Although some are off limits and reserved exclusively for use by clubs and associations, you should have no trouble finding one near you for public use. Contact the various centres to find out about costs – some will let you use their facilities free of charge.

**Images of Geneva**

*Breathtaking mountain vistas mirrored in the crystal clear waters of the lake, the cobbled streets of the Old Town contrasted against the bustling modernity of one of the world's business capitals; Geneva is a treasure trove of beautiful views. Images of Geneva is a stunning collection of photographs of both the familiar and undiscovered sights of this remarkable city.*

### Centre Sportif de la Queue d'Arve

Location → Rue François-Dussaud     **022 418 44 44**
Hours → Check for timings
Web/email → na     Map Ref → 15-B1

The Queue d'Arve sports centre has many excellent sporting facilities to offer. It has a good selection of badminton and tennis courts available that can be hired at a rate of SFr 13 per hour, and is also home to the Badminton Club Genève. There is a hockey rink, along with volleyball and basketball courts, while cycling fans can ride at the Vélodrome. For extreme sport addicts there is a climbing wall (difficulty 8B).

### Centre Sportif des Vernets

Location → Rue Hans-Wilsdorf, 4-6 · Acacias     **022 418 40 00**
Hours → Check for timings
Web/email → na     Map Ref → 15-B2

The Vernets Sports Centre houses the Geneva Ice Rink, used by the national league ice hockey team 'Servette de Genève'. The rink is also open to members of the public who want to practice their skating skills. The centre has excellent swimming facilities, including three indoor and two outdoor pools. The pools are mainly reserved for clubs and schools, but check with the centre for various swimming options and swimming teams. There is also a gym for member and club use.

### Centre Sportif du Bois-des-Frères

Location → Châtelaine · Vernier     **022 796 44 64**
Hours → 08:00 – 22:00   Sat & Sun, 08:00 – 20:00
Web/email → na     Map Ref → 5-B3

The multipurpose Bois-des-Frères Centre features football pitches, running tracks, long jump pits, volleyball, handball and basketball courts, gym facilities, shooting and archery arenas.

### Centre Sportif du Bout-du-Monde

Location → Rte de Vessy, 12-14     **022 347 80 87**
Hours → Check for timings
Web/email → na     Map Ref → 9-A3

The Bout-du-Monde sports centre has everything to please sports fans from football pitches to fencing rooms to basketball and volleyball courts. The centre has an excellent athletics stadium that is open to everyone, but is sometimes reserved for large training groups. The centre also boasts a bicross terrain course for mountain bikes and bike training. There is also a 1.3 km cross country track and a climbing wall, which can be used by anybody who has the right equipment.

### Centre Sportif Sous-Moulin

Location → Rte de Sous-Moulin, 39 · Thônex     **022 305 00 00**
Hours → Check for timings
Web/email → www.cssm.ch     Map Ref → 9-D2

This sports centre covers about 96,000 square metres, so there is plenty of space for football pitches, general training zones, tennis courts, athletics tracks, long jump pits, hammer throwing, table tennis, bowls, martial arts, shooting, fully equipped gym, and even an ice skating rink. There's also a restaurant snack bar where you can recharge your energy levels after a tough workout.

### Varembé Sports Centre

Location → Varembé · Petit-Saconnex     **022 733 12 14**
Hours → Check for timings
Web/email → na     Map Ref → 5-D2

As well as having excellent swimming facilities, the Varembé Sports Centre also has a number of basketball courts, table tennis rooms, volley ball courts and a mini athletics centre. Most of these facilities are reserved for use by private clubs or schools, but the mini athletics centre (including the running track) can be used by anyone. The club

*Beach, Health & Sports Clubs*

*Activities*

## Club Membership Rates & Facilities

GENEVA

| Club Name | Location | Area | Tel. no. |
|---|---|---|---|
| California – Champel | Av. de Miremont | Champel | 022 347 81 86 |
| - Chêne-Vert | Rue de Genève | Chêne-Vert | 022 349 32 31 |
| - Eaux-Vives | Rue des Eaux-Vives | Eaux-Vives | 022 786 99 80 |
| Harmony Fitness club – Balexert | Balexert Shopping Centre | Balexert | 022 797 29 29 |
| - La Praille | La Praille Shopping Centre | Acacias | 022 308 58 58 |
| - Signy | Signy Shopping Centre | Signy | 022 363 88 55 |
| Hilton Fit Club | Noga Hilton Hotel | City centre | 022 731 05 40 |
| Holmes Place | Rue de Rhône | City centre | 022 818 47 70 |
| | 4th floor, Globus Dept. Store | | |
| Meyrin fitness centre | Prom. Champs-Fréchets | Meyrin | 022 783 04 94 |
| Rainbow | Rue Bautte | City centre | 022 731 10 63 |
| Silhouette fitness centre – Acacias | Rue de Grand-Bureau | Acacias | 022 343 78 70 |
| - ICC | Rte de Pré-Bois | Airport | 022 788 1688 |
| - Les Alpes | Rue Thalberg | City centre | 022 732 77 40 |
| - Manoir | Rte de Frontenex | Eaux-Vives | 022 787 57 57 |
| - Meyrin | Av. Cardinal Journet | Meyrin | 022 785 50 50 |
| - Mies Versoix | Rte Suisse | Mies | 022 779 07 66 |
| - Vermont | Rue de Vermont | Grand Pré/Servette | 022 733 20 75 |
| - Wilson | Rue Jean-Antoine Gautier | City centre | 022 732 80 50 |
| Top Forme | La Voie de Moens | Grand-Saconnex | 022 747 02 45 |

\*   Holmes Place – monthly fee plus annual 'inscription' fees.  For corporate membership, incription fee is wavered
\*\*   Harmony – Off peak fees are SFr 990 for morning and afternoon use.  SFr 790 for just afternoon use only
C.O – Can organise

Skiing

Beach, Health & Sports Clubs

Activities

SFr 10 ~ € 6

| Membership Rates | | Gym | | | | | | Activity | | Relaxation | | | | |
| --- | --- | --- | --- | --- | --- | --- | --- | --- | --- | --- | --- | --- | --- | --- |
| Full price | Off peak | Treadmills | Exercise bikes | Step machines | Rowing machines | Free weights | Resistance machines | Gym/Dance classes | Swimming pool | Massage | Sauna | Jacuzzi | Hammam/Steam room | Beauty salon |
| SFr 1,640 – entry to all 3 clubs | SFr 1,149 | ✓ | ✓ | ✓ | ✓ | ✓ | ✓ | ✓ | – | ✓ | ✓ | – | ✓ | ✓ |
| SFr 1,640 – entry to all 3 clubs | SFr 1,149 | ✓ | ✓ | ✓ | ✓ | ✓ | ✓ | ✓ | – | ✓ | ✓ | – | ✓ | ✓ |
| SFr 1,640 – entry to all 3 clubs | SFr 1,149 | ✓ | ✓ | ✓ | ✓ | ✓ | ✓ | ✓ | – | ✓ | ✓ | – | ✓ | ✓ |
| SFr 1,490 – entry to all 3 clubs | SFr 990 ** | ✓ | ✓ | ✓ | ✓ | ✓ | ✓ | ✓ | – | – | ✓ | – | ✓ | – |
| SFr 1,490 – entry to all 3 clubs | SFr 990 ** | ✓ | ✓ | ✓ | ✓ | ✓ | ✓ | ✓ | ✓ | – | ✓ | ✓ | ✓ | – |
| SFr 1,490 – entry to all 3 clubs | SFr 990 ** | ✓ | ✓ | ✓ | ✓ | ✓ | ✓ | ✓ | – | – | ✓ | – | ✓ | – |
| SFr 3,415 | na | ✓ | ✓ | ✓ | ✓ | ✓ | ✓ | ✓ | ✓ | ✓ | ✓ | – | ✓ | ✓ |
| SFr 170 (per month)* | SFr 135 (pm)* | ✓ | ✓ | ✓ | ✓ | ✓ | ✓ | ✓ | – | ✓ | ✓ | ✓ | ✓ | ✓ |
| SFr 2,040 (per year) | SFr 1,620 (py) | | | | | | | | | | | | | |
| SFr 849 | SFr 589 | ✓ | ✓ | ✓ | ✓ | ✓ | ✓ | ✓ | – | – | ✓ | – | ✓ | – |
| SFr 930 | SFr 770 | ✓ | ✓ | ✓ | ✓ | ✓ | ✓ | ✓ | – | – | ✓ | – | ✓ | – |
| SFr 1,189 – entry to all 8 clubs | SFr 899 | ✓ | ✓ | ✓ | ✓ | ✓ | ✓ | ✓ | – | – | ✓ | – | ✓ | ✓ |
| SFr 1,189 – entry to all 8 clubs | SFr 899 | ✓ | ✓ | ✓ | ✓ | ✓ | ✓ | ✓ | – | ✓ | ✓ | – | ✓ | ✓ |
| SFr 1,189 – entry to all 8 clubs | SFr 899 | ✓ | ✓ | ✓ | ✓ | ✓ | ✓ | ✓ | ✓ | ✓ | ✓ | ✓ | ✓ | ✓ |
| SFr 1,189 – entry to all 8 clubs | SFr 899 | ✓ | ✓ | ✓ | ✓ | ✓ | ✓ | ✓ | – | – | ✓ | ✓ | ✓ | – |
| SFr 1,189 – entry to all 8 clubs | SFr 899 | ✓ | ✓ | ✓ | ✓ | ✓ | ✓ | ✓ | – | ✓ | ✓ | – | – | ✓ |
| SFr 1,189 – entry to all 8 clubs | SFr 899 | ✓ | ✓ | ✓ | ✓ | ✓ | ✓ | ✓ | – | – | ✓ | – | – | – |
| SFr 1,189 – entry to all 8 clubs | SFr 899 | ✓ | ✓ | ✓ | ✓ | ✓ | ✓ | ✓ | ✓ | ✓ | ✓ | ✓ | ✓ | ✓ |
| SFr 1,900 | SFr 790 | ✓ | ✓ | ✓ | ✓ | ✓ | ✓ | ✓ | ✓ | C.O | ✓ | – | ✓ | C.O |

The hills are alive...

Activities — Beach, Health & Sports Clubs

has a number of football pitches (used by three different Geneva clubs) where you can often watch a match in progress.

## Expand Your Horizons

Making a fresh start in a new city is a wonderful opportunity to finally get round to learning a new hobby, mastering a foreign language, or trying a different activity. Geneva has a wide range of extracurricular activities for eternal students, from workshops to longer courses to special interest groups. You should be able to find something that fits into your schedule, and it's a great way to meet new people, so what are you waiting for?

## Art Classes

Other options ➔ Art Galleries [p.112]

### ARA Atelier d'Art

Location ➔ Pl. des Florentins, 1, Town Centre | 022 312 05 12
Hours ➔ Check for timings
Web/email ➔ www.ara-atelier.ch       Map Ref ➔ 14-A4

The goal of this art studio is to spread a passion for art through professional and motivated classes. Whether you are an experienced artist who wants to brush up on a specific technique, or you just want to try painting for pleasure, the studio has something for everyone. Classes are run for small groups and cover a large variety of different techniques and skills. Techniques covered in the courses include drawing, observation, colour, the human body, portrait, abstract, perspective and geometry.

### Atelier du Pommier

Location ➔ Ch. du Pommier, 7       | 022 690 66 55
Hours ➔ Check for timings
Web/email ➔ www.pommier.ch       Map Ref ➔ 5-D1

If you've always wanted to try your hand at pottery, this is a good starting point. The school was founded by Catherine Zanghi in 1999 and offers a host of pottery courses for children and adults at reasonable prices. Week-long summer workshops are also offered. Timings and course dates vary, and you have to call to book classes. The rates per class are SFr 25 for children and SFr 30 for adults. The one week summer workshops cost SFr 150 per person.

### Ecole Supérieure Des Beaux-Arts de Genève

Location ➔ Bd. Helvétique, 9 · Town Centre | 022 311 05 10
Hours ➔ Check for timings
Web/email ➔ www.hesge.ch/esba       Map Ref ➔ 15-E1

If you're passionate about art, the Ecole Supérieure des Beaux-Arts de Genève may be ideal for you. This full time course is for serious arts scholars, rather than those who paint as a hobby. The school is dedicated to the study of art at a high level and the competition for a place is quite tough. Various art forms are studies, including drawing, painting, engraving, sculpture, photography and cinema. Every year the school prepares 300 students for the Federal Visual Arts Diploma.

### Ecole-Club Migros

Location ➔ Rue du Prince, 5 · Town Centre | 022 319 61 61
Hours ➔ Check for timings
Web/email ➔ www.ecole-club.ch       Map Ref ➔ 13-E4

Promising artists will find plenty of arts and crafts activities at this club. There are classes in drawing, painting, ceramics, fashion, jewellery, photography and more. Within each discipline there is a range of subjects, such as oil painting, still lifes and water colours. Visit the Website for more information on classes.

## Ballet Classes

Other options ➔ Dance Classes [p.212]

### Ecole de Danse de Genève

Location ➔ Rue de la Coulouvrenière, 44 | 022 329 12 10
Hours ➔ Check for timings
Web/email ➔ www.ecolededansedegeneve.com  Map Ref ➔ 13-C4

The focus at this ballet school is preparing professional dancers who are capable of meeting the demands of today's choreographers. Most of the students are aged between 17 and 23 years, and already have a solid grasp of the basic techniques. The three year course in different disciplines is aimed at grooming them to professional level. Also, children from the age of five are taught the fundamental exercises in classical techniques at the school.

## Beauty Training

### Institut Bio-Aromatique

Location → Rue Le Corbusier, 11 · Eaux-Vives | 022 347 70 50
Hours → 09:00 – 19:00   Sat 09:00 – 14:00
Web/email → www.institut-bio-aromatique.com   Map Ref → 16-C2

Training courses in beauty and cosmetics, as well as massage, are offered at the Institut Bio-Aromatique. The beauty and cosmetics course lasts eight months (Monday – Friday, 08:30 – 12:00) and covers theory and practical issues such as anatomy, cosmetic products, beauty techniques, facial and body care, waxing, manicures, facials, hygiene and use of electric appliances for beauty treatment. If you're looking for something less time consuming, the massage course takes three months to complete with classes twice a week (Mondays and Thursdays, 19:30 – 22:30).

## Belly Dancing

This exotic dance form is becoming increasingly popular around the world and Geneva is no exception. Many health clubs and aerobics studios offer belly dancing classes, so check with them to find out where and when. See Health Clubs [p.206].

### Danse Orientale

Location → Ch. des Bois Jacquet, 8 · Aïre | 022 796 28 23
Hours → Check for timings
Web/email → www.orientdance.com   Map Ref → 8-A1

Classes for beginners and intermediates take place at the Salle Rythmique de L'ecole Des Ranches (in Vernier, next to the swimming pool). Your first lesson is free, but make sure you book well in advance. You'll need to wear a skirt or wide-legged trousers, and soft, comfortable shoes. You can borrow a dance belt for your first class. Individual classes cost SFr 20, or a package of ten classes costs SFr 180.

## Birdwatching Groups

### Groupe des Jeunes de Nos Oiseaux

Location → Rue de la Ferme, 12 · Plainpalais | 022 320 60 80
Hours → Check for timings
Web/email → www.ornitho.ch   Map Ref → 15-D3

The Groupe des Jeunes de Nos Oiseaux was founded in 1947 and caters for young ornithologists and nature lovers between the ages of 12 and 25. The group is structured in sections by canton, and each section is part of the larger Society for the Protection and Study of Birds, Nos Oiseaux. This group meets for regular mountain and countryside walks, scientific activities and excursions around Europe.

## Bridge

### Bridge Contact Club

Location → Bd. Saint-Georges, 72 | 022 329 23 98
Hours → Check for timings
Web/email → www2.dotbase.com/bridgecontact   Map Ref → 13-C4

The Bridge Contact Club is based in central Geneva and offers a full range classes, competitions and tournaments for bridge lovers. Beginners wanting to learn the game and experienced players can develop their skills at the Bridge School. Check with the club regarding class times and availability. Tournaments and competitions are also organised throughout the year, and newcomers are always welcome.

### Club de Bridge Rive Gauche, The

Location → Ch. de la Gravière, 4 · Acacias | 022 342 37 46
Hours → See below
Web/email → www.bridgerg.org   Map Ref → 15-B1

On Monday afternoons and Wednesday and Friday evenings, the Rive Gauche Bridge Club meets to play the old game in Acacias. The club also organises a number of tournaments and cups including the Escalade Tournament in December, the Rive Gauche Trophy in March, and the Flowers Tournament in May. For more information on other clubs in your area, visit the Website of the Swiss Bridge Federation at www.bridgefederation.ch.

Expand Your Horizons

Activities

## Chess

Lovers of this classic game will find a number of active clubs and schools in the city, with many informal clubs popping up within different organisations and companies. Some of these are listed here, but for thorough information, log on to www.geneve-echecs.ch. This Website covers anything and everything on the world of chess in Geneva – guides, happenings, clubs and more.

Checkmate in the park

### CERN Chess Club

| | |
|---|---|
| Location → Building 504, CERN · Meyrin | na |
| Hours → Check for timings | |
| Web/email → http://chess.cern.ch | Map Ref → 1-B4 |

The aim of the CERN Chess Club is to provide players in the area with a place to practice their favourite game and to meet other chess aficionados. The club gets together for regular tournaments, usually on the first and third Monday of each month. The club is open to CERN members as well as temporary visitors, and the level of play varies from beginner to expert. The club also organises friendly games and international tournaments.

### Club des Amateurs d'échecs de Genève

| | |
|---|---|
| Location → Quai du Seujet, 32, Town Centre | 022 731 46 75 |
| Hours → See below | |
| Web/email → www.geneve-echecs.ch/caeg | Map Ref → 13-C3 |

The Geneva Amateur Chess club has about 70 members on its books, with teams taking part in cantonal and national championships. Tournaments include the Amateurs Open which takes place at the club premises in June. In addition to official activities, which take place on Fridays from 19:30, the club also offers chess lessons for adults and juniors at different skill levels, and all classes are taught by reputable teachers.

## Cookery Classes

### Ecole-Club Migros

| | |
|---|---|
| Location → Rue du Prince, 5 · Town Centre | 022 319 61 61 |
| Hours → Check for timings | |
| Web/email → www.ecole-club.ch | Map Ref → 13-E4 |

If you love creative cooking, expand your horizons with a cooking class in exotic cuisines such as Chinese, Thai, Indian, Vietnamese, Moroccan and sushi. You'll also be able to brush up on more traditional cooking methods like Haute cuisine, hearty cooking, vegetarian cooking and cooking fish. For total beginners, there is even a course called 'Cooking for Idiots'! In addition to the cooking courses, you can also do various wine appreciation courses. All classes are run by specialists.

## Dance Classes

Dance classes are hugely popular in Geneva, and whether you prefer salsa, flamenco, rock 'n roll or the mambo, there's a class for you. Most clubs offer free trial sessions, just in case you're still trying to make up your mind. Many health clubs offer dance classes as part of their fitness programs. See Health Clubs [p.206].

### Cours Bravo

| | |
|---|---|
| Location → Various locations | 022 752 52 00 |
| Hours → Check for timings | |
| Web/email → www.coursbravo.ch | Map Ref → na |

The dance team at Cours Bravo is led by Beatrice Bravo (a certified Swiss dance instructor), and new dancers are welcome at their varied classes and dance evenings. Whether it's Latino dance (salsa, merengue, bachata, samba or paso-doble), ballroom dance (waltz, foxtrot or quickstep), Argentinean tango, rock, disco or even hip hop, Cours Bravo offers professional tuition for dancers of all ages and levels at different times during the day.

### Dance Aerobic

| | |
|---|---|
| Location ➜ Various Locations | 022 782 80 78 |
| Hours ➜ Check for timings | |
| Web/email ➜ www.danceaerobics.com | Map Ref ➜ 1-E4 |

Dance Aerobic classes offer a full body workout, combining cardiovascular exercise with dance choreography. For women wanting something slightly less strenuous, there are also Melody Fit Classes. All classes are created by women in Switzerland and the emphasis is on good health and wellbeing. The programs are original and professional, competitively priced, and you don't have to sign a lengthy membership contract.

### Ecole-Club Migros

| | |
|---|---|
| Location ➜ Rue du Prince, 5 · Town Centre | 022 319 61 61 |
| Hours ➜ Check for timings | |
| Web/email ➜ www.ecole-club.ch | Map Ref ➜ 13-E4 |

The Ecole-Club Migros offers courses in many leisure activities, but in their dance department you can learn African, Brazilian, modern and contemporary, hip hop, jazz, funk, Oriental and classic ballroom dance styles. The club has venues around the city centre and Balexert. Classes are led by professional instructors and cost SFr 4.50 for an hour.

### Geneva Dance Centre

| | |
|---|---|
| Location ➜ Rue Peillonnex, 2 · Chêne-Bourg | 022 348 49 77 |
| Hours ➜ Check for timings | |
| Web/email ➜ www.genevadancecenter.ch | Map Ref ➜ 9-D1 |

Although it has an excellent reputation as a classical ballet school, the Geneva Dance Centre also offers aerobic body toning and conditioning as one of its activities. Classes are for beginners and enthusiasts, and the common aim is to make the individual feel at ease with the workout and satisfied with the results. Refer to 'Aerobics' [p.169] for more information on the centre.

### How2Tango

| | |
|---|---|
| Location ➜ Petit-Lancy | 078 720 21 01 |
| Hours ➜ Check for timings | |
| Web/email ➜ www.how2tango.org | Map Ref ➜ 8-B2 |

Learn the sensual and theatrical art of the Tango at this school, where the goal is regular and quick progress without too much effort. Britta and Dominique welcome new dancers and attempt to demystify this dance, which is often assumed to be difficult and inaccessible. Classes at beginner, intermediate and advanced levels take place in the evenings and last for 90 minutes. The school is based at Centre Commercial Caroll.

### Kap'danse

| | |
|---|---|
| Location ➜ Rue de Lyon, 112 | 022 340 26 96 |
| Hours ➜ Check for timings | |
| Web/email ➜ www.kapdanse.ch | Map Ref ➜ 5-C3 |

Kap'danse is a dance school for beginners and competitive dancers, offering a full range of classes including ballroom, standard Latino, Argentinean tango, milona, vals criolla, Cuban and Puerto Rican salsa, rock and roll, hip hop, and they also have stretching and aerobic dance sessions. Led by Barbara Kappeler, a certified Swiss Federation instructor, the school comprises of an international team of specialists that are passionate about dance. Contact the school for a detailed breakdown of classes and timings.

> **Hot to Trot**
>
> Salsa is definitely one of the most popular dances in Geneva. Not only are there many salsa classes and specialist schools in the city, but there are also plenty of nightclubs where you can practice your salsa skills. For a comprehensive listing, log on to www.salsatempo.com. This Website is the definitive online guide to all things salsa in Geneva. Check out the schools list for links and contacts of individual schools and classes.

## Drama Groups

### Ecole de Cirque de Genève

| | |
|---|---|
| Location ➜ Rue de Genève, 64 · Chêne-Bourg | 022 348 97 07 |
| Hours ➜ Check for timings | |
| Web/email ➜ www.ecoledecirque-ge.ch | Map Ref ➜ 9-D1 |

The Geneva Circus School, located in the little area of Chêne-Bourg, has been around for nearly 15 years and organises summer workshops and different classes in various circus arts for children and adults. The school runs courses in the exciting fields of trapeze, acrobatics, cycling, juggling, clown and performance. Contact the school directly for more details.

Expand Your Horizons

Activities

### Ecole-Club Migros

Location ➔ Rue du Prince, 5 · Town Centre | 022 319 61 61
Hours ➔ Check for timings
Web/email ➔ www.ecole-club.ch        Map Ref ➔ 13-E4

The Ecole-Club Migros offers aspiring actors two different drama workshops. For newcomers wanting a good thespian foundation, there's the Atelier Theatre I course (eight lessons, each lasting three hours), which offers an introduction to classic and modern acting methods, improvisation, physical and vocal expression. Following this introduction course, participants can do the more comprehensive Atelier II course (25 three-hour sessions), which focuses on in-depth methods and preparations for performance.

### Geneva Amateur Operatic Society (GAOS)

Location ➔ Various | na
Hours ➔ Check for timings
Web/email ➔ www.gaos.ch        Map Ref ➔ na

The Geneva Amateur Operatic Society (now in its 33rd season) is the largest English speaking amateur musical society in Europe. With three to four major stage productions each season, ranging from light opera and musicals to music hall, cabaret and English pantomime, along with several evenings of light classical music and a choral group, there is plenty for all tastes both onstage and behind the scenes.

### Geneva English Drama Society (GEDS)

Location ➔ Meyrin | na
Hours ➔ Check for timings
Web/email ➔ www.geds.ch        Map Ref ➔ 1-E4

Now in its 69th year, the Geneva English Drama Society provides a diverse theatre programme with a wide variety of styles. A typical season includes four full stage productions and twenty staged play readings (one each fortnight), plus workshops and social events. The play readings sometimes attract as many as a hundred people, and provide onstage opportunities for both experienced and aspiring actors. Contact the membership secretary for more information about the group, via the Website.

## Language Schools

Parlez vous français? Habla usted Español? Sprechen Sie Deutch? If you'd like to learn a new language then there are a lot of language schools and courses available in Geneva. Apart from French (which many people learn out of necessity), Spanish classes are increasingly popular, as are Arabic. Many of the international organisations and multinationals offer language tuition as part of their recruitment packages, so you may find that this has been included as part of your deal.

### Ecole-Club Migros

Location ➔ Rue du Prince, 5 · Town Centre | 022 319 61 61
Hours ➔ Check for timings
Web/email ➔ www.ecole-club.ch        Map Ref ➔ 13-E4

The Ecole-Club Migros has an entire section dedicated to language tuition with classes to suit all levels from beginners to those looking to perfect their skills. Students have the chance to take recognised language exams through institutions such as Alliance Française, Goethe Institute and Cambridge. English, French, German, Italian, Spanish, Arabic, Chinese, Danish, Greek, Japanese, Turkish, Dutch, Polish, Portuguese, Russian, Swedish, Swiss German and Czech are all available.

### IFAGE

Location ➔ Place des Augustins, 19 | 022 807 30 50
Hours ➔ Check for timings
Web/email ➔ www.ifage.ch        Map Ref ➔ 15-D2

For French, English, German, Spanish, Italian, Portuguese, Arabic, Greek. Russian, Chinese, Swedish and even sign language, IFAGE can offer courses at all levels. You can follow a la carte courses and obtain internationally recognised diplomas, and many international organisations have chosen IFAGE as an official examination centre for Geneva and the region. Prospective language students are tested free of charge to identify their level of knowledge. For more information about classes or tutors, check out the Website.

### Inlingua

Location ➔ Rue du Léman , 6 · Town Centre | 022 732 40 20
Hours ➔ Check for timings
Web/email ➔ www.inlingua.ch        Map Ref ➔ 13-E2

Inlingua have courses in German, English, Arabic, Chinese, Spanish, French, Italian, Japanese, Dutch, Portuguese, Russian, Swedish or virtually any other language you want to learn. Available courses cover group or individual sessions, intensive modules, classes preparing for internationally recognised diploma examinations (like Cambridge, BEC, TOEFL, Alliance Française or Goethe Institute), and business classes. The school also offers accelerated learning programmes and international language trips.

### Université Populaire de Genève

Location ➜ Rue du Vuache, 23 · Town Centre | 022 339 05 00
Hours ➜ Check for timings
Web/email ➜ www.upcge.ch | Map Ref ➜ 13-C3

For the best value language classes in Geneva, they are hard to beat. For SFr 80 per academic year you can learn one of many languages at different levels. The Université Populaire is a training centre for adults and they are also a member of the Association des Universités Populaires Suisse (AUPS). Classes are taught by volunteer teachers and you can learn French, English, German, Italian, Spanish, and more languages are being added to their growing list.

## Libraries

Other options ➜ Books [p.139]

### Bibliothèque Publique et Universitaire de Genève

Location ➜ Promenade des Bastions | 022 418 28 00
Hours ➜ Check for timings
Web/email ➜ www.ville-ge.ch/bpu | Map Ref ➜ 15-D1

The Bibliothèque Publique et Universitaire de Genève was established by Calvin in 1559. Open to the public and to students of the university, it is constantly adapting and developing its services to suit current needs. A reading room and periodicals library are available for use on the premises, but if you want to take a book home you have to become a member. Membership costs SFr 10 and you'll need to show your residency permit or proof of domicile when applying.

### Bibliothèques Municipales de la Ville

Location ➜ Various all over the city | na
Hours ➜ Check with individual establishments
Web/email ➜ www.ville-ge.ch/bmu | Map Ref ➜ 13-D4

The Geneva Municipal Library Network is made up of a number of libraries spread across the city aimed at providing educational, cultural and leisure resources for public use. The central libraries include Cité, Servette, Pâquis, Jonction, Eaux-Vives and St Jean. The network also includes a sports

library, home service (022 418 92 74), mobile book bus, two discotheque music libraries and a mediatheque. You can direct all your queries to central administration at Rue de la Tour-de-Boël 10, or call them on 022 418 32 50.

### Library of the UN Office Geneva (UNOG)

Location ➜ Av de la Paix, 8 · Petit-Saconnex | 022 917 41 81
Hours ➜ Check for timings
Web/email ➜ www.unog.ch/library/start.htm | Map Ref ➜ 5-E2

The Library of the United Nations Office in Geneva was founded by the League of Nations in 1919. Primarily for use by UN staff members, the library is also open to people outside the UN such as government representatives, lawyers, scholars, journalists, businessmen and students. The library specialises in international law, international relations, economics, politics and social sciences and houses all the UN and League of Nations archives. The library also has an excellent online system with a vast number of e-resources. Tours can be arranged by special request.

## Music Lessons

Music is part of life in Geneva, and whether you're a guitar strummer, a rhythmic drummer or a high note hummer, you'll be able to find a music class that suits you. Even if you're just looking for someone who can (finally!) show you how to play 'Stairway to Heaven' in the right key, the city has schools, academies and tutors aplenty.

### Association pour la Musique de Recherche

Location ➜ Rue des Alpes, 10 · Town Centre | 022 716 56 30
Hours ➜ Check for timings
Web/email ➜ www.amr-geneve.ch | Map Ref ➜ 13-E2

AMR was set up to encourage the practice of musical improvisation in jazz and its derivatives, contemporary music and simple non-manuscript music. Under the leadership of experienced musicians, 'orchestras' are formed in September according to instruments, timetables and levels of participation. Every year AMR also organises an International Jazz Festival (usually in March or April) and the Cropettes Jazz Festival (in June) where visitors can enjoy quality jazz performances. Find out more about jazz, festivals and venues at the club's Website.

### Conservatoire de Musique de Genève

Location ➜ Pl. Neuve · Town Centre | 022 319 60 61
Hours ➜ 09:00 – 12:00 14:00 – 17:00 Sat & Sun closed
Web/email ➜ www.cmusge.ch  Map Ref ➜ 13-D4

The Geneva Music Conservatoire consists of two sections – professional, for serious musicians aspiring to make music a career, and amateur, for students that want to learn about music, theatre and dance. Lessons take place throughout the year (group for theory and basics, individual for instrument tuition) and in addition children, teenagers and young adults can take part in additional rehearsals, auditions, group activities and orchestras. A vast choice of instruments are available including pianos, keyboards, brass instruments, chord instruments, guitars, strings, percussion and wind instruments.

### Conservatoire Populaire de Musique

Location ➜ Bd. Saint-Georges, 36 | 022 329 67 22
Hours ➜ Check for timings
Web/email ➜ www.cpm-ge.org  Map Ref ➜ 13-C3

The Geneva Popular Music Conservatoire has over 150 teachers and 4,000 students. The Conservatoire is a non profit, private foundation whose goal it is to promote music, dance and theatre. Classes are reasonably priced, making them accessible to children, teenagers and adults at varying levels of musical expertise. The Conservatoire offers courses in general music, percussion, early music, jazz, electro-acoustic, dance, theatre and they also have a drum band. Call the Conservatoire for more information about admissions.

### Drum and Percussion Centre

Location ➜ Rte de Chêne, 67 · Chêne-Bougeries | 022 700 41 47
Hours ➜ Mon – Fri 15:00 – 19:00
Web/email ➜ www.drum.ch  Map Ref ➜ 6-B4

If want to start playing the drums or another percussion instrument, check out the Drum and Percussion Centre. Founded in 1988 by Al Widmoser, this school specialises in Latino and African percussion training using a variety of instruments including the drums, djembé, congas and the didgeridoo. Classes (for all levels from the age of six) involve technique training, sound appreciation and the sharing of musical pleasure. You can rent or buy equipment from the school and they also have practice rooms on the premises, which your neighbours should be pleased about!

### ETM

Location ➜ Rue de Malatrex, 32 · Town Centre | 022 344 44 22
Hours ➜ Check for timings
Web/email ➜ www.etm.ch  Map Ref ➜ 13-C3

The ETM (Ecole de Musiques Actuelles et Des Technologies Musicales) school is the only school in Geneva that offers courses in jazz, rock, blues, funk, fusion and other contemporary music disciplines. The school is open to children and adults of all ages and no previous musical or instrument knowledge is necessary to sign up. The goal is to offer complete training from beginner to professional level in a relaxing atmosphere. At the end of the course students put on concerts and even get the opportunity of recording their own CDs.

## Scrabble

Scrabble is taken quite seriously in Switzerland, where there are around 30 clubs. Clubs meet regularly to develop their wordsmith techniques and strategies. If nothing else, it's a great way to improve your French! Scrabble enthusiasts can sign up with one of Geneva's many Scrabble clubs by calling the Swiss Scrabble Federation on 024 499 24 42, sending an e-mail to jphell@omedia.ch, or visiting the Website at www.scrabble.ch).

### Geneva Based Scrabble Clubs

*MALAGNOU who meet every Wednesday evening at 20h00 at the 'Club des Aînés' (Older persons club), Route de Malagnou 40 (Contact Alain Fournier on 022/ 329 05 31 for more information)*

*LANCY who meet on Tuesdays at 20h00 and Fridays from 13h45 – 17h45 at the Great Lancy community hall (contact Liliane Kammacher on 022/ 794 06 88)*

*ONEX who meet on Tuesday from 14h00 and Wednesday from 19h45 at the 'Maison Onésienne', rue des Évaux, Onex (For more information, call Monique Khatchadourian on 022/ 757 40 04)*

## Singing

Other options ➜ Music Lessons [p.215]

### Atelier Catalyse

Location ➜ Eaux-Vives | 022 700 64 75
Hours ➜ Check for timings
Web/email ➜ www.catalyse.ch  Map Ref ➜ 12-A1

Set in an old warehouse in Eaux-Vives, Catalyse is a vast loft style club that's dedicated to vocal expression and creativity. Children can learn about music while having fun and adults can discover and exercise their vocals through singing, improvisation and Gospel sessions. Different artists also use the space to rehearse and put on performances. As well as the group and individual classes, Catalyse also offers workshops throughout the year aimed at the development of vocal creativity.

### Ecole-Club Migros

Location ➔ Rue du Prince, 5 · Town Centre | 022 319 61 61
Hours ➔ Check for timings
Web/email ➔ www.ecole-club.ch               Map Ref ➔ 13-E4

You can sing to your heart's content at the Ecole-Club Migros in one of their classes. Et si on chantait is a series of classes that use singing to help people feel better about themselves. Through singing and movement students work on breathing techniques to improve their vocals. Chanter sur Scene is another course offered by the school where students choose a repertoire of songs to sing on stage. There are several singing venues in Geneva, so call the club to see which one is nearest to you.

## Social Groups

If you're feeling homesick or just need to get out and meet some like minded people, a social group is just what the doctor ordered. With its cosmopolitan society, Geneva is home to a number of social and cultural groups, who always welcome new members. These groups are generally a great way to make new friends and network. If your particular interests are not covered by an existing group, then seize the day and start your own!

### American International Club of Geneva, The

Location ➔ Hôtel Intercontinental | 022 910 25 80
Hours ➔ Check for timings
Web/email ➔ www.amclub.ch               Map Ref ➔ 5-C2

The club is a great place to meet people, make friends and participate in business, social, civic and charity events. The club has a membership of over 1,200 people from the American and international community, representing aspects of corporate and independent business and diplomatic life in Geneva. Activities include monthly luncheons, sporting and social activities

as well as special Independence Day celebrations. The club's constitution requires that a majority of the voting members be US citizens, but non citizens are welcome too, as long as they're over 18.

### American International Women's Club

Location ➔ Rte de Chêne · Chêne-Bougeries | 022 736 01 20
Hours ➔ Office hours Mon – Fri 09:00 – 12:00
Web/email ➔ www.aiwcgeneva.org               Map Ref ➔ 16-E2

The AIWC organises a large number of activities such as language classes, sports, hobbies, family fun, volunteer work, social events, and excursions as well as support groups and lectures. To find out more, just attend one of their monthly coffee mornings for newcomers (call above number to check about times and venues). The club also organises regular 'Geneva for Beginners' sessions, introducing new arrivals to the ins and outs of the city.

### Anglo-Swiss Club of Geneva

Location ➔ Various locations | 022 788 09 96
Hours ➔ Check for timings
Web/email ➔ www.angloswissclubs.ch               Map Ref ➔ na

The Anglo-Swiss Club of Geneva welcomes not only British and Swiss people to its ranks, but also people from member countries of the Commonwealth for whom the English language serves as a medium of communication. The club organises a variety of cultural, recreational and social events on an almost monthly basis. Lectures are usually held at a Geneva hotel, accompanied by dinner, and cost in the region of SFr 45. The British Consulate in Geneva actively supports this club.

### Geneva Welcome Centre, The

Location ➔ Rte de Ferney, 106 · Petit-Saconnex | 022 918 02 70
Hours ➔ Check for timings
Web/email ➔ www.cagi.ch               Map Ref ➔ 5-D1

The Geneva Welcome Centre offers convenient assistance to international civil servants, members of permanent missions, consulates and NGOs (including their families), answering all their questions about the city. It also responds to queries from NGOs wishing to establish themselves in the region and initiates and supports the cultural and social exchanges between Geneva and its local communities.

Expand Your Horizons

**Activities**

# **freedom**ofchoice

lausanne - morges - nyon - genève - www.europlex.ch

# Going Out
## EXPLORER

# Going Out

---

**MUST KNOW**

The reviews in this chapter have been painstakingly written by dedicated reporters who have spent every night out on the town to bring you the lowdown on the most remarkable restaurants and the coolest clubs (it's a tough job, but somebody's got to do it!). The resulting reviews represent the opinions of each reporter - but have they got it wrong? Has your favourite hangout been slated? If so, hop onto your virtual soapbox and tell us the truth. Visit www.eatoutspeakout.com and have your say... we're listening!

---

**MUST DO**

Before you've even unpacked your bags, you should log on to www.sindy.ch and register as a Sindy member. Apart from throwing huge annual parties, like the Christmas Ball, they also organise regular get-togethers, adventure trips and special events. Funds raised from some Sindy events are donated to various Geneva based charity projects and organisations, so you are partying for a good cause! With over 6,000 members, Sindy is the fastest way to kick-start your social life.

---

**MUST KNOW**

Swiss cuisine centres around one of the sources of national pride - cheese. Some of the most famous dishes are largely cheese based. Fondue is a huge central pot of melted cheese, that everybody dips bits of bread into. Raclette is a big wedge of cheese held near a source of heat until it gets soft - then a layer is scraped off and served up! Croute au fromage is a thick slice of bread soaked in wine and smothered in cheese, then baked until sizzling. If you're looking for a slightly less cheesy dining experience, Geneva is home to a range of restaurants serving the world's most popular cuisines. See [p.236].

---

**MUST GO**

During the summer, Switzerland is home to several world class music festivals. The most famous is probably the Montreux Jazz Festival, which features some renowned international jazz musicians over a period of two weeks (usually in July). And don't miss the Paléo Festival in Nyon, which boasts past performances by some of the biggest names in contemporary music, such as REM, Oasis and Peter Gabriel. See www.montreuxjazz.com and www.paleo.ch for more info.

Table Of Contetns

Going Out

SFr 10 ~ € 6

1st Edition | GENEVA EXPLORER

## Going Out

While Geneva's social scene has all too often received bad international press for it's lack of nightlife you shouldn't always believe what you read in the papers. In fact the city plays host to a surprisigly wide range of social hangouts and entertainment and although it may not rival London, Paris or even nearby Lausanne in the party stakes there is still plenty on offer to keep your life social. The following section has been divided into two; the city's numerous restaurants are listed under Eating Out, while cafés, bars, pubs, nightclubs and 'cultural' entertainment such as theatre, cinema and comedy clubs, are under On the Town.

### Eating Out

With people from all corners of the globe residing in Geneva, an excellent variety of restaurants have found a home in this multi-cultural melting pot. Both budget and taste are well catered for and dining out is a popular pastime, whether it's couples courting or crowds cavorting!

Restaurants are plentiful in the city and you can eat and drink your way around the world in Geneva. At first glance along the lakeside or within the city's more prestigious restaurants you might get the impression you can afford no more than a glass of water, but Genevois café culture is alive and well and everyday diners still enjoy top quality fayre. For those with a healthy appetite and wallet to match there are quality establishments to rival counterparts of London, Paris or New York.

Most places open early in the evening at around 18:00, but generally aren't busy until about 20:00. Many of the more popular places do fill up quickly however so booking in advance is recommended. Many restaurants also have weekly buffet nights when you can eat, and sometimes drink, as much as you like for a great value, all inclusive price.

While French restaurants appear to have the menu monopoly you shouldn't miss out the slightly overshadowed Swiss restaurants. The Old Town especially plays host to a variety of comfy Swiss eateries. The ever-trendy Carouge attracts food fans in their droves with plenty of mouthwatering choices. Check out Eaux-Vives for some down to earth quality Italians and go bohemian in Paquis which has dozens of low-priced, authentic Arabic, East Asian, South American and African cafés and restaurants. For a bit of class and a lot of cash take a trip to the lakeside restaurants and hotels where the bill might make a sizeable dent in your finances but the food, service and ambience may just be worth it.

As for the obligatory takeaway option, at first glance it may seem that the Swiss in fact shun this international tradition but fear not - many of the restaurants are happy to wrap up a takeaway at pretty reasonable prices.

### Drinks

There's alcohol aplenty flowing through Geneva with hundreds of bars to chose from! Whatever your tipple, from wines and beers to something a little stronger, you'll find all your favourites  - and some great cocktails  - in the city. With France just kilometres away and excellent Swiss produce, restaurants generally have extensive quality wine lists – although some are a little pricey in the top end establishments.  In mid-range restaurants expect to pay SFr 20 – 30 for a decent bottle – this can rise into the hundreds for an extra special grand cru or wines in the swankier eateries. Still and sparkling mineral water prices in restaurants can also be hiked up, sometimes to SFr 10 per bottle. With Switzerland being famous for its clean water (you can drink it from the street fountains!), you can ask for a carafe of tap water which is good quality and leaves you with a few more francs to play with!  In supermarkets and other outlets, bottled water is usually less than SFr 1 per bottle, regardless of brand.

### Hygiene

The Swiss are well known for their clean living so dining hygiene is a top priority. Some more obsessive restaurant and shop owners have even been spotted vacuuming the pavement in front of their establishments.   Outlets are regularly checked by the Geneva authorities for hygiene, although of course there are some places that slip through the net – but they tend to stand out from the crowd, and not in a good way!

### Tax & Service Charges

Service charges are usually included in the menu prices so it is not really clear what percentage they are, but at least you don't get an added shock when you get the bill.  The fact that service charge is included is normally clearly indicated somewhere on the menu.

## Tipping

With service charges almost always included in the bill, tipping isn't really a big deal in Geneva, which makes a refreshing change form other cities where you feel obliged to leave a percentage of the bill – whatever the quality of service. In standard restaurants and cafés (and if the service has been fine) there's absolutely no pressure to tip but it's polite to leave something – this really can be a token few francs. Obviously excellent service might compel you to be a bit more generous but at the same time if the service is poor then there is definitely no reason to tip. In the more elite restaurants, tipping has become more expected and is often regarded by clientele as a status symbol, i.e., the bigger the tip, the bigger the wallet!

## Independent Reviews

We undertake independent reviews of all restaurants and bars that we include in this book. The following outlets have been visited by our freelance reporters and the views expressed are our own. The aim is to give a clear, realistic and, as far as possible, unbiased view (that we are permitted to print!). However, if we have unwittingly led you astray, please do let us know. We appreciate all feedback, positive, negative and otherwise. Please log on to www.Explorer-Publishing.com and share your views. Your comments are never ignored.

## Ratings

Rating restaurants is always a highly subjective business. Where appropriate, our reviewers have summarised their experiences (see the bottom of each entry) in terms of Food, Service, Venue, and Value. They were asked to consider their restaurant compared to other venues in that category, and in the same price range. In other words, you may notice that a local caféhas the same summary rating as a premium gourmet restaurant. This is not to say that they are equal to one other. Instead, this is a way of comparing restaurants that are similarly styled and priced to each other. We hope this will help you to make informed choices regardless of your taste or budget. Each rating is out of five - one dot means poor, two and a half means acceptable and five means fab:

Food●●●●○ Serv●●●○○ Venue●●●○○ Value●●●○○

For an explanation of the various symbols or icons listed against the individual reviews, refer to the Quick Reference Symbols below.

## Restaurant Listing Structure

With so many outlets serving food and drink listed in the *Geneva Explorer*, the choice can seem daunting. Listed alphabetically by region, then country, or commonly known style of cuisine, this section aims to add to the variety of your dining experience by giving as much information as possible on the individual outlets. For an 'at a glance' clarification of this listing, refer to the index at the beginning of this section.

As with all good, simple rules, there are exceptions. Restaurants in the international category usually serve such a variety of food that it is impossible to pin them down to one section. While a restaurant that specialises in cooking seafood in styles from all over the world will be found in Seafood, a Thai restaurant that cooks a lot of fish Thai style will still be listed under Thai! Makes sense? We hope so! Where a restaurant specialises in more than one type of cuisine, the review appears under the main category.

In order to avoid any confusion concerning a particular restaurant's listing, as a rule, any non English names retain their prefix (ie, Al, Le, La and El) in their alphabetical placement, while English names are listed by actual titles, ignoring prefixes such as 'The'. Bon appetit!

## Icons – Quick Reference

The prices indicated are calculated as the cost of a starter, main course and dessert for one person. This includes any relevant taxes, but excludes the cost of drinks. Another good cost indication is whether the outlet is licensed, the restaurant location (in a hotel or not), type of cuisine, etc. The SFr 150 icon indicates that an average meal should cost anywhere between SFr 100 to SFr 200, ie SFr 150 ± 50.

## Quick Reference Explorer Icons

 Explorer Recommended

 NO Credit Cards Accepted

 Alcohol Available

 Will Deliver

 Reservations Recommended

 Dress Smartly

 Outside Terrace

 Vegetarian Dishes

## Vegetarian Food

With nearby France being a carnivore's heaven (and a vegetarian's hell), vegetarians may be pleasantly surprised by the range and variety of meat-free cuisine that can be found in restaurants in Geneva. Although there are all the regular meat dishes available, Swiss cuisine does favour cheese and potato recipies and so there are generally a few dishes on most menus that are naturally vegetarian. The city also has a penchant for excellent salads – available almost everywhere – which will satify any herbivore's appetite.

Also, most outlets offer at least one or two specific vegetarian dishes. However, if you want a little more variety, the numerous Thai restaurants tend to have the best choices. However there are also excellent Italian, Mexican, Far Eastern and International restaurants all over the city offering vegetarian options. A word of warning: if you are a strict vegetarian, confirm that your meal is completely meat free as some restaurants cook their 'vegetarian' selection with animal fat or on the same grill as the meat dishes.

## Restaurants

## American

### Road Runner

Location → Rte de Chêne, 63 · Chêne-Bougeries | 022 735 64 20
Hours → 11:00 - 14:30   Sun 18:00-22:00
Web/email → www.roadrunner-restaurant.ch        Map Ref → 14-D4

    50

A loyal legion of young and trendy Genevois have made Road Runner their favoured hangout. Ordering is done at the counter, and freshly grilled authentic Swiss beef burgers are delivered a few minutes later. They taste great, but the downside is that Swiss beef is a little on the expensive side, especially for a burger joint. However this venue is hip in a diner kind of way and the burgers are so good they err on the side of gourmet.

Food ●●●●○ Serv ●●●○○ Venue ●●●○○ Value ●●●○○

## Arabic/Lebanese

Other options → **Belly Dancing [p.211]**

### Happy Days

Location → Bd. George-Favon, 32 · Les Délices | 022 328 52 18
Hours →   See below
Web/email → na                                   Map Ref → 13-C3

  25

Enter this family run restaurant and be greeted with a smile and the smell of garlic and onions

Alfresco eating

# RESTAURANT

*Also Bistro & bar with terrace,*
*seminar and banquet facilites*
*for 10 to 100 persons,*
*4 star hotel with 34 rooms.*

# The rendez-vous
# of food & wine
# connoisseurs!

*www.vendee.ch*

## HOSTELLERIE DE LA VENDÉE
CHEMIN DE LA VENDÉE 28 ■ 1213 PETIT-LANCY ■ RESERVATION: TEL. 022 792 04 11

cooking. It's easy to understand why Happy Days has been so successful for many years and has such a loyal clientele. Quality is the first concern, which means the menu changes according to the available produce. Go for the mousaka and stay for the baklava. 88

*Timings: Mon- Fri 11:00 - 15:00 (sit down) & 11:00 - 19:00 (Take away); Sat 14:00 - 17:00; Sun closed*

Food●●●○○Serv●●●○○Venue●●●○○Value●●●○○

## Brazilian

### Le Gaucho

Location → Ch. Malombré, 1 · Champel   |   022 346 11 50
Hours → 11:00 - 16:00 & 19:00 - 01:00
Web/email → na

Map Ref → 16-A1

Think quantity not quality. While a Brazilian grill restaurant may seem one of the best places to get meat, this is not one of them. The house speciality is an all you can eat cold buffet and hot meats from the grill which is average at best. Not the best option if you're wanting to impress, but if you're looking to fill an empty stomach, and have children you do not want to leave with a baby sitter, you have found the perfect location. 88

Food●●●○○○Serv●●●●○○Venue●●●○○○Value●●●○○○

Fêtes de Genève

## Chinese

### Jade Garden

Location → Giuseppe-Motta, 30 · Sécheron   |   022 734 56 27
Hours → 12:00 - 14:30 & 19:00 - 23:00  Sun closed
Web/email → na

Map Ref → 5-D2

 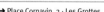

This Chinese restaurant has been a regular watering hole for the UN crowd for decades. Guaranteed parking, English speaking, air conditioned and there is even ice available for your coke. This restaurant knows how to serve to foreigners. You will never have bad service or a bad meal. However, don't expect anything extraordinary. It is a good bet when you're not in the mood to be adventurous. Not the best bargain in town for dinner, but they do have favourably priced lunchtime specials 88

Food●●●●○○Serv●●●●○○Venue●●●○○Value●●●●○○

### Kwai

Location → Place Cornavin, 2 · Les Grottes   |   022 732 60 30
Hours → 11:00 - 23:00
Web/email → na

Map Ref → 13-D2

Big portions, full of flavour, ready in a snap. Kwai, located near the train station, is a pleasant surprise. There are servers galore and their English might be easier to understand than their French. The staff are quick and friendly, bringing heaped plates of steaming Asian delights with a smile. Perfect for big eaters. While the venue is not overly attractive, it is casual and well spaced to allow for children, which sets it apart from many other Geneva restaurants. 88

Food●●●●○Serv●●●●○Venue●●●○○Value●●●●●

### Le Lin Xiang

Location → Rue du Port, 7 · Town Centre   |   022 311 33 30
Hours → 11:30 - 14:00 & 18:30 - 22:00
Web/email → na

Map Ref → 13-E4

You know it's good the second you walk in the door and an enticing aroma encircles you. The friendly owner takes great pride in his restaurant and while the menu is a little too familiar the quality is first class. The welcoming and casual atmosphere along with delicious dishes in hearty portions translate into full tables. All the dishes are well made, but the three course house speciality duck should not be missed.

Food ●●●●○ Serv ●●●●○ Venue ●●●○○ Value ●●●●○

## Le Thé

Location → Rue des Bains, 65
Hours → 12:00 - 22:00   Sun closed
Web/email → na

**079 436 77 18**

Map Ref → 13-C4

*Plate smashing is a form of expression, culturally acceptable only in Greek restaurants. You can now get your point across for all other eateries and still avoid costly lawsuits. Just log on to Eat Out Speak Out, UAE's first online restaurant review forum and freely spill all thoughts about the dining experience.*

*www.EatOutSpeakOut.com*

Two cosy dining rooms create an intimate setting highlighted by an interesting display of loose teas (red, white, green, & unusual herbal teas), cups and pots available for sale. The kitchen is tiny, but the results are excellent nonetheless. Small steaming plates of tasty food served à la carte, dim sum style. Popular by word of mouth (their phone number isn't actually listed in the phone book) reservations are recommended. Le Thé has earned its reputation as a hidden gem of Chinese tea and cuisine in Geneva.

*Other timings: Closes for 2 weeks every August (random each year).*

Food ●●●●○ Serv ●●●●○ Venue ●●●●○ Value ●●●●○

## Ethiopian

## La Gazelle D'Or

Location → Rue de Lyon, 55 · La Prairie
Hours → 11:30 - 14:30 & 18:30 - 24:00
Web/email → na

**022 340 33 50**

Map Ref → 13-B2

Authentically Ethiopian from the music and décor to the menu and service, a trip to La Gazelle D'Or takes you right out of Geneva. Popular with bohemian diners looking for something a little different, not only are the dishes traditionally Ethiopian but so is the way you eat them, by hand on shared plates. The menu is also in English and kids meals and drinks are ½ price until 22:00. This is also a great option for vegetarians who can dine at a fraction of the price.

Food ●●●●○ Serv ●●●●○ Venue ●●●●○ Value ●●●●○

## French

## Auberge de Floris

Location → Rte d'Hermance, 287 · Anières
Hours → Closed Sun & Mon
Web/email → www.auberge-de-floris.com

**022 751 20 20**

Map Ref → na

 75

Situated on the Left Bank, with beautiful views of the lake and the Jura mountain range, this Michelin-starred restaurant is delightful. Whether you go for a romantic night out, or a lazy lunch on the Terrace (during summer), your hosts, Inès and Claude Legras, make sure that you will leave with many happy memories of Auberge de Floris. If you're planning a boating trip on the lake, you can order a gourmet picnic basket to take with you - just place your order by phone, two hours in advance, and it will be delivered to you at the port of Anières

Food ●●●●○ Serv ●●●●○ Venue ●●●○○ Value ●●●○○

## Bistrot des Bergues

Location → Rue Kléberg, 8 · St-Gervais
Hours → 07:00 - 24:00   Sat 08:30 - 16:00  Sun closed
Web/email → na

**022 731 12 50**

Map Ref → 13-D3

75

There is an eclectic buzz at Bistrot des Bergues that gives this restaurant that something extra. Maybe it's the delicious dishes, created with care and attention. It could be the convivial atmosphere that attracts a beautiful crowd but remains casual. Then there is the intimacy, which despite slightly crammed tables, creates a romantic setting. It could be the fabulous lemon pie, which literally melts in the mouth. Or maybe it's just the ever-present owner, who is an added delight and adds to the attraction of this exciting eatery.

Food ●●●●○ Serv ●●●●○ Venue ●●●○○ Value ●●●○○

## Brasserie Lipp

Location → Rue de la Confédération, 8
Hours → 11:30 - 00:45
Web/email → www.brasserie-lipp.com

**022 311 10 11**

Map Ref → 13-D4

100

A prime location at the Confédération Centre, long hours, a happening bar, French cuisine, a large wine selection and yummy desserts means that Brasserie Lipp is very popular. Sometimes it's a bit noisy but service is efficient and timely and the buzz is what attracts tourists and locals alike. The menu has a lot to choose from and is printed in French and English. A convenient place for groups or night owls looking for a late dinner, Brasserie-Lipp has become a bit of a Geneva institution.●●

Food ●●●●○ Serv ●●●●○ Venue ●●●●○ Value ●●●●○

## Brasserie Parc des Eaux-Vives

Location ➜ Quai Gustave Ador, 82 Eaux-Vives | 022 849 75 75
Hours ➜ 12:00 - 14:30 & 19:00 - 22:30
Web/email ➜ www.parcdeseauxvives.ch          Map Ref ➜ 14-C3

For one of the most decadent evenings in Geneva, venture to the recently reborn mansion in the Parc des Eaux-Vives. After a fire the mansion has been completely refurbished and is now a brasserie, a Michelin star gastronomic restaurant and a small hotel. While the prices are outrageous at the other two, the brasserie is good value.●●

Food ●●●●○ Serv ●●●●○ Venue ●●●●○ Value ●●●●○

## Café des Bains

Location ➜ Rue des Bains, 26 · Plainpalais | 022 321 57 98
Hours ➜ 11:30 - 15:00 & 18:00 - 00:30 Sun & Mon closed
Web/email ➜ www.cafedesbains.com          Map Ref ➜ 15-C1

This café, in the modern art district of Geneva, is yet another gallery. However, this time the art is on

your plate. A unique menu, reflecting the season's offerings in creative combinations, might leave hefty eaters hungry. A favourite amongst the thirty-something crowd, it is a great place to see and be seen. Located across the street from SIP, a favourite nightspot, many begin a good soiree at Café des Bains and simply cross over to continue the festivities.●●

Food ●●●●○ Serv ●●●●○ Venue ●●●●○ Value ●●●○○

## Café des Négociants

Location ➜ Rue de la Filature, 29 · Carouge | 022 300 31 30
Hours ➜ 11:00 - 14:30 & 19:00 - 24:00 Sun am closed
Web/email ➜ na          Map Ref ➜ 15-D4

This restaurant is certainly trendy and their wine cellar is definitely a selling point - especially as you can play the connoisseur and descend into the cave to select your bottle. However the menu doesn't live up to the price tag and while it is interesting in concept the proof isn't quite in the pudding. The dishes lack flavour and the kitchen seems to have problems with serving hot dishes to large groups. The ambience makes up for the food, and if you keep the wine flowing then an enjoyable night is sure to be had.●●

**Note:** *Kitchen closes at 22:30*

Food ●●●○○ Serv ●●●●○ Venue ●●●●○ Value ●●○○○

## Café Universal

Location ➜ Bd. du Pont d'Arve, 26 · Plainpalais | 022 781 18 81
Hours ➜ 12:00 - 14:00 & 19:00-23:45 Mon eve & Sun closed
Web/email ➜ na          Map Ref ➜ 15-D1

The décor and ambience give Café Universal a decidedly French, urban feel, which can become noisy and smoky as the evening wears on. It's a small price to pay if you want to lounge about with Geneva's beautiful people. There is a good selection of salads, grilled meats and some interesting specialties. Depending on the night, dancing could erupt after dinner. Café Universal is a hip place that has a trendy character as well as an authentic feel. It's a popular place for a late dinner.

Food ●●●●○ Serv ●●●●○ Venue ●●●●○ Value ●●●○○

Liquid lunch

## Chez Jacky

Location → Rue Necker, 9 · St-Gervais | **022 732 86 80**
Hours → 12:00 - 14:00 & 19:00 - 22:00 Weekends closed
Web/email → restaurant@chezjacky.ch    Map Ref → 13-D3

 100

In a rather modern setting with attractively laid tables, French cuisine entices with fresh market produce. The Piccata à la Milanese and Saffron Risotto, Fillet of Perch served with Fennel and White Butter and Glazed Boneless Quail with Spices and Chutney are just some of the succulent savours awaiting you. Centrally positioned near the Gare de Cornavin, if you want to make an evening of it with some friends or are celebrating a special occasion, a room for parties is available for up to 15 guests.

Food ●●●●○ Serv ●●●●○ Venue ●●●●○ Value ●●●●○

## Chez Ma Cousine

Location → Place du Bourg-de-Four, 6 | **022 310 96 96**
Hours → 11:30 - 23:30 Sun 11:30 - 22:30
Web/email → na    Map Ref → 13-E4

25

If you feel like chicken tonight then there is one place with a menu sure to make your mouth water. Chez Ma Cousine has chicken, chicken and more chicken on offer. Their roast chicken with delicious thick cut potato wedges is a favourite with the regulars - especially at under SFr 15 a time. With

three outlets in Geneva, each with a café style atmosphere, Ma Cousine is busy and bustling and the service is excellent. Just don't fill up on too much chicken as the desserts are delightful too. Take away is also available.

*Other branches: Petit Saconnex – 2, Chemin du Petit-Saconnex (022 733 79 85 ), Lissignol – 5, Rue Lissignol (022 731 98 98).*

Food ●●●●○ Serv ●●●○○ Venue ●●●○○ Value ●●●●○

## L'Aïoli

Location → Rue Adrien-Lachenal, 6 · Eaux-Vives | **022 736 79 71**
Hours → 11:30 - 14:00  18:00 - 22:30  Sun closed
Web/email → na    Map Ref → 14-A4

    75

A casual environment and good food have made L'Aïoli a neighborhood favourite. Regional fare from Provence features prominently in the menu and the famous L'Aïoli garlic sauce is the signature of this French restaurant. The regional flavour is also expressed in the rustic décor and the patron looks like he just arrived from Provence. For lunch, the plate of the day is SFr 17.

*Other Timings: Mon-Fri 07:00 - 00:00; Sat 18:00-24:00*

Food ●●●●○ Serv ●●●○○ Venue ●●●●○ Value ●●●○○

## L'Auberge d'Hermance

Location → Rue du Midi, 12 · Hermance | **022 751 13 68**
Hours → 12:00 - 14:30 & 19:00 - 23:00
Web/email → www.hotel-hermance.ch    Map Ref → na

    100

Located a short drive from the Geneva city centre in the Medieval village of Hermance, L'Auberge favours attention to detail, offering fine dining perfect for special occassions. A European menu with eclectic touches, the salt encrusted chicken is delicious and a feat of culinary creation. The food, service, setting and special touches all make dining here a thoroughly enjoyable experience, but you certainly pay for it.

Food ●●●●○ Serv ●●●●○ Venue ●●●●○ Value ●●●○○

## L'Evidence

Location → Rue des Grottes, 13 · Les Grottes | **022 733 61 65**
Hours → 12:15 - 14:30 & 19:15 - 23:00
Web/email → na    Map Ref → 13-C3

 100

The L'Evidence menu impresses with fine dining cuisine that is both varied and inventive (take the tartar of sea bass with leeks, stew of saffron lobster and tornedos of duck with citrus fruits as examples). Set on the corner of the avant-garde Grottes area,

French

Going Out

L'Evidence offers a rich setting of exposed beams, warm colours and baroque type pictures on the walls. Service is with a smile and the impeccably dressed waiters complement the fashionable crowd without creating an overly pretentious atmosphere!

*Price guide:* Dish of the day CHF18. Menus from CHF 48 to CHF 75 (minimum 6 people). A la carte 70 CHF.

Food●●●●○ Serv●●●●○ Venue●●●●● Value●●●●○

## La Broche

Location → Rue du Stand, 36 **022 321 22 60**
Hours → 12:00 - 14:00 & 19:00 - 22:30  Sat closes 23:30
Web/email → labroche@bluewin.ch        Map Ref → 13-C4

   50

Appearances can be deceiving so don't let the grey stoned exterior of this restaurant dictate your first impressions of La Broche. The interior is in fact a wonderful mix of modern glass and dark wood set against grey stone with climbing green vines. Even better, if the weather decides to cooperate the large terrace makes for a great dinner setting. The food may seem a little limited but makes up for in taste what it lacks in variety.

Food●●●●○ Serv●●●●○ Venue●●●●○ Value●●●●○

## La Certitude

Location → Rue Pellegrino Rossi, 7 · Pâquis **022 738 27 26**
Hours → 12:00 - 14:30  19:00 - 23:00
Web/email → na                         Map Ref → 13-E2

100

This sister restaurant of L'Evidence is located in the so-called red light district of Geneva. However, there is certainly nothing seedy about La Certitude where the delightful menu and elegant setting impress a fine dining crowd. Candlelight and orchids dominate the ambience. They do meat well from tartar to the grill and have lovely accompaniments like mille-feuille of grilled vegetables. They are also skilled in preparing seafood from scallops to sole.

*Note:* Open until Midnight if you have made a reservation, open for coffee during the afternoon while the kitchen is closed 14:30 – 19:00

Food●●●●○ Serv●●●●○ Venue●●●●○ Value●●●○○

## La Perle du Lac

Location → Rue de Lausanne, 126 · Sécheron **022 909 10 20**
Hours → 12:00 - 14:00  19:00 - 21:30
Web/email → info@perledulac.ch        Map Ref → 5-E2

50

An idyllic setting right on the lakeside – the Perle du Lac has been drawing in couples and groups

looking for something extra special since 1930. With fine French cuisine - fois gras, lobster and truffles all feature highly – the restaurant is renowned for its excellent seafood and luxurious atmosphere although prices aren't cheap. In the summertime a beautiful terrace offers incredible panoramic views of the lake and Mont-Blanc mountain range as your backdrop.

Food●●●●● Serv●●●●○ Venue●●●●● Value●●●●●

## Le Chat Botté

Location → Quai du Mont-Blanc, 13 · Pâquis **022 716 66 66**
Hours → 12:00 - 15:00 & 19:00 - 21:45
Web/email → na                         Map Ref → 13-E2

 50

For high class, extreme comfort and excellent cuisine, Le Chat Botté is the ideal destination. The warm décor and spectacular lakeside location set the tone for this luxury eatery. Serving culinary delights such as spider crab, creamy asparagus soup, oven-roasted turbot, creamed potatoes with grilled almond oil and vinaigrette, the flavours are subtle and the standards high. The service is discreet and impeccable and fine weather brings with it hungry crowds desperate to get a table on the very popular terrace.

Food●●●●○ Serv●●●●○ Venue●●●●○ Value●●●●○

## Le Francis

Location → Bd. James-Fasy, 10 · St-Gervais **022 732 93 26**
Hours → 12:00 - 15:30 & 19:00 - 24:00  Sat & Sun closed
Web/email → na                         Map Ref → 13-D3

 75

If you can't make it to Brussels, Le Francis is a good alternate for mussels. Their house speciality, steamed mussels, comes with a choice of sauces - white wine and herbs, cream, onions, garlic and parsley, salmon and vodka flambé or Thai. If you're not a shellfish fan they also have a very good meat selection and creative salads.

Food●●●●○ Serv●●●●○ Venue●●●○○ Value●●●●○

## Le Pied de Cochon

Location → Place du Bourg-de-Four, 4 **022 310 47 97**
Hours → 12:00 - 14:00 & 19:00 - 22:00  Sat, Sun 12:00 - 22:00
Web/email → na                         Map Ref → 13-E4

 75

Despite the name (translated it means Pig's Foot) Le Pied de Cochon is in fact one of the classiest cosmopolitan restaurants in Geneva. Bow-tied waiters bustle their way between the tinkling cutlery of one of

French

Going Out

Geneva's much loved bistros, serving meaty Genevois and Lyonnais gutliners (Fr.35) and the namesake grilled pigs' trotters – for a clientele with more than a few francs to spare. Set in the heart of the Old Town, Le Pied de Cochon is well situated and a great option for a special occasion that can be followed by a leisurely stroll round this pretty part of town.

Food ●●●●○ Serv ●●●●○ Venue ●●●●○ Value ●●●●○

## Le Triporteur

Location → Rue de Carouge, 33 · Plainpalais | 022 321 21 81
Hours → 12:00 - 13:30 & 19:00 - 22:00 Sun & Mon closed
Web/email → na | Map Ref → 15-D2

A wooden interior sprinkled with contemporary lighting sets the relaxed yet inviting tone for subdued days and lively nights at Le Triporteur. Light breakfasts are served from 07:00 while the proceeding salads and main plates are certainly pleasing, both on the eye and the palate. Popularity comes from the restaurant's location on the Rue de Carouge, the no-fuss good food and convivial atmosphere.

*Other Timings:* Tue – Fri 07:00 – 12:00; Sat 9:00 – 12:00
Food ●●●●○ Serv ●●●●○ Venue ●●●●○ Value ●●●○○

## Les 5 Portes

Location → Rue de Zurich, 8 · Pâquis | 022 731 84 38
Hours → 12:00 - 14:00 & 18:00 - 22:30
Web/email → na | Map Ref → 13-E2

Mixing modern and eclectic décor with original wood features, this restaurant bar attracts a trendy crowd as well as regular locals who enjoy drinks and a great selection of tapas, many with a vegetarian twist. If you're looking for a bigger bite, the chef offers some excellent dishes including succulent steaks, pasta creations and interesting salads - all at a good price for great quality. For a real treat try the 'baked lobster', perfumed with exotic spices and garnished with fresh vegetables.

Food ●●●●○ Serv ●●●●○ Venue ●●●●○ Value ●●●●●

## Manor Cafeteria

Location → Rue de Cornavin, 6 · St-Gervais | 022 909 41 11
Hours → 08:30 - 18:45 Sun closed
Web/email → www.manor.ch | Map Ref → 13-D3

Shop till you drop, and when you do then drop in at the Manor Cafeteria. Located inside the Manor

department store, this is an easy stop during your busy day. Also an ideal option for those struggling with French because all you have to do is point at what you want. Take your pick from numerous options: fresh fruit and juices, salad bar, pasta bar, grill with meat and fish, cooked vegetables and desserts. All of the plates are made fresh daily.

Food ●●●●○ Serv ●●●○○ Venue ●●●●○ Value ●●●●●

Cornavin

## N'Oublie Pas Les Poissons Rouges

Location → Pl. des Eaux-Vives 2 · Town Centre | 022 735 22 50
Hours → See below
Web/email → www.poissonrouge.com | Map Ref → 14-A4

N'Oublie Pas Les Poissons Rouges attracts a hip, urban crowd in search of tasty dishes and a relaxed environment. The great location next to Rive and the comfortable sofas in the lounge (open at 17:00) create a tranquil hideaway amid a hive of activity. The menu is diverse with sushi, burgers, red meat, tapas and of course, fish. N'Oublie Pas Les Poissons Rouges is a fun getaway for exotic drinks in a comfortable environment with good food.

*Lunch & Dinner Timings:* Mon - Fri 12:00 - 14:30, Mon - Sat 19:00 – 23:30

*Other Timings:* Mon - Fri 07:00 - 15:00, Mon - Thu 17:00 - 01:00, Fri & Sat 17:00 - 02:00; Closed Sun

Food ●●●○○ Serv ●●●●○ Venue ●●●○○ Value ●●●●○

French

Going Out

### Remor

Location → Pl. du Cirque, 3 · Plainpalais
Hours → 11:30 - 24:00   Sun closed
Web/email → na

**022 328 12 70**

Map Ref → 13-C4

   50

Remor attracts a cacophony of cosmopolitan clientele, mixing the sophisticated with the sometimes throughly offbeat. You'll find the after theatre crowd, the occasional banker, expats, locals and the odd bohemian artist. The walls are adorned with French posters and work from local artists and the proprietors obviously have flair, particularly with the homemade ice creams and sorbets which are a favourite late night dessert. The outside terrace fills up in the evening with after work drinkers.

Food●●●●○Serv●●●●○Venue●●●●●Value●●●●○

## Indian

### Le Darshana

Location → Rue Adrien-Lachenal, 5
Hours → 12:00 - 14:30 & 19:00 - 22:30  Sun closed
Web/email → na

**022 736 36 48**

Map Ref → 14-A1

    50

A friendly atmosphere and attentive staff serves up a solid selection of Indian food. Le Darshana's décor, ambience and good service make a refreshing change from Geneva's European staple. The vegetarian main plates are good value, starting at just SFr 10, while the lunch buffet is only SFr 17. For the Indian connoisseur there is nothing new but you'll find something to satisfy most appetites.

Food●●●●○○Serv●●●●○○Venue●●●●○○Value●●●●○○

### Le Piment Vert

Location → Pl. Grenus, 4 · St-Gervais
Hours → 11:30 - 21:30   Sat 12:00 - 17:00  Sun closed
Web/email → na

**022 731 93 03**

Map Ref → 13-D3

   25

Piment Vert is well worth visiting for healthy fast food. Their food is fresh and colourful and perfect for a stop while shopping or to pick up food for home. A must try is the Thora Malo Kirata King Fish with Coconut Milk, delightfully light in texture despite its rich ingredients. For the less

adventurous, there are dishes you will recognise such as Chicken Tandoori.

Food●●●●○Serv●●●●○Venue●●●●○Value●●●●○

## Italian

### Fontana di Trevi

Location → Ch. de la Tourelle · Petit-Saconnex
Hours → 11:30 - 14:15 & 18:30 - 23:00
Web/email → na

**022 788 77 70**

Map Ref → 5-C2

    50

A great pizza and pasta joint in Petit Saconnex! Set within the Budé shopping centre, this great pizza and pasta joint has typical - but very inviting - Italian style décor, complete with photos of Rome's beautiful 'Fontana di Trevi' itself. There's also a very nice terrace that's perfect for long summer lunches. A wide choice of good quality dishes is available and the restaurant serves excellent and varied 'plat du jour', generally for under SFr 20.

Food●●●●○Serv●●●●○Venue●●●●○Value●●●●○

Street café

### L'Age d'Or

Location → Rue Cornavin, 11 · St-Gervais
Hours → 10:00 - 00:30
Web/email → na

**022 731 30 93**

Map Ref → 13-D3

   50

While they may not be on the gigantic side, the pizzas at L'Age d Or make up for in taste what they lack in size. The pasta and salads are equally

Going Out

Indian | Italian

impressive while the list of desserts is enough to satisfy even the sweetest of tooths. The railway theme and opulent Orient Express style decoration is kitsch but with leather seats, mirrors, chandeliers and subdued lighting, it works. Staff are cordial, efficient and pleasant, and make this popular restaurant worth a visit or two. ⓑⓦ

Food●●●●○Serv●●●○○Venue●●●●○Value●●●●○

## La Maison Rouge

Location ➔ Rue des Noirettes, 17 · Carouge | 022 342 00 42
Hours ➔ Mon - Fri 12:00 - 14:00 & 18:00 - 24:00
Web/email ➔ www.lamaisonrouge.ch          Map Ref ➔ 15-C3

 75

This restaurant is situated in a distinctive red house in Carouge, and has one of the best wine lists in town. Once you've selected your bottle, try the delicious Italian cuisine, made with the freshest ingredients. The décor is very pleasing, with wooden floors, a marble bar, and fashionably mismatched furniture. Reasonable prices (main courses are priced from SFr 20) and exceptional service round off a great experience. ⓑⓦ

Food●●●●○Serv●●●●○Venue●●●○○Value●●●●○

## La Primavera

Location ➔ Rte de Meyrin, 8 · Servette | 022 734 01 02
Hours ➔ 08:30 - 24:00
Web/email ➔ na          Map Ref ➔ 5-D3

 75

This may look like any other local Italian restaurant but Franco, the welcoming owner, puts his heart and soul into making certain you have a wonderful time in his establishment. His plates are copious, filled with flavour and exuding quality. He does not cut corners on ingredients, which you can experience first hand from one of his many salads or wood fired pizzas. You will enjoy the food, but you will come back because of Franco. ⓑⓦ

Food●●●●○Serv●●●●○Venue●●●○○Value●●●●○

## La Trattoria

Location ➔ Rue de la Servette,1 · Les Grottes | 022 734 94 76
Hours ➔ 09:30 - 14:30 & 17:30 - 24:00
Web/email ➔ na          Map Ref ➔ 13-C2

 75

A long-time Geneva fixture and as popular as ever, this authentic bustling Italian provides big portions, a varied menu and no nonsense service.

Oven-baked pizzas will satisfy the biggest of appetites and there are plenty to choose from. As for pasta dishes the 'Penne à la Sicilienne' with aubergine and garlic overload is a must. And if you manage to get the the bottom of your huge serving you will be brought another one right away! ⓑⓦ

Food●●●●●Serv●●●○○Venue●●●●○Value●●●○○

## Espresso Club

Location ➔ Rue de Pâquis, 25 · Pâquis | 022 738 84 88
Hours ➔ Call for timings
Web/email ➔ na          Map Ref ➔ 13-E2

 50

A relaxed atmosphere (you eat sitting round the bar) and a wide variety of good quality oven baked pizzas as well as pasta dishes make Espresso Club a great option for easy dining. Frequented by locals and inquisitive newcomers, the bar has a cosy family feel as you all tuck into your pizzas in a big round table that hugs the bar. You'll never go thirsty with Italian beers and some decent wines right on your doorstep, all for a very reasonable price. ⓑⓦ

Food●●●●○Serv●●●○○Venue●●●●○Value●●●●○

## Senso

Location ➔ Rue du Rhône 56 · Town Centre | 022 310 39 90
Hours ➔ Call for timings
Web/email ➔ www.senso-living.ch          Map Ref ➔ 13-E3

25

This extremely chic venue feels like anything but a chain, which it just happens to be. Located also in Singapore and New Dehli, the owners seem to have discovered the formula for success. Come for drinks in the laid back lounge bar or dress up for a dinner with the beautiful crowd. Knowledgeable servers accompany you throughout the evening with suggestions hard to ignore. The wine list is a little overpriced but the enticing menu which changes frequently makes expensive tipples a small price to pay for perfection. ⓑⓑ

Food●●●●○Serv●●●●○Venue●●●●○Value●●●○○

*Plate smashing is a form of expression, culturally acceptable only in Greek restaurants. You can now get your point across for all other eateries and still avoid costly lawsuits. Just log on to **Eat Out Speak Out**, UAE's first online restaurant review forum and freely spill all thoughts about the dining experience.*
www.**EatOutSpeakOut**.com

Italian

Going Out

## Japanese

### Miyako

Location → Rue de Chantepoulet, 11 | **022 738 01 20**
Hours → 12:00 - 14:30 & 19:00 - 22:30  Sun closed
Web/email → www.miyako.ch
Map Ref → 13-D2

**100**

Miyako invites you not only to sample the delights of Japanese cuisine but also experience the art of preparation. Talented chefs at the sushi bar create miniature sculptures while the teppanyaki wizards whirl knives and spatulas and serve up a slice of Japanese perfection. For intimate evenings you can reserve one of the private tatami rooms.

Food ●●●●○ Serv ●●●●○ Venue ●●●●○ Value ●●●○○

### Sushi Train

Location → Rue Neuve-du-Molard, 21 | **022 310 27 27**
Hours → 12:00 - 14:30 & 19:00 - 23:00  Sun, Mon eve closed
Web/email → na
Map Ref → 13-E4

**75**

Conveyor belt sushi can be novel if you like Japanese food but if it's variety you want then head for the black lacquered low tables and stools at the back. They aren't the most comfortable but traditional Japanese meals will satisfy. Look out for daily half-price sushi specials.

Food ●●●●○ Serv ●●●○○ Venue ●●●○○ Value ●●●●○

Sushi

## Mexican

### Fiesta Mexicana

Location → Balexert Shopping Centre | **022 796 88 41**
Hours → 08:00 - 24:00
Web/email → na
Map Ref → 5-B2

**75**

Fiesta Mexicana is located inside the Balexert mall, but offers more than food court fare. Plates are generously decorated with delicious extras and frozen margaritas are served by the pitcher. If you need more reasons to go, they are located next to the movies, open on Sundays and have underground parking.

Food ●●●○○ Serv ●●●○○ Venue ●●●○○ Value ●●●○○

> ### *Fondue versus Raclette*
>
> *Fondue is the most famous Swiss meal. However, another delicious, though often overlooked, traditional dairy delight is raclette. Raclette, derived from the French word meaning 'to scrape', involves scraping melted cheese over potatoes, pickles, meats, or just about anything else that you fancy.*

### Fruits et Passions

Location → Rue de la Servette, 16 · Les Grottes | **022 733 14 42**
Hours → 12:00 - 14:30 & 19:00 - 23:00  Mon closed
Web/email → na
Map Ref → 13-C2

**75**

Colours and aromas add to the light-hearted feel of this restaurant where drinks glasses chink and the atmosphere revels. Rowdy it is not, but fun is certainly had here on a nightly basis with great drinks and even better food.

Food ●●●●○ Serv ●●●○○ Venue ●●●●○ Value ●●●○○

### La Diligence

Location → Rue Pécolat, 2 · Town Centre | **022 732 44 95**
Hours → 08:00 - 24:00
Web/email → na
Map Ref → 13-D2

**50**

For a taste of Mexico the Diligence, set just off the rue de Mont-Blanc, offers a colourful interior and a variety of dishes to make your mouth water. Spicy nachos washed down with cool margaritas will get you in the mood – then follow up with the excellent fajitas or any of the well portioned main courses accompanied by a surpisingly good selection of Mexican wines. Reasonable prices and friendly service are an added bonus of this typical, yet good quality Mexican.

Food●●●●○Serv●●●●○Venue●●●○○Value●●●●○

## Le Bleu Nuit

Location ➔ Rue du Vieux Billard, 4 · 022 328 34 44
Hours ➔ See below
Web/email ➔ na · Map Ref ➔ 13-C4

The smart and simple atmosphere, friendly service and artisanal fare have created a loyal clientele at Le Bleu Nuit. Because everything is homemade, they occasionally run out of items, but don't despair as your second option is sure to be just as satisfying. It serves Mexican food on weekends and French on weekdays. An easy place for a business lunch or a leisurely evening meal.

**Other Timings:** Mon-Thu 11:00 – 01:00; Fri 11:00 – 02:00; Sat-Sun 18:00 - 01:00

Food●●●●○Serv●●●●○Venue●●●○○Value●●●●○

## Los Tacos

Location ➔ Rue de la Faïencerie, 8 · Carouge · 022 342 03 03
Hours ➔ 09:00 - 12:00 13:30 - 17:30 Sat & Sun closed
Web/email ➔ na · Map Ref ➔ 8-D3

Los Tacos could quite possibly be the best Mexican in Geneva. The food is fresh, delicious and varied, the hand made tortillas, salsa, chorizo, enchiladas and tacos tempt your taste buds on the well covered menu while the margaritas add a little fun to your Mexican Fiesta.

Food●●●●●Serv○○○○○Venue○○○○○Value●●●●○

## Mañana

Location ➔ Rue Chaponnière, 3 · Pâquis · 022 732 21 31
Hours ➔ 12:00 - 14:00 18:00 - 23:30
Web/email ➔ www.manana.ch · Map Ref ➔ 13-D2

Not far from the station, waitresses in in colourful dresses welcome you into this lively venue. More Tex-Mex than Mexican with its barbecued ribs, fajitas and other specialities, but nevertheless all food is tasty and well prepared. This restaurant is popular with young professionals, students or people looking for a lively but reasonably priced eatery in the city. And once the sun goes down you can work off all those mealtime calories in the underground Cactus Bar where Geneva's young

crowd dances the night away.

Food●●●●○Serv●●●●○Venue●●●●○Value●●●●●

## Moroccan

Other options ➔ **Arabic/Lebanese [p.224]**

## La Mamounia

Location ➔ Bd. Georges-Favon · Plainpalais · 022 329 55 92
Hours ➔ 12:00 - 14:30 19:00 - 23:00
Web/email ➔ na · Map Ref ➔ 13-C4

Despite its status as a chain restaurant La Mamounia offers the perfect culinary respite to the multitude of European restaurants in Geneva. The décor is worthy of an upmarket Marrakesh eatery and the delicious plates of cous cous and vegetables prepared in true Moroccan style satisfy the curious diner.

Food●●●●○Serv●●●○○Venue●●●●○Value●●●●○

## Steakhouses

## Café de Paris

Location ➔ Rue du Mont-Blanc, 26 · Cornavin · 022 732 84 50
Hours ➔ 11:00 - 23:00
Web/email ➔ na · Map Ref ➔ 13-D2

While the menu may be a little limited, at least Café de Paris doesn't profess to be all things to all diners. What it does pride itself on however is making a mean steak, and their entrecôte steak in a 'secret recipe' sauce served with golden brown chips and salad is rather good. Accompany your superior steak with one of the excellent red wines and indulge. Smart but inviting with well dressed and extremely efficient waiters, if you're a meat lover you will really love this restaurant.

Food●●●●●Serv●●●●○Venue●●●○○Value●●●○○

## Le Relais de l'Entrecote

Location ➔ Rue du Rhône, 49 · Town Centre · 022 310 60 04
Hours ➔ 12:00 - 14:30 & 19:00 - 23:00
Web/email ➔ na · Map Ref ➔ 13-E4

Minutes from the flower clock, this Paris style café is always full and smoky. Amongst other things, they serve a small salad, crispy shoe string French fries and entrecôte steak covered in a herb sauce. Just make sure you bring your appetite because not only do they have delicious desserts to round off the meal but before that, they come round with a second serving of steak and fries! No reservations.●

Food●●●●○Serv●●●●○Venue●●●○○Value●●●○○

## Swiss

### Café du Soleil

Location ➜ Pl. du Petit-Saconnex
Hours ➜ 07:00 - 24:00
Web/email ➜ www.cafedusoleil

022 733 34 17

Map Ref ➜ 5-D2

For fondue fanatics the dark wooded interior at Café Du Soleil is as Swiss as it gets. Rumoured to be one of the oldest restaurants in Geneva, it certainly looks a little aged. The ambience, however, is lovingly embraced and the need for reservations reflects this. Café de Soleil does not take credit cards so make sure you have cash on you.●

Food●●●●○Serv●●●○○Venue●●●○○Value●●●●○

### Cave Valaisanne-Chalet Suisse

Location ➜ Bd. Georges Favon · Plainpalais
Hours ➜ 08:00 - 01:00
Web/email ➜ na

022 328 12 36

Map Ref ➜ 13-D4

For traditional Swiss kitsch, the Cave Valaisanne - Chalet Suisse is hard to beat. Designed for tourists seeking an authentic Swiss fondue, the chalet side has a dimly lit dark wood-beamed interior and as many cow bells and mountain scenes as they could fit in. The cave side is less contrived but it's all still very much an 'uber Swiss experience'. The food is standard Swiss cuisine and affordable and if you don't mind feeling like you'vie stepped into the set of a Heidi film then it's good old touristy fun!●

Food●●●○○○Serv●●●○○Venue●●●○○Value●●●○○

## Thai

Other options ➜ **Chinese [p.226]**

### Jeck's Place

Location ➜ Rue de Neuchâtel, 14 · Pâquis
Hours ➜ 12:00 - 14:00 & 18:00 - 22:00 Sat, Sun 18:00 - 22:00
Web/email ➜ na

022 731 33 03

Map Ref ➜ 13-D2

Although its location in a non-inspiring Pâquis street may not be a selling point, this small Thai

### Swiss Cuisine

Swiss cuisine is a combination of French and German cuisines - not quite as heavy as German, not quite as fine as French. A common perception of Swiss cuisine is that it is all about cheese and chocolate, and while this is not strictly accurate, cheese does feature in a great many classic Swiss dishes.

Swiss cheese is a source of national pride, and certain cheeses produced in Switzerland are renowned throughout the world as the best of the best. Gruyère is hard and tangy, and is commonly used in fondues. Emmental is undoubtedly one of the most famous Swiss cheeses; it is hard, mild and it has distinctive holes in it. Vacherin can be hard or soft, but either way it is made from cow's milk in France or Switzerland (usually in the Jura region). Commonly, fondues call for a blend of Gruyère, Emmental and Vacherin, depending on the recipe.

Cheese fondue is a famous Swiss dish, although it is complicated and not often prepared at home. It is a blend of three Swiss cheeses, white wine and garlic, into which cubes of bread are dipped. The cheese mixture must be kept warm throughout the meal and so it is necessary to have a special fondue set, which includes a burner. If it's all a little bit cheesy for your tastes, you can have a meat or seafood fondue, where small pieces of meat or seafood are individually deep fried in hot oil. And chocoholics will love a chocolate fondue, where bits of biscuit and fruit are dipped into a lovely hot pot of melted chocolate.

Another well known cheesy Swiss dish is Raclette; a big chunk of hard cheese is held near a burner until it softens enough for a layer to be scraped off - this melted cheese is then eaten with sliced meats, pickles and potatoes. Rosti is a potato dish, which in the past was commonly eaten for breakfast but is now enjoyed as a side dish with lunch or dinner. The potatoes are grated, mixed with oil and shaped into rounds or patties before being baked or shallow fried. Sometimes additional ingredients, such as apple, meat, cheese or onions are added.

Different regions in Switzerland each have their own specialities. Geneva's typical cuisine has been influenced by its environment and geography. The historical importance of the lake is reflected on restaurant menus, where you'll find plenty of dishes featuring freshwater fish such as char and perch. And with France as a next door neighbour, it's no surprise that many local dishes are French in flavour.

Swiss | Thai

**Going Out**

restaurant is a true hidden gem. Wood and rattan décor complements excellent quality oriental food (some say the best in Geneva) at surprsingly affordable prices. The house speciality is a range of Singaporean dishes, mixing influences from Malaysia, China and India and Jeck's has built up a loyal customer following so the atmosphere is familiar and inviting.◉

Food●●●●●Serv●●●●○Venue●●●●○Value●●●●○

### Nyamuk

Location ➔ Rue des Bains, 52　|　022 328 50 52
Hours ➔ 12:00 - 14:00 & 19:00 - 22:00  Sun closed
Web/email ➔ na　　　　　　　　Map Ref ➔ 13-C4

The food at Le Nyamuk is as interesting as it is tasty while the seating is comfortable and spacious and the ambience relaxed. The walls are decorated with paintings from local artists, and if you become inspired by your cuisine you can visit Geneva's sole travel-only bookshop under the same roof for some further Thai investigation. Then there is the travel agency also located here if you feel the need to book that trip to Koh Samui!

Food●●●●○Serv●●●○○Venue●●●●○Value●●●●○

### Sala Thai

Location ➔ Rue Maurice-Braillard · Sécheron　|　022 733 39 33
Hours ➔ 12:00 - 14:00 & 19:00 - 22:00
Web/email ➔ na　　　　　　　　Map Ref ➔ 5-D2

Between Petit Saconnex and the Varembé area of the city, Sala Thai offers a wide variety of dishes of excellent quality, and the fantastic summer terrace is a lunchtime favourite. Try the delicious (and as spicy as you request) Thai green or red curries or one of the lighter (but equally delicious) Phad Thai dishes. Décor is traditional rustic Thai style with waiters and waitresses in national dress. For an even greater Thai experience ask to be seated in the little 'Sala Thai' – small wooden kiosks – where you can eat cross legged, seated on the floor.

Food●●●●○Serv●●●●○Venue●●●●○Value●●●●○

### Sam Lor Thai

Location ➔ Rue de Monthoux, 17 · Pâquis　|　022 738 80 55
Hours ➔ 12:00 - 14:00 & 19:00 - 23:00
Web/email ➔ na　　　　　　　　Map Ref ➔ 13-E2

The atmosphere, décor and service at Sam Lor Thai is what makes this restaurant special. For an

especially authentic experience dine traditional style - cross legged at low tables or at the 'boat' bench. The food is of a very high standard and there is a large range to chose from – delicious rich flavours that range from sweet and sour to seriously spicy will more than satisfy your tastebuds. A good wine selection is also available and reservations are required.◉

Food●●●●●Serv●●●●●Venue●●●●●Value●●●●●

### Vietnamese

Other options ➔ **Chinese [p.226]**

### Bat Dat

Location ➔ 71 bis Rue des Rois · Town Centre　|　022 328 26 10
Hours ➔ 12:00 - 14:30 & 19:00 - 24:00  Sat pm & Sun closed
Web/email ➔ na　　　　　　　　Map Ref ➔ 13-C4

A healthy and delicious variation on traditional Asian cuisine. This beautiful and peaceful venue will entertain your taste buds and your eyes. Fresh orchids and scattered candles set the scene while the aromas of exotic dishes tantalise. For those who fear the heat factor with certain spicy Asian dishes, Bat Dat is for you. Focusing on freshness, the spice level is significantly lower in these Vietnamese dishes. The food presentation is first class, the venue enticing and the service warm and friendly.◉

Food●●●●○Serv●●●●○Venue●●●●○Value●●●●○

A mosaic mural

Going Out | Thai | Vietnamese

## Dinner Cruises

What could be better than combining a stunning cruise on the Lake with a delicious dinner? There are a number of magnificent steamers to choose from where you can relax in an elegant dining room whilst the sights of Geneva drift by. Live entertainment comes in the form of sailing boats, windsurfers and water-skiers who share the waters, and the idyllic scenery acts as the perfect backdrop. Check out the variety of cruises leaving from the Quai du Mont-Blanc and next to the Jardin Anglais. Cruises normally take place from June to mid-September. For specific events check out the 'Paguis' company (opposite the Hotel Beau Rivage on the Quai du Mont-Blanc) that offers Swiss folklore and dinner cruise packages (022 311 25 21) and Bateau le Valais (022 311 32 88).

## Cafés & Coffee Shops

Café culture is alive and kicking in Geneva, with a plethora of inviting and varied establishments where you can grab a coffee, meet your friends and watch the world go by. Almost every corner has its own café, which comes to life in the summer with street and lakeside open terraces filling up with tourists and locals alike. In all areas of the city you'll find somewhere to rest, sip your coffee, read the newspapers and people-watch to your heart's content. And with Italy and France close neighbours, the choice and quality of coffee is pretty excellent – you'll be ordering your second cup before you know it!

### Alliance Gourmande

Location ➔ Pl. de Grenus, 10 · St-Gervais | 022 901 10 03
Hours ➔ 09:00 - 22:00   Sun closed
Web/email ➔ www.alliancegourmande.com      Map Ref ➔ 13-D3

Alliance Gourmande has somewhat of a split personality - for some it is a café, for others a restaurant or wine bar, while many customers come to buy spices. Recently renovated, it is clean, light and open and offers a non-smoking section. Their specialties include foie gras, paella and world-renowned Pata Negra (dried ham). Rich coffees and croissants are served in the morning. Colourful salads and creative plat du jour are beautifully presented at lunchtime. However at night they serve tapas to accompany a nice glass of wine.
Food●●●●○Serv●●●●○Venue●●●●○Value●●●●○

### C.A.L.M. Comme à la Maison

Location ➔ Rue Ancienne, 36 · Carouge | 022 301 22 20
Hours ➔ 09:00 - 20:00
Web/email ➔ omachado@dplanet.ch      Map Ref ➔ 8-E3

A hip eatery located in Carouge, this busy café specialises in lunches (serving mainly quiche, salads and sandwiches) and is popular for tea, coffee, and cakes at all hours. As you enter, the décor makes you feel as if you are enjoying the comfort of a friend's home. A large two level terrace more than doubles the space in good weather. On rainy days however, the weekend brunch crowd gets a little bunched up.
Food●●●●○Serv●●●●○Venue●●●●●Value●●●●○

### Café Art's

Location ➔ Rue des Pâquis, 17 · Les Pâquis | 022 738 07 97
Hours ➔ 11:00 - 02:00  Sat, Sun 08:00 - 02:00
Web/email ➔ na      Map Ref ➔ 13-E2

Café Art's mixes culture, class and cool and serves a young, pop-culture clientele. The café has an arty décor with a lounge area where you could spend all day chilling out reading the papers and ordering countless coffees. If you get a bit peckish there is a refreshing salad and panini menu to choose from at reasonable prices. Call in to Café Art's after work, after shopping or on a lazy Sunday and relax in the calm cool atmosphere. Highly recommended.
Food●●●●●Serv●●●●●Venue●●●●●Value●●●●○

Shady Lunch

Going Out    Dinner Cruises | Cafés and Coffee Shops

## Globus Au Molard

Location ➔ Pl. du Molard · Town Centre | 022 319 54 57
Hours ➔ 09:00 - 19:00 Thu closes at 21:00 Sun closed
Web/email ➔ na                          Map Ref ➔ 13-E4

Great food and excellent coffee are compulsory sustenance for Geneva's shopaholics, and Globus Au Molard has both. Recently refurbished the café is ultra modern with a varied choice of food from ciabattas and baguettes to pasta and sushi. Chic and cheerful, many loyal patrons skip the sandwiches, despite their excellent quality, and go straight for the delicious desserts and scrumptious pastry guaranteed to bring a smile to your face! Service is quick and professional, although you don't have to rush the shop talk!

Food●●●●○Serv●●●○○Venue●●●●○Value●●●●○

## L.A. Café

Location ➔ Rue de Berne, 15 · Pâquis | 022 909 86 26
Hours ➔ 07:00 - 02:00
Web/email ➔ na                          Map Ref ➔ 13-D2

Billed as a 'café and cocktail bar' the L.A. Café is hardly the most inspiring evening destination in the city. Set a few minutes from the station and within the Capitole Hotel, the bar is more of a last resort than a premier destination but if kitsch fluorescent lighting, cheesy music and meat markets are your thing the this is the spot. Cocktails are varied but pretty expensive so stick to the bottled beer if you're on a budget.

Food○○○○○Serv●●●○○Venue●●○○○Value●●○○○

## La Sixième Heure

Location ➔ Pl. des Philosophes · Plainpalais | 022 320 73 69
Hours ➔ 12:00 - 14:30 19:00 - 22:00 Sun closed
Web/email ➔ na                          Map Ref ➔ 15-D1

A welcoming and convivial ambience is created by refined food and delightful décor in a spacious setting. The culinary offerings are diverse and the attention to detail is evident in every dish, especially the freshly made desserts. If you fall in love with La Sixieme Heure you can even buy the chair or plate you were using and take it home. A visit to this relaxed venue is a worthy culinary experience.

*Other Timings: 08:30 – 23:00 Mon-Sat*

Food●●●●○Serv●●●○○Venue●●●●○Value●●●●○

## Les Recyclables

Location ➔ Rue de Carouge, 53 · Plainpalais | 022 328 23 72
Hours ➔ See below
Web/email ➔ www.recyclables.ch         Map Ref ➔ 15-D2

If you don't mind ordering from a counter, simple, fresh and good quality food soon arrives at your table in this café/secondhand book shop. With its bohemian atmosphere you instantly feel at home as you sip tea, sample cakes and flip through the thousands of books on the shelves. The homemade soup tastes especially delicious on a rainy afternoon.

*Timings: The library is open from 9:30 to 18:30, Monday to Friday and 9:00 to 17:00 on Saturday. The café is open 09:00 - 23:00 daily (except Sundays).*

Food●●●○○Serv●●●●○Venue●●●●○Value●●●○○

Café

## Willi's

Location ➔ Rue du Mont-Blanc,11 · Cornavin | 022 732 77 09
Hours ➔ 07:00 - 02:30
Web/email ➔ na                          Map Ref ➔ 13-D2

For Saturday morning coffee and watching the Geneva world go by, Willi's café bar is the perfect spot. Set in the middle of the Rue de Mont-Blanc, the pretty street side terrace is a great vantage point for savouring your coffee and enjoying a spot of voyeurism! Inside the décor is attractive and comfortable and the service is friendly and welcoming. Check out the cocktails which are reputed to be of a very high standard, and enjoy the excellent coffee - all for reasonable city prices.

Food●●●○○Serv●●●●○Venue●●●●○Value●●●●○

## Café Bars

The following outlets are those that merge the casual feel of a café with the vibey atmosphere of a bar. So they make great lunchtime hangouts for a café-style meal, but by night they liven up a bit and become places that people go to for a few drinks.

### Café Baroque / B club

Location ➜ Pl. de la Fusterie, 12 · Town Centre | 022 311 05 15
Hours ➜ 12:00 - 02:00
Web/email ➜ na
Map Ref ➜ 13-D3

 50

Full of fashionable, beautiful people, Café Baroque boasts modern décor and luxurious furnishings, not to mention prices to match the clientele. This is definitely a place to be seen, whether during the day for coffee, in the early evening for an aperitif or for a final tipple before heading downstairs to the trendy B-Club to sip champagne and show off your moves. Just be warned the place can get packed, and the more beautiful you are the sooner you're likely to be served! ☞

Food●●●●○Serv●●●●○Venue●●●●●Value●●●●○

### Café Bizarre

Location ➜ Rue du Temple, 5 · St-Gervais | 022 738 33 33
Hours ➜ 17:00 - 02:00 Mon - Sat
Web/email ➜ na
Map Ref ➜ 13-D3

25

Set outside the main city streets, Café Bizzare is a real hidden gem and definitely worth a visit. A funky and well designed modern décor and the extremely friendly, laidback staff make this bar a favourite

Your table is ready...

with a young professional crowd who like to get together for a drink, a chat and to listen to the cool sounds from the regular live DJs. Light snacks such as excellent french bread open sandwiches and other tapas treats are available at all hours and prices are among the most reasonable in the city (a pint of beer is around SFr 6). The bar attracts a regular crowd and theme evenings, like 'Indian Night', are also extremely popular. ☞

Food●●●●○Serv●●●●●Venue●●●●●Value●●●●●

### Café Marcel

Location ➜ Rue de la Rôtisserie · Town Centre | 022 310 22 40
Hours ➜ 11:30 - 14:30 & 18:00 - 03:00
Web/email ➜ na
Map Ref ➜ 13-D4

50

Red walls, long white curtains in bay windows, white metal furniture, minimalist décor and no pretentions – Café Marcel is stylish yet unassuming, with an uber modern feel. Reminiscent of a Parisian hangout, the bar attracts cool customers who want to catch up and chill out to live DJ sounds. Friendly and good humoured staff set this bar aside from some of the more uptight trendy Geneva haunts. ☞

Food●●●●○○Serv●●●●○Venue●●●●○Value●●●●○

### Demi Lune Café

Location ➜ Rue Etienne Dumont, 3 · Old Town | 022 312 12 90
Hours ➜ 11:00 - 01:00 Fri, Sat 11:00 - 02:00
Web/email ➜ www.demilune.ch
Map Ref ➜ 13-E4

50

Hugely popular, the Demi Lune is a great place to come for your 'pre-clubbing' drinks or Sunday morning chill out session. Stylish Mediterranean décor and a lounge area await – an ideal place to kick back with friends and sample the delightful cocktails. If you're feeling peckish there's a tasty menu featuring hot and cold tapas, hamburgers and salads, and service is always with a smile. Busy at the weekends, if you want a seat it's best to arrive early. ☞

Food●●●●○Serv●●●●○Venue●●●●○Value●●●●○

### L'Antidote

Location ➜ Rue de la Rôtisserie · Town Centre | 022 311 11 33
Hours ➜ 11:30 - 02:00
Web/email ➜ na
Map Ref ➜ 13-E4

   50

L'Antidote keeps true to its name as a remedy to the stresses of modern life. Frequented by Geneva's beautiful crowd, who sip designer drinks to match their Manilo Blahniks, the bar boasts an excellent light menu with a variety of fantastic salads perfect for the fashionista's diet. Overlooking the Place du Molard and the Rue de la Rôtisserie, the terrace becomes a veritable catwalk during the summer with model types sipping cocktails and sampling some of the best sushi in the city.

Food ●●●●○ Serv ●●●●○ Venue ●●●●○ Value ●●●●○

---

### La Clémence

Location → Pl. du Bourg-de-Four, 20  |  **022 310 10 96**
Hours → 07:00 - 24:00  Sat 07:00 - 02:00
Web/email → na  |  Map Ref → 13-E4

 **25**

Set in the heart of the Old Town in the Place du Bourg-de-Four, La Clemence manages to attract passers by and turn them into regular visitors. In the summer the beautiful and large terrace is always crammed full of customers quenching their thirst or chilling in the sun. Located right next to the fountain, the Clemence is a favoured meeting point and a great spot to catch the numerous passing carnivals, musical performances and street parades that take place over the summer. On a Sunday, arrive early for a coffee and a croissant and linger the day away.

Food ●●●●○ Serv ●●●●○ Venue ●●●●○ Value ●●●●○

---

### Les Bains des Pâquis

Location → Quai du Mont-Blanc · Pâquis  |  **022 732 29 74**
Hours → 10:00 - 20:00
Web/email → na  |  Map Ref → 13-E2

 **25**

*Plate smashing is a form of expression, culturally acceptable only in Greek restaurants. You can now get your point across for all other eateries and still avoid costly lawsuits. Just log on to Eat Out Speak Out, UAE's first online restaurant review forum and freely spill all thoughts about the dining experience.*
*www.EatOutSpeakOut.com*

Whatever the season, a visit to the Bains des Pâquis café bar is definitely worth the trip. In summer, soak up the sun on the wooden decks, then jump in the lake to cool off before indulging in a while host of tasty treats! Be warned though, the summer queues are crazy but the food is worth the wait. There's always an excellent plat du jour (such as Moroccan chicken and cous cous at a very decent SFr 12) and a good quality selection of salads and irresistible sweets. The fresh fruit juices and cool beers are the perfect

cure for a sunshine thirst. Don't, however, let the cold winter months put you off, as fantastic champagne fondues and other winter warmers are available at very reasonable prices.

Food ●●●●○ Serv ●●●●○ Venue ●●●●● Value ●●●●●

## Internet Cafés

With a huge international community, Internet cafés are an essential fixture in Geneva. Various bars and cafés double up as Internet hubs with prices of about SFr 6 per hour (sometimes you have to buy a drink too). The best location is generally the Gare de Cornivan railway station which has a large Internet café area and probably the best prices in town (average price SFr 5 per hour and less for students). The large Fnac store in the city centre also offers Internet access in its rather funky café so you can click before you shop!

## Food on the Go

## Bakeries

If you're a pastry junkie you'll love Geneva! Like its French and Italian neighbours, Switzerland is crammed full of quality bakeries on every corner selling delicious breads, croissants, pastries, and all sorts of other yummy sweet and savoury snacks. Filled French bread and croissants and quiches are popular lunch-on-the-go options although more and more places are now offering a greater variety including paninis, sliced bread combos, pasta and salad mixes and pies. For a real deli treat, check out the newly opened café/deli in the Globus department store (enter through the store on Rue du Rhône or through its side door direct into the deli on Place du Molard) – for excellent quality food with window bar stools where you can watch everyday Geneva pass by.

---

### Le Pain Quotidien

Location → Bd. Helvétique, 3, Rive  |  **022 736 36 90**
Hours → 07:00 - 18:00  Sun 08:00 - 18:00
Web/email → na  |  Map Ref → 13-C4

  **50**

Le Pain Quotidien's coffees, freshly squeezed orange juice, excellent breads and good selection of pastries are served in an informal setting. Healthy and fresh soups, quiches, salads and sandwiches are also available. Saturday and Sunday brunches are as much a social occasion as they are a reason to enjoy the good food. ●

*Other branches: bd. Georges-Favon 32 Plainpalais(781 81 90)*
Food●●●●○ Serv●●●●○ Venue●●●●○ Value●●●○○

Bakery

## Parties at Home

### Caterers

A range of catering companies are available in the city to suit every kind of party range from casual buffet to distinguished sit down dinners. A new addition to the catering crew is *Globus* – the large department store in the city centre has just opened an excellent food hall and is highly recommended for outside catering (50, Rue du Rhône 1204 Genève, tel 310 27 44). Other Geneva favourites include the Coop Catering service (022 939 46 99) and the Migros party service (022 307 53 17 / 022 307 55 28), all offering an excellent variety of products at quite reasonable prices. For fine dining options (with prices to suit, of course) Hotels Beau Rivage (022 716 66 66) and Noga Hilton (022 908 90 81) also have excellent catering services.

### Party Organisers

Other options → **Party Accessories [p.155]**

| **Sindy** | |
|---|---|
| Location → Various locations | na |
| Hours → Various | |
| Web/email → www.sindy.ch | Map Ref → na |

Sindy is a non-profit group run by about 20 volunteers. Their aim is to make Geneva a more fun place for both expats and locals, by organising special events and activities. In the past they have thrown mega parties, hosted salsa weekends, and organised many other events like Sunday brunches, Christmas balls and adventure trips. They currently have around 6,000 members, and Sindy welcomes all young professionals (aged 25 and over) to join their mailing list. To find out more, and to register your name on the mailing list, visit the above Website or send an email to sindy.geneva@usa.net

## On the Town

The general description of Geneva nightlife is that it's unlikely to get your pulse racing – but this isn't necessarily true. While it may pale in comparison to London or Paris, if you listen to the word on the street there are some good party venues that will keep you out until the very early hours! There are hundreds of pubs and bars of all varieties from traditional Swiss and French venues (which can be a bit sombre but serve good wine) to theme bars. There is also the usual ubiquitous Irish establishments and some swankier offerings with fantastic décor. For hardcore clubbers it's true that you need to look carefully and avoid the dodgier 'black window' establishments which tend to be sleazy lap dancing venues set up to attract the visiting business crowd. A few quality places do exist (for example the Liquid Club and the SIP in Plainpalais) and you can always head off to the more cutting edge establishments in Lausanne if Geneva doesn't do it for you!

Food on the run

Geneva also plays host to internationally renowned classical music and opera events, with a world famous orchestra dividing its time between Geneva and Lausanne, as well as major international performers. Dance and drama are also well accounted for with a number of quality theatres in the city and in Carouge. The *Fêtes de Genève* is the city's premier annual arts festival, held in early August on the lakeside, with music of all kinds as well as theatre, funfairs and street entertainers.

What's on listings are published weekly in Genève-Agenda, the free city guide available from the tourist office and hotels. You can get tickets for most shows from either City-Disc at the station (022 900 18 50), or UBS Ticket Corner, 5 Rue de la Corraterie (022 376 62 65).

Most bars are open all night during March's Motor Show weekend, August's Fêtes de Genève, and L'Escalade in December when venues come alive with the usual crowd of revellers and even those die hard stay-at-homers!

## Bars

There are bars aplenty in Geneva with a wide variety of styles. Whether you're looking for a quiet bar with a subdued atmosphere, a funky joint with a hive of activity, a cocktail haunt with excellent Caiprinhas or just a good old beer hole – there's all this and more in the city. Most bars stick to (admittedly higher than average) city prices and many also serve snacks and food. Known for its 'young, posh and loaded' crowd, Geneva has a collection of upmarket establishments where Manilo Blahniks are required to get your foot in the door!

### Door Policy

With such a wide array of nationalities and cultural diversity in Geneva, most of the general city bars and nightclubs are pretty much open to anyone with no strict 'members only' rules. However there are some exclusive Geneva establishments requiring membership and if your name's not on the list you're definitely not coming in! Generally if you're in the rich set then you'll probably already have your membership – and if not, don't spend time worrying about it – there are plenty of other swanky places ready to accept you without you having to beg mercilessly, bribe doormen, or pretend you're Madonna's second cousin twice removed!

### Dress Code

Most of the 'general' establishments (meaning mid-price, no fancy chandeliers, pub-style venues) have a reasonably relaxed attitude to their clients' dress and you can get away with jeans and trainers without too much bother. However, with all those designer labels lining the main shopping streets it's hardly surprising that Geneva embraces dressing to impress. You don't have to be totally draped in Dior (although it might help) but for the swankier bars and nightclubs you may want to opt for catwalk couture - or close to it.

### Specials

Many places hold occasional promotions with different themes and offers. You can get all the old favourites – Ladies' nights, Back to School, 80's, Latino, etc., – at a variety of different establishments, including many of the nightclubs. Keep your eye out for special nights, generally promoted in the local publications or on flyers and posters around the city. Quiz nights are pretty popular at the English and Irish bars and attract quite a following.

### General Bars

Other options → **Café Bars [p.240]**

#### Café Cuba

| Location → Pl. du Cirque, 1 · Plainpalais | **022 328 42 60** |
| Hours → 07:00 - 01:00 Sat, Sun 07:00 - 02:00 | |
| Web/email → na | Map Ref → 13-C4 |

  **50**

Live it up Latino style at Café Cuba - a Latin feel restaurant/bar covering three floors with an explosive interior and excitable clientele! Check out the excellent cocktail list for marvellous Mojitos and colourful Caipirinhas as well as many other mouthwatering concoctions. Varied and tasty tapas are on offer as well as a Mexican themed menu including dishes such as fajitas. A great place to meet, eat and dance the night away.

Food ●●●○○ Serv ●●●●○ Venue ●●●●○ Value ●●●○○

#### L'Alhambar

| Location → Rue de la Rôtisserie,10 | **022 312 13 13** |
| Hours → 17:00 - 02:00  Sun 11:00 - 24:00 | |
| Web/email → www.alhambar.com | Map Ref → 13-E4 |

 **50**

Located above the Alhambra theatre, this stylish and popular bar attracts a young and funky clientele. Chandeliers and antique-style sofas

**Going Out** · Bars | General Bars

complement the eclectic mix of young party hard trendsetters, all here to impress. Music is varied with jazz, soul, funk and dance DJs drawing in the crowds. Look out for special theme nights (such as Bollywood, Movie stars, etc.) which if nothing else, are a good laugh and perfect for birthdays or hen and stag parties. And when the party's over, Sunday brunch will help with the hangover!

Food ●●●●○ Serv ●●●●○ Venue ●●●●● Value ●●●●●

## L'Ethno

Location ➜ Rue Bovy-Lysberg,1 · Plainpalais | 022 310 25 21
Hours ➜ 12:00 - 02:00   Sun 17:00 - 02:00
Web/email ➜ www.ethnobar.ch
Map Ref ➜ 13-D4

🍴 🍷 **50**

With its trendy, earthy décor and cool atmosphere, Café Ethno attracts a young and fashionable crowd. Drop in for a glass of excellent wine or one of the funky cocktails, and sample the tasty tapas and panini at reasonable prices. Service is friendly and casual, and the feeling is generally laidback - groups of friends huddle around tables or chill out in big armchairs near the bar. Definitely one of the most stylish and unpretentious bars in Geneva and well worth a visit.

Food ●●●●○ Serv ●●●●○ Venue ●●●●● Value ●●●●○

## La Bohême

Location ➜ Bd. Helvétique, 36 · Eaux-Vives | 022 700 46 00
Hours ➜ 10:00 - 02:00
Web/email ➜ na
Map Ref ➜ 14-A4

🍷 **75**

If you're a bit of a drama queen (or king!), La Bohême might be just up your alley. Dramatic, mock-baroque

'Mine's a pint, please!'

---

décor complete with velvet curtains, life-size animal figurines, chaise longues and golden chandeliers attract a varied crowd, from business drinkers, groups of friends and a few Lotharios! The cuisine is French and of standard quality although lacking somewhat in variety, making this more of a place you might happen to end up in rather than choose as a top restaurant destination.

Food ●●○○○ Serv ●●●○○ Venue ●●●○○ Value ●●●○○

## La Terrasse

Location ➜ Quai du Mont-Blanc, 31 · Pâquis | 022 796 20 40
Hours ➜ 12:00 - 23:00
Web/email ➜ na
Map Ref ➜ 14-A2

🍴 🍷 🚫 **25**

In the summer months La Terasse is an absolute favourite with the Geneva crowd. Open from the beginning of May until end of August, the bar offers all your old favourites plus a few fancy summer cocktails. Sit out on the wooden decks right on the lake, or picnic on the grassy areas and relax in the glow of summer. The atmosphere is fun and friendly with everyone that's anyone getting down to La Terrasse to chill out on balmy summer evenings. A favourite meeting place and excellent people watching spot.

Food ○○○○○ Serv ●●●●○ Venue ●●●●● Value ●●●●○

## Le Chat Noir

Location ➜ Rue Vautier, 13 · Carouge | 022 343 49 98
Hours ➜ 18:00 - 04:00   Sat, Sun 20:00 - 05:00
Web/email ➜ na
Map Ref ➜ 15-D4

🍴 🍷 **50**

In very trendy Carouge, the Chat Noir is probably one of the best night spots for all round quality entertainment. The Bohemian bar – with an extremely cool summer terrace – attracts a cultured crowd. Le Chat Noir has been promoting artists and music through the Association de Soutien des Musiques Vivantes (ASMV) since 1994. The club promises (and delivers) a high quality eclectic programme (rock, jazz, blues, pop, electronic, etc.) with almost 100 groups per year ranging from local to international artists.

Food ○○○○○ Serv ●●●●○ Venue ●●●●● Value ●●●●○

## Le Petit Baroque

Location ➜ Pl. de la Fusterie, 12 · St-Gervais | 022 311 05 65
Hours ➜ 12:00 - 14:00   19:00 - 23:45
Web/email ➜ www.lebaroque.com
Map Ref ➜ 13-D3

🍷 **125**

With its very trendy clientele, theatrical décor, huge red curtains, stone staircase, wrought iron furniture

General Bars

Going Out

and chandeliers the atmosphere at Le Petit Baroque is high chic. As for the food, chef Yves Schmid – a Genevois with Korean roots - serves up a delectable array of top quality dishes that use the excellent produce rather than complex recipes to do the real work. In the summer don't miss the fantastic truffle risotto, perfect with a glass of wine. **BW**

Food ●●●●● Serv ●●●●○ Venue ●●●●○ Value ●●●○○

### Les Brasseurs

Location → Pl. Cornavin, 20 · Cornavin  022 731 02 06
Hours → 11:30 - 01:00 Sat, Sun 11:30 - 02:00
Web/email → na  Map Ref → 13-D2

🍴 🍷 **50**

If you like beer you'll love Brasseurs as it is the only brewery pub in the city. Opposite the Gare de Cornavin the bar has numerous brews including regular house lager, bitter and stout as well as seasonal specials. Whether it's just a half or a massive 5 pint 'beer tube', you'll get service with a smile and really reasonable prices. For the best Brasseurs experience, accompany your beer with a delicious 'Flammenkueche' – a kind of pizza or flat bread with cheese and onions. Cheers! **BW**

Food ●●●●○ Serv ●●●●○ Venue ●●●●○ Value ●●●●○

### No Limits

Location → Rue Chantemerle, 1  +33-4 50 92 40 92
Hours →  12:00 - 14:30 & 19:30 - 22:30
Web/email → www.restaurant-nolimit.com  Map Ref → na

 **25**

Located just over the border, No Limits is a replica of an American chain restaurant. It has booths, sports paraphernalia, large screens playing sporting extreme videos. As for the bar nuts, you get to throw your peanut shells on the floor - very liberating! It's a perfect stop after a long day of shopping as it is kid friendly and located right in the heart of the shopping district of Ville la Grand.

*Timings: Restaurant is open daily 12:00 - 14:30 (last order 13:30) & 19:30 - 22:30.* **SB**

Food ●●●○○ Serv ●●●●○ Venue ●●●●○ Value ●●●●○

### Santa Cruz

Location → Rue du Stand, 40  022 320 80 60
Hours → 20:00 - 02:00 Sun - Tue closed
Web/email → www.santacruz.ch  Map Ref → 13-C4

🍷 **50**

Get into the Latino spirit at Santa Cruz. This reasonably sized bar/disco is a popular haunt for a few sangrias and a spot of salsa. After you have strutted your stuff you can settle down at the bar for a cool cocktail or a crafty cerveza and keep your eye out for any potential J-Lo's! ●

Food ●○○○○ Serv ●●●●○ Venue ●●●○○ Value ●●●○○

## Upmarket Bars

### Arthur's Rive Gauche

Location → Rue du Rhône, 7-9 · St-Gervais  022 810 32 60
Hours → 07:30 - 02:00
Web/email → na  Map Ref → 13-D3

👔 🍴 🍷 **50**

For city centre chic, Arthur's has luxurious décor, fancy seating and extremely well dressed bar staff. Set next to the river side, clients can enjoy summer sunning on the terrace and winter warmth inside. The drinks menu is extremely varied with wine and champagne particular favourites, and great coffees for lazy weekend mornings. Evening prices are a little on the steep side but for something a little bit swish, Arthur's is definitely worth a visit. They also serve a decent food menu. **BW**

Food ●●●○○ Serv ●●●○○ Venue ●●●●○ Value ●●●●○

## Pubs

English and Irish pubs stay true to their names in Geneva and give locals and tourists a slice of home - complete with beer stained carpets, bar stools and plenty of beers! Pubs are real favourites for sports fans who can while away the hours catching their favourite football or rugby team, downing a few ales and scoffing a good old pub lunch. Frequent folk music sessions in the Irish establishments are crowd pleasers and guarantee a great *craic*!

### Mr Pickwick's

Location → Rue de Lausanne, 80 · Les Pâquis  022 731 67 97
Hours → 10:00 - 02:00
Web/email → www.mr-pickwick.ch  Map Ref → 5-E3

🍷 **50**

Catering for English pub-goers but attracting a varied crowd Mr Pickwicks has a good choice of draught beers, quality pub grub (available at all hours) and televisions airing English premiership football and rugby matches. Regular entertainment with live bands, karaoke and themed evenings make this a fun and friendly place to catch up with your mates and sink a few beers. **BW**

Food ●●●●○ Serv ●●●●○ Venue ●●●●○ Value ●●●○○

## Irish Pubs

### Charly O'Neills

Location → Rue Hoffmann, 18 · Servette   |   **022 740 45 30**
Hours → 17:00 - 02:00  Sat, Sun 13:00 - 02:00
Web/email → www.ireland.ch         Map Ref → 5-D3

 **50**

For a bit of good old-fashioned Irish *craic* and a lot of Guinness, get down to Charly's - a home from home bar that's a favourite with the international crowd. Whatever the season, this traditional Irish pub is always packed with people getting together for a quick pint, to watch the football and sometimes even have a sing along around the piano! Good quality pub grub is also available if you're peckish and regular entertainment (live bands, pub quizzes) keeps the regulars coming back for more. **BW**

Food ●●●●○○ Serv ●●●●●○ Venue ●●●●●○ Value ●●●○○

### Flanagan's Irish Bar

Location → Rue du Cheval Blanc, 4 · Old Town  |  **022 310 13 14**
Hours → 17:00 - 02:00
Web/email → na         Map Ref → 13-D4

 **50**

Set in the heart of the Old Town, Flanagan's gets a thumbs up as the obligatory Irish pub. Call in for a quick pint and you'll find yourself staying till the early hours in the downstairs nightclub/bar. This is a great easy going option that won't cost you an arm and a leg - just your sobriety! **BW**

Food ●●●●○ Serv ●●●●○ Venue ●●●○○ Value ●●●●○

### Mulligan's

Location → Rue Grenus, 14 · Town Centre  |  **022 732 85 76**
Hours → 17:00 - 01:00
Web/email → na         Map Ref → 13-D3

**50**

For a great pint of Guinness and regular live Irish folk music, Mulligan's makes for a relaxed evening. Set in Place du Grenus opposite the Manor department store – the pub is ideally situated for a post shopping pint or early evening festivities. A great place to meet people and a home away from

home for the international crowd, the bar also shows big game football and rugby matches and hosts regular live music performances. **BW**

Food ●○○○○ Serv ●●●●● Venue ●●●○○ Value ●●●○○

## Nightclubs

Although many club critics will have you believe Geneva is a sleepy town with no hope for a decent nightlife, there are in fact a number of popular clubs around the city that keep the throngs of clubbers filling the dance floor well into the early hours. There's something for everyone – whether it's commercial cheese, eighties favourites, serious techno, Latino grooves, jazzy jams or upmarket sounds you're looking for.  Clubs and dancing venues are dotted all over the city centre, the Old Town and Pâquis.  Plainpalais on the Left Bank of the lake is also pretty nightclub congested although the calibre of these hot spots is up for debate!  A number of international DJs visit Geneva clubs so keep a look out for their names on flyers and in local publications.  If you've exhausted the Geneva selection, you could always take a trip down lake to Lausanne where the party people reportedly live it up lavishly, or venture out to the famous 'Macumba' complex that claims to be the biggest club in Europe (see review below).

### Liquid

Location → Quai des Forces Motrices, 4  |  **022 329 01 29**
Hours → 00:00 - 05:00  Wed - Sat only
Web/email → www.liquidclub.ch     Map Ref → 13-C3

**25**

One of the liveliest clubs in the city, Liquid sees Swiss and international DJs stepping up to the decks to a rhythm hungry crowd.  Music style is generally house/dance but a variety of 'theme' evenings take place on Thursdays while on Wednesday nights happy hour lasts until 02:00. On the last Saturday of every other month, the trendy gay and lesbian 'Virage' night is held. **BW**

### Macumba

Location → Rte d'Annecy, 403  |  **+33-4 50 49 23 50**
Hours → Ring venue for timings
Web/email → www.macumba.net     Map Ref → na

 **25**

Promoted as 'the biggest club in Europe', Macumba is a multi-level extravaganza for everyone from hardcore clubbers to occassional toe-tappers. A multiplex of different themed rooms, ambiences and styles, there really is something for everyone in this huge establishment. To name just a few, there is Macumba for dance and techno, then there is the Tropical club for rock and pop, Club 30/40 churns out the cheese, the Irish bar does karaoke, the Villa goes Spanish style while the Lounge is for the trendsetters.

### Shaker's

| | |
|---|---|
| Location → Rue de la Boulangerie, 3 | 022 310 55 98 |
| Hours → 22:00 - 05:00 Sun & Mon closed | |
| Web/email → www.shakers.ch | Map Ref → 13-D4 |

🍷 75

Those looking to make a move go to Shaker's. It might not officially be a singles bar but by the look of the dance floor boys and girls are on the look out for luurvve! With testosterone in the air, R&B, Latino, House and Disco beats shaking the dance floor and a whole host of tempting cocktails this club is far from prententious and what you see is what you get - unless you're wearing beer goggles! (BW)

### SIP Soul Influenced Product

| | |
|---|---|
| Location → Rue des Vieux-Grenadiers, 10 · Plainpalais | na |
| Hours → 21:00 - 04:00 Thu - Sat only | |
| Web/email → www.lasip.ch | Map Ref → 15-C1 |

🚫 25

Previously rather exclusive and accessible only to the trendiest of trend setters, SIP is now slightly more relaxed and as long as you're well dressed and reasonably sober, you should get in. It's worth the effort - this former industrial site is now a loft-style wonderland with modern furnishings. The first floor sports a DJ playing chill out music, and upstairs there is a dance floor featuring eclectic music mixes.

## Entertainment

### Cabaret & Strip Shows

Geneva has its fair share of cabaret shows, strip clubs and hostess bars, particularly in Pâquis. Some are tame, some are sleazy, and some are just downright silly, but these establishments remain popular, particularly with the transient business community.

## Casinos

Casinos are exceptionally popular in Geneva. Cash-loaded visitors and fortune seekers crowd round the tables to try their luck. Elegance and style are the order of the day at Geneva casinos, so get dressed up and keep vulgar displays of cash to a minimum!

## Cinemas

Going to the movies is a regular evening pastime, and there are many cinemas around the city ranging from the fancy 13 screen complex at the Balexert Shopping Centre to smaller, bohemian style halls hidden away on city streets. Most cinemas (not Balexert) still practice the old fashioned ten minute intermission, so don't be surprised if half way through your film, the lights go up and everyone pops outside for a break. Most films are released in Switzerland at the same time as they are in the US and UK, so you don't have to wait for months to see the latest blockbusters. If you hate watching a film with dodgy dubbing, look out for the 'VO' sign - this stands for 'Version Originale', so you get to see the movie in its original form, normally in English. A night at the cinema can hurt the pocket a bit, but you can wait until 'cheap seats' days (usually Monday and/or Wednesday) when prices are more reasonable (around SFr 10 – 12).

Film fans should not miss the annual Ciné Lac Festival during the summer, where a huge, outdoor

*About time your favourite waiter got a pat on the posterior for good service? Prompt a pay raise or promotion by shouting 'good service' from the rooftops! Eat Out Speak Out is the perfect way to get your 'pat' across. Not only will we publish your 'pat' online, we'll also make sure that it is transported straight from your hands to the 'back' of the establishment.*

### Cinemas

| Cinemas | |
|---|---|
| Balexert | 022 979 01 00 |
| Broadway | 022 731 15 89 |
| Cac Voltaire | 022 320 78 78 |
| Camera Movie | 022 732 51 22 |
| Central | 022 908 04 30 |
| Hollywood | 022 310 65 32 |
| Les Grottes | 022 740 09 88 |
| Les Rex | 0900 900 156 |
| Les 7 Rialto | 0900 900 156 |
| Plaza | 022 732 57 09 |
| Splendid | 022 732 73 73 |

**Nightclubs | Cinemas**

**Going Out**

screen is erected on the lakeside, showing a range of movies including old favourites, cult classics and new releases. Visit the Ciné Lac Website at www.cinelac.ch or call 0840 04 04.

## Concerts

Genevans love music, and concerts and musical events take place throughout the year at different venues and bars. The summer ushers in an explosion of events including jazz festivals, classical recitals and some of the biggest names in international music. In June, the hugely popular Fête de la Musique sees bands setting up all over Geneva for a three-day extravaganza, and the annual Fêtes de Genève (usually beginning at the end of July) features a variety of concerts.

### Music Festivals

**Paléo Festival:** It started out as a folk festival in 1976, and today it features cutting edge pop and rock acts in a high octane party atmosphere. Now heading for its 30th anniversary, the festival is one of Europe's biggest open air music events. Past acts have included Oasis, Travis, Supergrass, Texas, Peter Gabriel, Alanis Morissette and REM. The festival is held in Nyon and is one of the essential Swiss summer events – for more information, visit www.paleo.ch.

**Montreux Jazz Festival:** This world famous event attracts hundreds of thousands of jazz lovers every year, and stretches over two glorious summer weeks (the 2005 festival is planned for 1 – 16 July). Apart from the main acts, there is also an interesting fringe festival, which features plenty of

free concerts and market stalls in this lovely lakeside town (about an hour from Geneva by car). Visit www.montreuxjazz.com.

**Caribana Festival:** This three day festival of rock, pop and alternative music is held in June, and provides a warm-up for the Paléo Festival. It is headlined by some big acts (2004 saw performances by Nickelback and Simple Minds). For more information, visit the Website at www.caribana.ch.

**Fêtes de Genève :** This series of musical events runs from the end of July until around the 8th of August, but warm-up events start taking place a good few weeks before. Stages are set up around the city and musicians of all levels of fame and talent entertain crowds on a nightly basis. Check out the official Website at www.fetes-de-geneve.ch.

**Fête de la Musique:** Each year in mid June, Geneva transforms into a musical metropolis for this festive event. You can drift from stage to stage catching some great musical acts, or just grab a cocktail and chill out on the lawns until the early hours. The dates for the 2005 festival are set for the 17th – 19th June – be there! Visit www.fetedelamusique.ch for more information.

In addition to the above festivals, there are other musical events organised by Ville de Genève in July and August. These concerts include classical and jazz music, as well as other styles. Concerts are held at the Hôtel de Ville (the town hall), the Victoria Hall and on the Ella Fitzgerald stage at the La Grange park. Bookings should be made at the town hall one hour before each concert. For more information, and a programme of events, call Ville de Genève on 022 418 65 00 or visit their Website at www.ville-ge.ch/culture.

Alternatively if you head over to the International Red Cross and Red Crescent Museum in July and August, you can watch some interesting concerts in an intimate setting. The programme features mainly classical music and jazz, with the occasional world music concert thrown in. Concerts start daily at 12:30. For further information and a programme listing, visit www.micr.ch.

## Theatre

Compulsive theatre goers will be able to get their fix in Geneva, where there is a wide choice of quality venues and an interesting variety of shows during the year. Opera is hugely popular and is well worth a visit, even if it's just to ogle the splendid interior of the Grand Théâtre de Genève on Place Neuve. Other theatre halls are also

It's time to go out!

exquisite and offer varied programmes. Most performances are in French, but if it's English theatre you're looking for, the Geneva English Drama Society (GEDS) and the Geneva Amateur Operatic Society (GAOS) stage regular shows.

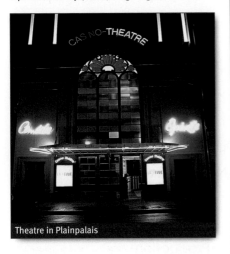
Theatre in Plainpalais

## Gay Scene

Geneva's gay scene is thriving, with plenty of bars, clubs and restaurants to choose from. Some establishments promote themselves as 'gay only', although others have more relaxed entrance policies and encourage a friendly mix of gays and heteros. If you're new to Geneva, you should definitely check out Dialogai (www.dialogai.org) - it's the oldest gay association in town and offers a big welcome and information on special evenings and activities. It also has a relaxed café/bar where you can chill out, enjoy a drink or browse through the library.

### Bar Nathan

Location → Rue Baudit, 6 · Les Grottes | **022 733 78 76**
Hours → 17:00 - 02:00
Web/email → na    Map Ref → 13-C2

Nathan is a trendy club where the décor mixes contemporary steel with traditional wood, and features cosy corner lounges. In addition to its fashionable interior, the bar also features temporary exhibitions, selections of gay magazines, a tapas menu and a whole list of elegant cocktails. Acid jazz and techno fill the dance floor on Wednesdays.

### Le Concorde

Location → Rue de Berne, 3 · Pâquis | **022 731 96 80**
Hours → 07:00 - 22:00, Sat 09.00 - 02.00, Sun 15.00 - 02.00
Web/email → na    Map Ref → 13-D2

The laidback Le Concorde, situated in the infamous Rue de Berne, is one of the oldest gay bars in the city. It remains popular with a varied clientele.

### Le Déclic

Location → Bd. du Pont d'Arve, 28 | **022 320 59 14**
Hours → 17:00 - 02:00 Sat 21:00 - 02:00 Sun closed
Web/email → na    Map Ref → 15-D2

Seasons may pass, fashions may come and go, but Le Déclic has stood the test of time. It is considered to be one of the 'nicest' bars in the region, with a great dance floor, lightshows and a giant TV screen. The huge cocktail menu has over 40 concoctions to choose from, all guaranteed to get you in the mood for dancing. The club regularly hosts special DJs.

### Le Prétexte

Location → Rue du Prince, 9 · Town Centre | **022 310 14 28**
Hours → 23:00 - 05:00 Wed - Sat
Web/email → www.lepretexte.com    Map Ref → 13-E4

Venture through the huge wooden door into an eclectic wonderland of stylish baroque furniture, oriental mosaics and seventies kitsch. The party atmosphere is irresistible and the unique 'shower show' livens things up even more. The club holds various theme nights on Thursdays, and there's a strip show on Tuesday and Wednesday nights.

### Lolipop

Location → Rue Goetz Monin, 10 · Plainpalais | **022 320 59 65**
Hours → 21:00 - 02:00 Sun 21:00 - 05.00 +
Web/email → na    Map Ref → 15-E2

The vaulted cellars and shiny colours of Lolipop (formerly 'Thermos) provide a happy flashback to the saucy seventies. This is the biggest gay bar in Switzerland, with 210 m$^2$ of labyrinth style halls on two levels. The atmosphere is friendly and the clientele definitely fall into the 'young and trendy' category.

# Maps

# Maps

## User's Guide

To further assist you in locating your destination, we have superimposed additional information, such as main roads, roundabouts and landmarks, on the maps. Many places listed throughout the guidebook also have a map reference alongside, so you know precisely where you need to go (or what you need to tell the taxi driver).

While the overview map on this page is at a scale of approximately 1:300,000 (1 cm = 1.3 km), all other maps range from 1:10,000 (1 cm = 100 m) to 1:20,000 (1cm = 200 m).

## Technical Info - Satellite Images

The maps in this section are based on rectified QuickBird satellite imagery taken in 2003.

The QuickBird satellite was launched in October 2001 and is operated by DigitalGlobe(tm), a private company based in Colorado (USA). Today, DigitalGlobe's QuickBird satellite provides the highest resolution (61 cm), largest swath width and largest onboard storage of any currently available or planned commercial satellite.

MAPS geosystems are the Digital Globe master resellers for the Middle East, West, Central and East Africa. They also provide a wide range of mapping services and systems. For more information, visit www.digitalglobe.com (QuickBird) and www.maps-geosystems.com (mapping services) or contact MAPS geosystems on (+971 0) 6 572 5411.

## Online Maps

If you want to surf for maps online, a good starting point is http://www.ville-ge.ch/fr/outils/maps.htm – this site features a comprehensive A to Z of Geneva's roads and streets, and even the individual buildings and house numbers. Choose one and the map zooms in to show you the exact location. The Geneva Tourism Website – www.geneve–tourisme.ch – also has links to online maps, and www.geneva.ch/Map is also worth a visit.

Also try www.mappy.com and www.map24.com.

## Community & Street Index

The following is a list of the main roads and communities in Geneva, which are referenced on the map pages. Many roads are longer than one grid reference, in which case the main grid reference has been given.

| Geneva | Map Ref |
|---|---|
| Aïre-la-Ville | 7-A1 |
| Bardonnex | 11-B2 |
| Bellevue | 2-D2 |
| Bernex | 4-D4, 7-D2 |
| Carouge | 15-D4 |
| Cartigny | 7-A3 |
| Chêne-Bourg | 9-D1 |
| Chêne-Bougeries | 6-C4, 16-E2 |
| Collonge-Bellerive | 3-E3 |
| Cologny | 14-E2 |
| Confignon | 7-E4, 8-A3 |
| Genthod | 3-A1 |
| Laconnex | 7-A4, 10-A1 |
| Lancy | 8-C2 |
| Le Grand-Saconnex | 2-C3, 5-C1 |
| Les Eaux-Vives | 14-B3 |
| Les Grottes | 5-D2 |
| Meyrin | 1-D4, 4-D1, 5-A1 |
| Moillebeau | 5-D2 |
| Monnetier | 12-E1 |
| Onex | 8-A2 |
| Perly-Certoux | 10-E1 |
| Plan-les-Ouates | 8-B4, 11-B1 |
| Pregny-Chambésy | 2-E4 |
| Satigny | 4-A1 |
| Soral | 10-A3 |
| Trônex | 9-D2 |
| Vandoeuvres | 6-E2 |
| Vernier | 5-A3, 9-B4 |

| France | Map Ref |
|---|---|
| Bossey | 12-B2 |
| Collonges-sous-Salève | 12-A3 |
| Ferney-Voltaire | 2-B2 |
| Gaillard | 9-D3 |
| Prévessin-Moëns | 1-D2 |
| Saleve | 12-E3 |
| St-Genis-Pouilly | 1-A2 |
| St-Julien-en-Genevois | 10-D3 |

SFr 10 ~ € 6

1ˢᵗ Edition | GENEVA **EXPLORER**

Introduction

Maps

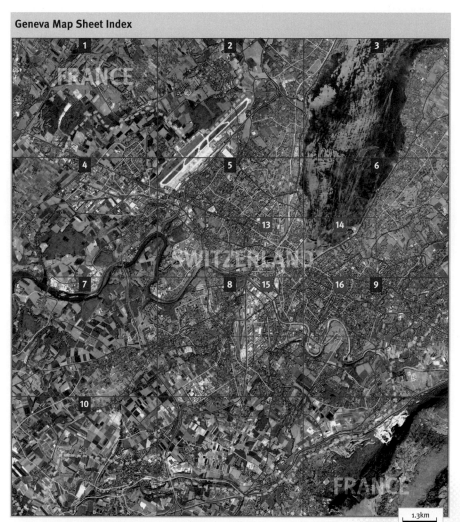

1.3km

## Map Legend

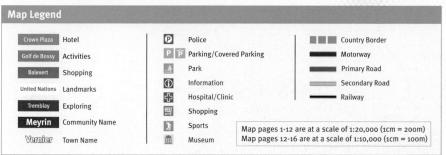

| | |
|---|---|
| Crown Plaza | Hotel |
| Golf de Bossy | Activities |
| Balexert | Shopping |
| United Nations | Landmarks |
| Tremblay | Exploring |
| **Meyrin** | Community Name |
| *Vernier* | Town Name |

| | |
|---|---|
| Ⓟ | Police |
| P Ⓟ | Parking/Covered Parking |
| ♣ | Park |
| ⓘ | Information |
| ✚ | Hospital/Clinic |
| ▦ | Shopping |
| 🏃 | Sports |
| 🏛 | Museum |

| | |
|---|---|
| ▬▬▬ | Country Border |
| ▬▬▬ | Motorway |
| ▬▬▬ | Primary Road |
| ▬▬▬ | Secondary Road |
| ▬▬▬ | Railway |

Map pages 1-12 are at a scale of 1:20,000 (1cm = 200m)
Map pages 12-16 are at a scale of 1:10,000 (1cm = 100m)

Plan reproduit avec l'autorisation de la Direction cantonale de la mensuration officielle du 8 décembre 2004.

**Autorisation 59/2004**

Geneva Map Sheet Index

Maps

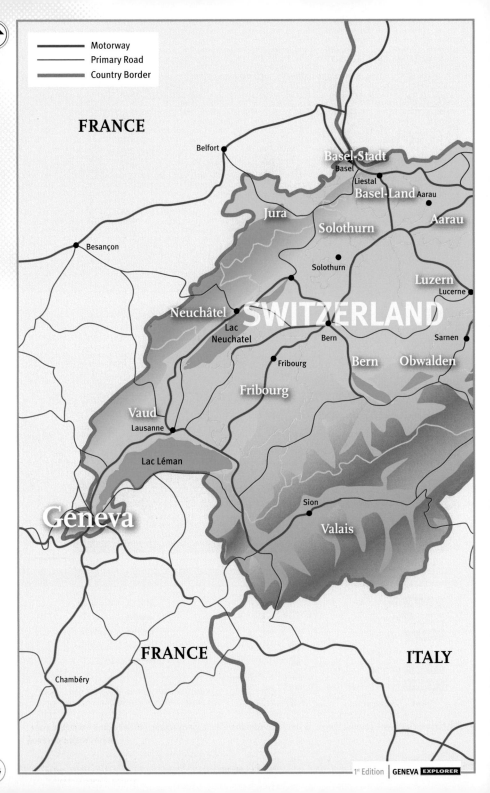

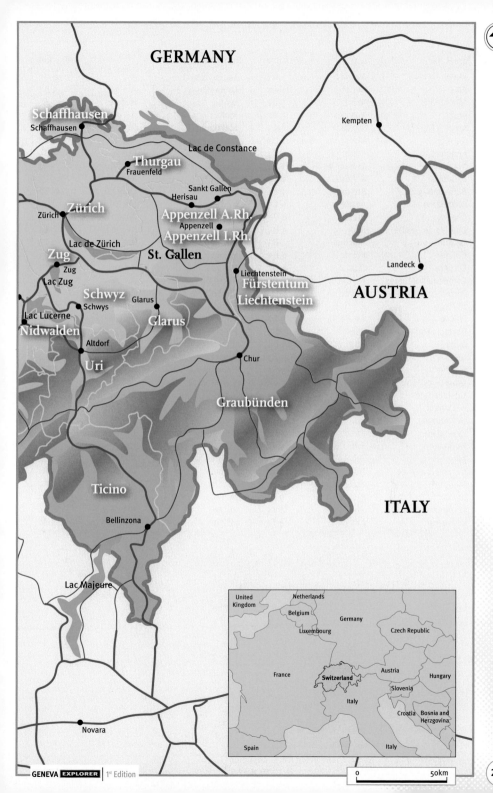

GERMANY

Schaffhausen
Schaffhausen

Lac de Constance

Thurgau
Frauenfeld

Sankt Gallen
Herisau

Zürich
Zürich

Appenzell A.Rh.
Appenzell
Appenzell I.Rh.

Lac de Zürich

St. Gallen

Zug
Zug

Lac Zug

Liechtenstein

Fürstentum
Liechtenstein

AUSTRIA

Kempten

Landeck

Schwyz
Schwys

Glarus

Lac Lucerne

Glarus

Nidwalden

Altdorf

Uri

Chur

Graubünden

Ticino

Bellinzona

ITALY

Lac Majeure

Novara

United Kingdom
Netherlands
Belgium
Luxembourg
Germany
Czech Republic
France
Austria
Slovenia
Hungary
Switzerland
Italy
Croatia
Bosnia and Herzgovina
Spain
Italy

0          50km

SWITZERLAND

Maps

| Street Name | | Map Ref | Street Name | | Map Ref |
|---|---|---|---|---|---|
| Ain | Av. de l' | 5-B3 | Louis- Aubert | Av. | 16-B3 |
| Aïre | Av. d' | 13-A3 | Louis- Casaï | Av. | 5-B2 |
| Aïre-la-Ville | Rte d' | 3-E2 | Lyon | Rue de | 13-A2 |
| Alpes | Rue des | 13-E2 | Mail | Av. du | 13-D4 |
| Amandolier | Av. de l' | 16-C1 | Malagnou | Rte de | 16-D2 |
| Annecy | Rte d' | 11-D3 | Mandement | Rte du | 4-C1 |
| Annemasse | Rte d' | 11-E3 | Meyrin | Rte de | 1-B4 |
| Arande | Sentier de l' | 11-B2 | Mont-Blanc | Pont du | 13-E3 |
| Batailleux | Rte des | 2-C4 | Mont-Blanc | Rue de | 13-E3 |
| Bois-de-Bay | Rte du | 7-C1 | Mont-Blanc | Quai du | 13-E2 |
| Châtelaine | Av. de | 5-C3 | Nant-d'Avril | Rte du | 4-D2 |
| Chancy | Rte de | 8-B2 | Pailly | Av. du | 5-B3 |
| Charles de Gaulle | Rue | 5-B4 | Paix | Av. de la | 5-E2 |
| Charmilles | Rue des | 13-B3 | Pas-de-l'Echelle | Rte du | 9-C3 |
| Chêne | Rte de | 6-B4 | Peney | Rte de | 4-D3 |
| Cologny | Quai de | 6-C2 | Philosophes | Bd des | 15-D1 |
| Communes-Réunies | Av. des | 8-C3 | Pictet De Rochemont | Av. | 14-B4 |
| Drize | Rte de | 8-D4 | Pont d'Arve | Bd. du | 15-D1 |
| Fayards | Rte des | 2-D1 | Pont-Butin | Rte du | 5-B4 |
| France | Av. de | 5-E2 | Pré- Bois | Rte de | 5-B1 |
| François-Diday | Rue | 13-D3 | Promenades | Bd. des | 8-D2 |
| G. Favon | Bd. | 13-D4 | Rieu | Chemin | 16-C2 |
| Genève | Av. de | 10-E3 | Romells | Rte des | 2-E2 |
| Geneve | Rue de | 9-D1 | Saint Julien | Rte de | 8-C4 |
| Giuseppe-Motta | Av. | 5-D2 | Servette | Rue de la | 13-B1 |
| Gustave Ador | Quai | 14-A3 | Terrassière | Rue de la | 14-B4 |
| H. Dunant | Av. | 15-D1 | Thônex | Av. de | 9-D2 |
| Helvétique | Bd. | 15-E1 | Thonon | Rte de | 3-E3 |
| Hermance | Rte d' | 12-D2 | Tranchées | Bd des | 16-A1 |
| Hoffmann | Rue | 13-B1 | Traz | La Voie-des- | 2-C3 |
| James-Fazy | Bd. | 13-D2 | Trois Lacs | Rte des | 12-D2 |
| Jacques Dalcroze | Bd. | 15-E1 | Verbois | Rte de | 7-A1 |
| Jeunes | Rte des | 15-B2 | Vernier | Rte de | 5-A2 |
| Jussy | Rte de | 9-E1 | Voltaire | Rue | 13-C3 |
| Lausanne | Rte de | 2-E4 | Vorge | Rte de la | 2-C4 |
| Lausanne | Rue de | 13-E1 | Wilson | Quai | 14-A1 |

SFr 10 ~ € 6     1ˢᵗ Edition | GENEVA EXPLORER

Community & Street Index

Maps

# Geneva & Surrounding Area

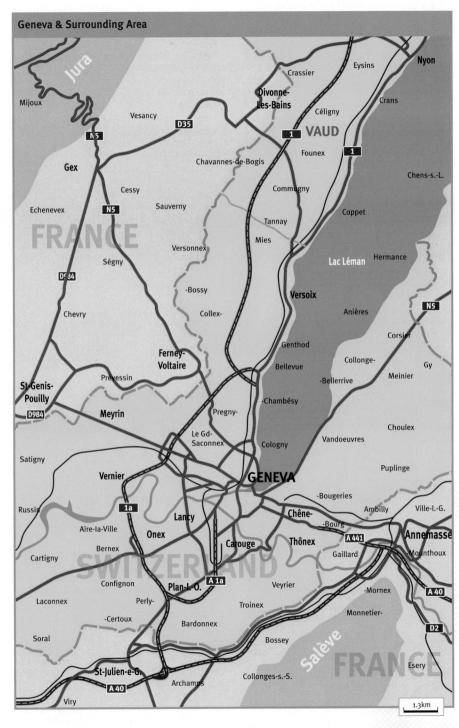

Maps

Geneva & Surrounding Area Map

N

Imagery courtesy of MAPS geosystems – Master Reseller for *Digital Globe*

1

2

FRANCE

C.E.R.N.(Prévissin)

D35

ST GENIS-POUILLY

Rue de l'Eglise

Rue de Pouilly

3

Route de l'Europe

4

Route de Meyrin

C.E.R.N.

C.E.R.N. Clubs

Bourdigny-Choully

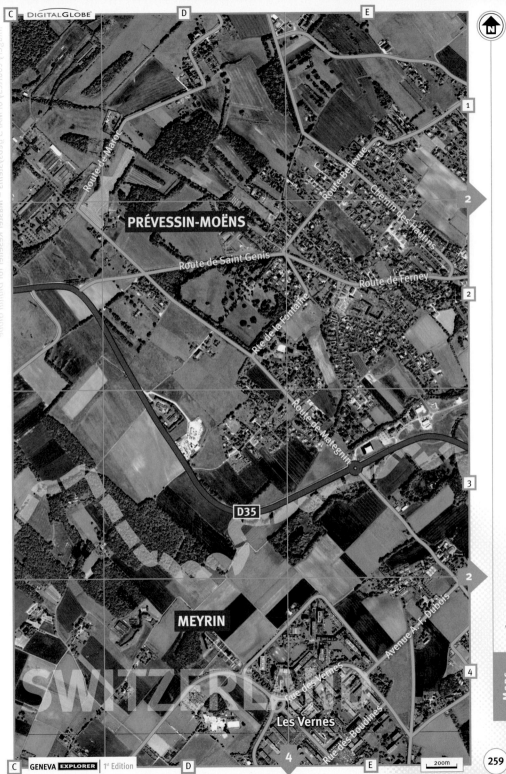

DIGITALGLOBE

1

N

2

Route de Maroc

PRÉVESSIN-MOËNS

Route de Saint Genis

Route Bellevue

Chemin des Hautins

Route de Ferney

2

Rte de la Fontaine

Route de Mategnin

D35

3

MEYRIN

2

Avenue A.-F.-Dubois

SWITZERLAND

4

Les Vernes

Rue des Vernes

Rue des Boudines

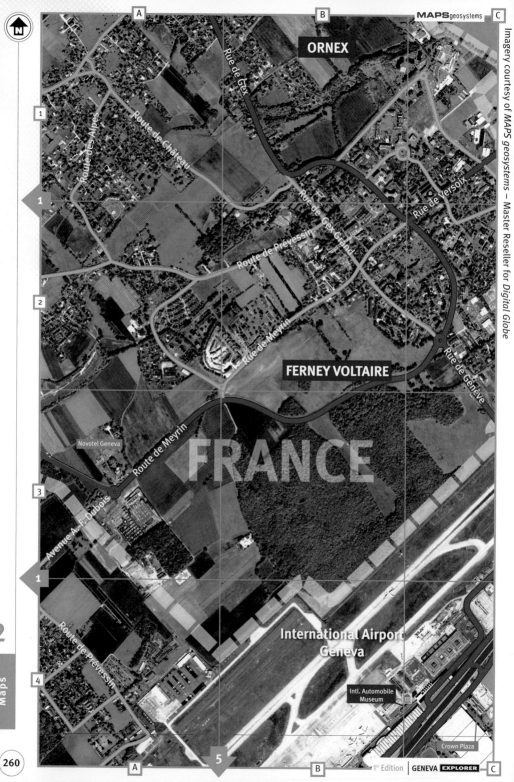

Imagery courtesy of MAPS geosystems – Master Reseller for Digital Globe

ORNEX

Rue de Gex

Route des Alpes

Route de Château

Rue de Versoix

Route de Prévessin

Rue de Gex Grand

Rue de Meyrin

FERNEY VOLTAIRE

Rue de Genève

Novotel Geneva

Route de Meyrin

FRANCE

Avenue A.-F.-Dubois

Route de Prévessin

International Airport
Geneva

Intl. Automobile
Museum

Crown Plaza

2

Maps

1st Edition | GENEVA EXPLORER

C D E

1

Route des Fayards

Route de Virelotip

Route de Colovrex

**1**

Route de Collex

Route de Valavran

Réserve, la

**BELLEVUE**

3

Route de Valavran

2

Route des Romells

3

Avenue de la Forétaille

Chemin de Valérie

Chemin de Chambésy

Chemin de Mechory

3

**LE GRAND-SACONNEX**

**PREGNY-CHAMBÉSY**

2

Route de Colovrex

Route de Prégny

SWITZERLAND

Route de Ferney

P

Route de Lausanne

4

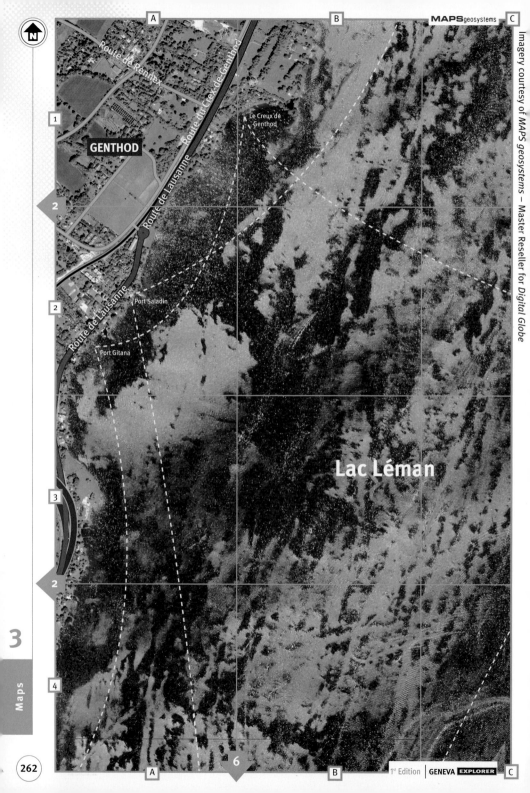

Route de Rennex

Route du Crex-de-Genthod

1

Le Creux de Genthod

GENTHOD

2

Route de Lausanne

2

Route de Lausanne

Port Saladin

Port Gitana

Lac Léman

3

2

3

Maps

4

6

Imagery courtesy of MAPS geosystems – Master Reseller for Digital Globe

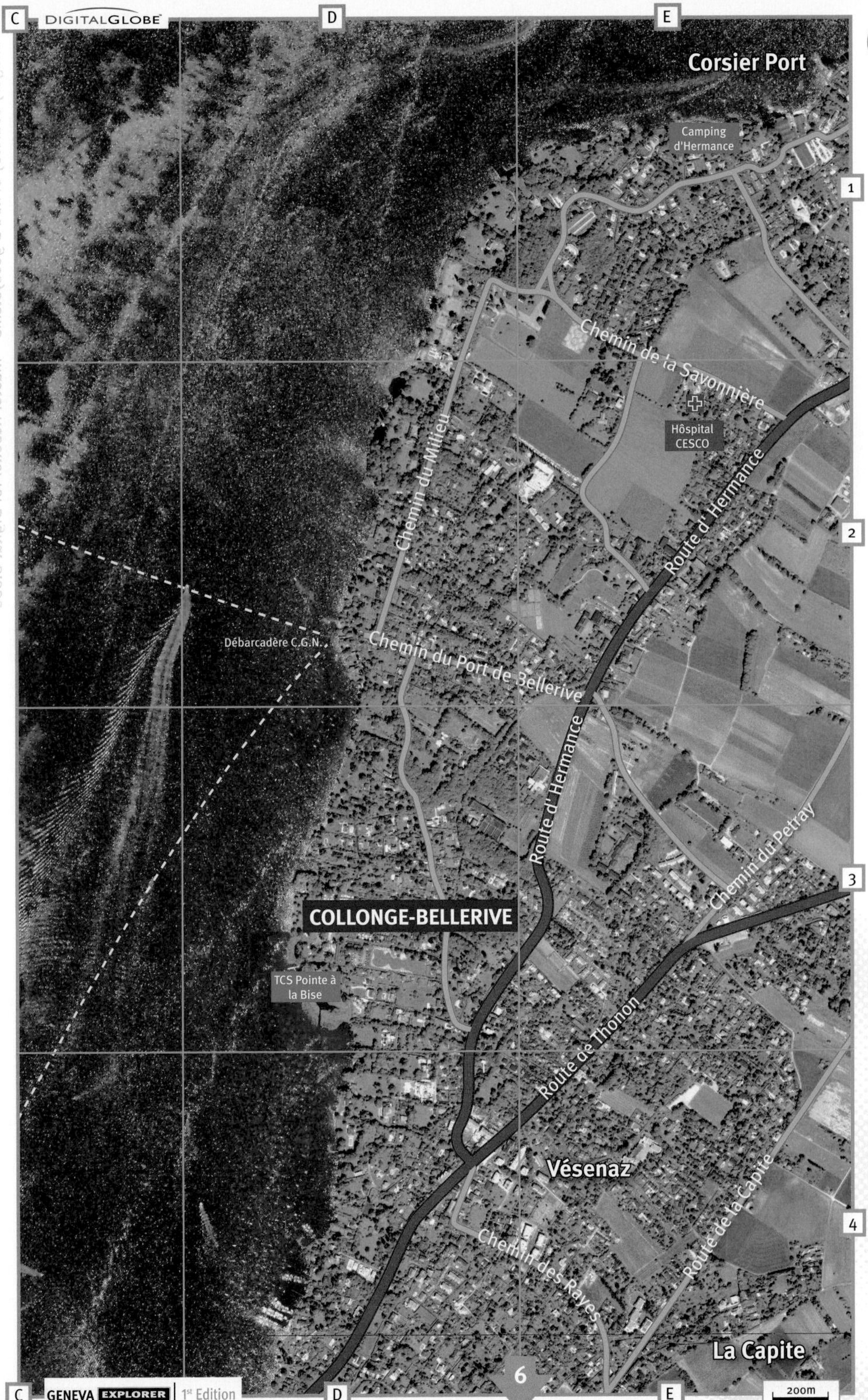

C | D | E

**Corsier Port**

Camping
d'Hermance

1

Chemin de la Savonnière

Hôspital
CESCO

2

Chemin du Milieu

Route d'Hermance

Débarcadère C.G.N.

Chemin du Port de Bellerive

Route d'Hermance

Chemin du Petray

3

**COLLONGE-BELLERIVE**

TCS Pointe à
la Bise

Route de Thonon

Route de la Capite

**Vésenaz**

4

Chemin des Raves

**La Capite**

3

Maps

Imagery courtesy of MAPS geosystems – Master Reseller for Digital Globe

1

C.E.R.N.

**SATIGNY**

**Bourdigny-Dessus**

Route du Mandement

Rue du Pré-Bouvier

Route de Satigny

Route de Satigny

**Bourdigny-Dessous**

Route de la Gare

Route d' Aire-la-Ville

**SATIGNY**

Route de Peney

Domaine de
Chateauvieux

**Peney-Dessus**

4

Maps

7

**MEYRIN**

Les Vernes

Hôp. de la Tour

Mairie Centre

Rue De Livron

Rue Lect

Avenue de Vaudagne

Route de Meyrin

Jardin Alpin

Rue des Vorets

Rue Lect

Rue des Inst. Mondiales

Chemin du Grand Puits

Chemin du Vieux Bureau

Route du Nant-d'Avril

Rue de la Bergère

Chemin Adrien Stoessel

Route de Satigny

Route de Montfleury

Route de Vernier

Chemin du Sorbier

Route de Peney

Route de Peney

Tunnel de Vernier

Le Rhône

Loëx

1a

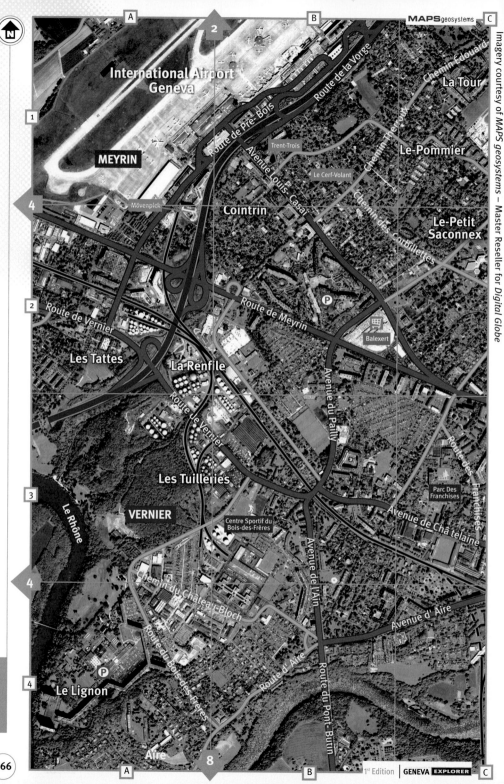

Imagery courtesy of MAPS geosystems – Master Reseller for *Digital Globe*

2

La Tour

Chemin Édouard

Route de la Vorge

1

International Airport
Geneva

Route de Pre- Bois

Trent-Trois

Le-Pommier

Chemin Thevoux

MEYRIN

Le Cerf-Volant

4

Avenue Louis- Casaï

Cointrin

Chemin des Corbillettes

Le-Petit
Saconnex

Mövenpick

2 Route de Vernier

Route de Meyrin

P

Balexert

Les Tattes

La Renfile

Avenue du Pailly

Route de Vernier

Route des Franchises

Les Tuilleries

Parc Des
Franchises

3

VERNIER

Le Rhône

Centre Sportif du
Bois-des-Frères

Avenue de Châtelaine

4

Avenue de l'Aín

Chemin du Châteal-Bloch

Avenue d' Aíre

5

Route du Bois-des-Frères

4

P

Le Lignon

Route d' Aíre

Route du Pont- Butin

Aíre

8

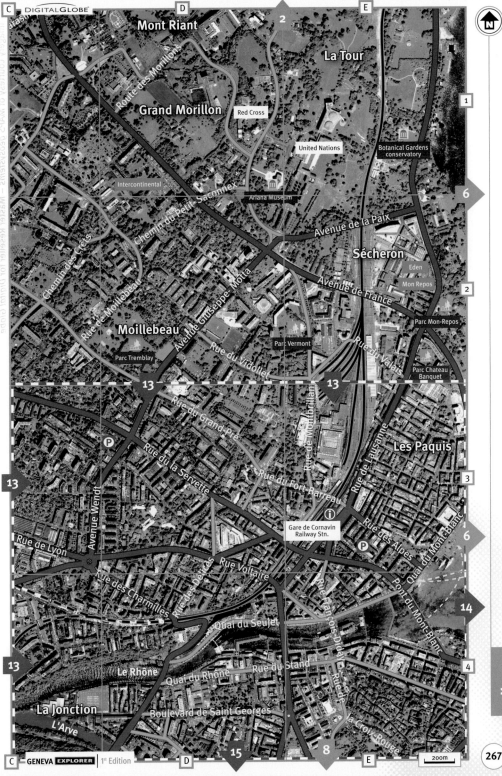

DIGITALGLOBE

Mont Riant

La Tour

1

Grand Morillon

Red Cross

United Nations

Botanical Gardens conservatory

Intercontinental

Ariana Museum

6

Avenue de la Paix

Sécheron

Eden

Mon Repos

Chemin du Petit-Saconnex

Avenue de France

2

Chemin des Crêts

Rue de Moillebeau

Avenue Giuseppe-Motta

Parc Mon-Repos

Moillebeau

Rue du Vidollet

Parc Vermont

Rue du Valais

Parc Chateau Banquet

Parc Tremblay

13

13

Rue du Montbrillant

Rue du Grand-Pré

Les Paquis

P

Rue de la Servette

Rue de Lausanne

13

Rue du Fort-Barreau

3

Avenue Wendt

Rue des Alpes

6

Rue de Lyon

Gare de Cornavin Railway Stn.

P

Quai du Mont-Blanc

Rue Voltaire

Rue des Charmilles

Rue des Bains

Rue François-Dizard

Pont du Mont-Blanc

14

Quai du Seujet

Le Rhône

Quai du Rhône

Rue du Stand

4

13

La Jonction

Boulevard de Saint Georges

Rue de la Croix-Rouge

L'Arve

5

Maps

Imagery courtesy of MAPS geosystems – Master Reseller for Digital Globe

Le Reposoir

1

5

**Lac Léman**

Montalègre

2

Débarcadère
Mouettes Genevoises

Quai de Cologny

14      14

Geneva-Plage

Quai Wilson

3

Rampe de Colony

14

Port Noir

**GENEVA**

Débarcadère
C.G.N.

13

Quai Gustave-ADOR

**COLOGNY**

Parc des
Eaux-Vives

Parc La Granges

Route de Frontenex

Chemi

5

**Les Eaux-Vives**

14

4   Rue du Rhône

P

Sagittta

P

Pax

Calvy

P

Diplomate

DIGITALGLOBE

N

**3**

Route de Thonon

Chemin des prunes

Ruth

Route de la Capite

**1**

Route de Meinier

**COLOGNY**

Golf Club de Geneva

**VANDOEUVRES**

Hôp. de Jour

**2**

Route de Choulex

Chemin des Hauts-Crêts

**Chougny**

Route de Vandoeuvres

**3**

Chemin de la Seymaz

**Bel Air**

de la Gradelle

Route Jean-Jacques-Rigaud

Avenue A.-M.-Mirany

Avenue A.-M.-Mirany

Clinique psychiatrique

**4**

**CHÊNE-BOUGERIES**

Avenue de bel Air

**9**

**6**

Maps

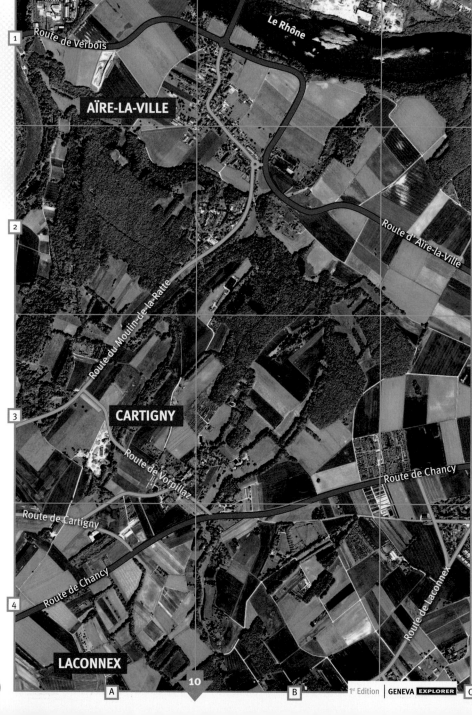

N

Route du Bois-de-Bay

Le Rhône

1

Route de Verbois

**AÏRE-LA-VILLE**

2

Route d' Aïre-la-Ville

Route du Moulin-de-la-Ratte

3

**CARTIGNY**

Route de Vorpillaz

Route de Chancy

Route de Cartigny

Route de Chancy

4

Route de Laconnex

**LACONNEX**

Imagery courtesy of MAPS geosystems – Master Reseller for *Digital Globe*

7

Maps

A           B           C

1ˢᵗ Edition | **GENEVA** **EXPLORER**

DIGITALGLOBE

4

1a

Hôp. Loëx

Route de Loëx

Les Evaux

8

BERNEX

2

3

Route de Soral

P

Rue de Bernex

8

CONFIGNON

BERNEX

4

Lully

Route de Soral

Plaine de l' Aire

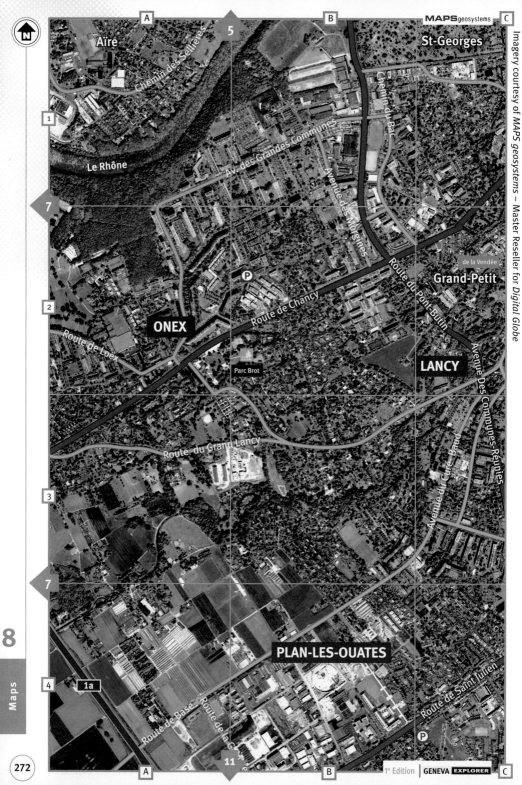

Aïre

St-Georges

Chemin des Sellières

Le Rhône

Av. des Grandes Communes

Chemin du Bac

Imagery courtesy of MAPS geosystems – Master Reseller for Digital Globe

de la Vendée

Grand-Petit

Route de Chancy

Route du Pont-Butin

ONEX

Route de Loëx

Parc Brot

LANCY

Avenue Des Communes-Réunies

Route du Grand Lancy

Avenue du Cure-Baud

PLAN-LES-OUATES

1a

Route de Base

Route de la C...

Route de Saint Julien

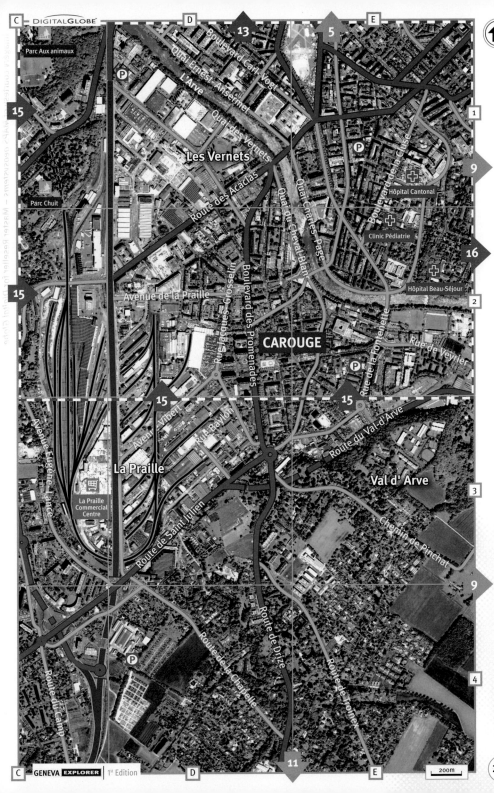

Parc Aux animaux

Parc Chuit

Boulevard Carl-Vogt

Quai Ernest-Ansermet

L'Arve

Quai des Vernets

**Les Vernets**

Route des Acacias

Quai Charles-Page

Quai du Cheval-Blanc

Boulevard des Promenades

Rue Jacques-Gosselin

Avenue de la Praille

**CAROUGE**

Boulevard de la Cluse

Hôpital Cantonal

Clinic Pédiatrie

Hôpital Beau-Séjour

Rue de la Fontenette

Rue de Veyrier

Avenue Eugène-Lance

Avenue Vibert

Rue Baylon

**La Praille**

La Praille
Commercial
Centre

Route de Saint-Julien

Route du Val-d'Arve

**Val d' Arve**

Chemin de Pinchat

Route du Camp

Route de la Chapelle

Route de Drize

Route de Troinex

200m

8

Maps

C   D   E

13   5

15

1

9

16

2

15   15

3

9

4

11

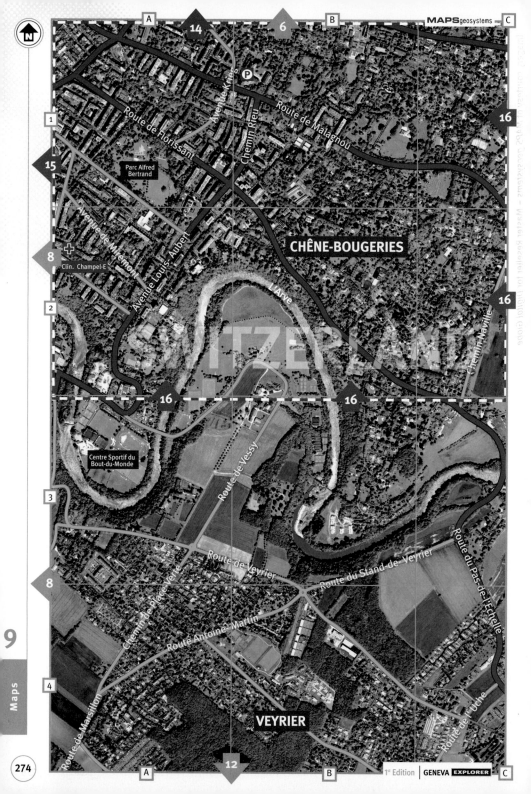

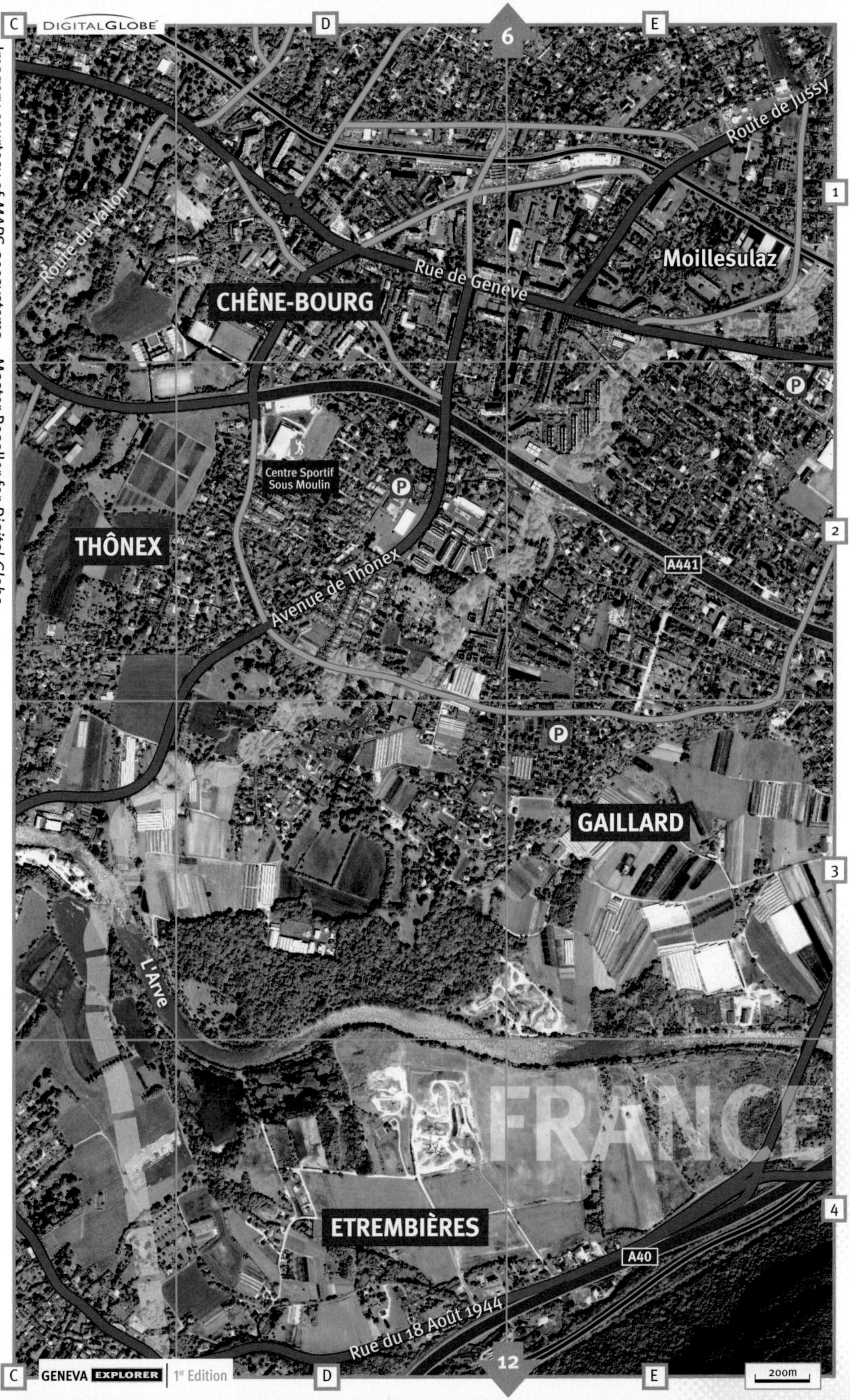

C D 6 E

Route de Jussy

1

Route du Vallon

Rue de Genève

CHÊNE-BOURG

Moillesulaz

P

Centre Sportif
Sous Moulin

P

2

THÔNEX

Avenue de Thônex

A441

P

GAILLARD

3

L'Arve

FRANCE

9

ETREMBIÈRES

4

A40

Rue du 18 Août 1944

C D 12 E 200m

Maps

N

LACONNEX

1

Route de Laconnex

Route de Pré-Laurel

Route de la Vy-Neuve

Route de Soral

SWITZERLAND

2

Route de la Parraille

Route-des-Lolliers

SORAL

3

Thairy

10

Maps

4

A40

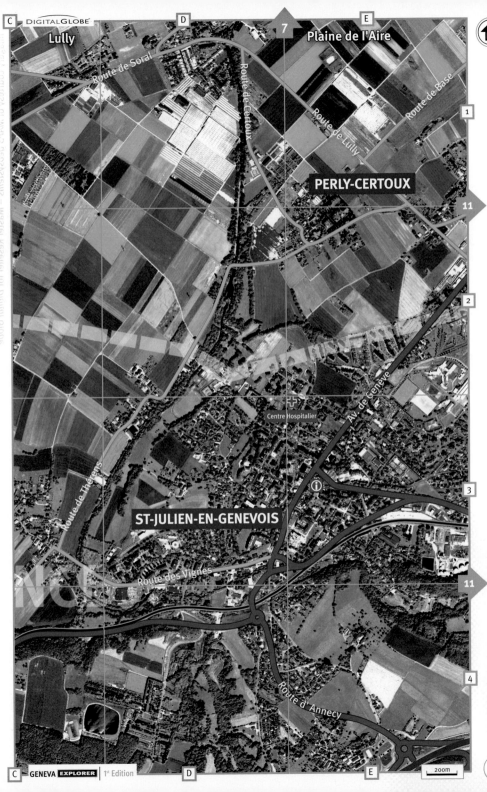

Route de Soral

Route de Certoux

Route de Lully

Route de Base

**PERLY-CERTOUX**

1

11

2

Av. de Genève

Centre Hospitalier

3

Route de Théreins

**ST-JULIEN-EN-GENEVOIS**

Route des Vignes

11

Route d'Annecy

4

Imagery courtesy of MAPS geosystems – Master Reseller for Digital Globe

1

Chemin des Mattines

Arare

**PLAN-LES-OUATES**

10

Route de Certoux

Route de Saint-Julien

Route de Cugny

Compesières

Route des Ravières

2

SWITZERLAND

Charrot

A401

**BARDONNEX**

3

10

**ST-JULIEN-EN-GENEVOIS**

P

11

Maps

4

A40

FRANCE

**TROINEX**

Route d'Annecy

Route du Saconnex d'Arve

Route de Pierre

Route des Hospitaliers

Croix-de-Rozon

**BARDONNEX**

Landecy

Route d'Annemasse

Route d'Annecy

Route d'Annecy

**ARCHAMPS**

11

Maps

Chemin des Marais

9

VEYRIER

1

SWITZERLAND

Route de Bossey

R. Charles-de-Gaulle

11

A40

Route du Pas- de – l'Echelle

2

Route de Crevin

Golf de Bossey

BOSSEY

Route de Bellevue

Mont-Salève

FRANCE

3

11

12

Maps

COLLONGES-SOUS-SALÈVE

4

1st Edition | GENEVA EXPLORER

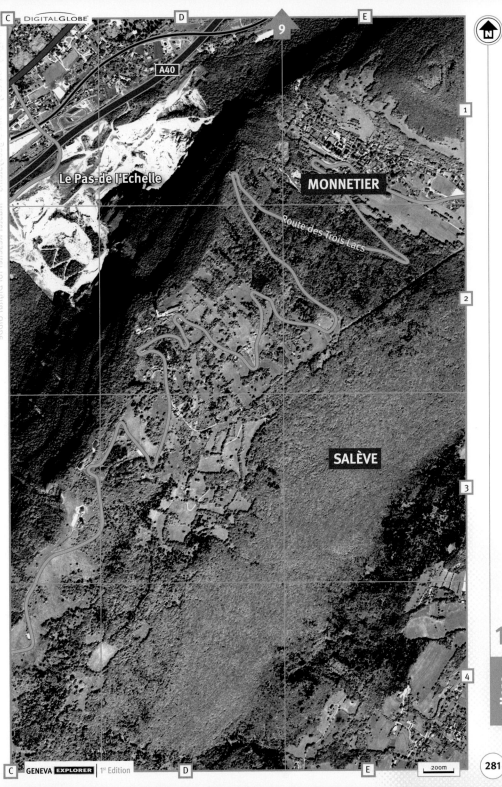

9

A40

Le Pas-de-l'Echelle

MONNETIER

Route des Trois Lacs

SALÈVE

1

2

3

4

12

Maps

200m

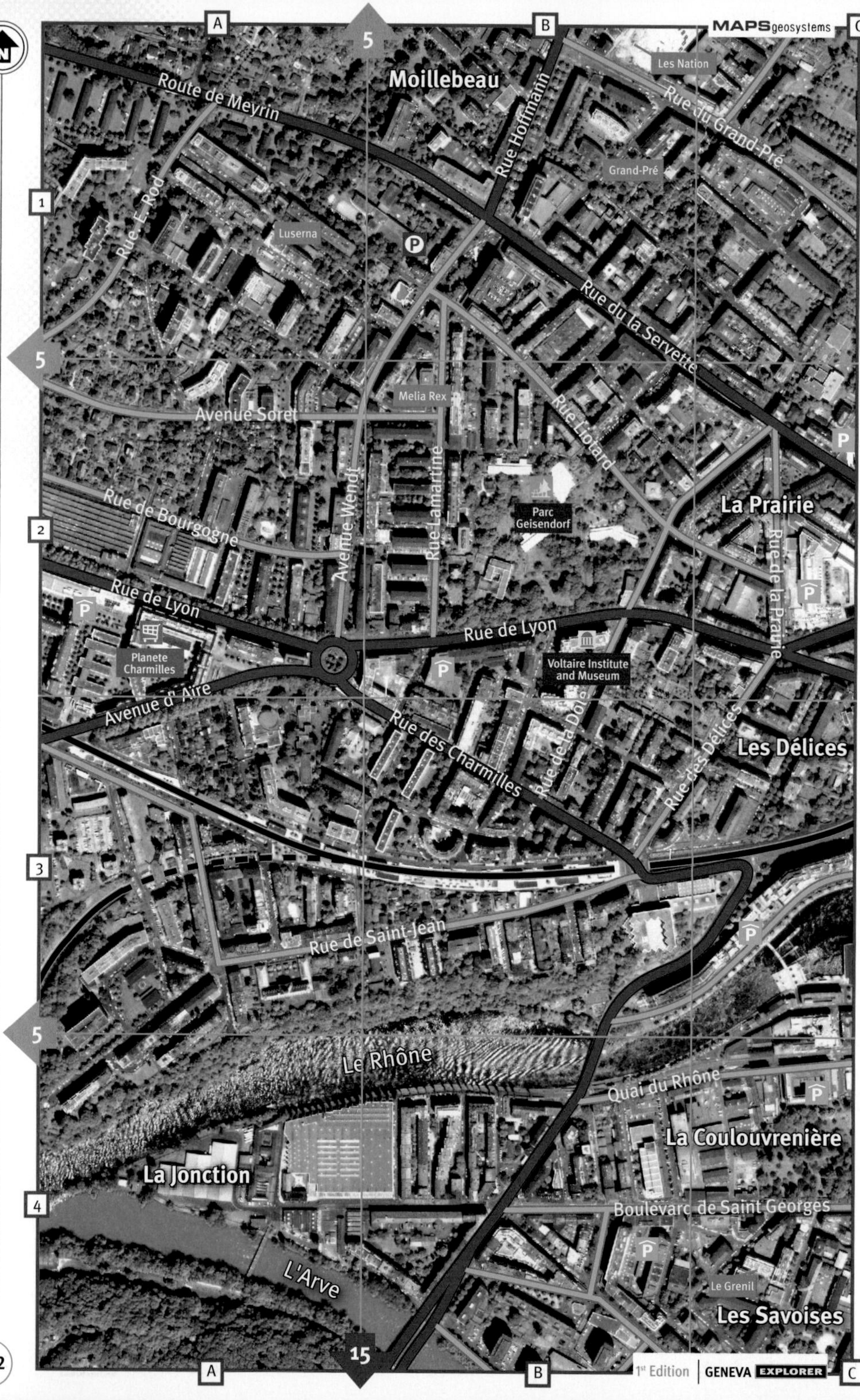

N

Route de Meyrin

Moillebeau

Les Nation

Rue Hoffmann

Rue du Grand-Pré

Grand-Pré

Rue de l'Ecole

Luserna

P

Rue du la Servette

Melia Rex

Rue Liotard

Avenue Soret

La Prairie

Rue de Bourgogne

Avenue Wendt

Rue Lamartine

Parc Geisendorf

Rue de la Prairie

Rue de Lyon

P

Rue de Lyon

P

Planete Charmilles

Voltaire Institute and Museum

Les Délices

Avenue d' Aire

Rue des Charmilles

Rue de la Dol

Rue des Délices

Rue de Saint-Jean

P

Le Rhône

Quai du Rhône

La Coulouvrenière

P

La Jonction

Boulevard de Saint Georges

P

L'Arve

Le Grenil

Les Savoises

N

Imagery courtesy of *MAPS geosystems* – Master Reseller for *Digital Globe*

1

13

Quai Wilson

Lac Lêman

2

Port des Eaux-Vives

Jet d'Eav

Parc La Grange

3

Pierres du Niton

P

Quai Gustave Ador

Churchill

Rue des Eaux-Vives

Rue du Trente et Un Décembre

Les Eaux-Vives

Avenue William Favre

13

Jardin Anglais

Rue P. Fatio

Rue F. Versonnex

Boulevard Helvétique

P

14

Maps

4

P

Century Best
Western

Avenue Pictet-de-Rochemont

P

P

P

Gare des Eaux-Vives

P

Villereuse

Rue de la Terrassière

P

P

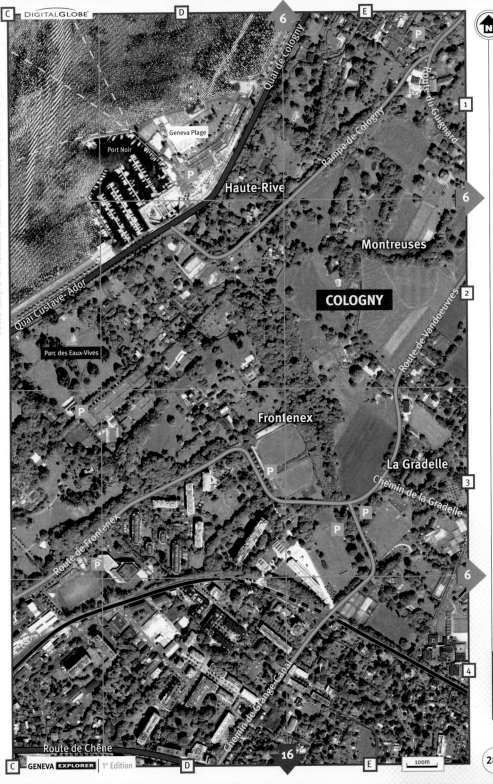

6

Quai de Cologny

Route du Guignard

1

Rampe de Cologny

Geneva Plage

Port Noir

P

Haute-Rive

6

Montreuses

Quai Gustave-Ador

COLOGNY

2

Route de Vandoeuvres

Parc des Eaux-Vives

P

Frontenex

La Gradelle

P

Chemin de la Gradelle

3

P

P

6

Route de Frontenex

P

14

Chemin de Grange-Canal

4

Route de Chêne

Maps

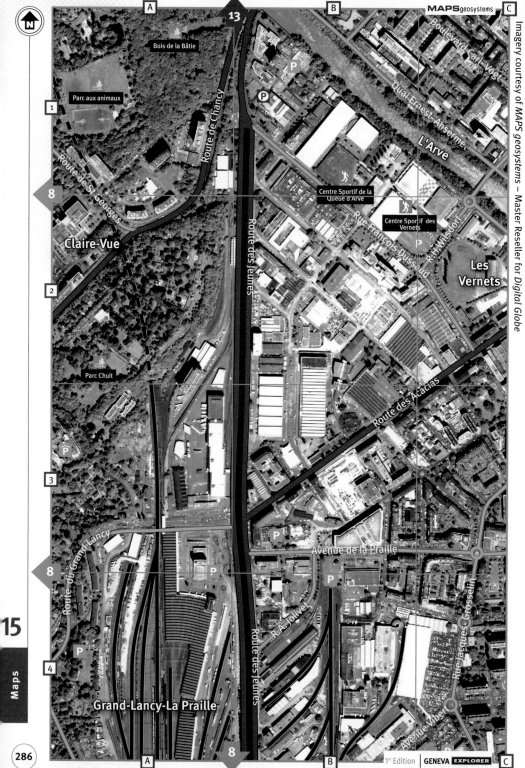

A

B

C

Imagery courtesy of MAPS geosystems – Master Reseller for Digital Globe

Bois de la Bâtie

P

Parc aux animaux

1

P

Boulevard Carl-Vogt

Quai Ernest-Ansermet

Route de Chancy

Route de St-Georges

8

L'Arve

Centre Sportif de la
Queue d'Arve

Claire-Vue

Centre Sportif des
Vernets

Rue François Dussaud

R. H. Wilsdorf

Les
Vernets

Route des Jeunes

2

P

Parc Chuit

Route des Acacias

3

P

Avenue de la Praille

Route du Grand-Lancy

8

P

A

15

P

R.-A.-Jolivet

Route des Jeunes

Rue Jacques-Grosselin

4

P

Grand-Lancy-La Praille

Avenue Vibert

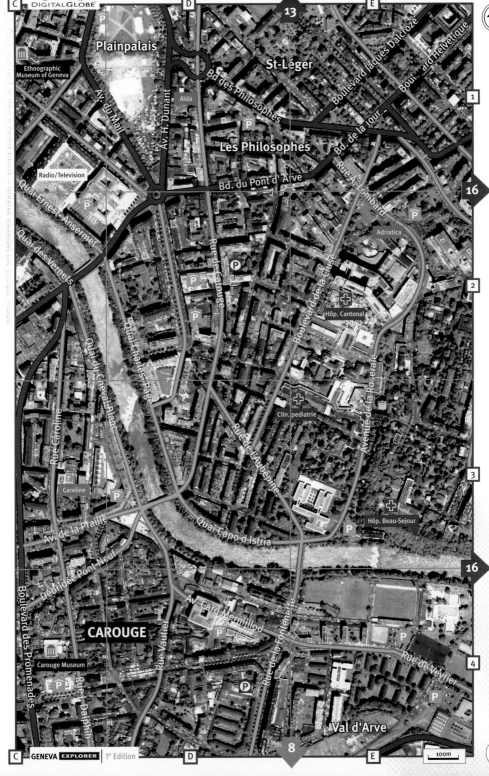

DIGITALGLOBE

**Plainpalais**

St-Léger

Ethnographic
Museum of Geneva

Bd des Philosophes

Aïda

Av. H. Dunant

Av. du Mail

**Les Philosophes**

Bd. de la tour

Boulevard Jaques Dalcroze

Boulevard Helvetique

1

Radio/Television

Bd. du Pont d'Arve

Rue A. Lombard

16

Quai Ernest-Ansermet

Adriatica

Quai des Vernets

Rue de Carouge

Boulevard de la Cluse

Hôp. Cantonal

2

Quai Charles-Page

Quai du Cheval-Blanc

Rue Caroline

Clin. pediatrie

Avenue de la Roseraie

Rue de l'Aubepine

3

Caroline

Av. de la Praille

Quai Capo d'Istria

Hôp. Beau-Sejour

P

16

Débridée Pont-Neuf

Boulevard des Promenades

Av. Card Mermillod

Rue Vautier

Rue de la Fontenette

**CAROUGE**

Rue de Veyrier

4

Carouge Museum

Rue Dalphin

**Val d'Arve**

15

Maps

100m

287

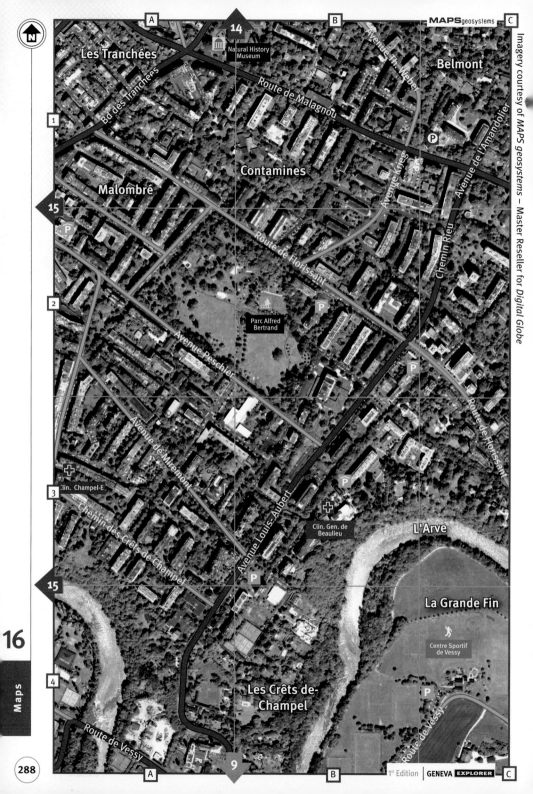

MAPS geosystems

N

Les Tranchées

Natural History Museum

**14**

Belmont

Bd des Tranchées

Route de Malagnou

Contamines

Malombré

Avenue Th. Weber

Avenue Krieg

Avenue de l'Amandolier

Chemin Rieu

Route de Florissant

Avenue Peschier

Parc Alfred Bertrand

Route de Florissant

Avenue de Miremont

Clin. Champel-E

Clin. Gen. de Beaulieu

L'Arve

Chemin des Crêts de Champel

Avenue Louis-Aubert

La Grande Fin

Centre Sportif de Vessy

Les Crêts de-Champel

Route de Vessy

Route de Vessy

**9**

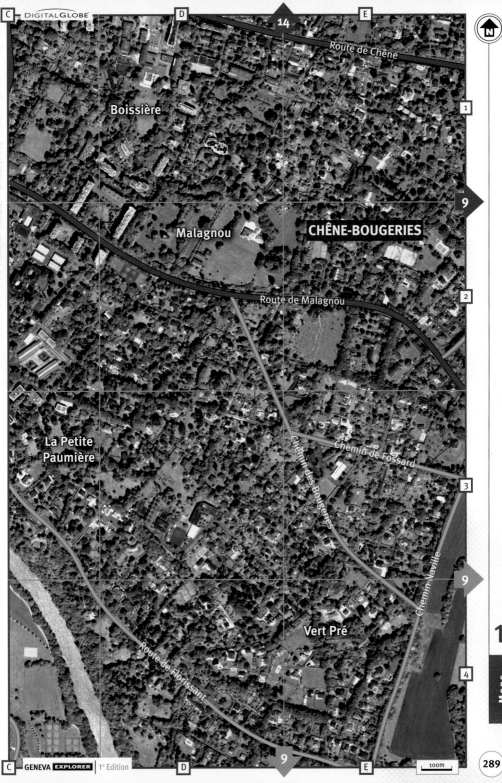

Route de Chêne

Boissière

CHÊNE-BOUGERIES

Malagnou

Route de Malagnou

La Petite
Paumière

Chemin de Fossard

Chemin des Bougeries

Chemin Naville

Vert Pré

Route de Florissant

100m

16

Maps

# DIGITALGLOBE™

C L E A R L Y   T H E   B E S T

61 cm QuickBird Imagery is the highest resolution satellite imagery available. We offer products and resorces to both existing GIS users and the entire next generation of mapping and multimedia applications.

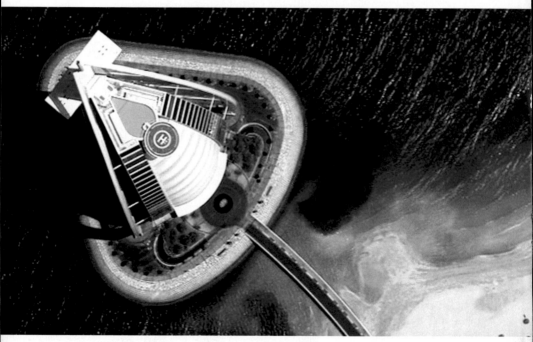

Burj Al Arab, Scale 1:2500, dated May 2003 © DigitalGlobe

## MAPSgeosystems

### DigitalGlobe's Master Reseller serving the Middle East and East, Central and West Africa

MAPS (UAE), Corniche Plaza 1, P.O. Box 5232, Sharjah, UAE.
Tel : +971 6 5725411, Fax : +971 6 5724057
www.maps-geosystems.com

For further details, please contact quickbird@maps-geosystems.com

# Index

**EXPLORER**

Index

SFr 10 ~ € 6

Index

# NOTES

# NOTES

€1 ~ SFr 1.5

Index

A-Z

# NOTES